The BERKSHIRE Book

A Complete Guide

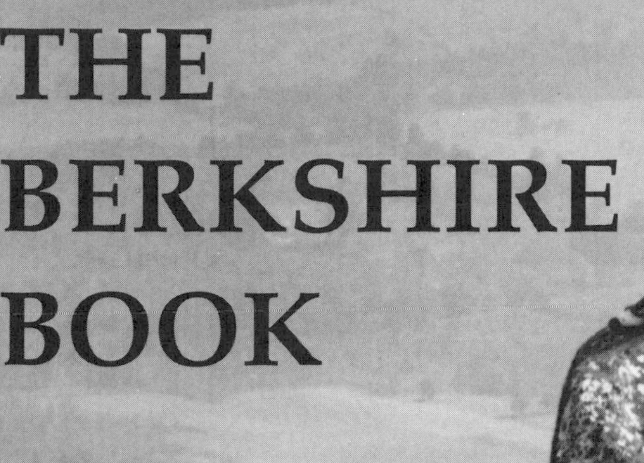

THE BERKSHIRE BOOK

A Complete Guide

Second Edition

Jonathan Sternfield

Berkshire House, Publishers
Great Barrington, Massachusetts

ON THE COVER AND THE TITLE PAGE

Front Cover Landscape — *View of Mount Greylock from Rte. 7, near Mount Greylock Regional High School, Williamstown; Inset--Chef Maurice Champagne, the Mill on the Floss, New Ashford; Hubbard Street Dance, Gordon Meyer, courtesy Jacob's Pillow, Becket; The Egremont Inn, South Egremont; Berkshire Downhill Skier, Paul Rocheleau, courtesy Berkshire Visitors Bureau.*

Title Page — *Hikers on Monument Mountain, Great Barrington, c. 1920 (photo by H. Armstrong Roberts).*

Back Cover — *Naumkeag, Stockbridge (photo by Mimi MacDonald); "Freedom from Want," Norman Rockwell, © Estate of Norman Rockwell, courtesy Norman Rockwell Museum, Stockbridge; Williamstown Theatre Festival.*

ISBN 0-936399-00-7
ISSN 1052-7907

Editors: David Emblidge, Virginia Rowe
Design of original text for Great Destination series: Janice Lindstrom
Cover design: Jane McWhorter

Berkshire House, Publishers
Box 915, Great Barrington, MA 01230
Manufactured in the United States of America

First printing 1991
10 9 8 7 6 5 4 3 2 1

The GREAT DESTINATIONS Series

- The Berkshire Book: A Complete Guide
- The Santa Fe & Taos Book: A Complete Guide
- The Napa & Sonoma Book: A Complete Guide (forthcoming)

Berkshire is a Great Place
Or
The Berkshires are a Great Place

If you listen closely when you're in this county, you'll hear people saying "The Berkshires is . . . ," just about as often as "The Berkshires are . . . " Which is right? Both are pretty common, and we see no clear way to declare a winner. In this book, we have opted to avoid the issue as much as possible, only occasionally using "The Berkshires" as a plural collective noun (as in "The Berkshires are . . . "). We join those hereabouts who, in recent years, have re-introduced what we think is a charming older use of the word "Berkshire," one based in the not-too-distant past. In this usage, we can say, "Berkshire is a great place."

Many Berkshire friends helped to produce this book, but even with all of their participation, we haven't covered everything. Subsequent editions of *The Berkshire Book* will continue to refine the ways we present information for the local resident and the visitor alike. The book's first edition brought forth a lot of praise, a little criticism, and many helpful suggestions. Readers are encouraged to contact the publisher with corrections or new ideas.

Introduction

Lenox has had its usual tonic effect on me, and I feel like a new edition, revised and corrected...

This was Berkshire's revitalizing influence on EdithWharton, in 1902, and we feel that tonic effect, too, nearly a century later, coming around again in a new edition, revised and corrected. Much in Berkshire has changed, much is the same. Great traditions have carried on, new ones have begun. An almost unimaginably artful tapestry of culture has gotten finer, more detailed and varied. A recreational bounty has been augmented, and dozens of new excellent restaurants have opened.

We feel encouraged. The first edition of *The Berkshire Book* was well received, our judgments confirmed, our candor praised. There was a call for more. Since Berkshire itself has become even more refined, shouldn't the book follow suit? Here you have it, then, *The new, improved Berkshire Book*, featuring detailed street and site maps of Great Barrington, Stockbridge, Lenox, Pittsfield, North Adams and Williamstown.

We've filled in a few gaps, adding football and fitness facilities to our *Recreation* chapter, and we've caught up with the times too, noting the new mountainbikers and snowboarders.

> *Berkshire, by common consent, is not only a good place to be born in, but a good place to live in, and a good place to die in, as well. It is also prominently recognized as a good place to go out from, and an equally good place to come back to.*
> *A Berkshire birth is something to be proud of; a Berkshire sojourn a delight, a rest, a recreation, a circumstance of pleasant memory, ever after; and a Berkshire residence a rich and enjoyable life experience.*
>
> The Book of Berkshire, 1887

"In old times, authors were proud of the privilege of dedicating their works to majesty," wrote Berkshire author Herman Melville in the 1850s to the nearby Sophia, wife of Berkshire author Nathaniel Hawthorne. Melville continued, calling such a dedication, "A right noble custom, which we of Berkshire must revive. For whether we will or no, Majesty is all around us here in Berkshire, sitting as in a grand Congress of Vienna of majestical hilltops . . . "

Pure nature is a Berkshire tradition, but so is the careful grooming and tending of nature. A village improvement speaker at the Laurel Hill Society meeting in Stockbridge in 1853 put it this way: "We mean to work till every street shall be graded, every sidewalk shaded, every noxious weed eradicated, every watercourse laid and perfected, and every nook and corner beautified — in short, till Art combined with Nature shall have rendered our town the most beautiful and attractive spot in our ancient commonwealth."

"Art combined with Nature," that is the essence of Berkshire life, an essence that led novelist Henry James to write of his visits to Lenox novelist Edith Wharton: "This renews the vision of the Massachusetts Berkshire, land beyond any other in America today . . . " Ever since the 19th-century influx of artists and art patrons, Berkshire culture has had a ripe medium in which to flourish. The legacy for us today is an almost unbelievably rich cultural life, from soaring symphonies at Tanglewood to breathtaking dance artistry at Jacob's Pillow; from the folksy characters of Norman Rockwell's paintings to the elegant austerity of Shaker ways and means; from the dramatic heights of acclaimed theatrical stars at Williamstown Theatre Festival and Berkshire Theatre Festival in Stockbridge to no less lofty moments in Pittsfield, at the Berkshire Public Theatre, and in Lenox, at Shakespeare & Co. Berkshire is home to other museums too, like the Clark in Williamstown, with its dozens of Renoirs, and the Berkshire Museum in Pittsfield, with its Calder mobiles and natural history exhibits.

And the cultural brilliance doesn't set with the sun. Pop music comes to life after dark, from guitar-strumming folksingers to blues and jazz groups, from hard rockers to new wavers, all playing at a variety of pubs, clubs, taverns, bars, restaurants and boogie joints.

There is lodging to suit every taste here, from the baronial Berkshire "cottages," such as Wheatleigh and Blantyre, to the rusticity of dozens of quaint houses offering a simple bed and breakfast. For those who prefer to sleep closer to nature, the county's state parks are a camper's delight. Berkshire has its restaurants too —hundreds of them — from haute cuisine to home cookin', with true winners in every category.

In recreation the region gets its greatest attention from skiers, drawn by the county's fine downhill and cross-country ski runs. For hikers, the Appalachian Trail traverses the entire county. And in warmer weather, Berkshire golf courses, tennis courts, and lakes come alive with sportspeople, eager to play.

"New England is America," says Englishwoman Tina Packer, artistic director of Shakespeare & Co., "but it's very like England. One of the reasons I like living in the Berkshires is that although you're in the country, the company is very good, and a lot of fine minds live here."

So many fine minds and so rich a culture, that Berkshire presents a cultural quilt in need of some firm stitching. Fortunately, I had the help of many exceptionally capable Berkshire friends. Together we've revised, updated and expanded our new-fangled guidebook, one we hope will be read and re-read, not just referred to; and one we hope will be highly useful for first-time and veteran visitors to the Berkshires, as well as for folks who've lived here a good long time.

Among my writing assistants, none was more important than Suzi Forbes Chase, who produced the lodging chapter. An author of travel books, Suzi also has hands-on lodging experience, having worked for the Sheraton Hotels; the Plaza, in New

York; and the Red Lion Inn, in Stockbridge. She brought her trained eye to virtually every inn, bed and breakfast, hotel, motel, bungalow and campground in Berkshire County. Her vivid compendium of descriptions truly gives you "The Keys to Your Room," before you get here.

"What to See, What to Do," the chapter on Berkshire artistic life, is based on years of attendance at many of the events; on insider's information; on personal interviews with public relations and artistic directors, art gallery owners, and artists; and finally on a massive amount of book research, including histories, biographies and letters.

I had the most help in preparing the restaurant and specialty food outlet chapter, "Pleasing the Palate." Here, we set out to document well-known Berkshire culinary delights and to go much further, exploring the menus of dozens of the county's fanciest and funkiest eateries and food purveyors. Most reviews are based on many visits to a restaurant, over many years; some establishments, however, were visited only once. To keep our reviews more uniform, we have framed them around our most recent dining experience. Our editorial budget paid for all our meals; we were in no way indebted to any restaurant, and we never announced our visit or intention. During the meals, we often had extensive conversations with waiters, managers and sometimes the chefs themselves.

For this edition, my gourmet expedition was assisted by one of our co-publishers, David Emblidge, a food lover who spent a year tasting life in France; our other co-publisher, Church Davis, a wine connoisseur who has dined in most of America's finest inns; Dan Klein, Great Barrington novelist, occasional food reviewer for *New England Monthly* and creator of Samara's Sesame Tahini Sauce; and Peter and Fran Buttenheim, now Williamstown residents (he's director of Williams College Alumni Campaigns, and she's a gourmet chef and writer). Together we produced the longest, most extensive collection of in-depth reviews, covering the widest range of dining styles, cuisines, food presentation and pricing ever published for the Berkshires.

Throughout the making of this second edition, Mary Osak served as my able and personable researcher. She sent questionnaires to everybody in the first edition and everybody we wanted in the second. Then she phoned them and double-checked everything. In her spare time, she handled dozens of other details, always efficiently and with good cheer.

From start to finish, we've aimed to create a comprehensive, reliable guide for one of America's premier places to live or vacation. We wish you every pleasure as you come to know the Berkshires better, and we hope our *Berkshire Book* continues to serve you as a trusted friend.

Jonathan Sternfield
Great Barrington, Massachusetts

THE WAY THIS BOOK WORKS

Entries are located by subject in the appropriate chapters. Among the chapters, arrangements vary to suit the needs of subject matter. Most material is arranged in three geographical groupings with SOUTH COUNTY offerings first, then those in CENTRAL COUNTY, and finally NORTH COUNTY. A few nearby but OUTSIDE-the-COUNTY listings appear, too. Within those geographic groupings, listings are arranged alphabetically — first by town or topic, and then by establishments' names. Some entries, such as those in *Shopping* are arranged by type; hence all the craft shops appear together. Each chapter has its own introduction, and the specific arrangement of that chapter is spelled out there.

Factual information was researched at the latest possible time before publication, but be advised that many of these "facts" are subject to change. Chefs and innkeepers come and go. When in doubt, phone ahead.

Specific information (such as address and location, telephone number, hours of business and summary of special features) is presented in the lefthand column or is otherwise shown separately, adjacent to descriptions of various entries throughout the book.

With few exceptions, specific prices are not given. Because pricing is constantly changing, we have noted price *ranges*, in two key chapters, the ones on lodging and dining.

Lodging prices are on a per room rate, double occupancy, in the high seasons (summer, fall foliage and ski months). Low season rates are likely to be 20-40% less. We urge you always to phone ahead for updated prices and other information and for reservations.

Restaurant prices indicate the cost of an individual's meal which includes appetizer, entrée and dessert but does not include cocktails, wine, tax or tip. Restaurants with a *prix fixe* menu are noted accordingly.

Price Codes

	Lodging	*Dining*
Inexpensive	Up to $65	Up to $15
Moderate	$65 - $95	$15 - $20
Expensive	$95 - $150	$20 - $30
Very Expensive	Over $150	Over $30

Credit Cards are abbreviated as follows: AE — American Express CB — Carte Blanche D — Discover DC — Diner's Club MC — MasterCard V — Visa

There is one telephone area code for all of Berkshire: 413. For all numbers in the 413 area, we cite local exchanges only; for numbers outside the 413 area, we give their area codes.

INFORMATION BOOTHS

In warmer weather, many Berkshire towns feature Tourist Information Booths. Year-round, tourist information can be obtained from the **Berkshire Visitors Bureau,** Berkshire Common: bottom level, Hilton Hotel, West St., Pittsfield; 443-9186. Open Mon.-Fri., 8:30-4:30.

Gt. Barrington Information Booth: 362 Main St., 528-1510. Open Tues.-Sat., 9-11:30, 12:30-5: Sun., 12:30-6.

Lee Information Booth: Main St. at the park; 243-0852. Open Mon.-Thurs., 11-5, Fri. and Sat., 11-6, Sun. 10-2.

Massachusetts Turnpike: at Burger King, Eastbound Mile marker 8, Lee; 243-4929.

Lenox Chamber of Commerce, Information Office: Lenox Academy, 75 Main St.; 637-3646. Open Mon.-Thurs., 10-4: Fri. and Sat., 10-6; Sun., 10-2.

Northern Berkshire Chamber of Commerce: Main office, 69 Main St., N. Adams; 663-3735. Open Mon.-Fri., 9-5. Tour booth located on Union St.; open 7 days, 10-4.

Pittsfield Information Booth: Bank Row. Open Mon.-Sat., 8-8; Sun., 8-5.

Stockbridge Information Booth: Main St.; 298-3344. Open 7 days, 10-5.

W. Stockbridge Information: Town Hall, center of town; 232-7080. Open Mon.-Fri., 8:30-12.

Williamstown Information Booth: Route 7; 458-4922. Open daily 10-6.

BERKSHIRE TOWNS

Berkshire is frequently divided into three sections: South, Central, and North. Though still chiefly pastoral, the county is punctuated with industry, most notably in Pittsfield, Adams and North Adams. Generally, the farther north you travel, the more rural and wild the country becomes — with the Adamses and Williamstown being the exceptions. In South County you'll find clusters of lively little towns; Stockbridge is the classic Colonial and Great Barrington the enduring economic crossroad. In the county's Central region, Lenox, — with all its palatial estates and Tanglewood — is the cultural hub; though both Pittsfield and Becket have substantial cultural offerings too. In North County, Williamstown has been called "Art Town U.S.A." for its density of fine art, and it has recently been voted the best college town in America. About 137,000 people live in Berkshire year-round, but in summer, in autumn-leaf season and in snowy ski weather, many thousands more come to enjoy. The original Berkshire is in England, south of Oxford, and there it's pronounced "Bark-sheer." "Berk" derives from "bark," related, of course, to trees or forest; "shire" means "hilly country county."

North County
Adams (Population: 9,578)
Cheshire (3,534)
Clarksburg (1,649)
Florida (746)
New Ashford (208)
North Adams (15,980)
Savoy (608)
Williamstown (8,117)

Central County
Becket (1,737)
Dalton (7,268)
Hancock (676)
Hinsdale (2,025)
Lanesborough (3,186)
Lenox (5,557)
Peru (717)
Pittsfield (47,536)
Richmond (1,605)
Washington (614)
Windsor (770)

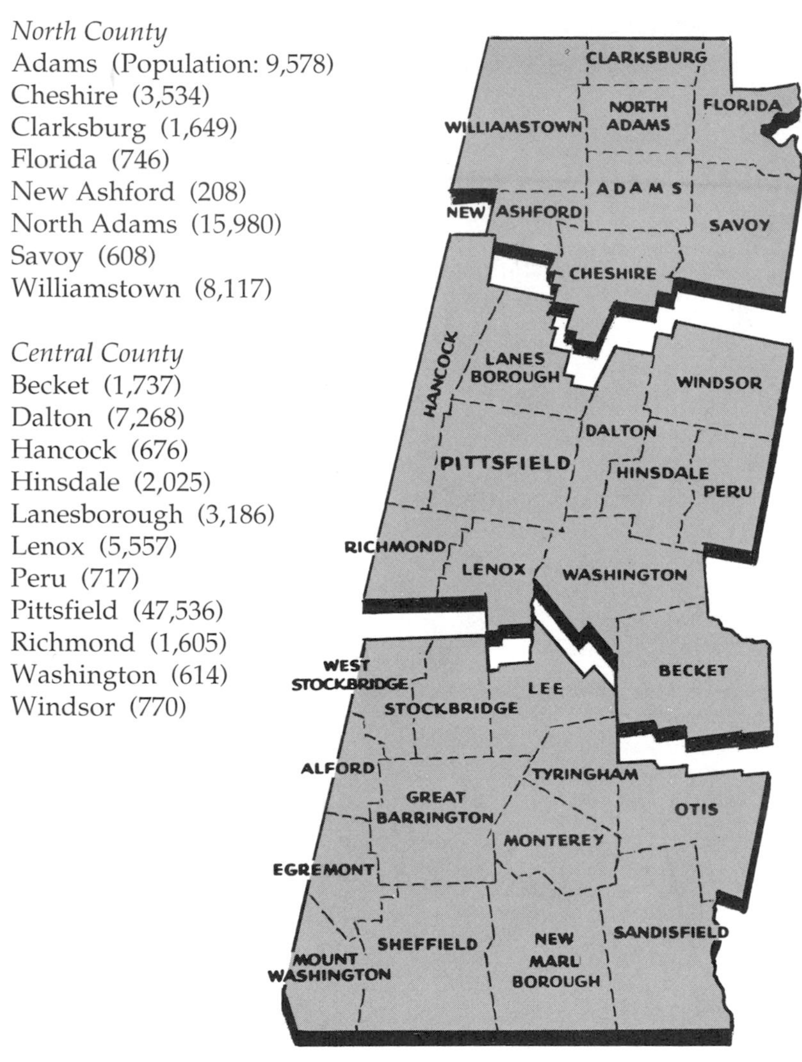

South County
Alford (394)
Egremont (1,060)
Great Barrington (7,014)
Lee (6,052)
Monterey (985)
Mount Washington (115)
New Marlborough (1,098)
Otis (963)
Sandisfield (764)
Sheffield (3,100)
Stockbridge (2,536)
Tyringham (338)
West Stockbridge (1,425)

Contents

CHAPTER ONE

From the Glaciers to the Present

HISTORY

"Save Time and Distance: Take the Hoosac Tunnel."

Berkshire's early history is a story of water and ice, of mountains and wildlife forming a beautiful, but inaccessible "place apart." It is a story of hunters seeking game and eventually a refuge. Later, it becomes the story of religious pilgrims in search of sanctuary, of artists and art patrons coming to be inspired and renewed. It is a saga of industry tapping the region's waterways and cutting into its woodlands. And it is a tale of farmers and engineers, housewives and schoolchildren, poets and actors, craftsmen and shopkeepers, dancers and dreamers.

There is also a new Berkshire history being written, one of restoration, revival and recreation. Where once the old was regularly pushed aside to make way for the new, now it is again revered, and often revitalized. Historic buildings like the Mount and Bellefontaine in Lenox, are being brought back to life. Working from a great tradition, the arts in Berkshire are excelling and expanding — in their seasons, in variety and in sheer number of offerings.

Lively issues are at hand in the hills: how to balance year-round economic viability with overbearing commercialization of the villages; when to stop condominium and time-sharing development. The county is still a haven for zealous religious groups, and though there are few Shakers left, there are several popular groups in Berkshire, whose members put their spirituality *first*, day in, day out.

Being three-quarters covered with trees, today's Berkshire is more forested than it has been in a hundred years. Its area of protected lands, nearly 15%, is on the rise. Industries come and go, without much overall growth, and air pollution continues to be minimal. General Electric remains the backbone of the urban economy here, but it is an increasingly high-tech operation, leaving some traditional assembly line workers behind. Berkshire arts and recreational facilities have burgeoned; the county is now fun during four seasons of the year, day or night. Thus, what was wild and hilly has been selectively cultivated, and now all of Berkshire is in bloom.

Note: Many of the cultural sites mentioned in this chapter are described at greater length elsewhere in this book; see the Index for page references.

NATURAL HISTORY

Tell me your landscape and I will tell you who you are.

Ortega y Gasset, Spanish philosopher

Berkshire's natural history starts over 500 million years ago, when the region was probably flatter, covered with mud, sand and the waters of an inland sea. Just as underwater life was beginning, shifting continental plates caused undersea upheavals, thrusting land masses upwards into the open air. From the decaying primitive sea life, limestone formed; from the sand and mud developed schist, gneiss and quartz.

Then the glaciers came. From the north and northwest, vast tidal waves of slow-moving ice crept into the region, smoothing and gouging, sculpting the landscape. Gradually, the ice melted, leaving rushing rivers, and huge lakes in areas like Great Barrington, Williamstown and Tyringham. But the snows in the northlands began to fall constantly again, and once more the oceans of ice slowly swept into the region. Three more times this cycle repeated: glacial dominance and melting. Without vegetation, this smooth-surfaced Berkshire was a place of howling winds, sandblasting the landscape. As climatic conditions tempered in this latest melting period, vegetation began to grow again, about 11,000 B.C. The grasses and bushes further tempered the climate, and from the boggy marshland, trees such as spruce sprang up, then pine and birch, and finally hardwoods such as oak and maple.

As trees and other vegetation softened the landscape, and as the land itself began to dry out, animals from neighboring regions moved into Berkshire. And not long after that came descendants of the Asians who first called this continent home. These original native Americans were foragers at first, but after developing tools, they then crafted weapons and became hunters. The remains of a 12,000-year-old mastodon were recently found in South Egremont and nearby were scattered arrowheads of the same age. Bow hunting came early to Berkshire.

What the native Americans and animals found back then in Berkshire is close to what we find today: a glacial landscape, with hills and mountains smoothed to a fraction of their former height, with lakes like Onota and Pontoosuc whose basins were scoured by the ice, with steep bowl-shaped cirques like Greylock's "Hopper" (visible from Rte. 7) carved deep into mountainside, with massive rock slabs like those in Ice Glen and at the foot of Monument Mountain, and with widely strewn rocks and boulders almost everywhere. Every spring, a new harvest of rocks appears in the fields, brought up by frost and plow. And those old stone walls partitioning the pastures served not only as fencing, but as rock depositories for farmers attempting to keep their fertile fields free of glacial "pebbles."

The overall topography of Berkshire shows the glacial path clearly. Deep north-to-south furrows are bounded by two north-to-south mountain chains, with two

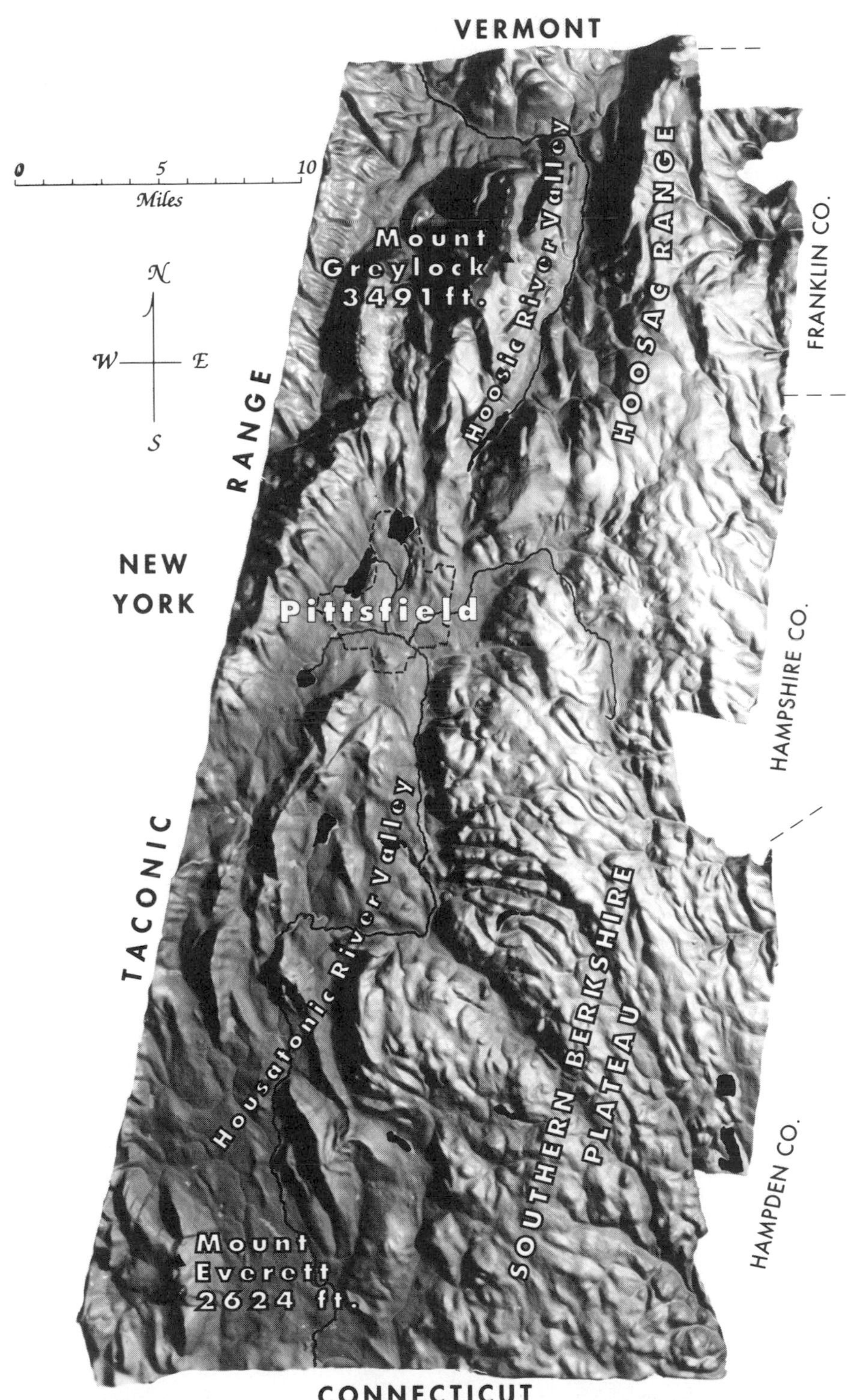

From the relief map by Bartlett Hendricks, courtesy Berkshire Museum.

major rivers running through the valleys. The contours of social and economic history in the region have always followed this lay of the land. On the east is the Hoosac Range, high, rugged country that came to be called "the Berkshire Barrier" because it blocked easy access for pioneers coming over from the Connecticut River valley. On the west, toward the New York border, is the Taconic Range, ruled over by Mt. Greylock (3,491 ft.) in the north and Mt. Everett (2,600 ft.) in the south.

The Housatonic River rises above Pittsfield and flows south through Berkshire, down to Stratford, Connecticut, and out into Long Island Sound. The Hoosic River, flowing northward from Hoosac Lake and tributaries, passes through the Adamses and into Vermont on its way to the Hudson River, above Albany. Because the rivers provided power for mills and generators and because the adjoining land was so fertile, Berkshire history became very much a "waterwheel" — sculpted by glacier and erosion, driven in our time by industry and recreation.

Americans !

Encourage your own Manufactories, and they will Improve.

LADIES, ſave your RAGS.

AS the Subſcribers have it in contemplation to erect a PAPER-MILL in *Dalton*, the enſuing ſpring; and the buſineſs being very beneficial to the community at large, they flatter themſelves that they ſhall meet with due encouragement. And that every woman, who has the good of her country, and the intereſt of her own family at heart, will patronize them, by ſaving her rags, and ſending them to their Manufactory, or to the neareſt Storekeeper—for which the Subſcribers will give a generous price.

HENRY WISWALL,
ZENAS CRANE,
JOHN WILLARD.

***Worceſter*, Feb. 8, 1801.**

"Americans! Encourage your own Manufactories and they will Improve. Ladies, save your RAGS." The 1801 ad that started the Crane Paper empire.

People who visit the Berkshires today only for high culture or fine food, or even for robust skiing, and who don't walk the trails or sit still on the hilltops miss what is perhaps the better half of the local entertainment. The sheer variety of Berkshire habitats and animal families is staggering. Though wildlife in Berkshire was undoubtedly richer before the arrival of people, there are still herds of deer, the occasional moose (sometimes appearing in an urban backyard), and black bear, red and gray fox, a few coyotes, bobcats, even eastern cougars, as well as more common beaver and mink. Berkshire has rare salamanders, extant only in these wetlands because the area's naturally high lime content counteracts the effects of acid rain, allowing the fragile creatures one last safe habitat. Giant blue heron, with wings six feet across, can be seen here on isolated ponds, and ruffed grouse, quail and wild turkey occupy the woods. Though formal gardens at historic homes are beautiful, not to be missed are the delicate alpine flowers on the tops of the tallest mountains, like Greylock, above the tree line.

In this geologically momentary melt between glacial flows, Berkshire is green, welcoming and beautiful.

* * *

Want to know more about Berkshire natural history? Lauren Stevens' *Hikes & Walks in the Berkshire Hills* has a nice overview, informed by the author's extensive trail experience and consultation with Williams College geologist, Paul Karabinos. The pamphlet *A Canoe Guide to the Housatonic* provides some good color commentary on the local ecology. The ***Berkshire Museum*** is the county's center for natural history study, and includes Bartlett Hendricks' wall-sized raised relief topographic map of the county. For field trips, try any of the "Nature Preserves" (see Chapter Six, *Recreation*). And in the summer, the Appalachian Mountain Club runs excellent nature study programs at sky-high ***Bascom Lodge*** atop Mt. Greylock.

Gone to the Country

In the mid-19th century, Henry Ward Beecher, New York's most celebrated preacher, built a home called Blossom Farm in Lenox, at Wyndhurst, now called Cranwell (on Rte. 20). Beecher's admiration for the scenic beauty of the area led him to write a series of newspaper articles called "The Star Papers." Here is a brief, ebullient account from 1855, celebrating Beecher's arrival in Berkshire.

> *Thus we sped on, from station to station, the hills growing larger all the way, until, at three o'clock, we reached Lenox....Bright bay Charley was waiting for his master; and our farm horses and wagon (think of that!) were waiting for the baggage, and soon we were trotting away, and greeting, as we went, each field, each stately elm, and round maple....As we rose along the ascending road, the hills began to emerge on every side, and as we drew near our dwelling, up rose, far in the north, old Grey-Lock, the patriarch of a wide family of hills, happily settled down about him. As far to the south, dim and blue, the dome of Mount Washington stood, and still stands, the head and glory of innumerable unnamed hills. Between these two great northern and southern landmarks, a distance of more than sixty miles, lies the Berkshire valley. Not such a valley as you think of along the Connecticut, — wide meadows, flat and fat; but such a valley as the ocean would be, if, when its waves were running tumultuous and high, it were suddenly transfixed and solidified. The most level portion of this region, if removed to Illinois, would be an eminent hill....The endless variety of such a country never ceases to astonish and please. At every ten steps the aspect changes; every variation of every atmosphere, and therefore every hour of the day, produces new effects. It is everlasting company to you. It is, indeed, just like some choice companion, of rich heart and genial imagination, never twice alike, in mood, in conversation, in radiant sobriety, or half-bright sadness; bold, tender, deep, various!*

SOCIAL HISTORY

History is to the community what memory is to the individual.

Shaker saying

From the outset, Berkshire's social history was greatly influenced by the effects of its natural history. Set off by imposing mountain ranges and beset by fierce winters, the area became home to migrant wildlife around 10,000 B.C., and shortly thereafter, was visited by roving bands of Amerindian hunters in search of game. Over the next 11,000 years, Berkshire was a summer hunting ground for many of these peoples, and for some, the area provided the materials to begin agriculture.

Among the woodland Indians, the Mahican lived along the Hudson River and ventured to Berkshire for the summer hunt. They called the major river here the *Hooestonic* ("the river beyond the mountains"), and from it, they fished shad, herring and salmon in the springtime. The Mahican built weirs to trap fish in the Housatonic's tributaries and also fished with hand nets from dugout canoes on the river. They gathered mussels from the rocky river bottoms and smoke-cured them together with their surplus fish for winter storage. They hunted duck and geese; and they maintained gardens in the river's floodplain which was fertilized annually by the spring flood.

After the Dutch established a fur trading outpost at Fort Orange (now Albany, New York) in 1624, the Mahican fell into conflict with the neighboring Mohawk. The two tribes went to war over the valuable fur trade, and by 1628, the Mahican had been driven from the west bank of the Hudson, settling permanently in Berkshire.

In 1676, the first European of record set foot in Berkshire, when Major John Talcott overtook a raiding band of about 150 Indians "neare unto Ousatunick" (Great Barrington). It was the last significant battle of King Phillip's War, and Major Talcott preserved both Colonial security and his perfect unbeaten battle record.

Fate did not smile upon the Mahican. Smallpox dramatically reduced their ranks in 1690. Not long after, Dutch farmers migrated east from the Hudson Valley and settled in Berkshire, near what is now the town of Mount Washington. There are still Dutch town names in South County, such as Van Deusenville (in Great Barrington).

In 1724, a small band of Mahican led by chiefs Konkapot and Umpachenee sold their lands along the Housatonic River (including what is now Sheffield, Great Barrington, Egremont, Mount Washington, Alford, and parts of Lee, Stockbridge and West Stockbridge). The buyers were the Parsons, proprietors through the Colonial Commonwealth of Massachusetts; the price, "£460, 3 bbls. of cider, and 30 qts. of rum." In a matter of months, scores of English settlers moved into Berkshire, to the Sheffield grant known as Lower Housatonic Township. The earliest homesteads were built at some distance from the Housatonic, on the second river terrace. This allowed the fertile floodplain to be used for agriculture and kept the settlers away from the malarial lowlands.

In the mid-1730s, the Rev. John Sergeant came from Yale College to proselytize and educate the hundreds of Mahican who lived around *W-nahk-ta-kook* ("Great Meadow"), later called Indian Town and then Stockbridge. He learned their language and won the respect of the Indians. Ten years later (1744), Berkshire was opened to cross-country road travel for the first time, when the "Great Road" was laid out between Boston and Albany, crossing the county at Great Barrington. In 1749 John Sergeant died; and soon the Mahican faded.

There seemed something of a renewal when the Rev. Jonathan Edwards came to Stockbridge two years later. With his fiery preaching style, Edwards had stirred up the "Great Awakening," a religious revival sweeping New England. His zeal, however, had offended parishioners at his previous pulpit in Northampton, and Edwards had been dismissed. Exiled, in effect, to Stockbridge, he now had a small but well-schooled congregation. One of America's earliest philosophers of religion, Edwards published *Freedom of the Will*, in 1754, Berkshire's first book.

With the conclusion of the French and Indian War, marked by the British victory over the French at Quebec (1759), Berkshire was no longer so vulnerable to invading Indian attack. After British solidification of power in the area, the royal governor, Sir Francis Bernard, created the county. Striking off a section from the already-existing Hampshire County, the governor declared this one "Berkshire," after his home county in England. The date was July 1, 1761 — Berkshire was born, in America, in Massachusetts.

As his tribe dwindled to fewer than 400, Konkapot, at age 94, stepped down as chief of the rechristened "Stockbridge Indians." Two years later, in early 1773, a group of townspeople and lawyers met in the Sheffield study of Col. John Ashley.

The wooden rake man, Lee, about 1865.

Courtesy Berkshire Historical Society

There, in one of the earliest public assertions of American freedom, they drafted "The Sheffield Declaration," stating to Britain and all the world that "Mankind in a State of Nature are equal, free and independent of each other . . ." By the following year, ferment in the county against the British was reaching fever pitch. In July, a county convention met under the chairmanship of Col. Ashley; and from this meeting, "the Stockbridge Non-Intercourse Articles" of 1774 were drafted, complaining that "whereas the Parliament of Great Britain have of late undertaken to give and grant away our money without our knowledge or consent . . ., we will not import, purchase or consume . . ." any British goods. By mid-August, British oppression had mounted, and on the 16th, the people of Berkshire would take it no longer. Fifteen-hundred strong, they staged a peaceful sit-down strike around the Great Barrington Courthouse, preventing the royal judges from meeting. It was the first open resistance to British rule in America.

In April, 1775, a regiment of Berkshire Minutemen under Col. John Paterson of Lenox started out for Cambridge to aid in the Revolutionary effort. And in May, former Sheffield resident Ethan Allen led his Green Mountain Boys and 57 Berkshire men in a successful surprise attack on Fort Ticonderoga. That following winter (1776), Gen. Henry Knox led Continental troops and over 100 oxen, dragging captured Ticonderoga cannon, through Berkshire on the way to Gen. George Washington in Cambridge. Aided by this additional weaponry, Washington was able to drive the British from Boston.

Once the United States was established, all sorts of religious, cultural and industrial developments began to take place in Berkshire. In 1779, one Mrs. John Fisk was excommunicated from the church in Stockbridge for marrying a Revolutionary War officer accused of habitually using profane language. A *cause célèbre* in Massachusetts' Congregationalism, the case pitted Calvinist orthodoxy against church liberals, a regional division with parallels to the contours of the ongoing national debate between Federalists and Jeffersonians. At the county courthouse in Great Barrington in 1781, Theodore Sedgwick of Stockbridge — who brought distinction to the county by serving in both houses of Congress — won the freedom of Col. John Ashley's slave, Mum Bett, said to be the first American slave freed by law. By 1784, the Indian community in Berkshire was nearing its end, having collapsed socially and economically. Beginning that year, the Mahicans were forced into westward migration, leaving only their Housatonic legends behind them. In the 1790s, the Shakers established colonies in Hancock and Tyringham, Williams College opened, and marble quarrying started in West Stockbridge.

Hancock's signature building – the round Shaker stone barn (1826)

The farmers of Cheshire pooled the entire town's milk production for a day in 1801, and produced the Great Cheshire Cheese, a 1,235 pound, barrel-shaped cheddar that was hauled by oxen to Albany, and then by boat to Washington, for presentation to President Jefferson. Industry took a firm hold in Berkshire that year as well. Zenas Crane began paper production in Dalton, and David Estes opened the first textile mill in North Adams. By the sides of Berkshire's rivers, plants of a new sort were sprouting.

Spanish merino sheep were introduced into Berkshire — the first in New England — and with their wool woven into fine worsted in the county's state-of-the-art mills, Berkshire broadcloth was fashioned into President Madison's inauguration suit in 1813. Shortly thereafter, the first stage route in the county was established, running from Greenfield to North Adams, Williamstown and Albany. And the writers began to come. First there was poet William Cullen Bryant in Great Barrington (1820). As he attempted to divine the art of poetry while earning his living as a lawyer, his new friend, Catherine Sedgwick, in Stockbridge published her first novel, *A New England Tale*, to critical acclaim. By stagecoach, Alexis de Tocqueville visited the Sedgwicks in Stockbridge in 1831. Not long after, trains came huffing into the hills, one of them bringing Henry Wadsworth Longfellow to honeymoon in Pittsfield. Dr. Oliver Wendell Holmes built a home on ancestral lands at Canoe Meadows and began to spend his summers in Berkshire. Then, in 1850, Herman Melville bought Arrowhead Farm in Pittsfield. Nathaniel Hawthorne moved from Salem to Lenox and took up residence at Tanglewood. Shortly thereafter, Dr. Holmes introduced Hawthorne to Melville on the occasion of a climb up Monument Mountain; the two great writers' imaginations were entwined thereafter.

In 1851, construction was begun on the Hoosac Tunnel (between the Berkshire towns of Florida and North Adams), a project that was to last decades — and tragically take hundreds of lives. It was a tunnel that was destined to be the longest in America and the one through which most tunneling technology was developed. Here, nitroglycerine was used for the first time, speeding the work, but also the demise of many workers.

But before those essentially creative explosions were silenced, there were many totally destructive ones sounding in the Civil War. Five days after the Confederate forces opened fire on Fort Sumter, Berkshire militiamen were on their way south to defend the republic. These first county recruits stayed three months and saw little action; other Berkshire regiments took their place, fighting often in the coming months, through 1865, as far south as the state of Florida. In that same year, President Lincoln was assassinated, and Berkshire mourned.

After two unsuccessful attempts, Cyrus Field of Stockbridge and his engineers finally laid a cable across the Atlantic, in 1866, connecting American communications with Europe. A year later, in America's leading paper town, Lee, paper fabrication from wood pulp rather than rags was demonstrated for the first time in the United States.

Industry was now booming in Berkshire. Aided by plentiful water power, textile and paper plants lined the rivers. Fueled by the county's abundant forests, iron smelters and other heavy industries cut deep into the Berkshire woodland. It was not long before nearly 75% of the county's timber was gone, and the hills were nearly bald. In 1875, the Hoosac Tunnel was finally completed, opening North County to interstate commerce; and shortly thereafter, in 1879, Crane & Co. of Dalton obtained an exclusive contract with the federal government to produce American currency paper, a contract involving a lot of money, both blank and printed.

In 1886, William Stanley installed the world's first commercial electric system, in the town of Great Barrington, where 25 shops along Main Street were lighted. Five years later, an electric trolley system was introduced in Pittsfield, running from Park Square to Pontoosuc Lake. Soon, this quiet, reliable transport would interconnect most of the county.

The decade of the 1880s ushered in Berkshire's Gilded Age as well, the age in which millionaires came to the hills to play and build their dream "cottages." In all, some 75 extraordinary mansions had been added to the Berkshire landscape. The Berkshire community would never again be a cultural backwater: European and urban tastes had come to live in the hills.

Novelist Edith Wharton's "cottage," the Mount, completed in 1902.

Courtesy Lenox library.

Making even grander strokes in Berkshire land acquisition was William C. Whitney, secretary of the navy under President Grover Cleveland. In 1896, in the Berkshire town of Washington, Whitney established an 11,000-acre game preserve and stocked it with buffalo, moose and elk. The estate was later to become October Mountain State Forest, a giant wilderness in county center. In the fall of 1902, President Roosevelt visited Berkshire, but he barely escaped alive, sustaining minor injury after his coach overturned near the Pittsfield Country Club. That next summer, both ex-President Grover Cleveland and humorist Mark Twain summered in Tyringham. Eight years later, on July 4, 1911, as Pittsfield observed its gala 150th anniversary, President Taft spoke before a crowd of 50,000 at the railroad station. And later that same year, Edith Wharton's novella *Ethan Frome* was published, a critical and popular success that derived many of its dramatic and scenic details from life in the Berkshires.

Twentieth-century Berkshire has been marked with events principally in industry and the arts. Since 1903, General Electric has played a significant role in the county's industry, and all through this century, that role has developed as the industrial giant has diversified its product research and manufacturing. The huge electric transformers still produced in Pittsfield are descendants of the ones first demonstrated in Great Barrington by William Stanley.

In the arts, the Berkshire Playhouse (later to become today's Berkshire Theatre Festival) opened in Stockbridge in 1928, with Eva LeGallienne in *Cradle Song*. Ted Shawn established his School of Dance at Jacob's Pillow in Becket in 1932. The 1930s also saw and heard the first Berkshire Symphony Festival concerts,

Symphonic music comes to Berkshire: The New York Philharmonic at Hanna Farm, Interlaken, in 1934, establishing the model for Tanglewood.

Courtesy Stockbridge Historical Room.

preludes to Tanglewood. Downhill skiing debuted in Berkshire in 1935, as Bousquet opened runs in Pittsfield and arranged for "ski trains" from New York. Other mountains soon had trails carved across them, and Berkshire became a winter recreational mecca.

The 1950s saw the arrival of famed artist Norman Rockwell in Stockbridge, and the creation of the Sterling and Francine Clark Art Institute in Williamstown, a collection and facility of international import. The Williamstown Theatre Festival began performances, enlivening all of Berkshire with star-studded drama. In the '60s, two colleges were opened: Berkshire Community College, in Pittsfield, the first in a projected series of state junior colleges; and Simon's Rock College of Bard in Great Barrington, a progressive school that is now part of Bard College.

In the mid-sixties, General Electric made another breakthrough, this time in plastics, and the company subsequently developed a whole new family of polymers, which diversified the corporation still further and sent a regional invention — the astronauts' Lexan faceshields — to the moon — from the plastics laboratories in Pittsfield to Tranquility Crater. And in the last ten years, the arts have blossomed still more gloriously, with Shakespeare & Co. being born in Lenox, then ambitiously beginning the restoration and adaptation of the Mount, Edith Wharton's mansion. In Pittsfield, too, a company found its home when the Berkshire Public Theatre settled into restoring the old Union Square Theatre.

Culturally, Berkshire's rich smorgasbord has been recently enriched by the offerings of the Berkshire Performing Arts Center in Lenox — with shows ranging from the Paul Winter Consort to Laura Nyro — and by the ongoing activity of David Barg's L'Orchestra, bringing fine classical music to an eager three-season audience at various local sites. And in the health-recreational arena, the county's stock went sky-high with the arrival in Lenox of Canyon Ranch, one of the most luxurious and sophisticated spas in the world.

Berkshire's current events center around environmental protection and clean-up, condo development, shopping malls, bypasses, the proposed Greylock Glen recreational area and the Mass MoCA modern arts complex in North Adams. Some of these significant projects, notably the expansive Berkshire Mall in Lanesborough, are already realities; others, like Greylock Glen and MassMoCA are well along in the planning stages. Bypasses, rerouting Route 7's truck traffic around Stockbridge and Pittsfield, are often discussed, and just as often bypassed. Despite

GE's Concept House is about 30% plastic – employing polymers principally in the roof, windows, siding and plumbing.

Courtesy General Electric Plastics.

the grim reality that one of its principal rivers, the Housatonic, continues to be undrinkable, unfishable and unswimmable, a victim of toxic PCB's, Berkshire is still beautiful, still a magnet to hundreds of thousands of tourists, a magic homeland to tens of thousands of residents.

Under the watchful eye of the Berkshire Natural Resources Council and other environmental protection groups, the splendor of the landscape is being guarded and preserved. With the gradual shrinking of industry here, and tourism among the most stable of Berkshire businesses, protecting the rolling hills seems to make good economic as well as aesthetic sense. Once, the hills were decimated, shaved bald by paper and lumber mills, and by charcoal manufacturers. The hills are alive again, fully forested and soothing to the eye. In many respects, Berkshire seems to be breathing easier, to be coming back to its senses.

CHAPTER TWO

Getting Here, Getting Around

TRANSPORTATION

Courtesy the Snap Shop.

Railroad Street, Great Barrington, just before the advent of the automobile.

Traveling to the Berkshires can be fun these days, especially by car, but it wasn't always so. During Colonial times, when Berkshire County was a patchwork of farms, travel here was by horseback or stagecoach over rough dirt roads. Colonel Henry Knox found this out in 1776, when he had to cut his own trail across Berkshire while dragging cannon from Fort Ticonderoga to Cambridge.

Some passage towards Berkshire was afforded by both the Hudson and Connecticut rivers aboard sailing ships, but river travel did not become popular till 1825 when the steamboats began regular service. Both Albany and Hartford were connected to New York City by steamboat runs, the upper Connecticut River being outfitted with an elaborate system of locks to bypass the rapids.

With the harnessing of steam for riverboat power, it wasn't long before the iron horse came huffing into the Berkshire Hills. Rails were laid from New York to the Berkshires by the Housatonic Railroad; and two lines competed to the west: the Albany-West Stockbridge Line and the Hudson and Berkshire Line. From Boston, construction of the Western Railway up from Springfield was reportedly "delayed by competition between Stockbridge and Pittsfield for fixing of the route through their town. After surveys, Pittsfield won." During the summers of 1840-41, deep cuts in the hills were made and many bridges built. When the lines were completed, Berkshire was nine hours by train from Boston and about three hours from Albany. But many who had come to work on the railroads never took the train back. Hundreds of the Irish rail laborers from cities east and west grew to love the Berkshires and stayed on.

Perhaps sons of these rail workers influenced local transport too, for early in our own century, a remarkable system of electric trolley track was laid among hilltowns in the Berkshires, running from Williamstown south through North Adams and Adams, through Pittsfield, Lenox, Lee, Great Barrington and Sheffield. Quiet and reliable, this Berkshire Street Railway grew so popular that opulent parlor cars were constructed and put into service, running till 1932. When automobiles and buses were refined, the possibilities for public transport changed and paved roads were improved, unpaved ones were surfaced. Rail service to and within the Berkshires withered.

Present Possibilities

Amtrak serves Pittsfield from Boston, but you'd better be on time for that one, because there's only one train a day in each direction!

So, if a car is available, by all means, drive to the Berkshires. You'll want a car here to explore the back roads and byways, and by auto, the trip to the Berkshires can be enjoyed at your own pace. If an automobile is not your way, and you're not on the train east or west, bus is the next logical option, and these run regularly from New York, Hartford, Boston and Albany. If you're in a hurry to get to these hills, you can fly in, but alas, now only by private or charter plane to Great Barrington, Pittsfield or North Adams. Major airlines with regular service fly into both Bradley International near Hartford and to the Albany County Airport; from there, car rentals or limousine and bus service are available. For your convenience, a host of details about Berkshire transportation follows.

GETTING TO THESE HILLS

BY CAR

From Manhattan: Take the Major Deegan Expressway or the Henry Hudson Parkway to the Saw Mill River Parkway, then proceed north on one of the most beautiful roadways in the world, the Taconic State Parkway. For the southern Berkshires, exit the Taconic at "Hillsdale, Claverack, Rte. 23" and follow 23 east, towards Hillsdale and on to Great Barrington. For Stockbridge, Lee, and Lenox, (and all points in south and central county) proceed up Rte. 7. For Williamstown and all of northern Berkshire, you might want to proceed farther up the Taconic and exit at Rte. 295, leading to Stephentown, then follow Rte. 43 through Hancock.

From New Jersey, Pennsylvania and south: If local color is high on your list or you'd rather ramble northward, Rte. 22 north is a good choice, and you can pick it up as far south as Armonk or Bedford in Westchester County, New York. Rte. 22 is a road still proud of its diners: of particular note is the Red Rooster in Pawling, just north of I-684's end. Further upstate on Rte. 22, turn right at Hillsdale on Rte. 23 east toward Great Barrington. For the most direct route from New Jersey, Pennsylvania and south, take the New York Thruway to I-84 east; at the Taconic Parkway, go north to Rte. 23 for southern Berkshire, or drive on to Rte. 295 for northern Berkshire.

From Connecticut and/or the New York Metro Area: Rte. 7 north was an early stagecoach thoroughfare to Berkshire, and you join the same trail at Danbury, via I-684 and I-84. Driving up Rte. 7, you'll wend your way along the beautiful Housatonic River, north through New Milford, Kent, and Canaan and into Massachusetts through Ashley Falls (an especially good ride for picnics and antiques). To arrive in southeastern Berkshire, Rte. 8 is a quick and scenic drive as it follows the Farmington River north.

BERKSHIRE ACCESS

Using Tanglewood (on the Stockbridge—Lenox line) as the Berkshire reference point, the following cities are this close.

CITY	TIME	MILES
Albany	1 hr	50
Boston	2 1/2 hrs	135
Bridgeport	2 hrs	110
Danbury	1 3/4 hrs	85
Hartford	1 1/2 hrs	70
New Haven	2 1/2 hrs	115
Montreal	5 hrs	275
New York City	3 hrs	150
Philadelphia	4 1/2 hrs	230
Providence	2 1/2 hrs	125
Springfield	3/4 hr	35
Waterbury	1 1/2 hrs	75
Washington, DC	7 hrs	350
Worcester	1 3/4 hrs	90

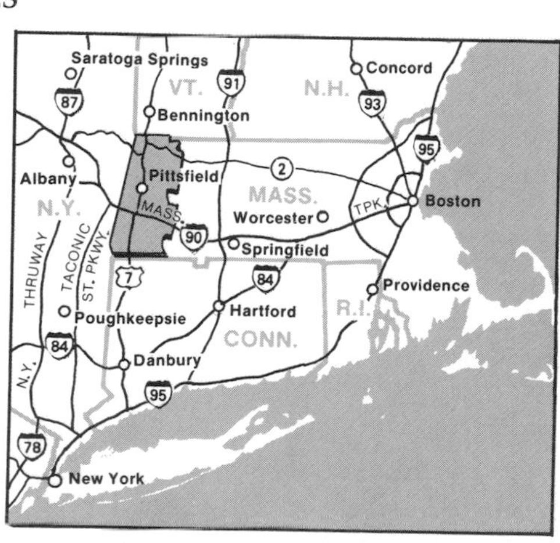

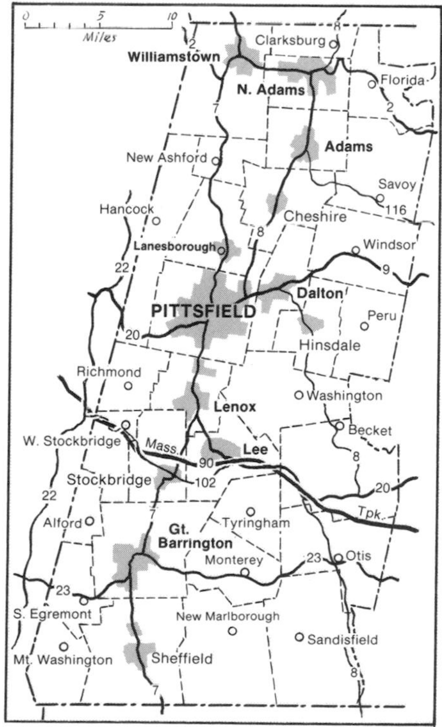

Berkshire County is 56 miles south to north, from Sheffield to Williamstown. Depending on the season and the weather, it's normally a two-hour leisurely drive up Rte. 7. Because of the mountain ranges that run along this route, east-west travel across the county remains much more difficult, with all the county's east-west routes (2 in the north; 9, midcounty; and 23 in the south) being tricky drives in freezing or snowy weather. Back roads in particular vary tremendously in condition and type, ranging from smooth macadam to rough dirt. On these back roads especially, drivers should keep an eye out for bicyclists, horseback riders, hikers, joggers and deer.

From Boston and east: The Massachusetts Turnpike is the quickest, easiest and one of the more scenic routes west to the southern Berkshires, and from Boston, there's no better bet. West of the Connecticut River, you can get off the turnpike at Exit 3 and take Rte. 202 south to 20 west and pick up Rte. 23 west at Woronoco for the best route to Otis Ridge, Butternut Basin and Catamount ski areas. Most people stay on the turnpike right into the Berkshires, exiting either at Lee or West Stockbridge.

A less rapid but more colorful route westward from Boston is Rte. 20, which cuts across southern Massachusetts, connecting with Lee. If you're coming west to the Berkshires from more northern latitudes, Rte. 9 from Northampton is a splendid drive, a high road, with long, lovely vistas and few towns. Still farther to the north, eastern entry to Berkshire County can be gained by driving the original Mohawk Trail, an Indian byway. Also known as Rte. 2, this is the most direct way to Jiminy Peak and Brodie Mountain skiing.

From Hartford: The quickest route by far is I-91 north to the Massachusetts Turnpike west. Then proceed as in directions for Massachusetts Turnpike travel from Boston. A slower but more pleasant drive is Rte. 44 west, up through Avon, Norfolk and Canaan, where you turn right and take Rte. 7 north into Berkshire County.

From Montreal or Albany: Leaving Canada, take I-87 (known as "the Northway") south to Albany, and exit at Rte. 7 to Rte. 2 toward Williamstown, or continue on I-87 south and I-90 east (they're the same south of Albany), connecting then to the Massachusetts Turnpike which is the continuation of I-90 east. Exit at either Canaan, NY or Lee.

BY BUS

From Manhattan: (3 1/2 hours) ***Bonanza*** (212-564-8484) serves the Berkshires out of New York City's ***Port Authority Bus Terminal*** at 40th St. between 8th and 9th Aves. Tickets may be purchased at the Greyhound ticket windows, (212-971-6363) near 8th Ave. Boarding is down the escalators at the center of the terminal, and then to the right, usually at Gate 13. Bonanza runs three buses daily: 8:45 a.m., 1:45 p.m., and 4:45 p.m. On Fiday afternoons, there's an express to the Berkshires, leaving Port Authority around 4:45 and arriving in Gt. Barrington about 7:50. There is also an additional Friday evening bus, leaving Port Authority at 6:45. The 1991 round trip ticket price is $44 to Gt. Barrington, with a same-day round trip priced at $33. Berkshire locales marked with an asterisk are Flag Stops, where you must wave to the bus driver in order to be picked up.

Berkshire Phone Numbers for New York Buses

Canaan, CT	Canaan Pharmacy, Main St.	203-824-5481
Gt. Barrington	Bill's Pharmacy, 362 Main St.	528-1590
Hillsdale, NY	*Junction Rtes. 22 & 23	800-556-3815
Lee	McClelland Drugs, 43 Main St.	243-0135
Lenox	New Dimensions, Walker St.	637-2588
New Ashford	*Entrance to Brodie Mt. Ski Area, Rte. 7	800-556-3815
N. Adams Terminal	Bus Terminal (Englander Coach Lines) Oasis Plaza, 148 American Legion Dr.	662-2016

Pittsfield	Bus Terminal, 57 S. Church St.	442-4451
Sheffield	*Rte. 7, First Agricultural Bank	800-556-3815
So. Egremont	*Gaslight Store	800-556-3815
Stockbridge	Chamber of Commerce Booth, Main St.	298-3344
Williamstown	Williams Inn, 1090 Main St.	458-2665

From Boston (3 1/2 hours): ***Bonanza, Englander*** and ***Greyhound*** serve the Berkshires from Boston out of the ***Greyhound Terminal*** at 10 St. James Ave. (617-423-5810). Bonanza/Greyhound services Lee, Lenox and Pittsfield; Englander services Williamstown and No. Adams. Greyhound/Trailways runs two buses daily to Pittsfield out of the ***Trailways Terminal*** at 555 Atlantic Ave. Trailways' 1991 weekday round-trip ticket price to Pittsfield is $26, weekend round-trip ticket, $30.

Berkshire Phone Numbers for Boston Buses

Lee	McClelland Drugs, 43 Main St.	243-0135
Lenox	Hagyard Pharmacy (Greyhound Agency) 4 Housatonic St.	637-0048
No. Adams Terminal	Englander Coach Lines, Oasis Plaza, 148 American Legion Dr.	664-4588 or 662-201
Pittsfield	Bus Terminal, 57 So. Church St.	442-4451
Williamstown	Williams Inn, 1090 Main St.	458-2665

From Hartford (1 3/4 hours): The ***Arrow Line*** runs one bus to Pittsfield daily, with a second on Friday and Sunday into Pittsfield from the ***Greyhound Terminal*** at 409 Church St., Hartford (203-547-1500). Arrow's 1991 round-trip ticket price is $38.

From Montreal (6 hours): ***Greyhound*** runs south to the Albany Greyhound Terminal. Connect to Pittsfield as noted below.

From Albany (1 hour): The ***Arrow Line*** runs two buses from Albany to Pittsfield on Friday and Sunday only; 1991 round-trip ticket price is $15. ***Bonanza*** runs two buses daily from Albany to Pittsfield. ***Greyhound*** runs one bus daily with an additional one on Friday and Sunday; 1991 round-trip ticket is $15 on Bonanza and $11 on Greyhound.

BY TRAIN

From Manhattan: Until World War II, the Housatonic Railroad ran ski trains from Manhattan to the Berkshires. And right up to 1971, Penn Central ran trains from New York City to the Berkshires, via Danbury. Since that time, however, rail service northward has no longer linked the Big Apple with the Berkshires. If you're inclined to ride the rails, ***Amtrak*** (800-872-7245) can help you get to the Berkshires, but not all the way. Their turboliner from Penn Central Station (7th and 32nd) runs frequently and smoothly along the Hudson River, a splendid ride. For southern Berkshire, stay aboard till Hudson, a river town recently restored; for northern Berkshire, carry on to Rensselaer. Reservations are necessary for some trains. For travel connections from Hudson or Rensselaer to the Berkshires, see "By Taxi or Limousine."

From Boston: Amtrak runs a single train daily through the Berkshires, starting from Boston's South Station. The Pittsfield depot has no actual station; it's just a shelter. (To find the depot: take West St. westwards past the Hilton; at the first light, turn right onto Center St.; take the next right onto Depot St.; the shelter is on the left.) Anyone boarding the train in Pittsfield must purchase tickets on the train; the 1991 round-trip ticket price ranges from $25 each way to $38 round trip, depending on time of travel and seat availability. Private compartments are also available, ranging from $46.50 supplementary for a single compartment to $79 supplementary for a double compartment.

From Montreal: Amtrak runs one train daily from Montreal through Albany. The 1991 round-trip ticket price is $60, excluding holiday periods. During the Thanksgiving, Christmas and New Year's seasons, the round-trip rate rises to $92. There is no same-day train connection from this run to the Berkshires; to get here by hired car, see "By Limousine or Taxi"; or see "By Bus."

From Albany: Amtrak has a single Pittsfield-bound train daily from the Albany/Rensselaer Depot on East St. (2 miles from downtown Albany). The 1991 ticket fare is $10 one way, and ranges from $15 to $17 round trip depending on time of travel and seat availability.

BY PLANE

If you own a small airplane or decide to charter one, you can fly directly to the Berkshires, landing at Gt. Barrington, Pittsfield or N. Adams airports.

From New York City: Feeling rich, traveling high with some friends or riding on the corporate account? There are several charter air companies in the metropolitan New York area that will fly you from La Guardia, JFK or other airports near New York to any of the Berkshire airports. Their 1991 estimated rates run from $675 to $1000 one way, for a twin-engine airplane (holds five plus the pilot). Airlines currently flying these routes include:

Aircraft Charter Group	800-553-3590
Chester Air, Chester, CT	800-752-6371
Long Island Airways	800-645-9572

and from Westchester County:

Panorama (White Plains airport)	914-328-9800
(if calling from New York City):	718-507-9800
Richmor Aviation	800-331-6101

From Boston: There are several charter flight companies that fly from Beantown to Berkshire. Their 1991 estimated rates run $275 to $600 for a twin-engine airplane (holds five plus the pilot). Some of those you can try are:

Aerotransit	508-777-3250
Bird Airfleet	508-372-6566
Wiggins Airways	617-762-5690 Ext. #251

From Hartford: Bradley International Airport in Hartford handles numerous domestic and international airlines, so you can fly to Bradley from nearly anywhere. From there, charter air service to the Berkshires is available through any of the companies listed under "From Boston" or through the Berkshire County companies listed below.

From Albany: Albany is terminus for a substantial volume of domestic jet traffic and, being under an hour from the Berkshires by car, is the closest you can get to these hills by jet. Charter connector flights from Albany to the Berkshires are available through ***Page Flight*** (518-869-0253) or through the Berkshire County companies listed below.

In Berkshire County: There are three aviation companies in Berkshire County which operate air taxi service to just about any other northeastern airport.

Berkshire Aviation	Gt. Barrington Airport	528-1010 or 528-1061
Lyon Aviation	Pittsfield Airport	443-6700
Esposito Flying Service	Harriman & West Airport, N. Adams	663-3330

These local carriers' 1991 rates for a twin-engine plane (holds five plus the pilot) averages $200 to Albany, $550 to Boston, $235 to Hartford, $700 to La Guardia or JFK, and $495 to Teterboro, New Jersey (at the foot of the George Washington Bridge). They also have single-engine planes (holds three plus pilot) for roughly 35-40% less, but these are dependent on weather conditions.

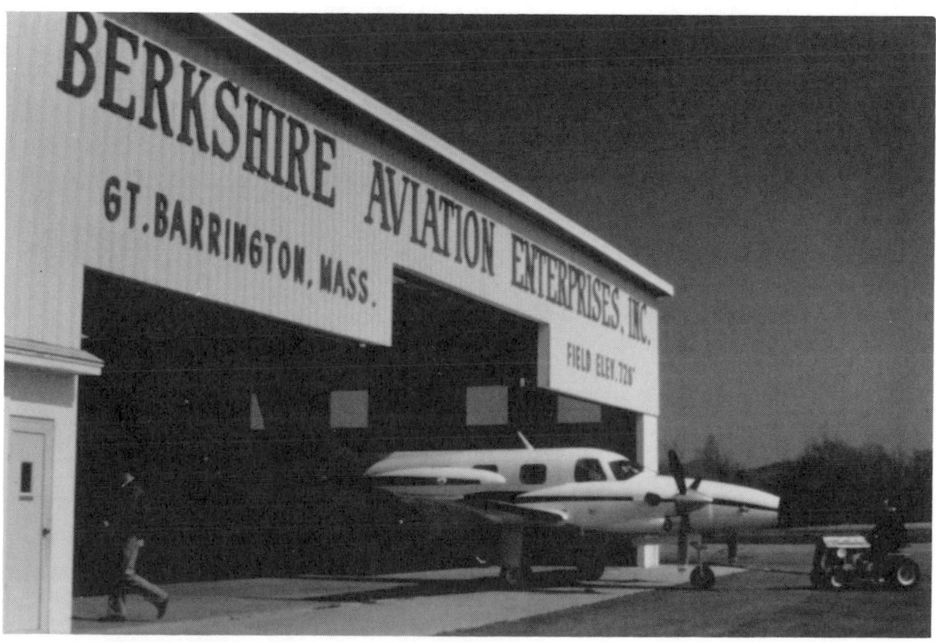

The start of a flight from the hills, at Great Barrington Airport.

BY LIMOUSINE OR TAXI

If you're with a group or want to pamper yourself, a limousine direct to Berkshire is the smoothest approach. There are many limousine services which will whisk you away from urban gridlock to the spaciousness of this hill country. The 1991 rates for this service run from $1.20 a mile for a comfortable town car to about $2.00 a mile for a luxury limousine — gratuity, tolls and parking are all extra. To estimate total cost, see the mileage chart at the beginning of "Berkshire Access."

From New York and its Airports:

Connecticut Limousine (Milford) 203-878-6867 or 878-2222
(picks up only at LaGuardia, Kennedy or Newark)
Kabot 718-545-2400 or 626-3700
Esquire 212-935-9700 or 737-7000

From Boston and Logan Airport:

Cooper 617-482-1000 or 800-342-2123 (outside MA)
Fifth Avenue 617-286-0555

From Hartford and Bradley Airport:

Carey, Aster Madison Avenue 800-735-4667
Ambassador 203-633-7300 or 800-395-LIMO
Buckley 203-953-8787
Elite 203-233-4423

From Albany, Albany Airport and Rensselaer:

AAA Limousine Service 518-456-5030
Diamond Limousine 518-283-8000 or 448-0844

To northern Berkshire (by reservation only)

Norm's Limousine Service 663-8300
Veteran's Taxi 663-6284
(fares range from $40 to $50 one way)

From Hudson, NY and its Amtrak Station:

Star City Taxi 518-828-3355

GETTING AROUND THE BERKSHIRES

Note: Individual town maps of Great Barrington, Stockbridge, Lenox, Pittsfield, North Adams and Williamstown can be found at the back of the book.

> *You are entering God's country, don't drive through like hell*
>
> *Sign near Otis*

Rte. 7 is Berkshire County's main roadway, connecting cities and towns from south to north. Driving in winter, you'll certainly need snow tires. In summer, the cruising is easy; but on certain weekends during Tanglewood season and fall foliage, temporary traffic delays in popular villages are likely. Whenever possible, park and walk. Friendly but firm traffic cops will suggest outlying parking areas. And motorists beware: several Berkshire towns have laws requiring a full stop for pedestrians in crosswalks.

BY BUS

Berkshire County is no longer served by the electrified Berkshire Street Railway, but the "B," a public bus system, has in some ways filled the gap. The buses run from early in the morning to early in the evening. A complete schedule can be obtained from the ***Berkshire Regional Transit Authority*** (499-2782 or 800-292-2782). Fares vary by distance. If you're visiting without a car, the ***"B"*** will provide plenty of access to other communities, but you will need to plan activities around the weekday (and slightly different weekend) bus schedules.

BY RENTED CAR

Car rental agencies abound in Berkshire. Most will not deliver cars — you must first go to their place of business to do the paperwork. One exception is Ugly Duckling Rent-A-Car. They will pick you up from the train, bus or wherever, then drive you back to their office to complete the paperwork. Berkshire car rentals are available through the following agencies.

Canaan, CT	Ugly Duckling (new and used)	203-824-5204
Cheshire	Bedard Brothers Auto	442-9596 or 800-696-5550
Gt. Barrington	Caffrey Motors	528-0848 or 800-698-0848
	Condor Chevrolet	528-2700
	Larkins Enterprises (used only)	528-2156
Pittsfield	Avis	442-2284 or 800-331-1212
	Hertz	499-4153 or 800-654-3131
	Johnson Rent-A-Car	443-6431 or 800-825-FORD
	National Car Rental	442-1543 or 800-CAR-RENT
	Pete's Rentals	445-5795 or 800-696-7383
	Rent-A-Wreck	447-8117
N. Adams	Mohawk Rentals	663-3729
	Scarafoni	663-6516
	Uncle Corporation	663-6663
Williamstown	B & L Service Station	458-8269

BY TAXI OR LIMOUSINE

Numerous taxi and limo companies serve Berkshire County. The following is a listing by town, with notations indicating if they have only taxis (T), only limos (L), or both (B).

Adams	Commonwealth Coach	743-5104 (L)
Great Barrington	Taxico	528-0911 (T)
Lee	Abbott's Limousine & Livery	243-1645 (L)
	Park Taxi	243-0020 (T)
Lenox	Aarow Taxi	499-8604 (T)
N. Adams	Berkshire Livery Service	662-2609 (L)
	Norm's Limousine Service	663-8300 or 663-3261 (B)
	Veteran's Taxi	663-8300 (B)
Pittsfield	Aarow Taxi	499-8604 (B)
	Airport & Limousine	443-7111 (L)
	Berkshire Limousine	499-3232 or 800-543-6776 (L)
	Rainbow Taxi	499-4300 (B)
Stockbridge	Stockbridge Livery	298-4848 (T)
Williamstown	Luxury Limo	458-9414 (L)

BY BICYCLE

Bicycling in the Berkshires gives an exciting intimacy with the rolling landscape. Though practical only in warmer weather, biking from town to town is still quite reasonable here. The 1991 bike rental prices vary widely — from $10 a day to $45 weekly to $90 a month, with bikes available through:

Pittsfield	Plaine's Ski & Cycle Center	499-0294
Williamstown	Spoke Bicycle & Repair	458-3456

ON FOOT

The Appalachian Trail enters southern Berkshire in the town of Mount Washington and runs over hill and dale, past Great Barrington, through Monterey and down into Tyringham Valley, then up near the town of Washington, through Dalton and Cheshire, over Mt. Greylock and toward Vermont, bypassing North Adams. If you've got the time, we've got the trail. See "Hiking" in Chapter six.

Many Berkshire towns are small enough for walking exploration, and three in particular are well suited to visiting without a vehicle: Stockbridge, Lenox and Williamstown. All are lovely villages, with good accommodations, fine dining, interesting shopping and first-rate cultural attractions within easy walking distance.

NEIGHBORS ALL AROUND

Though one tends to think of the Berkshires as a place apart, the county and its people frequently have close ties with neighboring communities. Travelers will want to connect with the neighbors, too, for Berkshire is surrounded by areas of extensive natural beauty, and certain nearby towns are loaded with good restaurants, old inns and cultural attractions.

TO THE SOUTH

The Litchfield Hills of northwest Connecticut are gentler than the Berkshire

Hills, but still make for good hiking. There is lovely architecture in this area, with many stately homes in Salisbury, Lakeville, Sharon, Litchfield and Norfolk. And there are music festivals as well, such as the ones at Norfolk and at Music Mountain in Falls Village. See "Music" in Chapter Four.

TO THE EAST

Halfway over the Berkshire highlands between the Housatonic River valley and the Connecticut River lies the jagged eastern county border, shared with Franklin County up north and Hampshire County down south. Besides this eastern area's natural splendor, an attractive array of cultural possibilities is located here. The "Five College Area" of Amherst, South Hadley and Northampton offers all the aesthetic and academic action anyone could want with the presence of Amherst, Hampshire, Mt. Holyoke and Smith Colleges as well as the University of Massachusetts.

TO THE NORTH

The Green Mountains of Vermont offer great skiing, hiking and camping. The town of Bennington makes an interesting stopover, with its museum (featuring Grandma Moses paintings), a fine college (Bennington), and Robert Frost's grave. There is also the extraordinary Bennington Pottery, where you can both buy and dine on their handsome stoneware. Rte. 7 up here continues as the spine of most communities, and a ride to architecturally stunning Manchester is worth the time; but consider the slower, less traveled Rte. 100 (the continuation of Massachusetts Rte. 8) threading through the mountainous midstate.

TO THE WEST

A less affluent neighboring area is Columbia County in New York State. This county of farms holds treasures for antiques and "untiques" hunters and those who like small, unpretentious, all-American towns. Berkshire is not far from the Hudson Valley, an area rich with history and with vineyards worth visiting. And then there's Albany, which offers big city, cultural entertainment such as the touring New York Metropolitan Opera, performing at the capital city's structurally unique theater, ***The Egg***. A bit farther north is Saratoga with its spas, its springs, its own summer arts festival (known as ***SPAC***) and its elegant and justly famous racecourse.

CHAPTER THREE
The Keys to Your Room
LODGING

Relaxing on the porch at the Red Lion Inn, Stockbridge.

As stagecoach travel through the Berkshires developed in the 18th century, the need for roadside lodgings grew; and of those original inns still welcoming wayfarers today, the ***New Boston Inn***, in New Marlboro, was likely the first. Built in 1737, this recently restored inn is about as authentic an early American lodging experience as you can find in New England. Quite close in age and attention to period detail is the ***Old Inn on the Green*** (1760), also in New Marlboro. This inn served as a tavern, a store and later as post office. Today it comforts travelers with a small number of authentically Colonial rooms and a superlative restaurant. Next came the ***Red Lion Inn*** (1773), in Stockbridge, which provided not only housing for sojourners but also a meeting place for pre-Revolutionary political activists eager to communicate their grievances to Britain. More than 200 years later, the Red Lion is still the best-known stopover on the Berkshire trail.

There are many other 18th-century Berkshire inns continuing to offer warmth and hospitality, with the invitation of a good night's sleep, often in a four-poster bed. There's the ***Village Inn*** in Lenox, built as a farmhouse in 1771; the ***Egremont Inn*** (1780) and the ***Weathervane Inn*** (1785) in South Egremont, the ***Elm Court Inn*** (1790) in North Egremont, and the ***Williamsville Inn*** in West Stockbridge, originally a farmhouse dating from 1797.

Is the 19th-century's sumptuous Gilded Age more your cup of tea? For you, Berkshire offers, among other possibilities, an Italian palazzo called ***Wheatleigh*** and a Tudor castle called ***Blantyre***, both in Lenox. Strikingly different in style, these palatial estates-turned-hotels share the ability to satisfy even the most refined of tastes and to do so with panache.

> *The guest will find Berkshire's hotel life most perfect . . . There is no landlord here, with a vast building, bragging of its 500 or 1,500 rooms and who rarely comes in contact with his guests; there is no place where the guests jostle each other as strangers and where they shift for themselves, as in large hotels. But, on the contrary, fellow guests become acquaintances, associates and friends; the landlord, with perhaps an assistant, gives personal attention to their wants, and in every way they are made to feel at home, and as it were, members of one large family. Hotel keeping is an art that has reached a high development in Berkshire.*
>
> The Book of Berkshire, 1889

Of course there are in Berkshire many lesser lodgings, shorter perhaps on romance but more reasonably priced. A great many are charmingly situated and competently run — entirely comfortable places where almost any traveler would be pleased to spend the night. There is an ever-growing number of guest houses, both in town and out, many offering bed and breakfast ("B&B"); there are the simpler inns where precious quiet is an everyday experience; and there are modern hotels and all grades of motels for those on a budget or with little concern for country charm. For outdoor folk, we include Berkshire's best campsites, your own patch of woodsy ground in the temple of trees.

To evaluate lodgings, we place a high value on hospitality, the personal attention and sincere care that can turn a visit into an unforgettable sojourn. We also assign value and significance to the architectural qualities of a property; to its historical renown and traditions; its care in furnishing and use of antiques or other art; to the views and the natural beauty right at its doorstep.

BERKSHIRE LODGING NOTES

Rates

Rate cards are generally printed early in the spring and will change slightly from year to year. Reminder: Price codes are based on a per room rate, double occupancy, during the high seasons (summer, fall foliage, skiing). Off-season rates are usually 20-40% lower.

Inexpensive	Up to $65
Moderate	$65 to $95
Expensive	$95 to $150
Very Expensive	Over $150

These rates exclude required room taxes or service charges which may be added to your bill.

Minimum Stay

Many of the better lodgings require a minimum stay of two or three nights on high season weekends. For a single night's stay in Berkshire at such times, the B&Bs or motels are the best bet. During the off-season, minimum-stay requirements relax and in most instances no longer apply.

Deposit/Cancellation

Deposits are usually required for a confirmed reservation. Policies regarding deposits, cancellations and refunds vary. It is always wise to inquire about these in advance. In the high season, lodging demand occasionally exceeds supply, so reservations for the more popular places need to be made months ahead.

Other Options

For last-minute or emergency lodging arrangements in Berkshire, here are some numbers to phone.
Berkshire Visitors Bureau: 443-9186
Bed & Breakfast USA: 528-2113
Berkshire Bed and Breakfast Connection: 268-7244
Covered Bridge Bed & Breakfast: 203-672-6052

Information Booths

For single-night stays in the high season or spur of the moment arrangements at other times, visit any of the tourist information booths listed in the Introduction.

LODGING SOUTH COUNTY

Egremont

North Egremont

BREAD & ROSES
Managers: Julie & Elliot Lowell.
528-1099.
Box 50, Star Rte. 65, Gt. Barrington, MA 01230.
Rte. 71, .5 mi. from jct. with Rte. 23.
Price: Moderate.
Credit Cards: None.
Handicap. Access: Limited.
Special Features: No smoking.

A charming, 1800s farmhouse, featuring five bed rooms, all with private bath and air conditioning, far from the madding crowd. Curl up in front of the cheery fireplace in the living room, perhaps with a book from the extensive library, or sit out on the spacious porch and listen to the babbling brook. Breakfasts from Julie's kitchen feature French Toast Grand Marnier and a souffle of spinach and mushrooms. French is spoken here, too. (Please note that children under 12 nor pets are allowed.)

ELM COURT INN
Managers: U. & G. Bieri.
528-0325.
Rte. 71, N. Egremont, MA 01252.
Price: Moderate.
Credit Cards: MC, V.

Immaculate, comfortable rooms above one of the more popular restaurants in South Berkshire. At the center of a quaint, quiet hamlet.

HIDDEN ACRES BED AND BREAKFAST
Managers: Daniel & Lorraine Miller.
528-1028.
RD4, Box 150, Gt. Barrington, MA 01230.
Rte. 71, N. 3 mi. to Rowe Rd., then 9/10 mi. to Tremont Dr.
Price: Moderate.
Credit Cards: None.

Perhaps the loudest noise you will hear at Hidden Acres is the sound of falling leaves. Stone walls, massive trees and five secluded acres invite walks, picnics and solitude. Full country breakfast is served in the large country kitchen. (Smoking is not allowed.)

South Egremont

BALDWIN HILL FARM B&B
Owners: Richard & Priscilla Burdsall.
528-4092.
RD3, Box 125, Gt. Barrington, MA 01230.
From center of S. Egremont, left on Baldwin Hill Rd., N.- S., to inn on left.
Price: Inexpensive to Moderate.
Credit Cards: MC, V.
Special Features: Pool, no children under 10.

If you have a secret desire to live on a farm, you'll love Baldwin Hill. This working farm, in a very rural setting, includes a Victorian farmhouse turned B&B and barns galore. Peace, quiet and tranquility abound on 500 acres perfect for hiking, cross-country skiing or reading by the fieldstone fireplace in winter or under a tree in summer. Four rooms, one with private bath, have views across fields to the mountains beyond. Full breakfast is served by friendly innkeepers, who take pride in this farm that has been in the family since 1910.

THE EGREMONT INN
Manager: John Black
528-2111.
Old Sheffield Rd., S. Egremont, MA 01258.
Side street off Rte. 23 in center of village.
Price: Moderate to Expensive.
Credit Cards: D, MC, V.
Special Features: Pool, tennis.

Coziness, low ceilings, fireplaces, broad porches, 21 delightful rooms furnished with antiques: these set the tone for this historic 1780 inn nestled on a quiet side street in the heart of a classic, old village. Scenery ranges from lovely to gorgeous. Pool and tennis courts for guests' use. Fine restaurant located on main floor.

TRAIL'S END GUESTS
Owners: Anne & Frank Hines.
528-3995.
678 S. Egremont Rd., Gt. Barrington, MA 01230.
On Rte. 23, just E. of S. Egremont.
Closed: Oct.-Apr.
Price: Inexpensive to Moderate.
Credit Cards: None.

This modern house is neat and trim inside and out. Just off Rte. 23, it has four rooms, all with private bath. Look for the handsome sleigh on the porch or in the yard.

THE WEATHERVANE INN
Managers: Anne & Vincent Murphy.
528-9580.
Box 388, S. Egremont, MA 01258.
Rte. 23, just E. of the village.
Price: Expensive; MAP available in summer.
Credit Cards: AE, MC, V.
Handicap. Access: Limited.
Special Features: Pool.

This is a comfortable, clean and very well-run operation set within a 1785 farmhouse. Your hosts are skilled at their trade and provide their version of Colonial lodging and home cooking in their cheery restaurant. Location is convenient to some of the best antiques shopping in the Berkshires, including one shop just behind the inn.

WINDFLOWER INN
Managers: Liebert & Ryan families.
528-2720.
684 S. Egremont Rd., Gt. Barrington, MA 01230.
Rte. 23, just E. of S. Egremont.
Price: Expensive (MAP).
Credit Cards: None.
Handicap. Access: Limited.
Special Features: Pool, no smoking in bedrooms or dining room.

One of the prettiest locations in South Berkshire complements the soothing, comfortable interior of this gracious and respected inn. Antiques furnish the common rooms as well as the bedrooms. All 13 rooms have private bath and six have fireplaces. Excellent prix-fixe restaurant on main floor of this family-run inn. Please note that MAP price includes full breakfast and dinner for two. Swimming pool.

Great Barrington

A VICTORIAN COTTAGE BED & BREAKFAST
Managers: Robert Eric Drennan & Rose Tannenbaum.
528-0328.
12 West Ave., Gt. Barrington, MA 01230.
From Main St., turn W. on Taconic to West Ave.
Price: Moderate to Expensive.
Credit Cards: None.
Special Features: No smoking.

A young couple with two very young children, purchased this Victorian home and carriage house in 1989. Bob, a skilled contractor, immediately began stripping the woodwork, repairing the bathrooms, and polishing. Now it's a bed and breakfast. Three rooms for rent have bay windows, one has a private bath and the other two share. The gorgeous antique quilts are family treasures. Breakfast is a spectacular affair. Bob actually gets up at 4:00 a.m. daily to bake bread, and that's just the beginning. There might be crêpes with a banana/rum sauce or huge, puffy German pancakes or, maybe, Eggs Benedict.

ARRAWOOD BED & BREAKFAST
Managers: Marilyn & Bill Newmark.
528-5868.
105 Taconic Ave., Gt. Barrington, MA 01230.
Corner of Taconic Ave. & Oak St.
Price: Inexpensive to Moderate.
Credit Cards: None.

This graciously restored Victorian home, is located on a lovely, residential street. Fireplaces in public rooms, a full, country breakfast and canopy beds in guest rooms are special touches. Informal elegance.

COFFING – BOSTWICK HOUSE
Proprietors: Diana & William Harwood.
528-4511.
98 Division St., Gt. Barrington, MA 01230.
Corner of Rte. 41 & Division St. 2 mi. N. of Gt. Barrington.
Price: Inexpensive to Moderate.
Credit Cards: None.

It's hard to imagine now, but the sleepy village of Van Deusenville was once a bustling town with mills, factories and a train station. Little remains except this large 1825 mansion of the village founder, now a six-room bed and breakfast. The guest rooms are spacious and well appointed, as are the public rooms, although the exterior of the main house and the outbuildings need repair. Breakfasts prepared by the owner, a local caterer, are sumptuous. Just down the street is the church where Alice of "Alice's Restaurant" fame lived.

ELLING'S B & B
Managers: Jo & Ray Elling.
528-4103.
RD3, Box 6, Gt. Barrington, MA 01230.
On a hill above Rte. 23, between S. Egremont & Gt. Barrington.

Your hosts here are seasoned, well-regarded veterans of the hospitality trade. Their six-room guest house is set on six, pastoral acres high on a hill overlooking the valley; their location is convenient to swimming, ski slopes, Tanglewood and the best of southern Berkshire. Recommended.

Price: Moderate.
Credit Cards: None.
Special Features: Badminton & horseshoes.

GREENMEADOWS
Managers: Frank Gioia & Susie Kaufman.
528-3897.
117 Division St., Gt. Barrington, MA 01230. N. of Gt. Barrington, 1/4 mi. W. of Rte. 41.
Price: Moderate.
Credit Cards: AE, MC, V.

A rural setting on a quiet, country road but the rooms are standard and the tiny breakfast room is the only public room. A suite in the former carriage house has a large deck overlooking pastoral fields, plus a full kitchen.

LITTLEJOHN MANOR B&B
Managers: Herbert Littlejohn, Jr. & Paul A. DuFour.
528-2882.
Newsboy Monument Lane, Gt. Barrington, MA 01230.
On Rte. 23, S. of town, en route to S. Egremont.
Price: Moderate.
Credit Cards: None.
Special Features: No pets.

This turn-of-the-century Victorian home is run in a very friendly way and furnished partially with antiques. One of the four bedrooms has a working fireplace and all share several baths. A hearty breakfast in the morning is complemented by afternoon tea served in the sitting room. Delightful flower and herb gardens.

ROUND HILL FARM BED & BREAKFAST
Owners: Thomas & Margaret Whitfield.
528-3366.
17 Round Hill Rd., Gt. Barrington, MA 01230.
From Alford Rd., left on Seekonk Rd. and then next left on Round Hill Rd. to farm.
Price: Moderate to Expensive.
Credit Cards: AE, MC, V.
Special Features: No smoking, no children under 16.

A "Non-Smoker's Bed & Breakfast," the Round Hill Farm is unique in many other ways as well. For starters, the farm is just that — a horse farm, with 300 acres crossed by the Alford Brook — where guests can walk, cross-country ski, picnic and swim. The classic hilltop farmhouse was built in 1907 and has five rooms, most with shared bath; some available in summer only. They are filled with treasured antiques and books and lovingly decorated, some with Laura Ashley fabrics.

In 1987 the Dairy Barn was converted into a four-room apartment and several additional guest rooms. They are light and airy and beautifully decorated with Laura Ashley, Pierre Deux, etc. The loft contains a collection of sculpted cows, some almost life-sized, that adds a touch of humor. There seems to be nothing the Whitfields have forgotten in their effort to meet guests' every need. They'll provide shoe polish, buttons and even needles for needlepoint.

SEEKONK PINES INN "BED & BREAKFAST"
Managers: Linda & Chris Best.
528-4192.
142 Seekonk Crossroad, Box 29A, RD1, Gt. Barrington, MA 01230.
Rte. 23, between S. Egremont & Gt. Barrington.
Price: Moderate.
Credit Cards: MC, V.
Special Features: Pool.

This 150-year-old former country estate, surrounded by meadows and well-groomed acreage, just keeps getting better. Furnished in Early American and just plain country, this inn is filled with personal touches. Linda is an artist and her watercolors brighten many of the rooms, as do her original stenciled floors and walls. Family quilts warm the beds. There's a swimming pool for hot summer days and several formal gardens for walking or reading. The healthy, hearty breakfast features home-grown berries and whole grains.

THORNEWOOD INN
Managers: Terry & David Thorne.
528-3828.
453 Stockbridge Rd., Gt. Barrington, MA 01230.
Rte. 7, just N. of Gt. Barrington.
Price: Moderate to Expensive.
Credit Cards: AE, D, MC, V.
Special Features: Pool.

Creativity and imagination are evident throughout this marvelous inn. It all started several years ago with the purchase of an old, run-down, but handsome Dutch Colonial. The owners have restored and expanded to create nine lovely guest rooms, all with private bath, and four delightful public rooms. The antiques used throughout include canopy beds, pier mirrors and original sinks. Their latest renovation includes the addition of a beautiful restaurant, with a view of the Berkshire hills. The full breakfast might include strawberry-stuffed French toast or apple pancakes.

TURNING POINT INN
Managers: Jamie, Irving & Shirley Yost.
528-4777.
RD2, Box 140, Gt. Barrington, MA 01230.
Rte. 23, E. of town.
Price: Moderate to Expensive.
Credit Cards: None.
Special Features: No smoking. Children welcome.

Very well-regarded lodging in a handsome brick and clapboard former stagecoach inn that's over 200 years old. Informal atmosphere. Full vegetarian breakfast served to inn guests. New two-bedroom cottage is perfect for families. Popular Butternut Basin ski area is less than a mile down the road.

Housatonic

BROOK COVE
Managers: Clifford & Barbara Perreault.
274-6653.
30 Linda Lane, Housatonic, MA 01236.
Rte. 41., 5.7 mi. from Exit #1 Mass Pike.
Price: Inexpensive to Moderate.
Credit Cards: AE, MC, V.
Handicap. Access: Yes.
Special Features: Hot tub available.

Definitely not your typical guest house. The Perreaults have one large apartment they rent by the night. Since the country property meanders down to the Williams River, the setting seems ideal for longer stays. Room price is for two, with an additional $6 for each person over that. Your hosts will be happy to provide breakfast for an additional $5 per person.

CHRISTINE'S GUEST HOUSE B&B
Hosts: Steve & Christine Kelsey.
274-6149.
325 N. Plain Rd., Housatonic, MA 01236.
Rte. 41 about 4 mi. N. of Gt. Barrington.
Price: Moderate.
Credit Cards: MC, V.
Special Features: No smoking.

A little jewel (three rooms, all with private bath), off the beaten path between Great Barrington and West Stockbridge. The rooms and the innkeepers are delightful. One room is decorated in white wicker, one has a cannonball bed and the other a four-poster. All are filled with handcrafted items. Cheese and crackers served in the afternoon. Full "surprise" breakfast. Very special.

Lee

(See also South Lee)

AARDENBURG ANTIQUES
Managers: David Hubregsen & Douglas Howes.
243-0001.
144 W. Park St., Lee, MA 01238.
On Stockbridge Rd., off Rte. 20.
Closed: Sept.-May.
Price: Moderate to Expensive.
Credit Cards: None.
Special Features: Tennis.

Listed in the National Register of Historic Places, this red house with gray trim and black shutters, dates to 1793. At one time it was the Hyde Park Academy for Boys, with Franklin Delano Roosevelt as one of its illustrious students. Now, besides being a bed and breakfast, it is an elegant antiques store, well worth visiting. Six guest rooms are furnished with antiques, but none have private baths. The house is situated on four acres high on a hill, with views of ornamental pools, landscaped grounds and tennis courts.

APPLEGATE
Managers: Nancy & Rick Cannata.
243-4451.
279 West Park St., Lee, MA 01238.
Between Lee & Stockbridge.
Price: Moderate to Very Expensive.
Credit Cards: MC, V.
Special Features: No smoking requested.

This magnificent, large, white, pillared Colonial is special in every way. From the gracious and delightful hosts — he a pilot and she a flight attendant — to the detailed attention they have lavished on their inn, a stay at Applegate will be a cherished treat. Public rooms are large, with fireplaces and bay windows. Inn dolls Martha, Heather and Claudia observe the activity from their antique rockers. Breakfast is served from a collection of antique cups. Guests are greeted in their rooms by crystal decanters filled with brandy and Belgium chocolates selected in Brussels by the owners. Six large guest rooms all have private bath and several have fireplaces; one even boasts a sauna/shower. From the screened-in porch filled with wicker furniture, the view across the pool, enclosed by a low rock wall, to the six landscaped acres beyond, is tranquility itself.

BLACK SWAN INN
Managers: Sallie Kate & George Kish.
243-2700 or (800) 876-SWAN.
Rte. 20W, Lee, MA 01238.
On Laurel Lake, N. of Lee.
Price: Moderate to Very Expensive.
Credit Cards: AE, CB, DC, MC, V, D.
Handicap. Access: Yes.
Special Features: Pool. On lake.

From the outside, this 52-room "inn" looks decidedly like a motel, but its location on placid Laurel Lake, its private balconies, Colonial decor, quaint beds, and friendly hospitality provide an innlike atmosphere. Lovely restaurant, swimming pool, and exercise room with sauna. There are boat rentals for boating on the lake. Close to Tanglewood, hiking trails, etc.

CHAMBÉRY INN
Owners: Joe & Lynn Toole.
243-2221.
Box 319, Lee, MA 01238. On Main St. (Rte. 20) in Lee.
Price: Moderate to Very Expensive.
Credit Cards: AE, MC, V.
Handicap. Access: Yes.

Joe Toole is an unabashed romantic, and we all are allowed to benefit. The Chambéry Inn began life as a schoolhouse in 1885, when five nuns arrived from France to teach the youngsters of St. Mary's Parish in Lee. Joe's grandfather was in the first class. Concerned that it was scheduled for the wrecker's ball and enchanted by its remarkable history, Joe assumed the gargantuan task of moving the schoolhouse to its present location. He left the proportion of the rooms as they were, which is BIG, with 13-foot ceilings and massive windows. There are nine rooms, six are suites with fireplaces; all have large private baths with whirlpools, and king or queen beds. The furniture, including canopy beds, is Amish handcrafted cherry. A charming feature in the suites is the original blackboards. Joe invited former students and teachers to share their remembrances of school life at St. Mary's. It's probably a "one-of-a-kind" in the United States.

THE DONAHOES
Manager: Mary Donahoe.
243-1496.
Box 231, Lee, MA 01238.
Off Rte. 102, S. of Lee, on Fairview & Davis Sts.
Price: Moderate.
Credit Cards: None.
Special Features: No children, no pets.

Country setting in a Shaker Colonial high on a hill above Rte. 102, connecting Stockbridge and Lee. Great location for theater and concert fans. Small number of rooms insures quiet stay.

The gracious front doorway at Haus Andreas.

HAUS ANDREAS
Managers: Gerhard & Lilliane Schmid.
243-3298.
RR1, Box 435, Lee, MA 01238.
Just outside village of Lee on Stockbridge Rd.
Price: Expensive to Very Expensive.
Credit Cards: MC, V.
Special Features: Heated pool, tennis, bicycles, golf nearby.

No expense was spared in renovating this 1800s house, built by a Revolutionary War soldier and initially restored by George Westinghouse in the early 1900s. The small estate became the 1942 summer sanctuary for Queen Wilhelmina of the Netherlands, her daughter Princess Juliana and granddaughters Beatrix and Irene. The house is secluded, with eight rooms, all with private bath. Continental breakfast.

INN ON LAUREL LAKE
Manager: Bernard Morris.
243-9749; 243-1436.
Rte. 20W, Lee, MA 01238.
Rte. 20, few mi. W. of Lee.
Closed: Mar.-Apr.
Price: Moderate to Very Expensive.
Credit Cards: None.
Special Features: Private beach, tennis, sauna.

On the shore of Laurel Lake, this 80-year-old country property has attracted a loyal following with its comfortable bedrooms and sitting rooms, filled with an impressive collection of record albums and books. The tennis court, sauna and private beach add to guests' playtime possibilities. Proximity of major highway needs to be noted. Children under 10, as well as dogs, are *verboten.*

JIRAK'S GUEST HOUSE
Manager: Margaret Jirak.
243-3201.
60 Laurel St., Lee, MA 01238.
Rte. 20, W. of Lee.
Price: Moderate to Expensive.
Credit Cards: None.

Restored Victorian home on a busy thoroughfare. Family-run guest house with six comfortable rooms; one with private bath. Friendly atmosphere. Full breakfast.

KINGSLEIGH 1840 BED & BREAKFAST
Managers: Linda & Arthur Segal.
243-3317.
32 Park St. Lee, MA 01238.
Rte. 20, center of Lee.
Price: Inexpensive to Moderate.
Credit Cards: AE, MC, V.

An 1840 Victorian, newly decorated and air conditioned. Four rooms with comfortable appointments. In heart of town, close to restaurants but on a heavily traveled main street. Can't miss its bright yellow paint with slate blue trim.

MORGAN HOUSE
Managers: Beth & Bill Orford.
243-0181.
33 Main St., Lee, MA 01238.
Town Center.
Price: Inexpensive to Expensive.
Credit Cards: AE, CB, D, DC, MC, V.

Venerable, attractive stagecoach stop of yesteryear with lovely though small rooms. High on hospitality and with many a tasteful touch in the decor, the inn holds several liabilities in the form of a busy, sometimes noisy restaurant on the first floor and an even busier Main Street immediately beyond the front door.

PARSONAGE ON THE GREEN
Owners: David Renner & Michelle Moore.
243-4364.
20 Park Pl., Lee, MA 01238.
Just off the village green, beside Congregational Church.
Price: Inexpensive to Moderate.
Credit Cards: MC, V.

This white, central-hall Colonial houses four guest rooms, all with shared bath. Cozy, attractive decor and furnishings. The public rooms include both living room and parlor with fireplaces. Wine and cheese are served Friday and Saturday nights. David is an accomplished chef at one of the most highly respected local restaurants. Prepare for a ***surprise*** continental breakfast.

THE PLACE
Managers: Richard Rice & Charles Petrie.
243-4465.
51 Park St., Lee, MA 01238.
Opposite park in town center.
Price: Expensive to Very Expensive.
Credit Cards: AE, MC, V.
Handicap. Access: Limited.

A Victorian in the heart of town, this house has recently been renovated inside and out by new owners. The inn portion features four rooms, two with private bath, and a suite with two bedrooms. Fine restaurant on main floor.

PROSPECT HILL HOUSE
Managers: Marge & Chuck Driscoll.
243-3460.
1A S. Prospect St., Lee, MA 01238.
Just off Park St.
Closed: Nov.-May.
Price: Inexpensive.
Credit Cards: None.

This Cape Colonial on one acre at the end of a street, offers a quiet setting, near the golf course. Four rooms, most with shared bath. Common room has fireplace. Full breakfast served.

RAMSEY HOUSE
Managers: Mickey & Dick Ramsey.
243-1598.
203 W. Park St., Lee, MA 01238.
Up hill W. of town center.
Price: Moderate to Expensive.
Credit Cards: MC, V.

An 1895 Colonial in residential area above town. Antique-furnished rooms are quite special, some with canopied or four-poster beds and private bath. Golf and tennis across the street at small club. Congenial hosts pay particular attention to their guests. Modified continental breakfast includes freshly baked breads and perhaps a baked apple.

South Lee

THE FEDERAL HOUSE
Managers: Robin & Kenneth Almgren.
243-1824.
Rte. 102, S. Lee, MA 01260.
Just E. of Stockbridge.
Price: Moderate to Expensive.
Credit Cards: AE, DC, MC, V.

Brick Federal house, built in 1824, has been beautifully restored. In this historic property, the six guest rooms sit above a respected restaurant. Graceful, small and charming rooms feature antique furnishings. All have private bath and air conditioning, and several have fireplaces. Owned and operated by a dynamic young couple who combine good taste and culinary talents.

MERRELL TAVERN INN
Managers: Faith & Charles Reynolds.
243-1794.
Box 318, Rte. 102, S. Lee, MA 01260.
Just E. of Stockbridge.
Price: Moderate to Expensive.
Credit Cards: AE, MC, V.

As you walk through the massive door of this 1800s brick inn, you're transported back in time. For years it served as a stagecoach stop on the busy Boston-Albany Pike, until it outlived its usefulness. It lay idle and boarded up for over 100 years until purchased by the Reynolds in late 1980. Now lovingly and carefully restored, the inn is listed on the National Register of Historic Places. The ten bedrooms are furnished with four-poster and canopy beds and all have private baths; four have fireplaces. The Old Tavern Room features the original circular Colonial bar. A groomed lawn in back leads to the banks of the Housatonic River.

Colonial antiques highlight the entry at Merrell Tavern Inn.

Paul Rocheleau, courtesy Merrell Tavern Inn.

OAK N' SPRUCE LODGE
Manager: Paul DiCroce.
243-3500.
Meadow St., S. Lee, MA 01260.
Off Rte. 102, on Meadow St., N. of village.
Price: Moderate to Expensive.
Credit Cards: AE, MC, V.

A full-service, but by no means fancy resort. Golf, swimming, tennis, health club and stocked trout stream are attractions. For rent are 53 hotel rooms and 100 condominiums. Restaurant and bar in main building. Beautiful natural scenery offsets the hodgepodge architecture and interiors. Very casual atmosphere, occasionally punctured by a large sales staff aggressively selling time-shares.

Monterey

MOUNTAIN TRAILS B&B
Managers: John & Maureen Congdon.
528-2928.
Rtes. 23 & 57, Monterey, MA 01245.
At the jct. of Rtes. 23 & 57.
Price: Inexpensive to Moderate.
Credit Cards: None.
Handicap. Access: Yes.

A four-room B&B in the country. Two rooms have private bath, and two share. A full breakfast is served. Especially loved by hikers as the Appalachian Trail and Beartown State Forest are nearby. It's also a place where children are welcome.

New Marlborough

MILLSTONES
Managers: Dorothy Mills & Beth Putnam.
229-8488.
Box 121A, Star Rte. 70, New Marlborough, MA 01230.
Rte. 57, 5.5 mi. E. of Rte. 23.
Price: Moderate.
Credit Cards: None.
Handicap. Access: Yes.

This turn-of-the-century kennel-master's home was part of the largest estate in town. The house now sits on seven groomed acres and features six bedrooms with period wallpaper and window dressings, comfortably furnished with antiques. Most rooms share a bath. The southside rooms overlook the hills and dales sloping towards Connecticut. The public rooms offer the added attraction of a piano, a respectable collection of books and magazines, and the warmth of a blazing fireplace in the colder months.

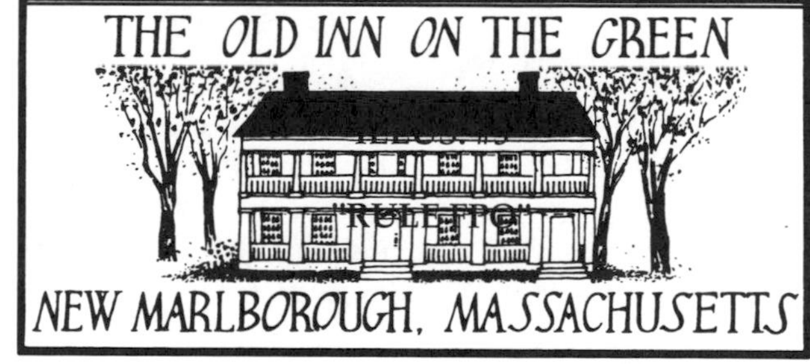

Courtesy Old Inn on the Green

THE OLD INN ON THE GREEN AND GEDNEY FARM
Innkeepers: Bradford Wagstaff & Leslie Miller.
229-3131.
Star Rte. 70, New Marlborough, MA 01230.
Rte. 57, in center of village.

A great location, rich in unaffected nostalgia and natural beauty, is the setting for this 18th-century inn. The village preserves a magical sense of a quieter past. Rooms in the inn have been lovingly restored, though sparingly furnished; and all share baths. Gedney Farm, a short walk from the inn, is new. Eight two-level suites have been carved out of a Normandy-style barn, built turn-of-the-century as a showplace for Percheron stallions and Jersey cattle. All suites feature fireplaces in the living rooms, large

Price: Moderate to Very Expensive.
Credit Cards: MC, V.

bedrooms and whirlpool tubs in the master baths. Restaurant in the inn is one of the finest in the Berkshires. Highly recommended.

RED BIRD INN
Managers: Don & Joyce Coffman.
229-2433.
Box 592, New Marlborough, MA 01230.
Adsit Crosby Rd., Rte. 57.
From Gt. Barrington, Rte. 23 E. to Rte. 57.
Price: Moderate.
Credit Cards: None.

A former stagecoach stop, the 18th-century Red Bird Inn, is located on a quiet country road. The rooms are furnished with antiques, decorated with Ralph Lauren and Laura Ashley, and retain their original wide plank floors, fireplaces and old ironwork. Some have private bath; some shared. A full breakfast is served.

Otis

GROUSE HOUSE
Managers: The Goulet Family.
269-4446.
Rte. 23, Otis, MA 01253. Near Rte. 8, on Rte. 23.
Closed: Mon.-Tues.
Price: Inexpensive.
Credit Cards: AE, MC, V.

Next door to Otis Ridge Ski area, Grouse house offers six rooms, all with shared baths. Reduced rate on lift tickets for guests of the house. Guests can get breakfast at the ski lodge, as no breakfast is served at the inn.

STONEWOOD INN
Managers: Joan & Howard Basis.
269-4894.
Mail: SR 62, Box 42, Monterey, MA 01245. E. of Gt. Barrington on Rte. 23 in W. Otis.
Price: Moderate to Expensive.
Credit Cards: None.

A gracious, 1880s country farmhouse, set on 15 pastoral acres, now owned by a decorator who has filled the rooms with antiques and country touches, in perfect harmony with the setting. There's a woodstove in the common room. Four large bedrooms share two baths. Only the mattresses — three king-size and one queen — are not antique, but are newly custom-made. There's an additional large suite, with private bath, suitable for four people. Full country breakfast may include baked apples, blueberry pancakes, or thick French toast.

Sandisfield

DAFFER'S MOUNTAIN INN
Managers: Jean & Bill Daffer.
258-4453.
Box 37, Rte. 57, Sandisfield, MA

Mostly a restaurant, but with seven rooms upstairs that share several baths. Congenially run by hosts who cater effectively to their guests' needs. In fall, the large sign reads "Hunters Welcome." Very informal. Friendly groups return year after year.

01255.
Closed: Mon.-Tues., also 4 wks. April/May.
Price: Inexpensive.
Credit Cards: MC, V.

NEW BOSTON INN
Innkeepers: Anne & Bill McCarthy.
258-4477.
Box 120, Sandisfield, MA 01255.
Rtes. 8 & 57, Sandisfield. In the village of New Boston.
Closed: Mar.
Price: Expensive.
Credit Cards: AE, MC, V.
Handicap. Access: Yes.
Special Features: Restaurant.

Built in 1737, the New Boston Inn has come back to life under the guidance of Bill and Ann McCarthy. This remarkable old stagecoach inn, listed in the National Register of Historic Places, underwent a loving and painstaking renovation in 1985, and the owners continue to make improvements. The eight guest rooms are, true to the period, snug. Low ceilings, wide-board floors and multi-paned windows hark back to the 18th century and, in most cases, are original. All rooms feature private baths and are decorated with early pine furniture and stenciling. All closets are cedar lined. Extensive library reflects Anne's former career as a librarian.

Our favorite space at the inn is the second-floor ballroom. After wandering through the cozy bedrooms, you enter the spacious ballroom under a barrel-vaulted ceiling. The sense of openness, grace and the continued presence of the past is romantic, especially the matching fireplaces at either end. True to form, the McCarthys are resisting the temptation to create three new rooms out of this one. They propose to maintain the ballroom as it is and to use it as a common room for guests and as a reception area for wedding parties and other festive gatherings.

Another historic delight is the taproom that adjoins the low-ceilinged dining room. The 22-inch-wide oak boards on the wall are called "king's wood" because they were illegally retained by the colonists after the deputies of the king of England went about marking trees for the royal sawmills. In this room as throughout the inn, the wooden molding, plaster walls, slanted floors, venerable windows and doorways (there is hardly a right angle in the place) provide a powerful charm and sense of history. What's more, the New Boston Inn has a resident ghost. She is real enough to have been reported in Yankee magazine: an Irish maiden, dressed in bridal black (that's what they wore back then), who was shot by a scorned suitor in an upstairs room.

Sandisfield may be one of the more remote towns in Berkshire, but the New Boston Inn's return to life will make the ride out there more than worthwhile.

Sheffield

A UNIQUE BED & BREAKFAST INN
Manager: May Stendardi.
229-3363.
Box 729, Sheffield, MA 01257.
Rte. 41, several mi. N. of CT state line.

Just up a short hill off scenic Rte. 41, this house offers four guest rooms, all with private bath. There's personal attention here, from the hand-ironed sheets to the flowers in the room. Delicious breakfast served.

Price: Moderate to Expensive.
Credit Cards: MC, V.

CENTURYHURST ANTIQUES & BED & BREAKFAST
Managers: Ronald & Judith Timm.
229-8131.
Box 486, Sheffield, MA 01257.
Main St., Rte. 7.
Price: Moderate.
Credit Cards: AE, MC, V.
Special Features: Pool. No smoking, no pets.

This grand old home, nestled among towering trees, is listed on the National Register of Historic Places. The inn features four guest rooms that share two baths. Continental breakfast. Swimming pool for summer relaxation. The antiques shop specializes in early Wedgwood, and American clocks. Also large gallery providing space for additional antiques dealers.

THE DEPOT
Managers: Dennis & Joan Sawyer.
229-8894.
Rte. 7A, Box 575, Sheffield, MA 01257.
From Rte. 7, follow Rte. 7A toward Ashley Falls.
Price: Inexpensive to Moderate.
Credit Cards: AE, MC, V.
Handicap. Access: Yes.

The owner's home once served as the Sheffield train station, but was moved to this location 19 years ago. The guest rooms are located in a separate guest house. Three of the five rooms have private bath; all have refrigerators — handy, as no breakfast is served.

IVANHOE COUNTRY HOUSE
Managers: Carole & Dick Maghery.
229-2143.
RD1, Box 158, Sheffield, MA 01257.
On Rte. 41, 4 mi. S. of Rte. 23; 10 mi. N. of Lakeville, CT.
Price: Moderate to Expensive.
Credit Cards: None.
Special Features: Swimming pool.

Set along one of the most scenic roads of South Berkshire, the Ivanhoe provides comfortable rooms, all with private bath, at reasonable prices. Continental breakfast served at your door. Take a dip in the pool before dinner, play the piano if you wish, enjoy the fire in the chestnut-paneled public room, and select from the many fine local restaurants for your evening meal. At the base of Race Mountain, traversed by the Appalachian Trail, 20 wooded acres hug this 1780-vintage country house. Golden retrievers are raised on property, and guests are welcome to bring their own dogs, for an additional $10.

ORCHARD SHADE
Owners: Debbie & Henry Thornton.
229-8463.
Box 669, Sheffield, MA 01257.
Maple Ave., N. of Christ Church on Main St.
Price: Inexpensive.
Credit Cards: AE, MC, V.

This venerable old 1840 house has operated as a bed and breakfast since 1888. Furnished with antiques, the public rooms have two spacious fireplaces to ward off the chill on cooler evenings. The large screened-in porch is perfect for relaxing after a busy day of Sheffield antiquing. Pets are not allowed.

STAGECOACH HILL INN
Manager: Danielle Pedretti.
229-8585.
Rte. 41, Sheffield, MA 01257.
On Rte. 41, several mi. N. of Lakeville, CT.
Closed: Wed. (summer); Tues.-Wed., (winter), and 3 wks. in March.
Price: Inexpensive to Moderate.
Credit Cards: AE, CB, DC, MC, V.
Handicap. Access: Yes.
Special Features: Pool.

A time machine. Nostalgia for bygone eras (especially Colonial times as evident in the decidedly English pub and restaurant), plus charm and comfort greet the fortunate visitor to this ideally situated hostelry. Choice of rooms in the main house or small chalets, all with private bath. A romantic hideaway. Recommended.

STAVELEIGH HOUSE
Owners: D. Marosy & M. Whitman.
229-2129.
Box 608, Sheffield, MA 01257.
Just S. of village, on Rte. 7.
Price: Moderate.
Credit Cards: None.
Handicap. Access: Yes.

This vintage 1821 house is set in the heart of Sheffield. Your hostesses believe in old-fashioned hospitality and have succeeded in creating a warm and comfortable interior, with hooked rugs, patchwork quilts and an immense collection of teddy bears. A full breakfast, with imaginative specialties, is featured.

Stockbridge

ARBOR ROSE BED & BREAKFAST
Owner: Christina Alsop.
298-4744.
Box 114, Stockbridge, MA 01262.
Yale Hill Rd., off E. Main St. (Rte. 102).
Price: Inexpensive to Expensive.
Credit Cards: MC, V.

The first thing you hear on entering the driveway to Arbor Rose is the soothing sound of rushing water. The house sits on a hill overlooking an 1800s mill and millpond—perfect for swimming in innertubes in summer and ice skating in winter. There are five rooms in the large white house, two with private bath and the rest with a shared bath. Charming decor is highlighted by colorful paintings by the owner's mother, Suzette Alsop, a noted local artist.

BERKSHIRE THISTLE
Manager: Jesse Cibelli.
298-5539.
Box 1295, Stockbridge, MA 01262.
Rte. 7, N. of village.
Price: Moderate to Expensive.
Credit Cards: AE, MC, V.

Although the location offers lovely views year-round, the house and rooms are of recent construction and more comfortable than charming. Easy access to theater, Tanglewood and great hiking trails. Swimming pool and picturesque pasture with grazing horses.

THE INN AT STOCKBRIDGE
Managers: Lee & Don Weitz.
298-3337.
Box 618, Stockbridge, MA 01262.
On Rte. 7, about 1 mi. N. of village.
Price: Expensive to Very Expensive.
Credit Cards: AE, MC, V.
Special Features: Pool.

A marvelous, secluded inn run by friendly, professional people. The large, white-columned house is decorated with impeccable taste, featuring priceless antiques, and many thoughtful touches. All seven rooms have private baths and are air conditioned. Wine and cheese are served in the living room (warmed by a fire in chilly weather) and breakfast in the formal dining room is incredible. Lee's cinnamon pull-apart coffee ring is out of this world. Special private dinners can be arranged on request.

Courtesy the Red Lion Inn.

THE RED LION INN
General Manager: Betsy M. Holtzinger.
298-5545.
Main St., Stockbridge, MA 01262.
Village center, Rtes. 7 & 102.
Price: Moderate to Very Expensive.
Credit Cards: AE, D, DC, MC, V.
Handicap. Access: Yes.
Special Features: Pool

In Colonial America, three years before the States became United, the Red Lion Inn first opened its doors to travelers on the stagecoach route linking Albany, Hartford and Boston.

Today, over two centuries later, the Red Lion continues to welcome visitors and locals, and still with consummate Colonial charm. The present inn, rebuilt after a fire in 1895, is a veritable icon of the Berkshires, representing graceful country lodging at its best.

Antique furniture and a fine collection of china teapots adorn the lobby. Each private room is decorated with unique period appointments, carefully coordinated by the inn's owner, Jane Fitzpatrick, also owner of Country Curtains. Recent improvements have concentrated on creating larger rooms and increasing the number of suites, consistent with guest requests.

The atmosphere is faithful to the rhythms of a simpler, slower time while providing all contemporary comforts. Sipping a cool drink on a hot summer's day on the famous porch of the Red Lion, or meeting your companion in front of the cheery fireplace in the lobby in winter, you can't help but feel you're at the very heart of the Berkshires. The Red Lion roars with a quiet Rockwell charm.

Throughout the inn, the loving attention to detail is evident in every aspect of its operation. It's easy to feel at home here because all the inn's top quality services are offered by a vibrant, eager-to-please staff. During your stay in summer, don't be surprised if you find your porch or courtyard company to be an actor or actress of note, who spends evenings nearby on the boards of the Berkshire Theatre Festival and nights at the inn.

The Red Lion Inn is not, however, a particularly tranquil place. The main building is full of activity and people, and the street right outside (Rtes. 7 & 102) is sometimes noisy with traffic. There's a conviviality and gaiety about the lobby that some folks love and others find annoying. If you're in the latter category, take heart. There are several sweet Red Lion cottages that form a complex around the inn: the Stafford House, the O'Brien House, the more remote Buck House and the newly acquired Stevens House, just up the street.

Reservations should be made in advance at this popular inn, especially in the summer. The rooms have many fine complements: an excellent formal dining room; the Lion's Den, a pub featuring nightly entertainment; a courtyard for summer meals under the trees, surrounded by bushels of impatiens; the Pink Kitty, an outstanding gift shop; and a Country Curtains retail store.

THE ROEDER HOUSE
Managers: Vernon & Diane Reuss.
298-4015.
Box 525, Stockbridge, MA 01262.
Rte. 183, just S. of Glendale village center.
Closed: Oct.-May.
Price: Expensive.
Credit Cards: AE, MC, V.

A delightful hideaway, in a small village far from the crowds, but close to summer attractions. Awaiting lucky house guests are large, exquisitely furnished rooms, all with private bath and filled with priceless antiques, including 4-poster queen-sized beds. The owners also run an antiques shop, and the entire house reflects their impeccable taste. Full breakfast is served on tables set with china, silver and crystal on the charming screened-in porch, weather permitting. Pool.

WOODSIDE BED & BREAKFAST
Manager: Paula Schutzmann.
298-4977.
Box 1096, Stockbridge, MA 01262.
Rte. 102, W. of town.
Price: Inexpensive to Moderate.
Credit Cards: MC, V.
Handicap. Access: Yes.

Here's an alternative to cozy and quaint — a country contemporary, comfortable and informal, just outside the village of Stockbridge. Four rooms have shared baths in this newer home located on an acre of land.

Note: See also **Kripalu Center** under "A Yoga Retreat" in Chapter 6.

Tyringham

THE GOLDEN GOOSE
Managers: Lilja Hinrichsen & Joe Rizzo
243-3008
Box 336, Tyringham, MA 01264.
On main st. of village.
Price: Moderate.
Credit Cards: AE

The town itself is worth the trip. Beautiful, surprising and secretive, Tyringham is a gift. The Golden Goose is a white Colonial hideaway, with five cozy rooms, three with private bath, and one studio apartment in a setting of absolute peace and quiet. The deck and picnic tables watch over the Appalachian Trail, so it's a perfect stopping place for Trail hikers. Wine and cheese served in the afternoon in the antique-furnished, fireplaced common rooms. A full breakfast served each morning. Recommended.

West Stockbridge

CARD LAKE COUNTRY INN
Innkeepers: Lynn & Larry Schiffman.
232-7120.
Box 449, W. Stockbridge, MA 01266
Main St., center of villiage.
Price: Moderate to Expensive.
Credit Cards: AE, MC, V.

Under new ownership since 1987, the inn offers eight guest rooms featuring brass and iron beds. Four rooms have private bath and four are shared. Village shops across street are artsy-craftsy. Noisy trucks on way to nearby turnpike may be disturbing.

THE CLADDAGH INN
Managers: Barbara & Jack O'Neil.
232-7092.
Main St., W. Stockbridge, MA 01266.
Price: Moderate.
Credit Cards: MC, V.

The Irish "Claddagh" symbol stands for loyalty, love and friendship and the O'Neils have translated that into a caring and conscientious American inn. In a cozy, country atmosphere, you'll find three rooms, all with private bath, furnished with antiques and fluffy terry robes. A soothing cordial awaits your arrival.

INN AT SHAKER MILL TAVERN
Owners: Gordon Rose & Jonathan Rick.
232-8565.
Box 87, W. Stockbridge, MA 01266.
On Rte. 102 in village.
Price: Inexpensive.
Credit Cards: AE, MC, V.
Handicap. Access: Limited.
Special Features: Full in-room meal service.

This may just be the best buy in the Berkshires. Enormous, modern deluxe rooms with two queen-sized beds (one with a patio) come complete with small kitchens. The suites have two full bedrooms, two full baths, large, fully stocked kitchen, living room, two TVs, laundry and just about anything else you might want. There are four rooms in a converted garage behind the popular restaurant, and four more units across the street, with patios or balconies right on the pond, are being planned. Two suites are also available in summer in the old West Stockbridge train station.

KASINDORF'S
Managers: Shirley & Meyer Kasindorf.
232-4603.
Box 526, W. Stockbridge, MA 01266.
Glendale Rd., off Rte. 41
Price: Moderate.
Credit Cards: AE.

A lovely, contemporary home set on five park-like acres. There are three rooms, one with private bath. Full breakfast served.

THE WILLIAMSVILLE INN
Owners: Gail & Kathleen Ryan
274-6118.
Rte. 41, W. Stockbridge, MA 01266.
On Rte. 41, 10 mi. N. of Gt. Barrington.
Price: Moderate to Very Expensive.
Credit Cards: AE, MC, V.

The gracious, white Colonial home was built in 1792 and retains the charm of a bygone era. There are nine guest rooms in the main house, two with fireplaces. Two cottages and four more units, all with woodstoves, in the converted barn, bring the room total to 15. All rooms have private bath. Fine restaurant on main floor, pool and clay tennis court give the inn added dimension.

LODGING CENTRAL COUNTY

Becket

CANTERBURY FARM
Managers: Linda & Dave Bacon.
623-8765.
Fred Snow Rd., Becket, MA 01223.
On country road off Rte. 8, 5 mi. N. of Rte. 20, E. of Lee.
Price: Inexpensive to Moderate.
Credit Cards: None.
Special Features: XC ski touring center.

This 200-year-old farm is the perfect hideaway for cross-country skiers. Eleven miles of tracked trails, rental equipment and lessons lure city fast-trackers to the country's slow tracks. Rooms furnished with antiques, braided rugs, personal warmth. Ask for the room with the fireplace. Gourmet, family breakfasts.

LONG HOUSE B & B
Owners: Roy & Joan Simmons.
623-8360.
High St. Becket, MA 01223.
Off main st. of Becket.
Price: Inexpensive.
Credit Cards: MC, V.

Since 1966, this charming 19th-century country home has welcomed guests. Four cozy rooms, one with private bath. Convenient to Jacob's Pillow, hiking and nature trails. Full breakfast offered. In summer, a weekly plan can be arranged.

Dalton

THE DALTON HOUSE
Hosts: Gary & Bernice Turetsky.
684-3854.
955 Main St., Dalton, MA 01226.
Price: Inexpensive to Expensive.
Credit Cards: AE, MC,V.
Special Features: Pool. No children under 7.

Main House and Carriage House rooms all have private baths; some have fireplaces. Set in a small New England village, the house has been partially furnished with antiques. New pool recently added, as well as picnic area. Breakfast served in new breakfast room.

Hancock

HANCOCK INN
Managers: Ellen & Chester Gorski.
738-5873.
Rte. 43, Hancock, MA 01237.
On Rte. 43, via Rte. 22, N. of New Lebanon, NY.
Closed: Mon., Tues., Wed.

Exceptionally cozy Victorian inn set in a quaint village that seems unaware of the 20th-century's arrival. A tastefully furnished, family-run establishment, the inn has the charm of a delightful, forgotten keepsake discovered one day in your grandmother's attic. Comfortable rooms above a respected and well-managed restaurant. Recommended.

Price: Inexpensive to Moderate.
Credit Cards: AE, MC, V.

JIMINY PEAK, THE MOUNTAIN RESORT
Manager: Donna Solada.
738-5500.
Brodie Mtn. Rd. Hancock, MA 01237.
Corey Rd., Hancock. Between Rte. 7 & Rte. 43.
Price: Very Expensive.
Credit Cards: AE, D, DC, MC, V.
Handicap. Access: Yes.

This relatively new, full-service resort, truly has it all. Even in the 105-unit Country Inn, all units are suites featuring kitchens, living rooms with queen-sized sofa beds and a master bedroom with queen-sized bed. There are also condominiums of various sizes and styles for rent. Add to that several restaurants, tennis, racquetball, swimming, health club, trout fishing, an Alpine Slide for summer and, best of all, great downhill and cross-country skiing in winter, and you've got one of the Berkshire's most complete resorts.

KIRKMEAD BED & BREAKFAST
Owners: Donald & Pat Bowman.
738-5420.
Box 169A, Stephentown, NY 12168.
From NY Rte. 22, in Stephentown, take Rte. 43 E. to Hancock, MA. Inn just across NY/MA state line.
Closed: Thanksgiving & Christmas.
Price: Inexpensive.
Credit Cards: None.
Special Features: No smoking.

Historic, 1767 stagecoach stop, has 21 comfortable rooms. All rooms have private bath. Informal atmosphere on 30 acres, with meandering brook. Breakfast around the large common table is ample and convivial. Complimentary bedtime snack.

Hinsdale

MAPLEWOOD B & B
Managers: Charlotte & Bob Baillargeon.
655-8167.
435 Maple St., Box 477, Hinsdale, MA 01235.
On Rte. 143.
Price: Inexpensive to Moderate.
Credit Cards: None.
Special Features: No smoking, hot tub.

Country setting; country style. The house is set on six acres with a small pond, and has four rooms, one with private bath. Full breakfast might feature fresh trout caught by Bob or corn pancakes with fresh, locally-made maple syrup. Antiques in many rooms.

Lanesborough

TOWNRY FARM
Managers: Cliff & Barb Feakes.
443-9285.
The Greylock Rd., Lanesborough, MA 01237.
Off Rte. 7, 3/4 mi. on way to Mt. Greylock.
Price: Inexpensive.
Credit Cards: None.

A working sheep ranch, a bakery and an inn are all tucked away on the 16 acres known as Townry Farm. Three rooms in the 1750 Colonial house share baths. The reasonable price includes full breakfast.

THE TUCKERED TURKEY
Managers: Dan & Marianne Sullivan.
442-0260 or 443-0564.
Old Cheshire Rd., Lanesborough, MA 01237.
From Rte. 7, turn E. on Summer St., then N. on Old Cheshire Rd.
Price: Moderate.
Credit Cards: None.

A 19th-century, restored Colonial farmhouse, set on close to four acres, with spacious views. Three antique-furnished rooms share baths. Guests are welcome to bring their children to play with the owner's three, aged 15, 6 and 2. Full breakfast served, along with a great sense of humor.

Lenox

THE APPLE TREE INN
Managers: Aurora & Greg Smith.
637-1477.
224 West St. Lenox, MA 01240.
On Rte. 183, S. of

Magically set, the Apple Tree Inn is indisputably the lodging that lies closest to the front gates of Tanglewood. Aurora and Greg Smith, innkeepers, have brought great warmth and hospitality to this inviting if not elegant country property. The guest rooms in the main house are down-comforter dainty,

Laying a fire for guests at the Apple Tree Inn.

Tanglewood Main Gate.
Price: Expensive to Very Expensive.
Credit Cards: AE, DC, MC, V.
Special Features: Restaurant, swimming pool, tennis court.

some with antique brass beds and fireplaces, some with shared baths. A separate unit with 20 additional rooms is of no evident charm, though the rooms are certainly convenient and clean.

The Apple Tree would be worth a visit for the views alone. There is no more magnificent panorama in the Berkshires than the views from the south rooms, from poolside or from the gazebo which now serves as a dining room. The downstairs parlor is thoughtfully appointed and very comfortable; the bar has rich wood paneling, stained glass windows and a huge hearth. A crowning touch is the landscaping, boasting hundreds of varieties of roses set among the apple trees — truly a visual feast throughout late spring and summer.

BIRCHWOOD INN
Managers: Arnold, Sandra & Laura Hittleman.
637-2600.
Box 2020, 7 Hubbard St., Lenox, MA 01240.
On corner of Main and Hubbard.
Price: Moderate to Very Expensive.
Credit Cards: MC, V.
Handicap. Access: Yes.

Elegant, mansion high on the hill overlooking the charm of Lenox. Under new management since 1987, there are ten rooms in the main house, eight with private bath, and two suites in the carriage house. A full gourmet breakfast, plus wine and cheese in the afternoon, are included.

BLANTYRE
Manager: Roderick Anderson.
637-3556 (Winter: 298-3806).
Box 995, Lenox, MA 01240.

There is, in Berkshire, no sanctuary so civilized as Blantyre. Regally set amidst 90 conscientiously groomed acres of lawns, trees and hedges, Blantyre offers its guests attentive and even ingenious service, great natural and architectural beauty, palatial furnishings and magnificent vistas. One would have to be fastidious indeed to find fault with this elegant, Tudor-style manse, created in 1902 as one of the original Lenox summer "cottages."

Built by New York City businessman Robert Paterson, Blantyre is a replica of his wife's ancestral home in the Scottish village of Blantyre, east of Glasgow. In the 1940s, the Lenox castle passed to filmmaker D.W. Griffith, who intended to make it into Hollywood East. That plan never materialized and Blantyre was purchased and sold several times from the 1950s to the '70s, falling further into disrepair.

Jack and Jane Fitzpatrick bought Blantyre in 1980 and, with their daughter, Ann, devoted a great deal of time and money to the task of resurrection. The success of their efforts cannot be contested, for Blantyre today is baronial yet hospitable, massive but comfortable, masculine yet delicately appointed, in all ways beyond expectation.

Off Rte. 20, several mi. NW of Lee.
Closed: Nov. 1–mid-May.
Price: Very Expensive.
Credit Cards: AE, DC, MC, V.
Handicap. Access: Limited.
Special Features: Grounds & building NOT open to public for casual viewing.

A member of the prestigious Relais et Chateaux, Blantyre was awarded the Relais et Chateaux Gold Medal in 1989, a very special award, bestowed on the hotel that receives the highest number of complimentary guest comments. The five original bedrooms, restored with impeccable taste, epitomes of comfort and warmth, are the essence of Blantyre's hospitality, providing splendid views of the Berkshire hills. These suite-size rooms with four-poster beds, fireplaces and artful bathrooms are the true "jewels" in Blantyre's crown. There are three other rooms on the same floor, created in the "nanny's wing" on a different scale, smaller but just as elegant. Twelve more rooms, all charming and painstakingly wrought, are neatly tucked away in the original Carriage House. There are also two cottages on the grounds, both cozy, endearingly whimsical and brilliantly situated.

Stately Blantyre. Frank Packlick, courtesy of Blantyre.

But Blantyre is more than superb accommodations. The gourmet dining room is magnificent, and not to be missed. The hotel maintains four Har-Tru tennis courts and two tournament-size bent-grass croquet courts. A delightful exercise room fashioned out of a former potting shed also provides a sauna and hot tub. Nearby is a lovely, landscaped swimming pool. A public 18-hole golf course surrounds the property, and Tanglewood is a mere three miles to the west.

BROOK FARM INN
Owners: Betty & Bob Jacob.
637-3013.
15 Hawthorne St., Lenox, MA 01240.
Just off Old Stockbridge Rd.
Price: Moderate to Expensive.
Credit Cards: MC, V.
Special Features: Pool.

"There is Poetry Here," the innkeeping Jacobs tell us, and they mean it. A 1,400-volume library is supplemented by 75 poets on tape. Poetry reading takes place every Saturday at 4:00 p.m., accompanied by tea and scones. Breakfast buffet and tea daily. Twelve antique-furnished rooms, all with private bath, are offered in this large Victorian home, close to many Berkshire attractions. Heated pool.

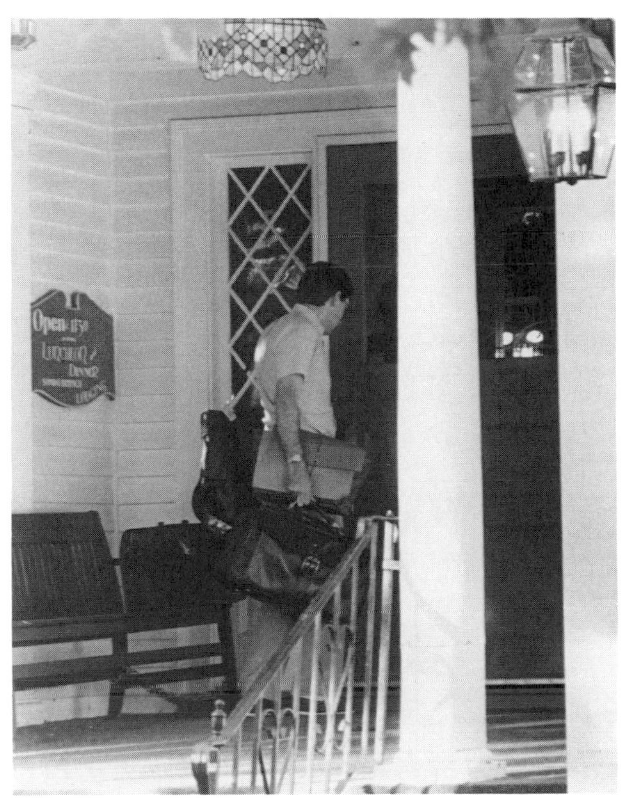

Beginning a Berkshire stay, at the Candlelight Inn.

CANDLELIGHT INN
Managers: Rebecca & John Hedgecock.
637-1555.
53 Walker St., Lenox, MA 01240.
On corner of Walker & Church Sts., near village center.
Price: Moderate to Expensive.
Credit Cards: AE, MC, V.

This comfortable, antique-furnished inn has eight large guest rooms, all with private bath, some retaining their original fixtures. Centrally located in the heart of Lenox, the inn features a charming restaurant on the main floor. Delightfully and professionally run by friendly hosts.

CLIFFWOOD INN
Owners/Managers: Scottie & Joy Farrelly.
637-3330.
25 Cliffwood St., Lenox, MA 01240.
Just off Main St., in village.
Price: Inexpensive to Very Expensive.
Credit Cards: None.
Special Features: Pool.

This very special inn, on a quiet, residential street, was built for an ambassador to France in the early 1890s. The elegant public rooms have tall ceilings, polished inlaid hardwood floors and grand fireplaces. The seven guest rooms have private baths and air conditioning, six even come with their own fireplaces. In summer, a continental breakfast is served on the spacious veranda overlooking the gardens and pool. On winter mornings, breakfast is served by a warming fire, in the oval dining room with its ornate wood-carved fireplace mantel. Wine, hors d'oeuvres and friendly conversation served early evening.

CORNELL INN
Manager: David Rolland.
637-0562.
197 Main St., Lenox, MA 01240.
On Rte. 7A, just N. of town.
Price: Moderate to Very Expensive.
Credit Cards: MC, V.
Handicap. Access: Yes.
Special Features: Spa with sauna, steam room, jacuzzi.

The Cornell Inn just keeps getting better. It began life in 1888 as a large, well-built Victorian and the owners keep making all the right improvements. Each of the nine bedrooms in the main house has its own bath, is furnished with brass or four-poster beds and several even have wood-burning fireplaces. In the converted carriage house are four newly built suites, each complete with kitchen, fireplace, sun deck, two bathrooms and much more.

CRANBERRY GOOSE
Managers: Ann McDonald & Margaret Ryan.
637-2812.
15 Cliffwood St., Lenox, MA 01240.
Just off Main St.
Price: Moderate to Expensive.
Credit Cards: None.

This large old house on a quiet, residential street is close to restaurants, shops and Tanglewood. Seven comfortable rooms, two with private bath. Fireplace in breakfast room. Spacious grounds.

EAST COUNTRY BERRY FARM
Manager: Rita Miller.
442-2057.
830 East St., Lenox, MA 01240.
Off Rtes. 7 & 20 at Holmes Rd.; right on Chapman Rd. to East St.; left to red farmhouse.
Price: Moderate to Expensive.
Credit Cards: AE, MC, V.

This unusual inn is a wonderful, historic farmhouse. Five rooms in all, with private baths, on 20 acres of peaceful countryside, with views of the mountains. Berry picking, wildflower walks, horseback riding, birdwatching, canoeing and bicycling are just a few of the possible pastimes. Continental buffet breakfast.

EASTOVER
Managers: Susan & Bob McNinch & Ticki Winsor.
637-0625.
430 East St., Lenox, MA 01240.
From Rte. 7 in Lenox, take Housatonic St. E., then left onto East St. for 2 mi.

Eastover makes no bones about it. Informality is key! Though it is surely not everyone's cup of tea, it is a very picturesque, amiable place that is admirably free of pretension. As another of the celebrated Lenox "cottages," this grand Gilded Age house is obviously living out of character but seems to be thriving.

You need not leave the sprawling grounds of this former estate to enjoy tennis, swimming, biking,

Price: Moderate AP;
wkly rates also.
Credit Cards: AE, CB, DC, MC, V.

volleyball, sauna, exercise room, horseback riding and all sorts of winter activities, including downhill and cross-country skiing and tobogganing on their own toboggan run.

Inspired by the remarkable spirit of the late founder, George Bisacca, the staff is up for anything as long as it's fun. To add to the festivities, there is dancing to live music during happy hour and again later in the evening. No liquor license here, so it's BYOB, but the band can play into the wee morning hours. This is not the place for the shy, the reclusive or those who don't quite feel dressed without a jacket and tie or a skirt and heels. For the good sport, the incurably casual or the curious, Eastover means relaxation, silliness and whatever the weekend's theme may be.

Mellowing out at Eastover.

Art Marasco

Wander the grounds, but beware of the American buffalo, English fallow deer, geese, burros and other pets of the singular Bisacca. The founder's collection of Civil War artifacts and the museum in the "Heritage Room" will fascinate boys of any age and revolt most others. Corny, oddly quaint and yet decidedly trendy, Eastover caters to families, couples-only and singles-only on different weeks and weekends. Call ahead to find out when you might go, depending on who you are. No matter what your status, Eastover has some fun planned for you.

THE GABLES INN
Manager: Frank Newton.
637-3416.
103 Walker St., Lenox, MA 01240.
In center of village.
Price: Inexpensive to Very Expensive.
Credit Cards: AE, MC, V.
Special Features: Pool.

Charming old home where Edith Wharton summered while her "cottage," the Mount, was being built. In the center of the village within walking distance of almost everything, including Tanglewood. There are 17 bedrooms, most with private baths; seven with fireplaces. A handsome house. Continental breakfast.

GARDEN GABLES INN
Owners: Mario & Lynn Mekinda.
637-0193.
141 Main St., Lenox, MA 01240.
Price: Inexpensive to Expensive.
Credit Cards: AE, MC, V.
Special Features: No children under 12. No pets.

Since its purchase in 1987 by the Mekinda family, this once-tired inn is breathing new life. All 12 rooms have been upgraded to include private bath and one has a whirlpool. The five acres of landscaped grounds include the largest outdoor pool in Berkshire County. Walking distance to Lenox shops and restaurants, and even to Tanglewood for the hardy. Breakfasts are extra special.

GATEWAYS INN
Manager: Vito Perulli.
637-2532.
71 Walker St., Lenox, MA 01240.
Just off Main St., in center of village.
Price: Expensive to Very Expensive.
Credit Cards: AE, DC, MC, V.

This Berkshire "cottage" was built in 1912 by Harley Proctor of Proctor and Gamble fame. Above an award-winning restaurant are spacious, elegant rooms, each with bath and fireplace, a four-poster here, a canopy there, and peace and quiet everywhere. Arthur Fiedler stayed here when performing at Tanglewood, and the "Fiedler Suite" is especially lovely.

PINE ACRES BED & BREAKFAST
Manager: Karen Fulco.
637-2292.
111 New Lenox Rd., Lenox, MA 01240.
Off Rtes. 7 & 20, S. of Pittsfield.
Price: Inexpensive.
Credit Cards: None.

A three-room bed and breakfast on a quiet back road. All rooms share baths. In summer, continental breakfast served on a wicker-furnished sun porch. Colonial decor in rooms.

ROOKWOOD INN
Innkeepers: Tom & Betsy Sherman.
637-9750.
19 Old Stockbridge Rd., Lenox, MA 01240.
Just off Main St. in center of town.
Price: Moderate to Expensive.
Credit Cards: AE.
Special Features: No smoking, no pets.

A grand 17-room Victorian painted lady, on a quiet street, but only one block from town center. All rooms have private bath and several include fireplaces. The two-level turret room is a marvelous secluded aerie. The innkeepers have two small children, so guests are welcome to bring their own.

SEVEN HILLS INN
Managers: Brian Butterworth.
637-0060 or 800-869-6518.
100 Plunkett St., Lenox, MA 01240.

Once the summer "cottage" of an eccentric dowager, this manor house-turned-inn changed hands again in 1987. Now owned by Baron Resources, Seven Hills is presently part of the "Country Inn Collection." From what we've seen, it looks good. Large public rooms include a full-service restaurant.

Off Rte. 7, next to the Mount.
Price: Moderate to Very Expensive.
Credit Cards: AE, CB, DC, MC, V.
Handicap. Access: Yes.
Special Features: Pool. Tennis.

Lovely pool on spacious grounds. All 15 rooms in the Manor House are large, with private baths, and five have working fireplaces. Please note: price includes breakfast and dinner. Conference rooms available for groups. Seven Hills specializes in parties, weddings and meetings.

UNDERLEDGE INN
Managers: The Lanoue Family.
637-0236.
76 Cliffwood St., Lenox, MA 01240.
Just off Main St.
Price: Moderate to Very Expensive.
Credit Cards: AE, MC, V.

Set high on a hill, off tree-lined Cliffwood St., this estate has 26-acre Kennedy Park at its back door. Perfect for hiking or cross-country skiing. The mansion was built in 1900, as a summer home for two wealthy sisters. Rooms are large and several feature fireplaces. The gracious front porch and sunny terrace are perfect places to relax and watch the sunset before driving along the pretty back road to Tanglewood, no more than a mile away.

THE VILLAGE INN
Managers: Clifford Rudisill & Ray Wilson.
637-0020.
Box 1810, 16 Church St., Lenox, MA 01240.
Off Walker St. in the center of town.
Price: Inexpensive to Expensive.
Credit Cards: AE, CB, DC, MC, V.
Handicap. Access: Yes.

Innkeepers Cliff Rudisill and Ray Wilson are cultivated, hospitable hosts, whose personal warmth complements this old, highly respected hostelry. Their pride in restoration and furnishings is evident in their recently completed eight-year renovation. The inn itself has been welcoming guests since 1771, when weary travelers arrived by horse-drawn coach.

Among the nice touches here are the hearty breakfasts served on the sunny porch (in warmer weather) and the English afternoon tea for which the Village Inn is justly famous. There is a full-scale restaurant, recently expanded to three rooms, two of which are reserved for non-smokers. All retain the delightful Colonial atmosphere.

The Village Inn by moonlight.

Bruce MacDonald, courtesy of the Village Inn.

WALKER HOUSE
Innkeepers: Peggy & Richard Houdek; Assoc. Innkeeper: Robert Wallace.
637-1271.
74 Walker St., Lenox, MA 01240.
Price: Inexpensive to Expensive.
Credit Cards: None.
Handicap. Access: Yes.

Comfortable, well-furnished, 1804-vintage Federal house operated by two genuinely friendly people. Grounds behind the house are gorgeous. Eight rooms all have private baths and are named for famous musicians. Sitting rooms offer an impressive collection of music and books. Within walking distance of Tanglewood, Lenox shops and restaurants.

Fountain and porte cochere at the entrance of Wheatleigh.

WHEATLEIGH
Managers: Susan & Linfield Simon.
637-0610.
Box 824, West Hawthorne Rd., Lenox, MA 01240.
From Rte. 183 in Lenox, left on Hawthorne Rd. to Wheatleigh sign.
Price: Expensive to Very Expensive.
Credit Cards: AE, DC, MC, V.
Special Features: Pool, tennis.

Wheatleigh is pure romance. An estate built for an heiress-turned-countess, it encourages flights of imagination. The grounds and setting are absolutely captivating. From the broad terrace, the manicured lawns slope down to a grassy stairway and then to a fountain. Straight ahead is an awesome view of the Stockbridge Bowl with the Berkshire hills in the distance. The pool is hidden away in a knoll surrounded by trees and the tennis court is off in another direction.

Owners Linfield and Susan Simon have preserved the expansive luxury of the interior space and decorative details in this turn-of-the-century mansion. The approach is by way of a winding driveway, then through an enclosed courtyard with a circular drive — reminiscent of a 16th-century private palazzo in the hills outside Florence. Once inside, the Great Hall is impressive with its magnificent Tiffany windows lining the grand staircase. The dark-wooded Conservatory with its cooling breezes is perfect for summer dining.

The 17 guest rooms are baronial in size and nine still have their wood-burning fireplaces. The bathrooms are splendid, several with original fixtures. Tastefully decorated throughout, only the Great Hall presents an unsettling effect. This room, decorated with stark chrome and leather furniture, is cold and uninviting. Too bad it's the first room seen by guests. Wheatleigh contains an award-winning, ***prix-fixe*** restaurant, complemented by an award-winning wine list.

WHISTLER'S INN
Managers: Richard & Joan Mears.
637-0975.
5 Greenwood St., Lenox, MA 01240.
On corner of Rte. 7A & Greenwood St.
Price: Moderate to Very Expensive.
Credit Cards: AE, MC, V.

Charming, much-admired guest house created within an 1820s English Tudor summer estate. Cultivated, accommodating hosts (Richard is an author; Joan is an artist) will put you at ease. Unaffected elegance and graciousness. The 11 bedrooms are quaint and cozy; interior is full of pleasant surprises, including an extensive library. From the stone-walled terrace it's possible to walk among the forgotten gardens of the remaining seven acres. Full breakfast is provided. Recommended.

The music room at Whistler's Inn.

Note: See also **Canyon Ranch** under "A Luxury Spa" in Chapter 6.

Peru

CHALET D'ALICIA
Managers: Alice & Richard Halvorsen.
655-8292.
East Windsor Rd., Peru, MA 01235.
Off Rte. 8, 3 mi. on Rte. 143, then left on E. Windsor Rd., 3 mi.
Price: Inexpensive.
Credit Cards: None.

Remote location in the wilds of the Berkshire hilltowns. Congenial home with three rooms, one with private bath. Full, country breakfast. Ideal for nature buffs, cross-country skiers, hunters, or simply for those seeking solitude. Friendly dogs and cats. Hot tub for total relaxation.

Pittsfield

AMERICAN HOUSE
Innkeeper: Joanne Spies.
442-0503.
306 South St., Pittsfield, MA 01201.
Rtes. 7 & 20 S. of Pittsfield 1 mi.
Price: Inexpensive to Moderate.
Credit Cards: None.

This charming 1898 Victorian, in the heart of Pittsfield, has been converted into a three-room bed and breakfast. One room has private bath, the other two share. Full breakfast provided by friendly innkeeper.

BERKSHIRE HILTON INN
Manager: Gerry van der Meer.
499-2000.
Berkshire Common, West St., Pittsfield, MA 01201.
Off Park Square.
Price: Moderate to Very Expensive.
Credit Cards: AE, DC, MC, V.
Handicap. Access: Yes.
Special Features: Pool.

Following a major renovation in 1989, this Hilton is far above the average. VIP rooms have a decidedly New England flair with prints on the walls, English-style furniture and chintz. Even the corridor carpeting is classy. To date, they have not hit the right restaurant combination, however. A publike casual restaurant, called the Park Square Grille, with photos of Pittsfield's old Park Square for decoration, complements the more formal restaurant. For businessmen, there's meeting space galore, from a grand ballroom to small meeting rooms.

COUNTRY HEARTS BED 'N' BREAKFAST
Managers: Jan & Steve Foose.
499-3201.
52 Broad St., Pittsfield, MA 01201.
S. of Park Square, 3 blocks.
Closed: Thanksgiving & Christmas.
Price: Inexpensive to Moderate.
Credit Cards: MC, V.

A three-room bed and breakfast, this home abounds with country touches, such as pretty, printed curtains, stenciling, and a wood stove. Relaxed informal atmosphere. Bountiful breakfast. The only thing that isn't country, is its location, which is in-town Pittsfield.

GREER BED & BREAKFAST
Managers: The Greers.
443-3669.
193 Wendell Ave., Pittsfield, MA 01201.
One block E. of South St.
Closed: Winter & spring.
Price: Moderate.
Credit Cards: None.

Surrounded by big, old mansions and carriage houses, this grey cedar-shake Colonial offers only two rooms, one with a private bath and one with a shared bath, but both have fireplaces. Full breakfast.

POMERANCE GUEST HOUSE
Manager: Stan Pomerance.
443-2303.
759 North St., Pittsfield, MA 01201.
Near Berkshire Medical Center.
Price: Inexpensive to Expensive.
Credit Cards: None.

A comfortable, no-nonsense guest house. Decorated in a whimsical, '40s-'50s style, the large rooms have walk-in closets and all share baths. No breakfast served.

WHITE HORSE INN
Managers: Darren & Regina Haman.
443-0961.
378 South St., Pittsfield, MA 01201.
Rte. 7, S. of town center.
Price: Moderate to Expensive.
Credit Cards: AE, MC, V.

Well-painted, attractive inn on busy main street, south of Pittsfield. All rooms have private bath and are individually decorated in various motifs. Small lavender flowers in #8, for example. Several rooms have fireplaces, bay windows and two double beds. Lots of green plants. Nicely landscaped back yard, perfect for picnics.

Richmond

BERKSHIRE HILLS COUNTRY INN
Manager: Ann Meyer.
698-3379.
Dean Hill Rd., Richmond, MA 01254.
Off Rte. 41.
Closed: Nov.-May.
Price: Inexpensive.
Credit Cards: None.

Great view of the Berkshires from this 147-acre hilltop property. The four rooms are comfortable; all share baths. Continental breakfast served. Children are not accepted.

ECHEZEAUX, A COUNTRY BED & BREAKFAST
Proprietors: Ronald Barron & Ina Wilhelm.
698-2802 (winter 617-965-3957).
Cheever Rd., Richmond, MA 01254.
At Cheever & Lenox Rds., 1/4 mi. off Swamp Rd.
Closed: Labor Day to last wkend. in June; 2 cottages available in fall.
Price: Moderate.
Credit Cards: None.

Delightful country retreat, owned by a member of the Boston Symphony Orchestra and frequently rented to other BSO members, this house often fills the surrounding hills with music. Main house has four antique-furnished rooms; two with private bath. Full breakfast is served.

MIDDLERISE BED & BREAKFAST
Managers: The White Family.
698-2687.
Box 17, Richmond, MA 01254.
State Rd., off Rte. 41.
Closed: Nov.-Feb.
Price: Moderate.
Credit Cards: None.

This renovated Cape-style house sits above the Richmond Valley and offers guests four cozy bedrooms, one with private bath. The rooms are quaintly furnished with antiques. Short drive to Tanglewood on one side and Hancock Shaker Village on the other.

PEIRSON PLACE
Manager: Margaret Kingman.
698-2750.
Rte. 41, State Rd. Richmond, MA 01254.
5 mi. N. of W. Stockbridge, beyond intersection with Rte. 295.
Price: Inexpensive to Expensive.
Credit Cards: AE, MC, V.
Handicap. Access: Yes.

Dating to 1772, this four-story former tannery, where boots for the officers of the Revolutionary War were made, sits on 200 acres in the country, near the charming, secluded village of Richmond. Ten rooms are available year-round, seven with private bath, and several with fireplaces. The room count increases to 15 in the summer. There's a private pond with boats, cross-country ski trails, and a sauna. Many out-buildings add charm. A fascinating history goes with the former tannery; ask the owner, whose family built it.

SEYCHELLES
Manager: Doane Perry.
698-2817.
Dublin Rd., Richmond, MA 01254.
Rte. 20 to Rte. 41S, then S. on Dublin Rd.
Price: Inexpensive to Expensive.
Credit Cards: MC, V.
Handicap. Access: Limited.

Delightful owners have lavished personal attention on this special home. Serene setting on 3 1/2 acres includes magnificent perennial garden, wildflower meadow, orchard and hidden retreats for guests. Two rooms in house have hand-made quilts, antiques, one room with private bath. In summer, full country breakfast is served on spacious porch.

Washington

BUCKSTEEP MANOR
Manager: Domenick Sacco.
623-5535.
Washington Mtn. Rd., Washington, MA 01223.
On Rte. 8 in the country.
Price: Moderate.
Credit Cards: MC, V.
Special Features: XC ski center.

Deep in the Washington Mountain woods, a cross-country skier's paradise. Several rooms in the main house share baths and are comfortably furnished. In the summer a few cottages increase the number of accommodations, adding to the rustic feeling of the property. Hiking, biking, and birding opportunities abound. Restaurant in summer season only. Great dancing and rock, country, bluegrass and reggae concerts in the Barn and on the lawn. Good vibes, funky buildings and that mellow, laid-back feeling predominates.

Windsor

WINDFIELDS FARM
Managers: Carolyn & Arnold Westwood.
684-3786
RRI, Box 170 Cummington, MA 01026.
Off Rte. 9, outside W. Cummington, 1.7 mi. N. on bush Rd. in Windsor
Closed: Mar. & Apr.
Price: Inexpensive.
Credit Cards: None.

Way out in the northern Berkshire hills, this country farmhouse offers a friendly welcome and two rooms with shared bath, furnished very comfortably with Scandinavian and antique designs. A swimming pond and miles of trails for hiking or skiing complete the picture. Hearty breakfast.

LODGING - NORTH COUNTY

Bascom Lodge, atop Mount Greylock.

Adams

BASCOM LODGE
Managers: Appalachian Mtn. Club; Jean McAlister.
743-1591 (Winter: 603-466-2727).
Rockwell Rd., Lanesborough, MA 01237.
On top of Mt. Greylock, off Rte. 7.
Price: Inexpensive.
Closed: Mid-Oct. to mid-May.
Credit Cards: MC, V.
Handicap. Access: Yes.

Let us now praise improbable places. Bascom Lodge, atop Mt. Greylock, is a marvel of dramatic beauty, adventure and bargain basement rates. Operated by the Appalachian Mountain Club and the Massachusetts Department of Environmental Management, the lodge at the 3,491-foot summit of the state's highest peak was built of stone and wood by the Civilian Conservation Corps during the Depression. Generations of hikers, birders and clever travelers have celebrated the accommodations and have returned again and again.

The stone fireplace and hand-cut oak beams cultivate a sense of adventure which the magnificent hills and trails confirm. This is lodging for the hearty, or at least, the sporting. Though linen is supplied, you might want to bring a sleeping bag or extra blanket.

The guest rooms are private or dormitory style; so, plan accordingly. Breakfast and dinner are served family style at a set time.

Workshops on topics ranging from birdwatching and backpacking to geology and photography are offered throughout the hiking season. We once even enjoyed a literary gathering up here, hearing selections from Thoreau's hiking notebooks read by a ruddy-faced AMC guide. While some rates at other more lavish places approach the upper end of the chart, the rates at Bascom don't even make it onto the bottom end! Well worth the climb.

North Adams

BLACKINTON MANOR
Hosts: Donna & Bill Furness.
663-9245.
1391 Massachusetts Ave., N. Adams, MA 01247.
One block off Rte. 2.
Price: Moderate.
Credit Cards: None.
Special Features: No smoking, pool.

Here's a romantic, 1832 Victorian, painted bright white with black wrought iron balconies. There are four rooms, some with private bath and the two queen-bedded rooms even have mountain views. A full breakfast is served by friendly innkeepers.

NORTH ADAMS INN
Manager: Ronald Sacco.
664-4561.
40 Main St., N. Adams, MA 01247.
Price: Moderate.
Credit Cards: AE, CB, DC, MC, V.
Handicap. Access: Yes.
Special Features: Indoor pool.

Centrally located in the heart of town, this 102-room facility specializes in package plans, but years of indifferent if not incompetent management have undermined both its reputation and future. It's now owned by a bankrupt bank in Oklahoma. The inn's manager tries very hard to make a difficult situation better. Since this hotel's prospects are in doubt, be sure to call in advance.

TWIN SISTERS INN
Manager: Gabriella Bond.
663-6933.
Box 412, 1111 S. State St., N. Adams, MA 01247.
In-town location.
Price: Inexpensive.
Credit Cards: None.

Set on 10 acres, this former carriage house now serves guests as a bed and breakfast. Four rooms share two baths. The large living room has a fireplace and there's a porch with a great view. Continental breakfast served.

Cheshire

THE WHITE RAINBOW INN
Managers: Carmen Furciniti & Matthew Kasuba.

This elegant, old country estate allows guests to sample true country living. There are four rooms, one with private bath. Two and a half acres include a colorful perennial garden. A continental breakfast

743-9254.
725 N. State Rd., Rte. 8, Cheshire, MA 01225.
Rte. 7 & 20 N. to Rte. 9, then E. to Rte. 8N. for 10 mi.
Price: Inexpensive.
Credit Cards: None.

is served in the formal dining room, and there's a common room complete with fireplace.

Williamstown

FIELD FARM GUEST HOUSE
Innkeepers: Miranda & Rick Krenzer.
458-3135.
554 Sloan Rd., Williamstown, MA 01267.
Rtes. 43 & 7, 1 mi. on right.
Price: Moderate.
Credit Cards: None.
Handicap. Access: Yes.

Property of the Trustees for Reservations, the inn is located on 254 acres of land, excellent for hiking and cross-country skiing. Five rooms all have private bath, two have working fireplaces, and three have sun decks. A swimming pool and tennis courts are added attractions.

LE JARDIN
Manager: Walter Hayn.
458-8032.
777 Cold Spring Rd., Williamstown, MA 01267.
On Rte. 7 a few mi. S. of town.
Closed: Jan.-Mar.
Price: Moderate.
Credit Cards: AE, MC, V.

Just south of the heart of Williamstown, on a wooded hillside above Rte. 7, Le Jardin offers gracious and cozy rooms in its large country farmhouse. Well-known restaurant on the first floor.

THE ORCHARDS
Owner: Chet Soling.
Resident Manager: Floyd Hunter.
458-9611.
222 Adams Rd. Williamstown, MA 01267.

This small luxury hotel, built on a former apple orchard, seems to be in a class all its own. The care and intelligent service of its owners is evident everywhere. Spacious rooms are furnished with English antiques and decorated in an English country style, and each has its own refrigerator. Some rooms

On Rte. 2, near N. Adams town line.
Price: Expensive.
Credit Cards: AE, CB, DC, MC, V.
Handicap. Access: Yes.
Special Features: Pool.

have wood-burning fireplaces and bay windows. Every bathroom is outfitted with fluffy robes. From the pastel stucco exterior to the soothing blend of interior colors, the entire hotel is in harmony.

The Orchards maintains an award-winning restaurant, an outdoor courtyard dining area in summer, creative room service and a complement of private meeting rooms.

[**Note:** As of this writing, the property was in some financial difficulty with the banks but was expecting to continue operations.]

WILLIAMS INN
Manager: Carl Faulkner.
458-9371.
Main St., Williamstown, MA 01267.
On the green off Rte. 7.
Price: Expensive.
Credit Cards: AE, D, DC, MC, V.
Handicap. Access: Yes.
Special Features: Indoor pool, sauna & spa.

What a shame the original Williams Inn burned to the ground. This unappealingly massive 100-room structure was built in the 1950s and relies for patronage mostly on parents of Williams College students and other captive audiences. Offers amenities of the better sort of chain motel. No disappointment here, as long as you prefer comfort to charm.

LODGING - OUTSIDE BERKSHIRE COUNTY

Salisbury, Connecticut

UNDER MOUNTAIN INN
Owners: Peter & Marged Higginson.
203-435-0242.
482 Under Mountain Rd.,(Rte. 41), Salisbury, CT 06068.
4 mi. N. on Rte. 41 from center of Salisbury.
Price: Moderate to Very Expensive.
Credit Cards: AE, D, MC, V.
Special Features: No pets. No children under 6. Non smoking rooms.

Have you been longing for a quiet day in the English countryside? Save the airfare and drive to the Under Mountain Inn, a 1730s Colonial set on three acres on a picturesque country road. Owner Peter Higginson is British — retired from the British Merchant Navy, in fact — and this veddy British inn is a reflection of his heritage.

The menu in the dining rooms, warmed by a fire in winter (I wonder if they burn peat?), features such English staples as steak and kidney pie, bangers and mash and shepherd's pie. On Sundays in summer, don't miss the fish and chips served with malt vinegar. The seven rooms in the inn are decorated with antiques and all have private baths. Hartley and Gibson sherry in the rooms, afternoon tea, and Gilchrist & Soames soaps all add to the British atmosphere. A wealth of British books in the parlor invite a quiet afternoon far removed from the hectic city pace. Tally Ho!

THE WHITE HART INN
Owner/Managers: Terry & Juliet Moore.
203-435-0030.
The Village Green, Box 385, Salisbury, CT 06068.
At intersection of Rtes. 41 & 44, in center of town.
Price: Moderate to Very Expensive.
Credit Cards: AE, CB, DC, MC, V.
Handicap. Access: Yes.
Special Features: Children welcome, Senior Citizen Discount.

Those indomitable restaurateurs, Terry and Juliet Moore (who also run the Old Mill in South Egremont), have restored this formerly abandoned and rather derelict landmark inn to polished perfection. The oldest portions of the inn were built sometime prior to 1810, when records indicate the farmhouse was converted to a tavern. The grand entrance hall, Hunt Room, formal dining room, tap room and garden room, all display an air of country elegance and comfort. Twenty-six charming rooms all offer private baths, air conditioning, phones and cable TV. Whether planning a wedding reception, business meeting, romantic weekend or escape from city pressures, the White Hart has it all. Recommended.

Averill Park, New York

THE GREGORY HOUSE
Hosts: Betty & Bob Jewell.
518-674-3774.
Rte. 43, Averill Park, NY 12018.
Price: Inexpensive to Moderate.
Credit Cards: AE, CB, D, MC, V.
Handicap. Access: Yes.

Country charm and congeniality abound here. Cozy, comfortable bedrooms set above and around a family-run restaurant. Great attention paid to guests' well-being, and the aromas from the kitchen are enticing. Close to Williamstown and North County's popular ski areas.

Berlin, New York

THE SEDGWICK INN
Innkeepers: Bob & Edie Evans.
518-658-2334.
Rte. 22, Box 250, Berlin, NY 12022.
Price: Moderate.
Credit Cards: AE, CB, MC, V.
Handicap. Access: Yes.

An 18th-century house with restaurant and small motel unit attached, set on 12 acres in the country. Privately owned and operated, this quaint, well-kept property offers comfortable rooms and proximity to Berkshire attractions. Rooms in the main house are preferred.

Canaan, New York

INN AT SHAKER MILL FARM
Host: Ingram Paperny.
518-794-9345.
Canaan, NY 12029.
Rte. 22, W. of town.
Price: Moderate to Expensive.
Credit Cards: MC, V.

A 150-year-old stone mill provides a backdrop for this country house dedicated to the gentle joys of leisure. Twenty comfortable rooms, all with bath, some with fireplace, surround cozy living rooms and a dining room open for dinner every weekend. A sauna, pond and private beach add to the pleasurable possibilities.

THE LACE HOUSE
Hosts: John & Sheila Clegg.
518-781-4669.
Rte. 22, Canaan, NY 12029.
Price: Inexpensive.
Credit Cards: AE, MC, V.

Hosting guests since 1823, this 1806 Victorian/Federal house is listed on the National Register of Historic Places. Its lacy embellishment inspired the name. Seven quaint bedrooms all share baths. A full breakfast is served to guests. (Note: Children under 10 are not allowed.)

Courtesy L'Hostellerie Bressane

Hillsdale, New York

L'HOSTELLERIE BRESSANE
Owners: Jean & Madeleine Morel.
518-325-3412.
Box 387, Hillsdale, NY 12529.
At junction of Rtes. 22 & 23.
Closed: Mon. (summer); Mon. & Tues.(winter).
Price: Moderate.
Credit Cards: None.

This Federal-period brick house strikes a noble profile above busy intersection in small upstate New York village. Six delightful, large rooms, two with bath, are thoughtfully furnished by your French hosts. The owner/chef, hailing from the Bresse region of France, operates an extraordinary restaurant on the ground floor.

SWISS HUTTE COUNTRY INN
Managers: Gert & Cindy Alper.
518-325-3333.
Rte 23, Hillsdale, NY. 12529
Price: Moderate to Very Expensive.
Credit Cards: MC, V.

At the entrance to the popular South County ski area, Catamount, this property boasts several tennis courts, a putting green, pool, lovely gardens and, of course, an inviting downhill slope in its front yard. Comfortable, well-furnished rooms are split between the original wooden chalet and a newer building. An award-winning restaurant completes the picture and is the pride of your hosts, the Alpers.

Stephentown, New York

MILL HOUSE INN
Owners: Frank & Romana Tallet.
518-733-5606.
Box 1079, Hancock, MA 01237.
Rte 43, W. Stephentown, NY.
Price: Moderate to Expensive.
Credit Cards: MC, V.
Handicap. Access: Yes

Old World touches in a former sawmill enhance this cozy, well-regarded country inn. Furnished with antiques, the rooms are warm and whimsical. A living room with fireplace offers warm comfort. Seven rooms and five suites, several with fireplaces of their own, all have private baths and air conditioning. Set on three peaceful, rural acres with formal gardens, stone walls, garden paths, and a pool, it's the perfect romantic escape – a touch of country with a European flair. Afternoon tea and continental breakfast served.

MOTELS

South County

BARRINGTON COURT MOTEL (Managers: Peter & Linda Gorman; 528-2340; 400 Stockbridge Rd., Rte. 7, Gt. Barrington, MA 01230; on Rte. 7, N. of Gt. Barrington.) Price: Expensive to Very expensive. AE, DC, MC, V. Handicap. access. 21 motel units and 2 suites, refrig., coffee makers in every room. Suites have kitchenettes, jacuzzi. Swimming pool.

BERKSHIRE MOTOR INN (Managers: Fred & Rita Chittenden; 528-3150; 372 Main St., Gt. Barrington, MA 01230; On Rte. 7, just S. of Town Hall.) Price: Inexpensive to Expensive. AE, D, MC, V. Health club and indoor pool on premises.

BRIARCLIFF MOTEL (Manager: Gail Brasee; 528-3000; 506 Stockbridge Rd., Gt. Barrington, MA 01230; on Rte 7, N. of town.) Price: Inexpensive to Moderate. AE, DC, MC, V. Handicap. access. 16 units on spacious landscaped grounds, with view of Monument Mtn.

GASLIGHT MOTOR LODGE (Owners: Barbara & John Cascio; 243-9701; Rte. 20, Greenwater Pond, Lee, MA 01238; 5 mi. E. of town.) Price: Moderate. MC, V. 8 units on pond with own swimming, paddle boats, row boats, ice skating, cross-country skiing and hiking, as the Appalachian Trail crosses property.

LANTERN HOUSE MOTEL (Manager: Curtis Ruppert; 528-2350; Stockbridge Rd., Box 97, Gt. Barrington, MA 01230; on Rte. 7, 1 mi. N. of Gt. Barrington.) Price: Moderate. (3-night weekend min. in summer). MC, V. Handicap. access. Pool.

LAUREL HILL MOTEL (Owners: Fred & Rita Chittenden; 243-0813; Box 285, Rte. 20, Lee, MA 01238; N. of Lee.) Price: Moderate to Expensive. AE, D, CB, DC, MC, V. 20 - unit motel with pool and view.

LEE MOTOR INN (Owner: Balvant Patel; 243-0501; Rte. 102, Box 426, Lee, MA 01238; between Stockbridge and Lee.) Price: Inexpensive to Very expensive. AE, D, DC, MC, V. 24 units in convenient location to Tanglewood, Berkshire Playhouse and other South County attractions.

MONUMENT MOUNTAIN MOTEL (Manager: Pat & Dick Roy; 528-3272; Stockbridge Rd., Gt. Barrington, MA 01230; on Rte. 7, just N. of Gt. Barrington.) Price: Inexpensive to Moderate. AE, D, DC, MC, V. Handicap. access. Far above an ordinary motel. Heated pool, lighted tennis courts, picnic tables, 20 acres that border the Housatonic River, spectacular flower gardens.

PILGRIM MOTOR INN (Manager: Ben Patel; 243-1328; 127 Housatonic St., Lee, MA 01238; on Rte. 20, E. of Lee.) Price: Inexpensive to Expensive. AE, DC, MC, V. 26 units. Pool.

PLEASANT VALLEY MOTEL (Owners/Manager: Suzie Patel; 232-8511; Rte. 102, W. Stockbridge, MA 01266; sandwiched between NY Thruway and Rte. 102.) Price: Moderate to Expensive. AE, MC, V. Handicap. access.

RIDGEVIEW MOTOR COURT (Managers: Anthony & Andrea Cavalier; 229-8080; Rte. 7A, Box 74, Ashley Falls, MA 01257; on Rte. 7A, S. of Sheffield.) Price: Inexpensive or weekly rates. No credit cards. Ten appealing little cabins on a quiet, country road. Rustic and a bit on the spartan side, but with a charm of their own.

SUNSET MOTEL (Owner/Managers: Ron & Puspa Patel; 243-0302; 114 Housatonic St., Lee, MA 01238; on Rte. 20, in town.) Price: Inexpensive to Expensive. AE, D, DC, MC, V. 22 units with AC, color cable TV, Pool. Convenient to Mass Pike, but may be noisy.

SUPER 8 MOTEL (Manager: Nancy Davis; 243-0143; 128 Housatonic St., Lee, MA 01238; just off Mass. Pike on Rte. 20.) Price: Inexpensive to Moderate. AE, D, DC, MC, V. Handicap. access. Non-smoking rooms, free coffee & paper. VCRs for rent. This two-level motel, next to a Burger King and conveniently close to the Mass Pike, opened in August, 1990; 49 attractive rooms, decorated in cranberry and grey, all have private baths. Some come with king-size bed and others with two doubles.

Central County

ALL SEASONS MOTOR INN - BERKSHIRES (Manager: Gregory Abbott; 637-4244; 390 Pittsfield Rd., Rte. 7, Lenox, MA 01240.) Price: Expensive. AE, D, DC, MC, V. Outdoor pool, tennis court. Restaurant & lounge.

BERKSHIRE NORTH COTTAGES (Managers: James & Mary Dowling; 442-7469; 121 S. Main St., Lanesborough, MA 01237.) Price: Inexpensive to Moderate. MC, V. 5 cottages, 3 with full kitchens, 2 with refrigerator only. Closed Nov.-mid-May.

HEART OF THE BERKSHIRES MOTEL (Owner: Sue Patel; 443-1255; 970 W. Housatonic St., Pittsfield, MA 01201; on Rte. 20, W. of town.) Price: Moderate, for 3-night minimum in summer. AE, D, MC, V. 16 units with outdoor pool, color cable TV & AC in all rooms.

HUNTSMAN MOTEL (Manager: Raman Patel; 442-8714; 1350 W. Housatonic St., Pittsfield, MA 01201; on Rte. 20, W. of town.) Price: Moderate. AE, MC, V. 14 units plus a suite with kitchen. All units have color cable TV.

INN AT VILLAGE SQUARE (Manager: Becky Pursell; 684-0860; 645 Main St., Dalton, MA 01226.) Price: Inexpensive. AE, D, MC, V. Handicap. access. A 16-unit motel, with a restaurant attached. Dining room and all rooms have recently been redecorated.

LAMPPOST MOTEL (Manager: Arvind Patel; 443-2979; Rte. 7, Box 335, Lanesborough, MA 01237; on Rte. 7, N. of Pittsfield.) Price: Moderate. AE, MC, V. 10 units, all with efficiency kitchens. Pool available.

LENOX MOTEL (Owner: Ish Bhatia; 499-0324; Rtes. 7 & 20, Box 713, Lenox, MA 01240; N. of Lenox.) Price: Expensive. AE, D, DC, MC, V. 17 units with AC, color cable TV and coffee in rooms. Pool.

MAYFLOWER MOTOR INN (Manager: "Jay" Patel; 443-4468; Rtes. 7 & 20, Box 952, Pittsfield – Lenox Rd., Lenox, MA 01240; N. of Lenox.) Price: Moderate to Expensive. AE, CB, D, DC, MC, V. Handicap. access. Swimming pool, some views.

MOUNTAIN VIEW MOTEL (Proprietor: Barbara A. Viklinetz; 442-1009; 499 S. Main St., Lanesborough, MA 01237; Rte. 7, N. of Pittsfield.) Price: Inexpensive to Moderate. AE, D, MC, V. Some handicap. access. Large rooms in motel. Cottages available year-round.

PINE HILL CABINS (Manager: Mary Diakiw; 447-7214; 269 Cheshire Rd., Pittsfield, MA 01201; on Rte. 8, N. of town.) Price: Inquire. No credit cards. 5 cabins, no kitchens, in remote location. Closed Oct.-May.

PITTSFIELD CITY MOTEL (Manager: Joe Hashim; 443-3000; 150 W. Housatonic St., Pittsfield, MA 01201; on Rte. 20, W. of town.) Price: Inexpensive. AE, D, MC, V. 38 units with AC, color cable TV in rooms. Pool.

PITTSFIELD TRAVELODGE (Manager: Beatrice Crocker; 443-5661, 800-255-3050; 16 Cheshire Rd., Pittsfield, MA 01201; at junction of Rtes. 8 & 9.) Near Berkshire Mall. Price: Inexpensive to Moderate. AE, CB, D, DC, MC, V. Handicap. access.

SUSSE CHALET MOTOR LODGE (Manager: Mike Halloran; 637-3560; Pittsfield Rd., Lenox, MA 01240; on Rtes. 7 and 20, N. of town.) Price: Moderate. AE, D, DC, MC, V. 70 units all with AC, color cable TV. Pool.

TANGLEWOOD MOTOR INN (Manager: Navin Shah; 442-4000; 626 Pittsfield, Rd., Lenox, MA 01240; on Rtes. 7 & 20, N. of town.) Price: Expensive. AE, D, MC, V. 22 units with AC, color cable TV. Pool.

WAGON WHEEL MOTEL (Manager: Sue Peter; 445-4532; Rtes. 7 & 20, Box 808, Lenox, MA 01240; 3 mi. N. of Lenox center.) Price: Moderate. AE, MC, V. Handicap. access. Some king-size waterbeds.

THE WEATHERVANE MOTEL (Manager: Navin Shah; 443-3230; 475 S. Main St., Lanesborough, MA 01237; on Rte. 7, S. of town.) Price: Moderate. AE, CB, D, MC, V. 17 units. Pool.

YANKEE MOTOR LODGE (Owners: The Trombley family; 499-3700; Pittsfield Rd., Lenox, MA 01240; on Rtes. 7 & 20, near Pittsfield town line.) Price: Expensive to Very expensive. AE, D, DC, MC, V. Handicap. access. This stylish, 61-unit motel has a heated pool with rock waterfall in center, 12 rooms with fireplaces, some queen-sized, four-poster beds, and manicured grounds.

North County

BERKSHIRE HILLS MOTEL (Managers: Jerry & Marguerite Vincz; 458-3950; Rte. 7, Williamstown, MA 01267; on Rtes. 7 & 2, 2 mi. S. of Williamstown.) Price: Inexpensive to Moderate. AE, MC, V. Brick, 2-story motel, spacious, landscaped grounds, heated pool, homemade complimentary continental breakfast, charming rooms and gracious, friendly innkeepers, keep guests returning year after year. Non-smoking rooms and king-size beds available.

BEST WESTERN SPRINGS MOTOR INN (Managers: The Grosso Family; 458-5945; Rte. 7, New Ashford, MA 01237; halfway between Pittsfield and Williamstown on Rte. 7.) Price: Moderate to Expensive. AE, CB, D, DC, MC, V. This is a well-run motel, conveniently located near several winter ski resorts. Standard motel rooms, complemented by several small chalets with fireplaces. The Grosso's award-winning restaurant across the street, makes this motel especially attractive.

CARRIAGE HOUSE MOTEL (Manager: Pat Deloye; 458-5359; Rte. 7, New Ashford, MA 01237.) Price: Inexpensive. AE, CB, D, DC, MC, V. Partial handicap. access. Owned by Brodie Mtn., this grey & yellow motel with 14 units, sits high on hill, behind a respected restaurant. Guests have access to a pool, indoor tennis & racquetball, woods, brook and trails.

CHIEF MOTEL (Owner: Tom Manship; 663-3325; 926 Mohawk Trail, N. Adams, MA 01247; on Rte. 2, E. of Williamstown.) Price: Inexpensive. 13 standard units are favorites with souvenir and game hunters. The views are worth the drive up.

CHIMNEY MIRROR MOTEL (Managers: Harm & Shirley Cyr; 458-5202; Rte. 2, Williamstown, MA 01267; just E. of town.) Price: Inexpensive. AE, MC, V. 18 units that recently changed ownership.

DUBLIN HOUSE MOTEL (Manager: Sandy Dolan; 443-4752; Rte. 7 at Brodie Mtn., New Ashford, MA 01267; near Lanesborough town line.) Price: Moderate. AE, D, DC, MC, V. Owned by Brodie Mtn. Ski Resort, this 21-unit motel offers convenience over charm, but right at the base of the slopes.

DUG OUT MOTEL (Managers: Mr. and Mrs. Gardner, and Melissa Pratt; 743-9737; 99 Howland Ave., Adams, MA 01220; on Rte. 8, going N. out of town.) Price: Inexpensive. MC, V. Several units have handicap. access. Basic motel unit on road between Adams and N. Adams. Restaurant no longer open.

1896 MOTEL (Manager: Sue Morelle; 458-8125; Cold Spring Rd., Williamstown, MA 01267; on Rte. 7.) Price: Inexpensive to Moderate. AE, D, DC, MC, V. Family owned and operated, the motel, with a very New England look, has 16 clean and comfortable rooms, with scenic Hemlock Brook at its front door. Generous complimentary continental breakfast.

FOUR ACRES MOTEL (Managers: Marjorie & Keith Wallace; 458-8158; 213 Main St., Williamstown, MA 01267; on Rte. 2.) Price: Inexpensive to Moderate. AE, CB, D, DC, MC, V. Handicap. access. Common room with fireplace, garden area with shuffleboard, meeting rooms.

GREEN VALLEY MOTEL (Manager: Catherine Sohl; 458-3864; Rte. 7 N., 1214 Simonds Rd., Williamstown, MA 01267; on Rte. 7, N. of town.) Price: Inexpensive. MC, V. 18 units.

JERICHO VALLEY MOTEL (Proprietor: Ed Hanify; 458-9511 or 1-800-JERICHO; Rte. 43, Box 239, Williamstown, MA 01267; 9 mi. S. of Williamstown, then 5 mi. W. on Rte. 43.) Price: Inexpensive to Moderate. AE, MC, V. Heated pool, on 350 mountain acres with spectacular views, fireplace lounge. Near Jiminy Peak and Brodie Mtn.

KERRY HOUSE MOTEL (Manager: Sandy Dolan; 443-4753; Rte. 7 at Brodie Mtn., New Ashford, MA 01267; near Lanesborough town line.) Price: Moderate. AE, D, DC, MC, V. Owned by Brodie Mtn. Ski Resort, this new 9-unit motel is located on the slopes of Brodie Mtn. Some efficiency apartments are available.

MAPLE TERRACE MOTEL (Managers: Ron Lagasse & Bill Francome; 458-9677; 555 Main St., Williamstown, MA 01267; on Rte 2, just E. of town green.) Price: Inexpensive to Moderate. AE, MC, V. Pool with mountain views. Spacious grounds well off the highway.

NEW ASHFORD MOTOR INN (Manager: Marguerite Gigliotti; 458-8041; Rte. 7, New Ashford, MA 01237; 1 mi. N. of Brodie Mtn.) Price: Inexpensive to Moderate. AE, MC, V. Handicap. access. Small motel made for the skier and traveler who does not insist on old-world charm.

NORTHSIDE INN & MOTEL (Managers: Linda & Fred Nagy; 458-8107; 45 N. St. Williamstown, MA 01267; on Rte. 7, N. of town.) Price: Inexpensive. AE, DC, MC, V. Handicap. access. 35 units with coffee shop for breakfast. Pool.

WHITCOMB SUMMIT MOTEL & RESORT (Manager: Indira Bhakta; 662-2625 or (508) 537-1741; Mohawk Trail, N. Adams, MA 01247; on Rte. 2, high above N. Adams in the mountains.) Price: Inexpensive. 18 units attract families and tourists who want a birds-eye view of the Mohawk Trail. All units have panoramic view. Souvenir shop with Indian theme. Small pool. Restaurant. Observation tower with 4-state view. Closed Nov.-May.

WIGWAM & WESTERN SUMMIT MOTEL (Managers: Hans & Inna Gertje; 663-3205; Mohawk Trail, Box 7, N. Adams, MA 01247; on Rte. 2 E. of town.) Price: Inexpensive. AE, D, MC, V. High atop the Mohawk Trail, 5 rural cottages offer fantastic views. Closed Nov.-May.

THE WILLOWS MOTEL (Managers: Schlesinger Family; 458-5768; 480 Main St., Williamstown, MA 01267; on Rte. 2 E. of town.) Price: Inexpensive. AE, D, MC, V. 16-room above average motel. Heated pool.

CAMPING

It's easy to get back to nature in the Berkshires. Nine of the county's state parks offer camping, with facilities ranging from showers and flush toilets to campsites that are little more than terraces hewn out of the mountainside. There are also more than a dozen private campgrounds in the area, and these usually offer more amenities, making a long summer stay quite comfortable. Wherever you camp, the rolling hills are a soothing sight for sore eyes.

> *The delights of camping? You will live outdoors, sleep on the fragrant spruce boughs under the transparent tent roof, lazily loaf in 'hammock grove,' and, by means of frequent walks compassing noble scenery, cultivate the most enormous of appetites.*
>
> The Book of Berkshire, 1889

Campsites in *state parks* are available on an unreserved basis, but please be aware that owing to budget restrictions at the state level, some state parks and forests may be closed. It is therefore a good idea to obtain complete information in advance from ***Massachusetts Environmental Management Department***, Region Five Headquarters, Box 1433, Pittsfield, MA 01201; telephone 442-8928.

Fees are as follows at all state parks and forests: Season pass $30; *Camping*: wilderness $5 per night; unimproved toilets $8; flush toilets $10; flush toilets with showers $12; electric hook-up $4; water utility fee $2; sewer utility fee $2; group camping $16; log cabins, one-room $16; three rooms $20; *Day use* per car $5 per day.

State campgrounds, noted below with an asterisk (*), are of two kinds: "Type-1" denotes facilities with showers and flush toilets; "Type-2" denotes those with outhouses.

South County

* **BEARTOWN STATE FOREST** (Manager: Thomas W. O'Brien; 528-0904; Blue Hill Rd., Monterey, MA 01245; Mailing Add: Box 97, Monterey, MA 01245; N. from Rte. 23 in Monterey.) On Benedict Pond; 10,555 acres, 12 Type-2 campsites, bicycling, boating, fishing, hiking, hunting, horseback riding trails, picnicking, xc skiing, snowmobiling, swimming.

CAMP OVERFLOW (269-4036; Box 150, Otis, MA 01253; 5 mi. from Rte. 8.) 100 sites, electric hookups, dumping station, camp store, fishing, swimming, boating, seasonal rates, right on Otis Reservoir.

LAUREL RIDGE FARM CAMPING AREA (269-4804; Old Blandford Rd., E. Otis, MA 01029.)

MAPLE GLADE CAMPGROUND (Managers: Thomas & Karen Shaffer; 243-1548; 165 Woodland Rd., Lee, MA 01238; across from October Mtn. State Forest.) 65 sites; $15 for tents, $17 with water. Small store, swimming pool.

* **MOUNT WASHINGTON STATE FOREST AND BASH BISH FALLS STATE PARK** (528-0330; East St., Mt. Washington, MA 01258; From S. Egremont, take Rte. 41 S., then next right onto Mt. Washington Rd. and follow signs.) 3,289 acres, including spectacular Bash Bish Falls, boating, bicycling, canoeing, 15 Type-2 wilderness campsites, fishing, hiking, horseback riding trails, hunting, snowmobiling, xc skiing. Nearby Mt. Everett State Forest offers three-state views from its road to the summit.

* **OCTOBER MOUNTAIN STATE FOREST** (243-1778; Woodland Rd., Lee, MA 01238.) Follow signs from Rte. 20 in Lee. 16,021 acres, 50 Type-1 campsites, bicycling, fishing, hiking, Appalachian Trail, horseback riding, hunting, xc skiing, snowmobiling. Some campsites wheelchair accessible.

PROSPECT LAKE PARK (528-4158; Prospect Lake Rd., N. Egremont, MA 01252.) 145 sites, tennis, swimming, boat rentals, basketball court, volleyball, snack bar, playground, and a 1916 New York Central Railroad caboose used as a lounge.

* **SANDISFIELD STATE FOREST** (Manager: Thomas W. O'Brien; 528-0904; West St., Sandisfield, MA 01255; off Rte. 57 at Pine Woods Rd., then to West St.) 11,000

acres, part of York Lake recreation area, which includes Campbells Falls and West Lake. West Lake has 10 Type-2 wilderness campsites open year-round at $5 per night. Rest of park offers wilderness hiking, bicycling, boating, fishing, hunting horseback riding trails, picnicking, xc skiing, snowmobiling, swimming.

* **TOLLAND STATE FOREST** (Manager: Bruce Taggart; 269-7268; Rte. 8, Otis, MA 01253; 5 mi. from Rte. 8.) 90 Type-1 campsites, on 8,000 acres, including lovely Otis Reservoir. Private, secluded campsites, some on the lake or overlooking lake. Bicycling, boating, fishing, hunting, hiking, horseback riding trails, picnicking, xc skiing, snowmobiling, swimming.

Central County

BISSELLVILLE ESTATE & CAMPGROUND (Owners: Eugene & Lorraine Brunet; 655-8396; Washington Rd. (Rte. 8), Hinsdale, MA 01235.) 35 campsites, 13 with sewer hookups. $14 campsites; 15 with sewer. Closed winter.

BONNIE BRAE CABINS AND CAMPSITES (Manager: Richard Halkowicz; (442-3754, 108 Broadway St., Pittsfield, MA 01201; 3 mi. N. of downtown Pittsfield, off Rte. 7 at Pontoosuc Lake.) Full hookups, free showers, trailer rentals, new pool, cabin rentals May 1-Oct. 31. Closed Nov. -Apr. 30.

BONNIE RIGG CAMPGROUND (Managers: Paul and Kathryn Neske; (623-5366; P.O. Box 14, Chester, MA 01011-0014; corner of Rtes. 8 & 20 in Becket.) 200 campsites, but by owner/ membership only. Call for information. Adult lounge, playground, swimming pool, sauna, jacuzzi.

BUCKSTEEP MANOR (623-5535; Washington Mtn. Rd., Becket, MA 01223; 10 mi. E. of Pittsfield, across from October Mtn. State Forest.) Showers, swimming pool, tennis, xc skiing, weekend restaurant.

* **MOUNT GREYLOCK STATE RESERVATION** (499-4262; Rockwell Rd., Lanesborough, MA 01237; from Rte. 7 in Lanesborough, take N. Main St. to Rockwell Rd.) 10,237 acres which includes the state's highest peak (see Lodging for historic Bascom Lodge). 100-mi. view from War Veterans Memorial Tower, 35 wilderness campsites, 45 mi. of trails including the Appalachian Trail, xc skiing, hunting, snowmobiling, picnicking.

* **PITTSFIELD STATE FOREST** (442-8992; Cascade St., Pittsfield, MA 01201; From Rte 7 take West St. to Cascade St.) 9,695 acres with streams, waterfalls, wildflowers, panoramic views, and famous Balance Rock. Two camping areas offer 31 Type-1 and Type-2 campsites, plus boating, canoeing, xc skiing, bicycling, fishing, hiking, picnicking, hunting, interpretive programs, snowmobiling, swimming and wheelchair-accessible picnic areas and trails.

PONTERRIL (Manager: John Barclay, Pittsfield YMCA; 499-0640; North St., Pittsfield, MA 01201; off E. Acres Rd. at Pontoosuc Lake N. of Pittsfield via Rte. 7.) 12 campsites, swimming pool, tennis, sailing and sailing instructions.

SUMMIT HILL CAMPGROUND (Manager: Vicki Roberts, 623-5761; Summit Hill Rd., Washington, MA 01235.) 110 campsites for tents and trailers, 83 sites with electricity and water, adult lounge, swimming pool and recreation hall. Closed in winter.

* **WINDSOR STATE FOREST** (698-0948; in winter 442-8928; River Rd., Windsor, MA 01270; Off Rte. 9 just E. of Windsor town line; off Rte. 116 in Savoy.) 1,626 acres with spectacular falls at Windsor Jambs. 24 Type-2 campsites, bicycling, fishing, hiking, hunting, picnicking, swimming, xc skiing, snowmobiling.

North County

BRODIE CAMPGROUNDS (Managers: Brodie Mtn; 443-4754; Brodie Mtn. Ski Resort, New Ashford, MA 01237; off Rte. 7, just N. of Lanesborough town line.) 120 campsites for tents and trailers, rented seasonally. Heated swimming pool, tennis, recreation hall.

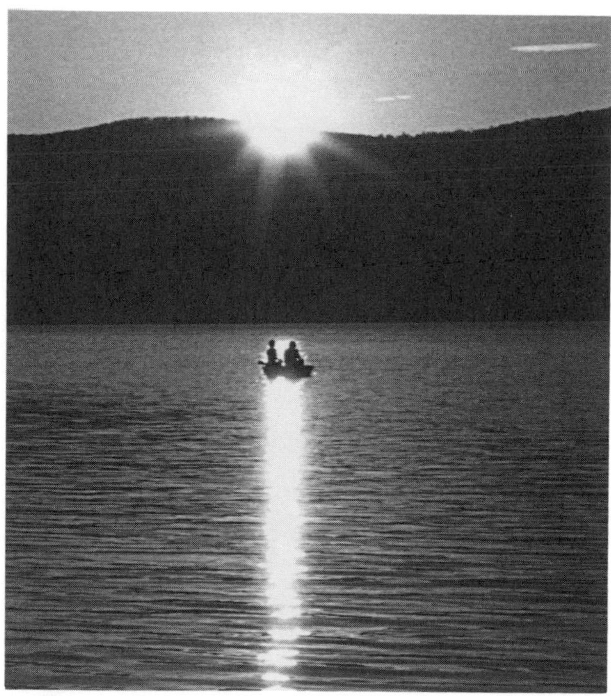

Many Berkshire campsites offer water sports and beautiful lake vistas as well.

Warren Fowler.

* **CLARKSBURG STATE PARK AND CLARKSBURG STATE FOREST** (664-8345, in winter 442-8928; Middle Rd., Clarksburg, MA 01247; From Rte. 8 N. take Middle Rd. in Clarksburg) 3,250 acres of unspoiled forestland with panoramic views; Mauserts Pond offers landscaped day-use area; 47 Type-2 campsites; boating, canoeing, xc skiing, fishing, hiking (Appalachian Trail), hunting, snowmobiling, picnicking, bicycling, swimming.

HISTORIC VALLEY PARK CAMPGROUND (Manager: Les Griffin; (664-9228; Box 751, N. Adams, MA 01247.) 100 campsites with electric and water hookups, laundry, camp store, recreation hall, hiking trails on beautiful Windsor Lake, public and private beaches with lifeguards.

PRIVACY CAMPGROUND (458-3125; Hancock Rd., Williamstown, MA 01267; on Rte. 43, 5 mi. S. of Rte. 7.) 475 acres, 35 sites, waterfall, pond, 10 mi. of hiking trails, paddle boats, volleyball, badminton, horseshoes, tetherball, basketball, table-tennis, campfires, waterwheel, windmill, trolley car, playground, recreation hall, sauna. 4 small cabins.

* **SAVOY MOUNTAIN STATE FOREST** (663-8469; Central Shaft Rd., Florida, MA 01256.) 10,500 acres, including Bog Pond and Tannery Falls; 45 Type-1 campsites in old apple orchard, 3 log cabins with grand stone chimneys, overlook South Pond and are available for year-round rental by writing RFD 2, N. Adams, MA 01247; picnicking, boating, bicycling, canoeing, xc skiing, fishing, hiking, interpretive programs, snowmobiling, swimming.

CHAPTER FOUR
What to See, What to Do
CULTURE

A French horn player at Tanglewood.

To glorify God's grandeur by gracefully combining Art and Nature — this was the goal of the Stockbridge Laurel Hill Society, as expressed in 1853. Thinking such as this represented an already well-developed Berkshire cultural awareness, with roots in Colonial times when the earliest local libraries, schools, churches and newspapers were the centers of cultural activity. But it was in the mid-19th century that the tradition of a Berkshire cultural bounty, as we know it today, really took shape.

It is an artistic abundance all out of proportion to the county's size and population. In music, dance, theater and other art forms, Berkshire has long had a cultural calendar of astonishing excellence and variety — especially for a mountainous area once thought of as remote. There are good reasons for this legacy.

In the mid-1800s, summers in the crowded eastern cities were not only unpleasant but frequently unhealthy. At the same time, particularly after the Civil War, improvements in transportation made the mountains much more accessible. And already in Berkshire, a few key families of taste, talent and money were setting the tone of cultural sophistication that you will still find here today. If you have come to Berkshire to escape the city, you are part of a grand old tradition created by writers seeking quiet; painters seeking picturesque landscapes; actors, musicians and dancers seeking summer audiences.

A local intelligentsia developed around Stockbridge and Lenox, helping to spark the Berkshire cultural bounty. No single family was more dynamic than the convivial and civic-minded Sedgwicks of Stockbridge, whose novelist daughter, Catherine, shares honors with poet William Cullen Bryant as Berkshire's first popular writer. The Sedgwick house and family still grace Stockbridge today. The presence of Herman Melville and Nathaniel Hawthorne in the 1850s strengthened the literary tone, as did the charm of the even more popular Oliver Wendell Holmes, who summered in Pittsfield. Adding a dash of 20th-century insight, Edith Wharton came, created a grand European lifestyle and the novels to go with it. The list of famous artistic residents is lengthy and impressive. Our Bibliography cites several engaging books which will tell you the whole fascinating story.

When the Berkshires became the "Inland Newport" during the late 19th century's Gilded Age, culture was imported here by the trainload. Architectural indulgences, furnishings, musical instruments and people to play them, paintings, chefs with their foreign cuisines, and landscape gardeners: the whole phenomenon of culture rode into Berkshire on the power of big money. Whatever we think these days about the implicit politics of it all, we are the beneficiaries of so much inherited culture. Some of the historic estates here have become cultural centers such as Tanglewood, for music, and the Mount, for theater. And yet, as if to remind us that beauty need not be ornate or expensive, the Shaker Village at Hancock is also a Berkshire cultural legacy of remarkable value and vitality. Don't miss it.

And finally, there is the philanthropy factor. The artistic institutions in Berkshire all have their patrons, large and small, typified by the Crane family and Crane Paper Co. of Dalton, which started the Berkshire Museum; by Francine and Sterling Clark, who created the Clark Art Institute in Williamstown; and by the Tappan family, which gave Tanglewood to the Boston Symphony Orchestra. There are *hosts* of others. We owe them all our thanks.

Many of the famous artists drawn to the Berkshires have lived here seasonally, like Edith Wharton, or year-round, like Norman Rockwell. Thousands more have come just to perform or exhibit. But on every one, Berkshire has left its mark. We asked Maestro Seiji Ozawa, conductor of the BSO, just what the Berkshires and Tanglewood mean to him. "Tanglewood has an absolutely special connotation for me," Ozawa replied. "It was the first place I ever saw in America since I came to Tanglewood as a student in 1960 at the invitation of Charles Munch. For me and the Orchestra, Tanglewood represents an opportunity to appreciate both the beauty of the Berkshires, and of the music we make here."

Art combined with Nature, up and down the county, from the fine woodwork in Colonist John Ashley's study at Ashley Falls to one of the few printed copies of the Declaration of Independence at Williams College's Chapin Library, from dioramas and Egyptian mummies at the Berkshire Museum in Pittsfield to simply beautiful fresh flower arrangements at the Berkshire Botanical Garden in Stockbridge (known for years heretofore as the Berkshire Garden Center). In performance halls, museums, libraries, theaters, nightclubs and historic homes, Berkshire is rich in art beyond measure.

The following descriptions will give you many ideas of where to go and what to do in Berkshire, but they will not tell you what's currently playing or showing.

For the larger seasonal schedules, such as Tanglewood, Jacob's Pillow, the museums, theaters and other concert series, it's best to write for information. We provide many addresses for you. Tanglewood issues its summer schedule on March 15th; other arts organizations soon follow. With such information in hand, you'll be better able to plan your own Berkshire festival. Telephoning is always a good idea for specifics, especially when you might travel a long way to see or hear a certain artist. Sold-out performances are not uncommon here. For cultural events as they happen, *The Berkshire Eagle* is the best bet. For seasonal coverage, see the newly revitalized *Berkshire Magazine*, now one of the best looking, best written regional magazines anywhere.

Church on the Hill (1805), Lenox.

ARCHITECTURE

If roaming through New England in search of handsome buildings is your idea of fun, then you'll find Berkshire County an inexhaustible delight. True, there are no skyscrapers, unless our tallest mountains deserve that name. True, you won't find the architecture of the Deep South or the Southwest here. But you will find in Berkshire virtually every other style that has ever been popular in North America, from Colonial times to the present. Few counties anywhere can claim this much architectural variety.

Berkshire is justly famous for the scores of mansions built during the opulent Gilded Age. Under "Historic Homes" in this chapter, in the chapters called *Restaurants* and *Lodging*, and elsewhere in this book, we describe several of the best surviving examples of these great "cottages," as they were called. See "Gilded Age" in the Index. But the saga of the sumptuous cottages isn't half the Berkshire building history.

Consider humbler examples: one-room schoolhouses, icons of America's simpler past. Still housing primary schools in some Berkshire towns, adapted to alternative uses in others, these white clapboard, bell-topped, frame structures are often handsome and always charming. Some of the best are the ones in Alford, Washington and Lanesborough (a stone structure, c. 1800).

There are numerous Berkshire villages that seem like architectural set pieces, so artfully coordinated are their building styles and locations. They seem quaint almost by design. The villages of ***Alford, New Marlborough, Stockbridge*** and ***Williamstown*** all have this look. There is a conspicuous absence of neon and plastic commercial clutter in these towns. Feelings of space and grace predominate. Yet also in each town, there is the clear sense that you are at the heart of a community where religion (churches), education (schoolhouses), government (town hall), domestic life (private homes) and the honor due the dead (cemeteries) all naturally fit together. People who live in cities or suburbs where all services are decentralized will find such Berkshire villages intriguing as well as architecturally beautiful. New Marlborough bears out all of this with its archetypical village green, surrounded in part by the Colonial-style ***Old Inn on the Green*** (1760), a fine Federal-style house (1824), and a Greek Revival-style ***Congregational Church*** (1839).

Then there are Berkshire farms. Almost any minor country road will lead you past splendid examples of gambrel-roofed barns or those New England rambling farmhouses that have spawned one extension after another. Often the oldest of these houses, or at least one of the farm's outbuildings, will be in the familiar saltbox (lean-to) shape. Some good rides for farm viewing include Routes 57 (New Marlborough), 41 (south from South Egremont or north from West Stockbridge), and 7 (north from Lanesborough). Dramatic Tudor-style barns from the Gilded Age are still in use at ***High Lawn Farm*** (on Lenox Rd., between Lee and Rte. 7, south of Lenox). But the most famous barn in Berkshire is the round stone barn at ***Hancock Shaker Village***, described under "Museums" in this chapter.

<u>South County</u> towns have many impressive buildings, among them several interesting industrial sites. A standout is the ***Rising Paper Mill*** (c. 1875; Rte. 183 in Housatonic, north of Great Barrington), with its handsome mansard slate roof. A similar mansard slate roof style is pushed to artful extremes on campus buildings at ***Simon's Rock College of Bard*** (Alford Rd., Great Barrington), resulting in structures that vaguely resemble Japanese pagodas. The mansard style also defines the shape of ***Monument Mountain Regional High School*** (Rte. 7, north of Great Barrington) — surely one of the most beautifully situated schools anywhere. But there is competition for that prize elsewhere in the county. ***The Berkshire School*** (Rte. 41, Sheffield) and ***Mount Greylock Regional High School*** (Rte. 7, south of Williamstown) both make effective uses of their mountain settings.

On its ***Congregational Church***, the village of Lee has the tallest wooden spire in the Berkshires. In South Lee (Rte. 102) is ***Merrell Tavern***, a Federal-period building still functioning as an inn, exquisitely maintained by the Society for the Preservation of New England Antiquities.

Sheffield, architecturally lovely and filled with antique shops, appropriately prides itself on having preserved the ***oldest (1837) covered bridge*** in Massachusetts (reached eastward off Rte. 7). Otis, a Berkshire hilltown, is graced with ***St. Paul's Church*** (1829), a fine example of the Gothic Revival style.

Stockbridge, of course, will dazzle even the most jaded architecture buff. Architect Stanford White's turn-of-the-century work appears in impressive diversity here: a casino (now the ***Berkshire Theatre Festival***, at Rte. 102 and Yale Hill Rd.); a mansion (***Naumkeag***, on Prospect Hill Rd.); a railroad station (now ***Ghinga***, a restaurant, on Rte. 7 south of the village); and a church (St. Paul's Episcopal, center of town). We describe the ***Mission House***, a Colonial "Historic Home," later in this chapter. Two other Stockbridge churches well worth a look are the red brick ***Congregational Church*** (Main St., next to Town Hall), and the Chapel at the ***Marian Fathers Seminary*** (on Eden Hill, off Prospect Hill Rd.). Whereas the interior of the Congregational Church has a powerful beauty in its simplicity, the Marian Fathers Chapel is beautiful for its finely crafted stone, woodwork, painting and fabrics — much of it done by transplanted European artisans.

Two outlying sites in Stockbridge are worth a drive. The district originally called Curtisville, now known as Interlaken (Rte. 183, north of Rte. 102), boasts several strikingly pretty 18th- and 19th-century homes and a remarkable former tavern-inn, as well as ***Citizens Hall*** with its Victorian Second Empire-style exterior details. The other building of note in rural Stockbridge is at ***Tanglewood's Lions' Gate*** (Hawthorne St., off Rte. 183) — where the replica of Nathaniel Hawthorne's ***"Little Red House,"*** overlooks Stockbridge Bowl and the distant mountains.

Finally, in South County, a ride out on the Tyringham Rd. (off Rte. 102, south of Lee) and then upland on Jerusalem Rd. will lead to ***"Jerusalem,"*** the remnants of a Shaker settlement dating from 1792. Five buildings remain but none is open as a museum (as is Hancock Shaker Village, described under "Museums"). Jerusalem Rd. begins in tiny Tyringham village. Along the Tyringham Valley Rd. is the ***Witch House***, a thatched-roof English cottage built by sculptor Henry Kitson in the late 1800s and known presently as Tyringham Art Gallery; see "Art Galleries," the next section in this chapter.

Central County abounds with notable architecture. In Dalton, a ride along Main St. (Rte. 9) provides views of the ***Crane Paper Mills*** (dating back to 1797) and several Crane family estates. In addition to other fine papers, Crane manufactures U.S. paper currency in these venerable mills. In 1816, Zenas Crane, company founder, built a dignified Federal-style house which still stands. There are also three 19th-century Richardsonian Romanesque churches on Main St. in Dalton proper.

In the hilltown of Hinsdale on Rte. 8 are some architectural surprises, vestiges of more prosperous, populous times when various mills were alive and well in the Berkshire highlands. The oldest (1798) Federal-style church in Berkshire is here. A Greek Revival town hall was built in 1848. The public library is in the high Gothic style, designed in 1868 by architect Leopold Eidlitz, who did St. George's Church in New York City and the New York State Capitol in Albany.

The only *stone* Early Gothic Revival church in the county is ***St. Luke's Chapel***, in Lanesborough (on Rte. 7). Like many other buildings cited in this book, St. Luke's is on the National Register of Historic Places.

Equal to any other village in Berkshire as an impressive architectural set piece is stately Lenox. This town has recently seen a commercial revival on its back streets that has spruced up the neighborhood, though some folks fear that such commercialization threatens its old New England charm. Recommended viewing in the historic center of the village includes the ***Lenox Academy*** (Federal style, 1803), the irresistibly photogenic ***Church on the Hill*** (1805), and the ***Lenox Library*** (1815; see "Libraries" in this chapter). All three buildings are on Main St. (Rte. 7A). ***The Curtis Hotel,*** dominating the center of town, is now a wonderfully restored and converted apartment complex. From the Gilded Age to recent times, the Curtis was one of Berkshire's classiest addresses for travelers. Not far from Lenox village, on Rte. 20 heading toward Lee, is the former ***Cranwell School*** with its architecturally daring chapel. Often used for musical events, ***Cranwell Chapel*** produces an inspiring uplift for the eyes and mind, rising from its sunken altar to its broad "floating" ceiling. Tall, narrow stained-glass windows encircle the sanctuary, enhancing the sense of spaciousness.

Pittsfield's architectural record is a distinguished though problematic one. Preservation and restoration nowadays receive good attention as you'll see on a walk around Park Square. There are clean lines in contemporary structures such as the ***Berkshire Athenaeum*** and ***Berkshire Common*** (shopping mall/offices/hotel). These new buildings integrate quite well, we think, with the ornate elegance of the old Venetian Gothic Athenaeum, with the two churches, with the bank buildings and with the courthouse—all dating from the 19th century. Park Square is an urban space which would make any city proud.

There have been unfortunate losses in Pittsfield, too. The Bulfinch church on Park Square, designed in 1794 by America's most famous Colonial architect, had been moved and then was demolished in 1939. Similarly, as train travel dwindled in the 20th century, the apparent need for a grand rail station did, too. Union Station (1914) with its vaulted ceiling and sense of drama was demolished in 1961. Today's Amtrak shelter on Depot St. is a far cry from the bygone comfort and dignity of Union Station.

Not even the Art Deco style escaped Berkshire builders' attention. ***The Berkshire Eagle newspaper building*** (1904; on Eagle St., off North St.) is a fine example of Art Deco, and it is set on a triangle, making it look like a miniature of Manhattan's Flatiron Building. Another important business structure in Pittsfield is the ***General Electric complex*** on the east side of town. Most of the plant's buildings are unremarkable to look at (though vitally important to the local economy). One, however, is worth a detour. The Plastics Division's new world headquarters is all shine and glitter. Address? "Plastics Ave.," of course (between Merrill Road and Dalton Ave.)

North County provides stark contrasts in architecture and much variety in the stories buildings tell about social history. The cities of Adams and North Adams are industrial and have seen better times. Urban renewal is proceeding, with a few of the abandoned textile mills converted to other uses, the idle ***Sprague Electric plant*** possibly being converted to the Mass MoCA museum. Still, in otherwise rather grim cityscapes, there are sights worth a visit. In North Adams, the ***Western Heritage Gateway State Park*** celebrates a 19th-century architectural and engineering wonder, the ***Hoosac Tunnel.*** See "Museums" in this chapter. The spires of North Adams' many churches are a pretty sight when descending into the city from the west on Rte 2. In Adams, history lovers will want a look at the ***Susan B. Anthony*** birthplace (1814; a private home near the corner of East Rd. and East St.); and the ***Quaker Meeting House*** (1782; near the end of Friends St.), another National Register of Historic Places building.

Williamstown, however, wins most of the architectural prizes in North County. Dozens of magnificent homes, an extraordinarily beautiful college, many quaint shops, and two masterfully designed art museums (the Clark Art Institute and the Williams College Museum of Art, both described under "Museums") — all this awaits you in Williamstown. ***West Hall*** (1790), at Williams College, is dignified and symbolizes the college's long history of loving attention to fine and sometimes dramatic buildings. A tour of the campus is well worth the time (597-3131 for information). ***The Williamstown Memorial Library*** (1815), which also houses the local history museum, is graced with elegant Palladian windows.

In Berkshire, a proud history still stands.

CINEMA

THE MAHAIWE

On September 26, 1905, a thousand people jammed the Mahaiwe Theater for its grand opening. In the ornate elegance of the new theater, they watched the Hopper DeWolf Company perform the comic opera *Happyland*. Eighty-five years later, the ornate elegance survives in proud if threadbare fashion, and the air of *Happyland* lives on. Once billed as the "most handsome theater in western New England," the Mahaiwe was first a stage for plays and vaudeville, with only an occasional silent film. When the talkies arrived, the Mahaiwe went to the movies. Now, under manager Al Schwartz's nurturing, the theater's getting spruced up again, showing a range of films from absolute fluff

Impresario Al Schwartz presides over the venerable Mahaiwe.

to Academy Award winners. In between, the Mahaiwe hosts special live concerts, from the exuberant dancers of Olga Dunn's company, to the symphonic triumphs of L'Orchestra. There are also occasional children's weekend movie matinees and the odd musical benefit, such as the one for Fairview Hospital, featuring vaudevillian June Havoc. This timeless, classic place has recently been renovated by Hoyts Cinema, an Australian conglomerate, which once considered demolishing it. After great hue and cry by the townsfolk, Hoyts realized that the only-slightly-profitable Mahaiwe is in fact a jewel in its crown. That's certainly the way we see it. ***The Mahaiwe***: 528-0100; 14 Castle St., Great Barrington, MA 01230.

CLARK FILM SERIES

The Clark Art Institute shows films on artists and on art history as well as movies of a more general interest. Call to get on their mailing list. Something for almost everyone here. ***The Clark Film Series***: 458-8109 or 458-9545; South St., Williamstown, MA 01267.

IMAGES CINEMA

North County's most dynamic movie house is back in business. Threatened by skyrocketing rents, Images pulled itself together in the summer of '89, principally with the help of Superman. Able to leap tall buildings in a single bound, this man of steel, also known as Williamstown resident, movie star Christopher Reeve, organized a fund-raising program that lifted the theater into a heavenly orbit. By showing top films and inviting their superstar talent (such as Paul Newman and Joanne Woodward) to come meet the people, Reeve helped save the day. So, not only does Images live, it thrives, opening in refurbished modernity for a fine future of feature films. Eclectic, exciting — the best from camp to classic. Mailing list available. ***Images Cinema***: 458-5612; 55 Spring St., Williamstown, MA 01267.

OTHER CINEMA

South County

Simon's Rock College of Bard (528-0771; Alford Rd., Great Barrington). Weekly classics and fun films, periodically open to the public. Phone on Friday afternoons for information.

Central County

Berkshire Cinema 10 (499-2558; Berkshire Mall, Rt. 8 and Old State Road, Lanesborough). Dolby stereo, Kintek stereo, action, adventure, drama, comedy, popcorn, and 10 screens.

Little Cinema (at Berkshire Museum, 443-7171; 39 South St., Pittsfield). Fine American and foreign films, nightly from late June through early September.

Pittsfield Cinema Center (443-9639; Rte. 20, W. Housatonic St., Pittsfield). Unlimited free parking and a choice of eleven, that's 11, different commercial flicks nightly. A teenage hangout, but often showing first-run films as early as New York or Boston.

North County

Coury's Drive-In (663-6222; 838 Curran Hwy., North Adams). In warmer seasons only.

Hoosac Drive-In Theatre (743-0670; 199 Howland Ave., Adams). In warmer seasons only. "NOW THRU SUN! 3 HORROR HITS! LIMIT 5 PER CAR!" Our favorite that night was *Don't Look in the Basement*. Get the picture?

Mohawk Theatre (663-5295; 11 Main St., North Adams).

North Adams Cinemas (663-5295; Rte. 8, Curran Highway). North County's multiplex, with six screens. All matinee and senior citizen seats, $2.50.

Williams College Museum of Art (597-2429; Williamstown). Often shows films in its auditorium, and these are free and open to the public.

Williams College (597-2277; Williamstown). Presents free American films in Bronfman Auditorium; and foreign films in Weston Language Center Lounge.

DANCE

JACOB'S PILLOW DANCE FESTIVAL
243-0745.
Box 287, Lee, MA 01238
Off Rte. 20, in Becket, 8 mi. E. of Lee.
Season: Summer only: Tues.-Sat.; occasional Sun. concerts.
Tickets: $15 to $22.50.
Gift shop.

America's first and oldest summer dance festival, Jacob's Pillow keeps step with the times, presenting the best in classical, modern, post-modern, jazz and ethnic dance. As a performance center, its schedule of offerings reads like a Who's Who of contemporary dance, featuring over the years: Merce Cunningham, Dame Margot Fonteyn, Peter Martins, Alicia Markova, Twyla Tharp, Alexander Godunov, Martha Graham, Paul Taylor, Alvin Ailey, and the Pilobolus troupe, among many others.

High on a hillside in Becket, at the farm that famed dancer Ted Shawn bought as a retreat, the creative heights of dance continue to be reached. Sit anywhere in the 600 seat barn-style theatre and the viewing is good, with open-beamed rusticity above and comfortable seats below. Sit anywhere and you will see athlete-artists who make you laugh or gasp, who move you as they move themselves. The inexpressible lightness of being seems afoot at the Pillow, and to watch performances there is to look in on creatures jousting with gravity in the most elegant and inventive ways, where stories are told wordlessly through bodies animated by music.

After successfully touring with his wife, Ruth St. Denis, and the "Denishawn" troupe in the 1920s, Ted Shawn worked to establish dance as a legitimate profession for men. Bolstered by powerful feelings of reverence for movement, Shawn sought to incorporate the strength of Greek soldiers trained in dance with the pagan religiosity of African and American Indian tribal dance. "I believe that dance is the oldest, noblest and most cogent of the arts," Shaw wrote in his "Credo." "I believe that true education in the art of dance is education of the

Two of the original Ted Shawn dancers, outside at Jacob's Pillow.

Courtesy of Jacob's Pillow.

whole man — his physical, mental and emotional natures are disciplined and nourished simultaneously in dance."

At his retreat in the Berkshires, Ted Shawn founded a world-class dance performance center and a school for dance. The school continues to flourish along with the festival, honoring its founder's heartfelt philosophy that the best performers in the world make the most inspirational dance instructors. In addition to performing here, many of the Pillow's visiting dance luminaries stay on to teach master classes in the compound's rustic studios.

Drive up to the Pillow early if you can and stroll among those studios where works are in progress, dancers are in development. Look through a window and watch bodies sway and strut, watch choreography created before your very eyes. As you watch, dancers will pass, dancing from studio to studio. Walk down to the Pillow's natural outdoor theater, "Inside/Out," and watch *avant-garde* and experimental pieces in rehearsal and in performance (free for the looking). And after savoring that dance *hors d'oeuvre,* you might want to sup at the Pillow. Happily, here too there are several lovely options. You can dine at the Pillow Cafe, feasting under a brightly colored tent, or you can take your dinner over to the picnic area and mingle with some of the dancers you will see performing in the Ted Shawn Theatre a while later.

Recent performances at the Pillow have included the witty Mark Morris, the elegant Miami City Ballet, the jazzy Hubbard Street Dance Company and the athletic Laura Dean Dancers, among others. But our favorite was the Native American Dance and Music Festival, featuring the dance, costume and music of the Crow, Cree, Creek, and Hawaiian Americans. With the completion of the Pillow's new Studio/Theatre, its dance season is now dramatically expanded.

Seating 150, the Studio/Theatre adds a separate 10-week schedule of international troupes, complementing the exciting dance scheduled for the Ted Shawn Theatre.

"Only when great content and great power of communication are combined do we have the great art of the dance — something that nourishes the soul as well as delights the eye," Ted Shawn wrote. "Great dance communicates ecstasy — by empathy the spectator is taken out of himself (ex-tase) and shares the ecstatic experience of the dancer, and he leaves the theatre a changed person with vision expanded...."

Pilobolus, one of the many national troupes appearing at Jacob's Pillow.

Clemens Kalischer, courtesy Jacob's Pillow.

BERKSHIRE BALLET
442-1307 & 445-5382.
210 Wendell Ave., Pittsfield, MA 01201 (Mail).
Concerts at various theaters.
Season: Intermittently year-round.
Tickets: $15.50 to $17; matinees, $13 to $15. Discounts for seniors, children & groups.
Gift shop: Boutique during performances.

The New York Times dance critic Jennifer Dunning put it positively in her recent review: "Berkshire Ballet can be counted on for impressively clear classical technique and fresh performing." Said the influential *Dance Magazine*: "Berkshire Ballet displays solid training, a distinctly soft, lyrical style and a wide choreographic range. In short, it is a company with integrity and taste."

Performing frequently at Berkshire Community College's Koussevitzky Theatre, Berkshire Ballet also tours the Northeast. Lavish productions of *Cinderella* and *Giselle* highlighted recent seasons, but our favorite was a performance of two world premieres: *Waltz in Time*, by Daryl Gray; and a stunning *Arrow of Time*, by Laura Dean. Dean's choreography threw the dancers into a perpetual whirlwind, transforming them to skittering creatures crisscrossing with arms akimbo. Fall and winter concerts followed, with the traditional *Nutcracker* being staged at BCC around Christmas time.

Ballet in the Berkshires? Absolutely!

OLGA DUNN DANCE CO., INC.
528-9674.
7 Alford Rd., Gt. Barrington, MA

Since its founding in 1977, the Olga Dunn Company has enjoyed such success that it spawned two offspring: the Young Company, and the Olga Dunn Dance Ensemble. Performing a free mix of

01230 (Mail).
317 Main St., 3rd Fl., Gt. Barrington, MA 01230.
Season: Year-round.
Tickets: $5 to $15.

exuberant, witty jazz and ballet, frequently with live musicians, the company has also toured area schools, exposing children to the creativity of dance and the excitement of movement. Their annual performances at the Mahaiwe, and at Great Barrington's Summerfest are some of the most popular highlights of the dance year. As Marge Champion, famed dancer and local Berkshire resident, put it: "The Olga Dunn Dance Company has become the radiating center of our experience in appreciating and participating in the art of dance."

OTHER DANCE

With the aura of Jacob's Pillow bringing the world's best dancers to the Berkshires, it's not surprising that little dance troupes would spring up here and there throughout the county.

In ***South County***, Great Barrington leads the dance. Many of the most innovative performances take place at the ***Simon's Rock "ARC,"*** the school's barn- theater on Alford Rd. For the past few winters, Simon's Rock (528-0771) has run a Winter Dance Festival, including formal and informal performances, dance workshops and master classes. Classes are given in the new skylit dance studio, and altogether, the event brings a huge jolt of dance energy to wintery Berkshire. Among the many dance groups that thrive in this fertile atmosphere is the ***Berkshire New Dance Collective,*** whose principal choreographer, Dawn Lane, has provided some arresting performances for South County dance buffs. ***The Barrington Ballet*** (528-4963) gives classes and occasional performances, as does the Mill River-based ***Anglo-American Ballet*** (229-8776). Eurythmy performances are sometimes given by the ***Rudolf Steiner School*** (528-4015) on W. Plain Rd. There is also a flourishing country and contra dance network in the Berkshires. Check the newspapers and bulletin boards for listings. Among the best of the callers is Penelope Naumann, of Housatonic.

In ***Central County,*** keep an eye on the special events schedule at ***Berkshire Public Theatre*** for dance happenings; the summertime festivals bring various troupes to Pittsfield, too.

In ***North County,*** the ***Williams College Dance Department*** sponsors various programs which keep North County hopping. The choreographer Merce Cunningham, accompanied by composer-musician John Cage, has also appeared at Williams College in one of those typical midwinter Berkshire arts bonanzas.

GALLERIES

Since the arrival in Berkshire of nationally recognized turn-of-the-century sculptors Daniel Chester French (who sculpted the Lincoln Memorial) and Sir Henry Hudson Kitson (who did *The Minute Man* at Lexington), the county has been home to an increasing number of talented visual artists. Perhaps best known of them all is famed illustrator and painter Norman Rockwell who came to live in Stockbridge in the 1950s. He found here the quintessence of New England. "Every artist has his own peculiar view of life," Rockwell later wrote in his autobiography. "The view of life I communicate in my pictures excludes the sordid and the ugly. I paint life as I would like it to be." (See "Museums" in this chapter for more about Rockwell.)

Life in the Berkshires already is as many of us would like it to be, and much of the art on display in local galleries reflects the uplifting reality of the landscape. Many artists focus on the undulating Berkshire hills and their ever-changing light. Of course, local galleries also show other themes and styles as well, from traditional still-life sketches to intriguing abstract paintings. Some galleries show Berkshire artists exclusively; others bring in works from artists the world over. Galleries in the Berkshires are like delicate flowers and bloom best in warm weather. Unless you're rambling, it's best to call ahead.

South County

SOUTH EGREMONT

Store Hill Gallery (528-1224; Rte. 23, between Kenver Ltd. and the Gaslight). The finest selection of oil, watercolor and acrylic paintings by Berkshire artists, including Elaine Anthony, Joe Barber, Audrey Blafield, John Hansegger, Philip Lekki, Stan Phillips, and painter/gallery director, Janet Rickus.

GREAT BARRINGTON

Galleria Arriba (528-4277; 40 Railroad St.). Contemporary Latin American art.

Lucien Aigner Studios (528-3610; 15 Dresser Ave.). Black and white photographs of Europe by the celebrated master photojournalist, Lucien Aigner.

Mill River Studio (528-9433; 620 S. Main St.). Posters and custom framing.

Shelly's Art Supplies and Framing (528-1721; 940 S. Main St.). Shelly's has moved, to the strip on Rt. 7, several miles south of town. Now our favorite framer and friends have their own building, an art barn if there ever was one. Etchings and oil paintings by Berkshire artist Shelly Fink, as well as hand-tinted 19th-century prints.

HOUSATONIC

Spazi Fine Art (274-3805; Rte. 183). This huge loft has been the recent scene of many group shows and artsy happenings, promising to become the center stage for the Berkshire art world.

SOUTH LEE

House of Earth Studio (243-1575; Rte. 102). Contemporary paintings in a rammed-earth studio.

MILL RIVER

The Gallery at Mill River (229-2018; Main St.). Paintings, sculpture, jewelry, crafts and prints.

MONTEREY

Hayloft Art Gallery (528-1806; Rte. 23). Berkshire watercolors, including popular townscapes, by local artist Leonard Webber.

SHEFFIELD

Westenhook Gallery (229-8101; Rte. 7). Mixed media. A recent highlight was a show of wonderful miniature paintings, drawings and etchings, none of which was bigger than 3 x 5 inches.

STOCKBRIDGE

7 Arts Gallery (298-5101; Main St.). Indonesian arts and crafts of the most playful, colorful variety imaginable.

Dolphin Studio (298-3735, W. Main St.). Creations by the ffrench family, including ceramics, collages, jewelry and Capreatures — furry, wooly capricious creatures by Crispina ffrench.

Holsten Galleries of Stockbridge (298-3044; Elm St., summer only). Outstanding contemporary objects of art: glass, ceramics, jewelry, paintings and wallhangings. One of the world's leading showrooms for sleek, sculptural glass.

Image Gallery (298-5500; Main St.). Modern arts (such as the intense and buoyant paintings of Stockbridge teacher, Leo Garel) and photography (usually by gallery-owner and master photographer, Clemens Kalisher).

Reuss Audubon Galleries (298-4074; Pine and Shamrock Sts.). This 19th-century house features a continuing, rotating exhibit of the "double elephant folio" bird prints from Audubon's Birds of America.

Ronrich Gallery (298-3556; Rte. 183, 2 mi. south of Tanglewood). Paintings and prints by American artists.

TYRINGHAM

Tyringham Art Galleries (243-3260; the Gingerbread House, Tyringham Rd.). Originally called "The Witch House", the studio of Sir Henry Hudson Kitson, this structure has a unique rolling thatched roof inspired by the hills; inside, contemporary paintings, sculpture and graphics. The gallery was up for sale as we went to press, so keep your eye on this one.

WEST STOCKBRIDGE

G/M Galleries (232-8519; Main St.). Exciting jewelry and unique art objects, as well as paintings and drawings.

Riversbend Gallery (274-6618; Rte. 41). 19th-century American paintings.

Central County

BECKET

Becket Arts Center of the Hilltowns (623-5339; Rte. 8). Local shows and programs.

The Gallery Up Yonder (623-8329; Yokum Pond Road). Mixed media.

Tully Filmus (623-5270; Rte. 8). Paintings, drawings and graphics by the accomplished Filmus family: Tully, Michael and Stephen.

HINSDALE

Stritch (655-8804; Shady Villa, Hinsdale). Indoor and outdoor sculpture, and paintings, by Berkshire artist John Stritch.

LENOX

Artuoso Gallery (637-0668; 22 Church St.). Contemporary Judaic art.

Sculptor John Stritch, at his Hinsdale studio.

Warren Fowler.

Brushwood Studio (637-2836; Brushwood Farm, Rtes. 7 & 20). Paintings, furniture and carved wooden horses make up one of the most intriguing collections in the county, gathered by artist-owner, Dudley Levenson.

Clark Whitney Gallery (637-2126; 25 Church St.). Contemporary art.

Ella Lerner Gallery (637-3315; 17 Franklin St.). 19th- and 20th-century paintings, drawings, graphics and sculpture in one of the area's oldest galleries.

Hado Studio Gallery (637-1088; 70 Church St.; summer only). Contemporary paintings and sculpture.

The Hand of Man (637-0632; at the Curtis Shops, Walker St.) A wide range of appealing crafts, photographs and paintings.

Hoadley Gallery (637-2814; 17 Church St.). Contemporary art crafts, with especially wonderful ceramics.

Towne Gallery (637-0053; 28 Walker St., Lenox). Regional paintings, graphics, sculptures and crafts; framing.

Ute Stebich Gallery (637-3566; 104 Main St.). Outstanding international collection of extraordinarily beautiful art, from primitive African, to sleek contemporary glass by Tom Patti. A must on any Lenox gallery hop.

PITTSFIELD

Berkshire Artisans (443-4322; 28 Renne Ave.; 1 block eastward off lower North St.). Exhibitions and workshops at the city's nonprofit municipal arts center.

North County

ADAMS

The Alley (743-7707; 25 Park St.). Prints and sculpture.

NORTH ADAMS

Ars Nova (663-3651; Building #1, above the General Store, Heritage Park). Exhibits of area artists.

Up Country Artisans (663-5802; Heritage Park). A continuous, ever-changing show of some of the Berkshire's best artists and artisans.

WILLIAMSTOWN

Beaverpond Gallery (738-5895; Rte. 43). Berkshire watercolors, custom framing, art classes.

Elysian Fields (458-4707; Eph's Alley, off Spring St.). Berkshire landscapes, artful jewelry and weavings.

HISTORIC HOMES

ARROWHEAD
442-1793.

© U.S. Postal Service.

In 1850, seeking to escape what he later called "the Babylonish brick-kiln of New York," Herman Melville gave in to his yearning "to feel the grass" and moved with his family to the Berkshires. He had visited the area as a boy when he came to stay with his uncle on a farm that is now the Pittsfield Country Club. By the time he moved to the Berkshires, Melville had already published two tales of his South Sea adventures, *Typee* and *Omoo*, and he had earned a reputation as a man "who had lived among cannibals."

But Melville longed to be known as a great writer, an artist who plumbs the depths of the human soul. And fresh from a new "close acquaintance" with the "divine" writings of Shakespeare, he took off on the grand literary whale hunt that was to be *Moby Dick*. "...at nights when I wake up and hear the wind shrieking, I almost fancy there is too much sail on the house, and I had better go on the roof and rig in the

780 Holmes Rd.,
Pittsfield, MA 01201.
Off Rte. 7, (about 1.5 mi.) near Pittsfield- Lenox line.
Season: Summer & Fall: Mon.-Sat. 10-4:40; Sun. 11-3:30; Winter: by appointment.
Fee: $3.50; senior citizens $3; students $2.
Gift shop.

chimney," he wrote to a friend from Arrowhead that first year. And though the house and hills were landlocked, they were expansive enough to allow Melville's imagination to flourish. "I have a sort of sea feeling here in the country, now that the ground is all covered with snow," he mused in a letter. "I look out of my window in the morning when I rise as I would out of a porthole of a ship in the Atlantic."

When he went to work in his upstairs study, Melville wrote looking northward at the Mt. Greylock range with its rolling form of a giant whale. Melville's study at Arrowhead is undoubtedly the most interesting room in the house. Here, you too can gaze pensively out toward formidable Greylock. Be sure to look around the room, as well. The implements of the writer's trade and duplicates of many important books in his library are right there. Melville used to lock himself in, ordering the women of the house to leave meals on a tray outside the door. Writing his big book was evidently a long, lonely voyage in itself.

Arrowhead is now the home of the Berkshire County Historical Society, which offers excellent guided tours. The other thoroughly "Melville" room is the kitchen, which is dominated by a grand stone hearth. The chimney above was immortalized in the charming Melville story "Me and My Chimney."

Elsewhere inside Arrowhead you'll see a full collection of 19th-century furnishings, many quite handsome but none really remarkable. The woodwork in the stairway is worth a long look. The drawing room and dining room on the main floor have a tidy polish and a look of prosperity, qualities hard to associate with the financially struggling Herman Melville.

Nonetheless, the Historical Society gets our applause for bringing Arrowhead to the public. The piazza is impressive as are the grounds; in fact, Arrowhead outdoors is a lovely picnic spot. The barn behind the house is the site of impressively varied cultural programs such as literary readings and historical talks. A film about Berkshire history is shown regularly. There is also a nature walk and an extensive herb garden on the grounds.

If you're hungry for more of the literary Melville than Arrowhead delivers, you must visit the Melville Room at the Berkshire Athenaeum on Wendell Ave., also in Pittsfield. See p.104 for more information.

THE MOUNT
Edith Wharton Restoration, Inc.
637-1899.
Box 974, Lenox, MA 01240.
On Plunkett St., Lenox, near southern jct.of.Rtes. 7 & 7A.
Season: Summer: Tues.-Sun. 10-5; Fall: Thurs.-

In February, 1901, the writer and heiress Edith Wharton arrived at the Curtis Hotel in Lenox for a week in the country. She had summered in the area for the preceding two years, and now, having found the "watering place trivialities of Newport" all but intolerable, sought a new site on which to realize the design principles incorporated in her book, *The Decoration of Houses*. By the time she returned to her Park Avenue home in New York, she had begun negotia-

Sun. 10-5.
Fee: $3.50, students $2; senior citizens $3.
Book/Gift shop.

© U.S. Postal Service.

tions on the 113-acre Laurel Lake Farm. In June, 1902, she bought the farm for $40,600. Her dapper but hapless husband, Teddy, contributed nothing.

"On a slope overlooking the dark waters and densely wooded shores of Laurel Lake," she later wrote, "we built a spacious and dignified house to which we gave the name of my great-grandfather's place, The Mount." The Georgian Revival house was modeled on Christopher Wren's Belton House in Lincolnshire, England, and at first, she retained an architect, her old associate, Ogden Codman. When his design fees grew exorbitant, she called upon Francis V.L. Hoppin to complete the job.

Edith supervised creation of the gardens, orchards, and buildings, while finishing her novel, *Disintegration.* The Mount was elegant throughout, boasting marble floors and fireplaces, and requiring 12 resident servants. Besides the 14 horses in their stables, the Whartons owned one of the earliest motorcars, a convenience that thrilled the visiting Henry James. In the fall of 1904, James and Wharton motored through Berkshire's autumnal splendor every day, enjoying social afternoons and evenings with visiting sophisticates. Wharton's writing successes, such as *The House of Mirth,* were celebrated, but her marriage was disintegrating, and by 1911, she had signed the papers that allowed her husband to sell the Mount. It was the end of her life in the Berkshires and in America.

"The Mount was to give me country cares and joys, long happy rides and drives through the wooded lanes of that loveliest region, the companionship of a few dear friends, and the freedom from trivial obligations which was necessary if I was to go on with my writing. The Mount was my first real home...and its blessed influence still lives in me."

Happily, its blessed influence lives on for all of us, as its physical and spiritual restoration continue. We spoke with Shakespeare & Co.'s artistic director, Tina Packer, perhaps the new mistress of the Mount. In 1978, Packer, with an ambitious group of actors and administrators, leased the abandoned Mount and began converting it to a theater (outdoors) and a historic home. By 1980, the theater, performing Shakespeare and plays based on Wharton's years at the Mount, had won national critical acclaim. Then the National Trust for Historic Preservation bought the Mount to save it from commercial exploitation. Shakespeare & Co. has stayed on; the house is run by Edith Wharton Restoration, Inc. (EWR).

We were privileged to speak to Tina Packer in Wharton's bedroom, where the author did most of her writing. "I do think there's some kind of link or empathetic reaction between myself, this house, and the sensibilities of Edith Wharton," Packer said. "To use the house as a kind of artistic energy center, I think would please her very much. And of course she built it for that; she built it in order to have her writing friends here and then be able to talk and exchange ideas and generally carry on."

In the summer, besides house and garden tours of the Mount, EWR and Shakespeare & Co. continue to offer plays centering on Wharton's life and writings. Recent presentations were: *Two By Wharton,* and *A Touch Of Satire,* both directed by Dennis Krausnick. *A Touch Of Satire* was a presentation of two one-act plays based on Wharton short stories, "The Temperate Zone," and "Expiation." These were both witty fun, well produced. *Two by Wharton,* featured a dramatization of Wharton's letters and thoughts, often in counterpoint to those of her friends Percy Lubbock and Henry James. The highlight of these plays was *Roman Fever,* in which the power and art of world-class actresses Tina Packer and Kristin Linklater was brought face to face. Bravo for Wharton, Linklater, Packer, EWR and Shakespeare & Co!

In between the one-act plays, matters get more convivial in the dining room, where, in palatial elegance, you're invited to share tea or coffee. Edith Wharton's powerfully gracious influence is everywhere.

NAUMKEAG
298-3239.
Box 792, Stockbridge, MA 01262.
Prospect Hill Rd., Stockbridge.
Season: Memorial Day-Labor Day: House & Garden Hours 10-4:15; Closed Mon. Labor Day-Columbus Day: House closed during the week, Gardens closed Mon.
Fee: House & Garden $5, House only $4, Gardens only $3, children 6-16 $1.
Gift Shop.

In the late 19th century during the Gilded Age, men and women of power played out their fantasies here, dotting the hillsides with dreamhouses. Some were outlandish (such as Shadowbrook, one of the largest houses ever built in America, eventually destroyed by fire); some were magnificent (such as Bellefontaine, an exact reproduction of the French Petit Trianon, now a part of Canyon Ranch spa). In between was the very livable mansion of the lawyer Joseph Choate, the summer "cottage" the Choate family came to call "Naumkeag" (a native Indian name for "place of rest").

The Choate family began visiting Berkshire in the summer of 1874, 10 years before they started building Naumkeag. As famous a lawyer as Joseph Choate was, here he was in the company of three even more renowned barristers: Supreme Court Justices (all of them Stockbridge residents), Field, Brewer and Brown. In Stockbridge then, Joseph Choate found both a retreat from New York City life and an enclave of great legal minds. Many times, Joseph Choate brought cases before his Justice neighbors in the Supreme Court, and very often, he won.

Choate's was an illustrious career. He defended such notable clients as Stanford University, Bell Telephone, and Pullman Car; he duelled with the government on behalf of the New York Indians, and fought against the graduated income tax, successfully postponing it for two decades.

In 1884, Choate finally persuaded David Dudley Field (his opponent in the Boss Tweed affair) to sell him the lower forty on the west side of Prospect Hill in Stockbridge. "What a luxury it will be to escape from the city," he wrote, "and to roll on the grass, ride over hills, and float in Stockbridge Bowl." By the autumn of 1886, Choate and his family were able to do all these things — their 26-room, shingled, gabled and dormered Norman-style "cottage" was complete. With architectural design by Stanford White and imaginative gardens by the landscaping pioneer, Nathaniel Barret, their summer home became yet another center of Choate's life. Below the house, they had their Fountain Steps, framed by birches; to the south, the Afternoon Garden, an outdoor room; further southward, the Chinese Pagoda and Linden Walk; uphill, the brick-walled Chinese Garden, where mosses and stone Buddhas gather with carved lions and dogs, all shaded by ginkgos; to the north, the topiary hedgework of the Evergreen Garden, and the fragrance and color of the Rose Garden. Naumkeag afforded felicitous country living in the grand manner.

In 1896, Choate's brother William and his wife founded the prestigious Choate School in Wallingford, Connecticut. The next year, President and Mrs. McKinley came to call on the Choates at Naumkeag, and not long after, the president asked Choate to succeed John Hay as ambassador to the Court of St. James. Years later, when he returned to a brass band welcome, Choate told a crowd that "There is more honest sunshine in a real October day in Stockbridge than there is in a whole winter in London."

After Choate died, the house eventually came into the hands of his daughter Mabel, who maintained it while adding somewhat to the gardens. Naumkeag, now under the auspices of the Trustees of Reservations, is still intact, including its gardens, furnishings, and an extraordinary porcelain collection, much of it from the Far East. The tours are excellent. Some years at Christmas, Naumkeag is enlivened with decorations and toys from the Choate era.

Joseph Choate was generous, but practical and witty. When the Stockbridge town fathers asked for a donation from him to build a fence around the cemetery, Choate denied them. "Nobody inside can get out," he said, "and no one on the outside wants to get in."

The Choate mansion, "Naumkeag."

Frank Packlick.

CHESTERWOOD
298-3579.
Box 827, Stockbridge, MA 01262.
Off Rte. 183, in Glendale.
Season: May-Oct. daily 10-5.
Fee: $4.50, children 18 & under, $1.
Gift shop.

Daniel Chester French was introduced to the Berkshires as a young art student at a school in the rural town of Richmond. When he was subsequently commissioned by the town of Concord to create his first public monument, the 25-year-old French sculpted *The Minute Man.* Its lifelike pose and exquisite sense of surface modeling won the artist national acclaim. He had produced his first American icon.

Years and scores of sculptures later, French sought a permanent country home to augment the New York City studio he maintained. In 1896, he and his wife, Mary, were shown the old Warner Farm and Boys School in the Glendale section of Stockbridge. After taking in the magnificent vista southwards, toward Monument Mountain, French pronounced it "the best dry view" he had ever seen and promptly arranged an advance on a current commission to buy the property. Thereafter, he and Mary spent half of each year in New York City, half in Glendale at Chesterwood. "[Glendale] is heaven," he said. "New York is — well, New York."

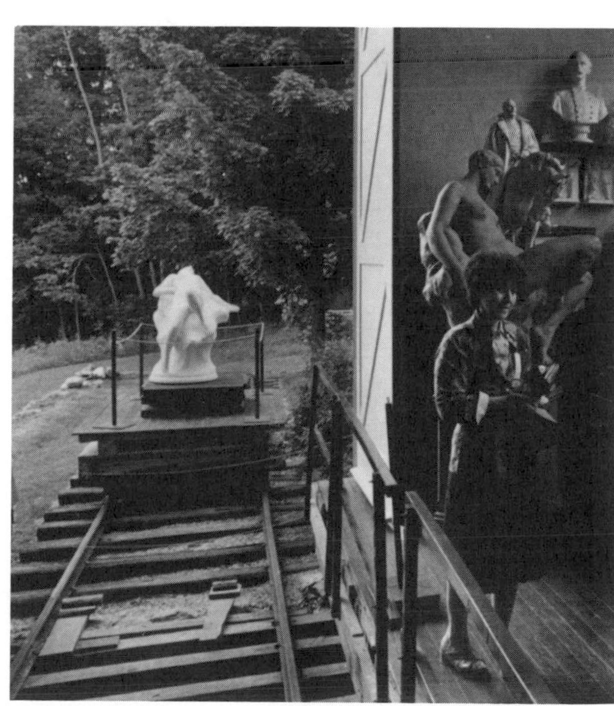

At the studio of Daniel Chester French, his erotic "Andromeda," in the light of day via the studio's railway.

Warren Fowler.

French not only sculpted great public monuments, he created a grand residence, studio and garden complex that is an enduring and eloquent tableau of his artistry. He spent his summers in an "ecstasy of delight over the loveliness" of his surroundings; it was here he created his masterpiece, the *Abraham Lincoln* which sits in the Lincoln Memorial in Washington. "What I wanted to convey," said French, "was the mental and physical strength of the great war President...." Visit Chesterwood today and you'll feel French's ability to carve that strength. In his studio, filled with memorabilia, you are invited to handle his sculpting tools. Centerpieces in the studio are his alabaster *Andromeda*, an arrestingly erotic work unknown to most Americans; and the fascinating "railway" he had laid to facilitate moving his works-in-progress out into the revealing daylight. There is still a palpable sense of the sculptor's presence.

French designed magnificent gardens, and these are maintained superlatively today after his fashion by the property's management, the National Trust for Historic Preservation. Periodically, some of the lawns around the mansion and studio are adorned with contemporary sculpture. Come for a morning or afternoon at Chesterwood (the guided tour is definitely worthwhile) and enter the rarefied milieu of a gentleman sculptor. His artistry will inspire you.

Classic Cars Come to Chesterwood

Cars as sculpture, that's the effect of an annual gathering of classics on the groomed lawns of Chesterwood. In late May or early June, the Berkshire County Car Club holds its yearly show, and for all you autoeroticists out there, this is a must. Just the curvaceous red sweep of a '60 Jag XK-150 convertible brings back a lusty innocence of teenage youth, when beauty and class were first recognized, when the art of everything began to be revealed. At the Chesterwood show, cars range from muscle cars of the '50s to stately limos of the '30s, from classic Jags to horseless carriages of the same vintage as Daniel Chester French.

THE MISSION HOUSE
298-3239.
Box 792, Stockbridge, MA 01262.
On the corner of Main & Sergeant Sts., in Stockbridge.

In 1735, an earnest minister from Yale came to the Berkshire wilderness to preach to the Mahican Indians. Establishing a settlement in the still-remote area, the sincere John Sergeant naturally drew the Indians to him, and thus began the town of Stockbridge. Sergeant learned the Indian language and preached two sermons in it every Sunday. In the springtime, he went out with the Indians to tap the sugar maples. His written account is the first in English to pass on this sugar production method. The minister frequently met with the Indians in the back of his simple cabin, spending long hours listening to their problems. Under Sergeant's leadership, the Stockbridge Mission flourished.

To please his wife, Abigail, Reverend Sergeant built what is now called Mission House, high on Prospect Hill. The tall and ornate "Connecticut doorway" that serves as the dwelling's front entry was carved in Westfield, Connecticut, and dragged by oxen 50 miles over rugged terrain to Stockbridge. It

Season: Summer: Tues.-Sun. 11-4; Closed Mon.
Fee: $3.50, children under 16, $1.

is not only a beautiful and noble doorway but also has special theological significance in that its panels represent the Ten Commandments, an open Bible and St. Andrews' Cross. This front door and the front rooms were Abigail's domain; in the back, a separate entry and long corridor allowed the Indians access to the Reverend's study.

When John Sergeant died in 1749, the Stockbridge Mission was not long for this world either, and by 1785, the Indians had been displaced from Stockbridge, driven out for the most part by land speculators like Abigail's father.

In 1927, Mission House was acquired by Mabel Choate, the art collector and philanthropist who was heir to Naumkeag (see p. 97). Choate had Mission House dismantled and moved to its present Main St. position, just a stone's throw from the site of John Sergeant's first log cabin. She then hired Boston landscape architect Fletcher Steele. Beside the restored, relocated Mission House, he planted an orderly, symmetrical 18th-century herb, flower and fruit garden that is as beautiful as it might be functional. There are today fruit trees of apple and quince; herbs such as lamb's ear, rue and southern wood; bright flowers; a grape arbor and a "salet garden" filled with garden greens.

The Trustees of Reservations maintain Mission House now. Tours of the house take you back to the 18th-century's furnishings and kitchen implements and the feeling of humble domesticity around the dominant central hearth.

COLONEL ASHLEY HOUSE
229-8600.
Box 128, Ashley Falls, MA 01222.
On Cooper Hill Rd., Ashley Falls, off Route 7A.
Season: Memorial Day-end of June; Labor Day-Columbus Day: Weekends only; rest of summer daily 1-5, exc. Mon. & Tues.
Fee: $3.50, children under 16, $1.

In his military role as colonel and as a political radical, John Ashley was destined to become as prominent a citizen as the Revolution would produce in Berkshire. But he began his Berkshire life decades earlier as a surveyor, trudging through the woods and swamps of Sheffield. With rod and chain, he and his cohorts mapped the wilderness.

Ashley loved what he saw, and by 1735 he had built a handsome home on the west bank of the Housatonic River, the oldest house still standing in Berkshire County. Framed of well-seasoned oak with chestnut rafters, it was the finest residence in Sheffield. Woodworkers from across the colony came to carve paneling and to fashion the gracefully curved staircase. Ashley's study, with its broad fireplace and sunburst cupboard, is a room whose craftsmanship inspires confidence. It was here that Ashley met with a group of his neighbors in early 1773 to draft "The Sheffield Declaration," stating to the world that all people were "equal, free and independent." In Ashley's study, they asserted their independence from Britain, some three years before Thomas Jefferson and associates drafted their declaration in Philadelphia.

Thanks to an excellent restoration and relocation (a quarter-mile from its original site), by the Trustees of Reservations, the Ashley House lives on. An herb garden flourishes outside while Colonial furnishings, a pottery collection and the original wood paneling survive inside. If you're antique hunting in the Sheffield — Ashley Falls area, Colonel Ashley House will complement your visit.

The Sheffield Declaration, 1773

Resolved that Mankind in a State of Nature are equal, free and independent of each other, and have a right to the undisturbed Enjoyment of their lives, their Liberty and Property.

Resolved that it is a well known and undoubted privilege of the British Constitution that every Subject hath not only a Right to the free and uncontrolled enjoyment and Improvement of his estate or property ....

Resolved that the late acts of the parlement of Great Britan expres porpos of Rating and regulating the colecting a Revenue in the Colonies; are unconstitutional as thereby the Just earning of our labours and Industry without Any Regard to our own consent are by mere power ravished from us .

THE WILLIAM CULLEN BRYANT HOMESTEAD
634-2244.
Off Rte. 9 on Rte. 112 South Cummington, MA 01026.
Season: Summer: Fri., Sat., Sun. & Holidays 1-5; Labor Day-Columbus Day: Sat., Sun. & Holidays 1-5.
Fee: $3.50; children 6-12, $2 under 6, free.

On a farm of 465 acres, in a small gambrel-roofed cabin of rough-hewn lumber, two miles from the frontier village of Cummington, William Cullen Bryant was born in 1794. Already a published poet, he went to Williams College but stayed only eight months, shortly thereafter taking up the law. From 1816 on, Cullen, as he was called, practiced law in Great Barrington.

Bryant was highly esteemed in Barrington, and he held several town offices, but he longed to exercise his poet's mind. To him, the locals were small-minded and tedious. Only the Stockbridge author, Catherine Sedgwick, seemed a kindred spirit. He had written about 30 well-respected poems while in Barrington, on such local themes as Monument Mountain's Indian legend, the Green River, and native waterfowl. These poems and the influence of Catherine Sedgwick's brothers helped Bryant become co-editor of *The New York Review* and *Athenaeum Magazine*, and, eventually, editor at the *New York Evening Post*, one of America's oldest and most influential newspapers.

Bryant occasionally returned to his Cummington homestead, using the house as a country retreat. He also added to the house considerably, and today it stands gracious, its 23 rooms still filled with furnishings such as Bryant's Empire maple canopied four-poster, a poet's bed, to be sure. Well managed by the Trustees of Reservations, the house is a bit overloaded with less than fascinating Bryant memorabilia. Read the poems first, or the tour's fine points will elude you.

THE MERWIN HOUSE
298-3039.
W. Main St., Stockbridge, MA 01262.
In the center of Stockbridge.
Season: June 1-Oct. 15; Tues., Thurs., Sat., Sun.,

"Tranquility" is the former home of Mrs. Vipont Merwin, and is a bit of 19th-century Berkshire refinement stopped in time. This charming brick mansion, built about 1825, is filled with period antiques (mostly Victorian); both the furnishings and collectibles reflect global travel and domestic dignity. Merwin House is maintained as a property of the Society for the Preservation of New England Antiqui-

Fee: $3, senior citizens $2.50, children over 12, $1.50.

ties. For Stockbridge strollers, evening views through the multipaned front windows give an inviting glimpse of an elegant world gone by.

SEARLES CASTLE

Mark Hopkins was a founder and treasurer of the Central Pacific Railroad, and when he died, his widow, Mary, consoled herself with the creation of a grand castle in Great Barrington. The 40-room, Stanford White-designed castle was constructed between 1882 and 1887 with locally cut blue dolomite. Upon its completion, Mary Hopkins married the stone structure's interior decorator, Edward Searles, a man 20 years her junior. Searles had spared no expense on the castle's interior, and many of the major rooms feature massive carved wood or marble fireplaces, each one unique. More than a hundred of the world's best artisans and craftsmen were brought on site to work with oak carvings, marble statues, atriums, columns and pillars.

When all the bills came in, they totalled $2.5 million, but Mary had the cash and Edward and the castle, with its Greek Revival temple, indoor pool, golf course and tennis court. First known as Barrington House, the castle has been a girl's school, an insurance company, and now serves as the home of the John Dewey Academy, a residential therapeutic high school. In 1982, Searles Castle was added to the National Register of Historic Places. Unfortunately closed to the public, partial views of the building and grounds are possible for pedestrians walking along Main Street.

Touring the Berkshire Mansions

For those who yearn to step back into Berkshire's Gilded Age, visits to Naumkeag, the Mount and Tanglewood, described in this chapter, will make an excellent start. Elsewhere in this book, under *Lodging* or *Restaurants*, other Gilded Age mansions are noted for their original beauty or their contemporary adaptations. But there is much more to know and to see — if you're willing to keep an eye out for certain opportunities. From time to time, local historical societies and garden clubs arrange visits to some of the best mansions, normally off-limits because they are private homes. Edith Wharton Restoration at the Mount (see pages 95 – 97) offers summer step-on guides who will lead your group on your bus to some of the great houses. In a three-and-a half-hour tour 23 mansions are visited, with light refreshments served in the gardens at Naumkeag.

You can also guide your own tour of the Gilded Age "cottages." Many are visible from the road and are well worth a look. Their owners' privacy should be respected, of course. The stories of Berkshire's Gilded Age are endlessly entertaining, and Carole Owens' *The Berkshire Cottages* tells them in lively detail. The business magnates, robber barons, philanthropists, architects and designers, artists in residence, and squadrons of domestic servants are all alive on Owens' pages. If you liked public television's "Upstairs, Downstairs", *The Berkshire Cottages* is your kind of book. Maps to guide your way are included. Recommended.

LIBRARIES

BERKSHIRE ATHENAEUM
499-9480.
One Wendell Ave.
Pittsfield, MA 01201.
Season: Year-round: Mon.-Thurs., 10-9, Fri.-Sat. 10-5; Closed Sun. July-Aug., open Mon., Wed., Fri., 10-5, Tues. & Thurs. 10-9. Sat. 10-1. Closed holidays.
Fee: Free.

The old Berkshire Athenaeum is a 19th-century specimen of the Venetian Gothic style, constructed next to the courthouse on Pittsfield's handsome Park Square. Built of Berkshire deep blue dolomite (a limestone) from Great Barrington, along with red sandstone from Longmeadow, Massachusetts, and red granite from Missouri, this Athenaeum was once Berkshire's central library and now serves Pittsfield's municipal courts.

The new Athenaeum is a three-level brick and glass facility featuring a perimeter stack system which allows a tall and airy reading room with natural clerestory lighting. Other attractive features include an outdoor reading terrace for adults and one for children.

The Athenaeum's collections are impressive and quite easy to use. There is an outstanding dance collection, a Local Authors Room and a Local History Room (where some of the research for this book was done). The music collection includes hundreds of albums and tapes of all types, many of them available for home listening. Similarly, mounted art prints are part of the circulating library. The crown jewel of the Athenaeum is its Herman Melville Room, a veritable treasure trove of Melville memorabilia, from carved scrimshaw depicting the terrifying Great White Whale to first editions of the author's works. Look for *Moby Dick* in Japanese! Here also you'll find autograph letters from Melville, photos of his Pittsfield Farm, Arrowhead (see p. 94), and the desk on which he wrote his last haunting work, *Billy Budd*.

The Athenaeum runs a broad range of programs, from the Bookmobile to an adult literacy project. Especially outstanding are its children's programs which in a recent year included 36 films, 37 story hours, three puppet shows, a summer reading program and a creative writing contest. Residents, year-round and part-time, from throughout Berkshire County are eligible for borrowers' cards.

CHAPIN LIBRARY OF RARE BOOKS
597-2462.
Box 426, Williamstown, MA 01267.
On the 2nd fl. of Stetson Hall, on Williams College campus.
Season: Year-round: 9-12, 1-5, exc. weekends & holidays. Open July 4.

One of the best rounded collections of rare books and manuscripts among American colleges is right here in Berkshire. If you're a collector, researcher, or literary enthusiast, Chapin Library has many impressive surprises waiting for you. Alfred Clark Chapin, Williams class of 1869, went on to become mayor of Brooklyn and to assemble an impressive library of first editions and manuscripts specifically for donation to Williams College. Since his presentation in 1915, other alumni have given their collections, and as result, the Chapin is strong in many significant fields.

At the Chapin is a fine copy of Eliot's *Indian Bible* (Cambridge, MA, 1661, 1663). Here also you'll find incunabula (the "babies" of all books, printed in the 15th century), Shakespeare in First Folio, first editions of Pope, Swift, Fielding, Defoe, Richardson, Sterne, Johnson, Scott, Byron, Burns, Browning, Keats, Shelley, Thackeray and Dickens. This last great storyteller is represented by ten of his most important novels, including *The Pickwick Papers* (written at age 24), all in their original paper parts. In American literature, there are notable first editions by authors such as Crane, Melville and Whitman (including every edition of his writings published during his lifetime).

The Chapin also has a fine T.S. Eliot collection and an autograph collection that includes letters of all the presidents of the United States from Washington to Nixon. In science, as in other collections, most of the notables are there: Tycho Brahe's *Astronomia* (1602); Harvey's *Anatomical Exercitations* (1653) and Darwin's *Origin of the Species* (1859), among many others. Here also is a Theodore Roosevelt collection, and one featuring graphic arts and fine printing, including the Kelmscott Chaucer.

Most powerful of all, however, is the Chapin's collection of documents from the American Revolution, many of which are on permanent display. Among the valuables are a copy of the Articles of Confederation of 1777, copies of two versions of the Bill of Rights, and a copy of the Committee of Style draft of the Constitution, with handwritten objections by one of its key members. In April 1983, Williams College stunned the academic and art auction world by successfully bidding on a recently discovered copy of the Declaration of Independence that had belonged to one of its signers. At a cost of $412,500, the college and alumni endowed the Chapin and the Berkshires with yet another cornerstone of American history.

SAWYER LIBRARY
597-2501.
Williams College, Williamstown, MA 01267.
In the center of Williams College campus.
Season: Year-round, closed weekends & school vacations.

Berkshire County's most comprehensive library, the Sawyer is an unmatched research resource. Here you'll find a wide array of the latest periodicals, shelves of newly released books, and a library staff as helpful as they come. The Sawyer is a very pleasant place in which to work, and unlike many college libraries, here most eyes are on the books.

LENOX LIBRARY
637-0197.
18 Main St., Lenox, MA 01240.
Season: Year-round; summer: Mon.-Sat. 10-5; rest of year, Tues.-Sat. 10-5; Thurs., open until 8.

Built in 1815 as the Berkshire County Courthouse, when Lenox was still the "shire town," this classic Greek Revival building became the Lenox Library Association in 1873. It is listed on the National Register of Historic Places, and if you're lucky enough to sit and read there some afternoon, you'll understand why. See especially the main reading room with its lofty illuminated ceiling, its amazing array of periodicals and impressive ornamental Christmas cactus. This is Old World reading at its

In the reading room at the Lenox library.

best. A solid collection of about 75,000 volumes plus a music room are available to the public. There is a closed collection of historical memorabilia, too, including the infamous sleigh in Edith Wharton's novella, Ethan Frome. A lovely outdoor park makes warm-weather reading much fun.

SIMON'S ROCK LIBRARY
528-0771, ext. 273.
Alford Rd., Gt. Barrington, MA 01230.
Season: Year-round, hours vary.

The Simon's Rock Library is certainly one of the best in South County, and the staff there has always been attentive to any of our research needs. The college it serves may be tiny, but don't be deceived: this library's holdings are exceedingly well chosen. This is a library of half a dozen rooms, on two floors, in three interconnected pagoda-style buildings — all in a sylvan setting. Here, you can see art books you have only dreamt about; here you can answer that lingering question about the divisions of a nanosecond. With their big skylights, the reading rooms are highly recommended for naturally lit wet-weather browsing. And fascinating art exhibits almost always grace the library's skylit gallery.

STOCKBRIDGE LIBRARY
298-5501.
Box 119, Stockbridge, MA 01262.
Main St., Stockbridge.
Season: Year-round, exc. Sun.

Parts of the Stockbridge Library date to 1864, and the reading room is one the most felicitous anywhere. Tall, stately, and obviously from another era, this book-lined salon sets the mood for study so strongly, it will woo you to sit a while and peruse. The children's section is also first-rate. Downstairs is a local history collection that will take you back in time, with the colorful Polly Pierce as your guide.

ALBERT SCHWEITZER CENTER LIBRARY
528-3124
Closed: Mon.
RFD 1, Hurlburt Rd., Gt. Barrington, MA 01230.
Season: Apr. 16 – Oct. 31. Tues. – Sat. 11-4. Sun. 12-4. Nov. 1 – Apr. 15. Sat. & Sun. 11 – 4. Groups by appt. weekdays.
Schweitzer books available for purchase.

In 1951, Austrian filmmaker Erica Anderson visited Albert Schweitzer in Lambarene, Gabon, Africa, at his hospital. So powerful was the impact of this great man on her, that she stayed on and returned often, taking many thousands of photographs, shooting an Academy Award documentary film on the good doctor, and just helping out. When Schweitzer died, he left Anderson $10,000 in thanks for her years of volunteer work. Using that gift, she set up the Friendship House in Great Barrington. Though she and Dr. Schweitzer are no longer alive, their spirits live on in the Berkshires.

Schweitzer was a musician, theologian, author, doctor and Nobel Peace Prize humanitarian, and is well represented in the collection of photos, writings and memorabilia at Friendship House. There are frequent programs about his work, and Anderson's film is shown regularly. The property and its activities exude Schweitzer's philosophy of "reverence for life."

MUSEUMS

THE BERKSHIRE MUSEUM
443-7171
39 South St., Pittsfield, MA 01201
Season: Year-round: Tues.-Sat. 10-5, Sun. 1-5; open Mon. July-Aug.: 10-5. member disc. available.
Gift shop.

Cultural hub for the whole county, Berkshire Museum continues to improve its strong collections of art, and of regional and natural history, as well as offering an exciting calendar of lectures, films, concerts, classes and field trips.

Founded in 1903 by Dalton paper maker and philanthropist, Zenas Crane, Berkshire Museum was repository for such enthusiastic buying by Crane that in its first ten years, the structure had to be expanded four times. So bounteous was Crane's giving that it stimulated other locally prominent families to donate their artistic wealth, too. Hence the museum now also shows the Hahn Collection of Early American Silver, the Gallatin Collection of Abstract Art, the Spalding Collection of Chinese Art, the Proctor Shell Collection, and the Cohn Collection of Minerals.

The collections are far ranging and impressive. There is 19th-century glass made in the towns of Berkshire and Cheshire, and there are pre-Christian glass bottles from Egypt, bottles with an aqua aura about them. In the Biology Room, there are exhibits of shells and aquatic life, fossils, mushrooms, reptiles and amphibians. Here also is "Uncle Beasley," the ten-foot-long model dinosaur who starred in the children's TV movie, *The Enormous Egg*. In the Bird Room, you can see mounted specimens of birds from the world over, with a special section on Berkshire birds. The owl exhibit in this room is especially captivating. Other galleries on the first floor include the Berkshire Animal Room, which presents

Face to face, at the Berkshire Museum.

Lisa Gamble Bartle, courtesy of the Berkshire Museum.

native mammal specimens; and a room showing the animals of the world in miniature, a collection of beautiful one-tenth scale dioramas by Louis Paul Jonas, Sr. These wonderful miniatures, teeming with animal life and frequently heightened by dramatic weather, give even the most traveled viewer a colorful glimpse into other ecosystems.

The museum's first floor also features a massive relief map of Berkshire County (see photograph, p. 3). Down the hall are Woodlands Indian art and artifacts, then exhibits on Early Man and his Tools. Also on display is one of the sledges with which Robert E. Peary reached the North Pole, along with arctic clothing worn on the expedition. Next comes the Berkshire Museum Corner Shop and finally, the Hall Photography Gallery, whose display changes monthly. Across the front hall on the museum's first floor is the Museum Theater, a 300-seat facility that is site for lectures, plays, concerts and the Little Cinema's admirable program of feature films. The theater is visually enlivened by two Alexander Calder mobiles.

Upstairs, the museum turns to fine arts and artifacts. In the American Portraiture and Decorative Arts Gallery, a long and powerful space, hang portraits by Copley, Stuart and Peale. The American Abstract Gallery features works by Calder, among others, and the British Gallery presents paintings by West and Reynolds. More classical 15th- to 18th-century European works hang in the next gallery, and among them is art by Patnir, DeHooch and Teniers. "Pa-hat," the ever-popular Egyptian mummy, lays resplendent in the next gallery, and she is surrounded by a first-rate collection of ancient reliefs and artifacts.

Other galleries on the museum's second floor accommodate changing exhibits drawn from its permanent art collection. In the Museum's center is the lofty and skylit Ellen Crane Memorial Room, a vast gallery hung with 19th-century landscape paintings of the Hudson River School, featuring works by Inness and Church.

Downstairs, in the museum's ten aquaria and nine vivaria, living fish and animals can be seen in approximations of their local habitats. On special occasions, children may pet Amy, the Armadillo.

The museum has a year-round calendar of programs, events, lectures and trips that could be a full-time education. "Art for Lunch" and "Animal Hour" are two of the series aimed at enriching local lives. Bus trips are run with destinations like

New York's Museum of Modern Art and the Frick for a pair of cubist shows.

Berkshire Museum also presents an impressive concert series, with unusual talents. Featured in a recent WinterSpring Concert was violin prodigy Livia Sohn, a 13-year-old, who has been a soloist with the Pittsburgh Symphony.

Music and movies, local history and art, artifacts and handcrafts, lectures and bus trips, plays and art openings: the sheer variety of cultural opportunities at Berkshire Museum make it a great regional treasure.

STERLING AND FRANCINE CLARK ART INSTITUTE
458-9545.
225 South St., Williamstown, MA 01267.
Season: Year-round: 10-5, exc. Mon.; open Memorial Day, Labor Day & Columbus Day.
Fee: Free admission.
Gift shop.

Sterling Clark acquired his first Renoir in 1916. By the time he was finished, he owned 36. He bought what he liked, not what was popular, and was sometimes able to purchase a masterpiece for a song. Such was the case with the renowned *Nymphs and Satyr*, a larger-than-life scene of idyllic eroticism by Bourguereau that greets you at the Clark, in the interior court, as you enter this magnificent house of art.

Around the corner from the Bourguereau are galleries filled with 19th-century American classics — by Winslow Homer, John Singer Sargent, Mary Cassat and Frederick Remington. Sterling Clark loved horses, so it's not surprising he loved his Remington showing the cavalry galloping forward, right out of the canvas. As obvious as that first Remington is, notice the subtleties of the lone horseman in another, *The Scout: Friends or Enemies?*

Albrecht Durer, Courtesy of The Clark Art Institute.

"Head of a Young Man" (1503) by Albrecht Durer, one of the Clark's many outstanding drawings.

Upstairs is the original Clark, the white Vermont marble neoclassic structure whose interior is finished in Italian marble, plaster and natural-finish oak. Both elegant and efficient, the setting was called by *Art News*, " ... very likely the best organized and most highly functional museum structure yet erected anywhere." Almost every gallery has some form of natural light, and the building is completely climate controlled. In addition, many galleries offer not only splendid paintings on the walls but peaceful views of the Berkshire hills as well.

The Clark is no mere painting gallery, however; it is an art museum, and as you walk among its colorful masterworks and their accompanying drawings and

"Stockbridge at Christmas"

prints, you'll also see some of the collection's antique furniture and silver, masterpieces of craftsmanship. The Clark is also one of the most important art education centers in America, an exquisite facility with a broad spectrum of lectures open to the public, serving as classroom to a Williams College graduate program in art history as well.

Besides its extensive art lecture series, the Clark presents chamber music and film programs (see p. 86). In its spare time, the Clark hosts mimes, puppeteers, one-person shows, poets and storytellers.

Even a short visit to the Clark is worth the trip, but linger if you can. Behold, the glories of mankind!

NORMAN ROCKWELL MUSEUM
298-3822.
Main St., Stockbridge, MA 01262.
Season: Year-round: 11-4 Mon.-Fri., 10-5 weekends & holidays.
Fee: Adults $5, Children $1, under 5, free.
Gift shop.

Norman Rockwell was a people painter, and besides capturing every nuance of skin color and texture, he sought to capture the inner person coming out, caught in one of life's special moments. The Corner House has the largest collection of Rockwell originals in the world (over 400). The museum changes its exhibit twice a year with a few exceptional paintings remaining on permanent display (for example, *Stockbridge at Christmas*). There are six galleries within this beautifully restored 18th-century house, and the tour is a delight. All sorts of colorful information is passed along (such as pointers about the portraits of Grandma Moses and Rockwell's family contained within one painting). Helpful hints are given about how to appreciate Rockwell's attention to detail: "Notice the ring finger on the old woman's hand; it's been indented by many years of wear ..."

Courtesy of Norman Rockwell Estate and Old Corner House; © 1967 Norman Rockwell Estate.

Norman Rockwell developed his paintings in a series of self-contained phases: first, a rough sketch; second, the gathering of models, costumes, background and props; third, individual sketches or photos of all parts; fourth a full-scale drawing in great detail; fifth, color sketches; and sixth, the final painting. The Corner House gives a clear impression of the artist's genius, and it is a must visit.

Wrote Roberta Smith of *The New York Times*, in a review of a recent Rockwell show in New York City: "Rockwell's talent, like that of a great athlete or child prodigy, was extraordinary — innate, consistent and unself-conscious, if frequently mechanical. Gifted with an eye for convincing detail and a movie director's feeling for narrative, he could condense elaborate plot lines into single images."

But things are soon to change in the land of Rockwell. The entire collection will move from Stockbridge center to a new site in the Glendale section. There, in a more modern gallery, more works can be shown, the paintings will be better protected, and more people will be able to see them comfortably. Currently, tours at the Corner House are a bit rushed due to the museum's popularity and the limited gallery space. No matter — all America is in Rockwell's paintings; don't be surprised if you see yourself there.

HANCOCK SHAKER VILLAGE
443-0188.
Box 898, Pittsfield, MA 01202.
Jct. Rtes. 20 & 41, 5 mi. W. of Pittsfield.
Season: Spring, Summer &

Founded in England in 1747, the Shakers originally called themselves the United Society of Believers in Christ's Second Appearing but soon became known as the Shaking Quakers for the tremblings they exhibited during religious dancing. In 1770, one of their members, Ann Lee, had a powerful vision, and as new leader of the sect, brought a

Fall: daily 9:30-5.
Fee: $7.50, children 6-12, $3.50, students & senior citizens $6.75, families $20.
Gift shops.

small band to America. Here around 1776, Ann Lee founded the first American Shaker community, at Niskayuna, near Albany.

They practiced a religion that was also their way of life and believed in a God that was both male and female. All property and labor was shared: "into one Joint interest and Union that all the Members Might have an Equal right and Privilege According to their Calling and needs in things Both Spiritual and temporal." The community consciously kept itself insular from the outside world. The sexes were treated equally, but kept separate, for celibacy was a basic Shaker tenet. Sins were confessed publicly, but because the Shakers were pacifists, punishment was never physical. Since the sect did not reproduce its own, converts or New Believers were important, and Mother Ann made frequent missionary journeys through Connecticut and Massachusetts, seeking souls.

As the following increased, a community was established in 1790 at Hancock, just west of Pittsfield. There, the community, called the City of Peace, grew and prospered, its residents seeking to achieve heavenly perfection on earth through a highly structured, cloistered life. "Spirit is the oar that moves the human will," said these Shakers; and for them, spiritual attentions accompanied every activity, every chore and joy. Design of clothing, furniture, implements and buildings was strictly functional, with beauty being almost synonymous with simplicity. "'Tis a gift to be simple," goes an old Shaker hymn, and such simplicity was a primary aim of both inner and outer life. "Beauty rests on utility," said their credo.

Of great beauty, then, is Hancock's symbol, the stunning Round Stone Barn. As splendid as the structure is to the eye, how much more splendid to the legs and arms of the single farmhand for whom the round barn was designed. With such an efficient architecture, one farmhand at the center could easily and quickly feed an entire herd of cattle.

When the sect was at its peak, in the mid-19th century, Hancock was one of 18 Shaker communities in New York, Massachusetts, Connecticut, New Hampshire, Maine, Ohio, Kentucky and Indiana. Hancock had a population of about 300 members who were divided into six "families." The agricultural base of the village was augmented by cottage industries, which fabricated such items as tin dustpans, flat brooms, oval boxes, baskets, hats, and bird's-eye maple chairs. But because of the strict codes of celibacy, Shaker population at Hancock declined steadily until 1960, when the last of the Hancock Shakers moved away.

Since that time, the village has come to life anew, being restored and recreated to accommodate visitors who wish to taste of the simple Shaker ways. The City of Peace, on over 1,000 acres of rolling farm and woodland, now acts as center of Shaker activities for adults and children including hands-on workshops, festive dinners and breakfasts, candlelit evening programs, special tours, and a three-day antiques show during Columbus Day weekend, to name a few.

At Shaker Village itself, you can tour 20 original Shaker buildings. And while you amble around the lovely old compound, you'll be able to see Shaker furniture, tools and machines, some of them attended by craftspeople working in the Shaker way. At the tinshop, you can watch the tinsmith make a handsome dustpan, working in

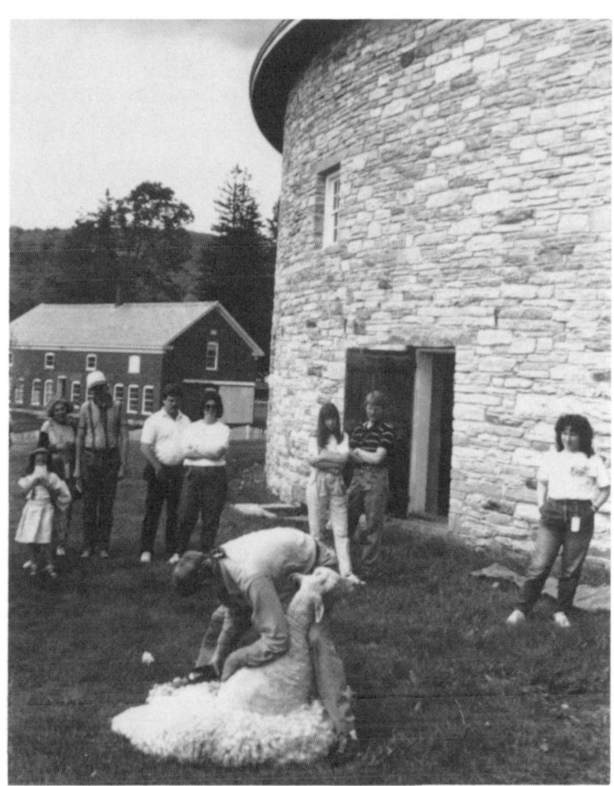

Traditional sheep shearing in the shadow of Hancock's round stone barn.

rhythms that are an unmistakable moving meditation. Or visit with the chair maker, the blacksmith or hat maker. In Hancock's workshops, you can learn to work like a Shaker, creating baskets or brooms, loaves of bread or oval boxes, hats or rugs, natural cosmetics or herb wreaths. Take in the gardens, both herbal and vegetable, and from any of the village farm workers, you can get a sense of the power of this Shaker simplicity.

WILLIAMS COLLEGE MUSEUM OF ART
597-2429.
Main St. (Rte.2), Williamstown, MA 01267.
Across from Gothic chapel: set back from street.
Season: Year-round: Mon.-Sat., 10-5, Sun. 1-5.
Closed: Thanksgiving, Christmas & New Year's.
Fee: Free.
Gift Shop

The Williams College Museum of Art is a 19th-century structure that is strikingly new. Behind its Greek Revival facade is a $4.5 million Charles Moore-designed building that opened in 1983. Combining wit and sophistication, the architect created a multileveled exhibition space that lends itself admirably to displaying many kinds of art. Moore's design for the building's rear facade is a continuation of his lighthearted approach, featuring what Williams students fondly call their "ironic columns."

Inside, the museum frequently shows its fine holdings in 19th- and 20th-century American art, highlighted by works of Grant Wood, Edward Hopper and Milton Avery. These latter paintings were the gifts of Williams alumnus Lawrence Bloedel, whose estate divided his collection between this museum and the Whitney in New York. And quite recently, the widow of American Impressionist Charles Prendergast donated works by her late husband and some by his talented brother, Maurice.

Visiting shows have been of high quality with major impact. Recently, Thomas Hart Benton's *America Today* murals were exhibited. These ten large murals depict American life in the late 1920s and manage to achieve a high degree of social-historical objectivity without sacrificing their art. While on exhibit at Williams and at the skilled hands of the Williamstown Regional Art Conservation Laboratory staff, the Benton paintings were cleaned and restored. The museum was able to display these important works while sharing with the public an opportunity to watch the restoration in progress — even occasionally allocating time for conservators to answer viewer questions. Concurrently, the museum showed contemporaries of Benton in one room and Depression Era color photographs in another. Films of the 1920s and '30s were screened, and the effect of all these complementary exhibits was to give the viewer a strong feeling for the sensibilities of the 1920s.

Through art, film, and lecture, the Williams College Museum of Art offers an integrated aesthetic experience. Our advice: when in Williamstown, stop off at both the Clark Art Institute and the college museum.

Mass MoCA - Op Art or Illusion?

The multimillion dollar Massachusetts Museum of Contemporary Art (Mass MoCA) is a planned non-profit retrofit of the Sprague Electric plant in North Adams, potentially one of the foremost modern art facilities in the world. Collections of huge paintings are anticipated to fill MassMoCA's huge walls. What more could a minimalist art aficionado want? Or do minimalists always want less? In any case, should the state legislature appropriate the money, and should the feasibility studies continue to look promising, North County could add another world-class art attraction, making Berkshire even brighter.

CRANE PAPER MUSEUM
685-2600.
30 South St., Dalton, MA 01226.
Off Rte. 9, behind Crane office, Dalton.
Season: June to Mid-Oct.
Fee: Free.

One of Berkshire's most important creations is money. Not the finished product, mind you, but the rag paper on which every U.S. bill is printed. The Crane Paper Company makes it, and from Berkshire County to the nation and then the world, these treasured notes circulate.

Because of the security surrounding the making of currency notes, and for safety reasons, the mills themselves are no longer open to the public. The Crane Paper Museum, established in 1929, is open, however, and it tells a fascinating industrial tale. This magical, one-room brick museum — ivy covered and set in a garden — is really a restored paper mill building. The exhibits inside are mostly scale models, historical photographs and paper samples. Crane produces only rag paper (nothing from wood pulp), and the exhibits show how the rags are soaked, softened, beaten to a pulp and dried into paper stock. The process of watermarking is explained, as are surface finishing (hard or soft) and anti-counterfeiting techniques. Also on display are historic documents, White House invitations, and U.S. and foreign currency, all printed on paper manufactured by Crane. At the end of your visit, you'll likely be offered an envelope of free Crane paper samples, including some of their luxurious stationery. It's that old "rags to riches" story come true again.

Paper money, one of Crane Paper's most successful products.

Courtesy of U.S. Treasury.

The Money Business

Among the most treasured items on Earth, American currency has been Berkshire born since 1879, when the second Zenas Crane obtained an exclusive contract with the U.S. Government. Developed in Dalton, the special rag paper had linen threads running lengthwise, making the paper tough, and very distinctive. Currency paper has remained little changed since its creation: basically, 25% domestic cotton, and 75% imported linen cuttings from England and Ireland. In the late 19th century, a few colored silk threads were added to the lengthwise linen, making the paper even more readily identifiable. Since then, the small quantity of red and blue silk fiber has been cut and randomly spread through the paper. Metallic and ultra-violet sensitive threads are a future possibility as the government and the paper-maker strive to keep up with the increased threat of conterfeiting brought on by color copiers and the like. Redesigned watermarks are another possibility.

However they do it, we've always found the result very satisfying. This is one Berkshire product that we can safely advise: Don't leave home without it! Printed in Washington D.C., these handsome engravings are suitable for framing, make dynamite gifts, and are redeemable in just about every establishment in the land. Great in the bank, in your pocket or wallet, a wad of these small prints inspires confidence, generosity and good will. Wave one of these Berkshire beauties at some big city bellhop, and watch him hop! There's power in this paper, and it all starts here in Berkshire. Whether you hide yours in a mattress or flash it at a casino, buy big buildings or a very used pick-up truck, pay for a massage or a roof repair, this attractive Berkshire notepaper connects us all.

STOCKBRIDGE LIBRARY HISTORICAL ROOM
298-5501.
Main St., Stockbridge, MA 01262.
Season: Year-round, exc. Sun.
Fee: Free.

Called *W-nahk-ta-kook* ("Great Meadow") by the Mahican Indians who settled there, the town of Stockbridge was incorporated by the English in 1739. A Colonial charter not only made the town official, but made it Indian property as well, and thereafter, it was known as "Indian Town." The history of this great meadow and its town, is displayed and explained in the Stockbridge Historical Room, a small museum in the basement of the Stockbridge Library. Here you'll see Indian artifacts, photos from the mid-1800s onwards, memorabilia from many famous residents and visitors to the village, and other intriguing historical bits which illuminate Stockbridge present.

WESTERN GATEWAY HERITAGE STATE PARK
663-6312.
9 Furnace St. Bypass, N. Adams, MA 01247. In N. Adams freightyard district.
Season: Year-round.
Fee: Free.
Gift shop & Restaurant.

Berkshire has always been somewhat isolated, nestled between long glacial ridges and separated from the rest of Massachusetts. In 1854, engineers and construction workers assaulted this situation, drilling and blasting a 4.3 mile long tunnel through the northeastern ridge. This Hoosac Tunnel was the first major tunneling work in the U.S., and many new methods were devised over the 20-year construction — but at a cost of over $20 million and more than 200 lives. The building of the tunnel and related railroad development made North Adams the largest city in Berkshire in 1900. "We hold the Western Gateway," says the North Adams seal, and at the turn of the century, more than half of Boston's freight came through the tunnel.

In 1980, the state of Massachusetts passed an act which provided for the creation of eight Heritage Parks, each of which is designed to serve as a catalyst and centerpiece for local urban revitalization. In North Adams, the result is Western Gateway Heritage State Park, a museum complex that celebrates the former Boston and Maine Freight House and the Hoosac Tunnel, both of which are on the National Register of Historic Places. Inside, you can see films, slide shows, written and visual histories of the railway and tunnel through the Hoosac barrier. Outside, there are shops, the restored freightyard and the church-spired charm of North Adams.

BERKSHIRE SCENIC RAILWAY MUSEUM
637-2210.
Box 2195, Lenox, MA 01240.
Willow Creek Rd. at the end of Housatonic St.
Season: June through Oct., weekends & holidays.
Museum & Gift Shop: Free.
Open: 10-3.

Good news! As of winter '91, prospects seem excellent for the return of the Scenic Railway. After having to suspend operations due to a business dispute, Berkshire Scenic Railway seems back on track, now that railway president John Herbert has linked up with railroad entrepreneur John Hanlon, who has purchased the 35-mile section of the Housatonic Railroad track from North Canaan, Connecticut, to Pittsfield. Eventually, Hanlon has hopes of restoring the rail links between Pittsfield and...New

York...and at any speed, that would be a fun run.

The Berkshire Scenic Railway ride is a thrill for even jaded locals, offering new views of familiar terrain, exciting glimpses of areas as yet unseen, and the delicious opportunity to be lost on your own home turf. In between train rides, you can find railroad memorabilia in the Railway Museum, an old-time railway station now undergoing restoration and currently housing an exhibit that includes railroading videos and a model railroad. Outside, a full-sized caboose is parked at the siding, just waiting to be coupled. Clackety-clackety, woo-woo, there'll be rails to ride again in Berkshire!

OTHER MUSEUMS IN WILLIAMSTOWN

Besides fine art and rare books, the many museums in Williamstown can take you in still other directions. You can go *back* at the ***Williamstown House of Local History*** (458-5369; Main St.), back in time through a collection of books, antiques and artifacts depicting Williamstown the way it was. You can go *out* at the ***Hopkins Farm Museum*** (597-2346; ***Hopkins Memorial Forest***, the Rosenberg Center, and Buxton Garden; Northwest Hill Rd.), out to such seasonal events as sheepshearing and maple sugaring, while the museum itself exhibits old photographs, farm machinery and tools. And you can go *up* at the 19th-century flintstone ***Hopkins Observatory*** (597-2188; Main St.), up to the stars via the projected shows at the ***Milham Planetarium*** (Fridays during the school year), or *back, out* and *up* to the real pulsars and quasars through the telescopes of America's second oldest collegiate observatory, in touch with the stars since 1836.

MUSIC

TANGLEWOOD
637-1666 or 637-1940.
Boston Symphony Orchestra, Tanglewood, Lenox, MA 01240.
Mail: 301 Massachusetts Ave., Boston, MA 02115.
On West St., Rte. 183, in Lenox.
Season: Summer only.
Tickets: $7-$12 lawn, $10-$58 shed.
Gift shop.

The rhapsody in green continues. Framed by towering pines, carpeted with lush lawns, endowed with spectacular mountain views, and animated by The Boston Symphony Orchestra and its students, Tanglewood remains *the* summer music festival in New England, an incomparable facility for all the world's musicians and music lovers. Whether you picnic on the lawn or sit closer to the BSO in the Shed, hearing music at Tanglewood can uplift and enlighten, can bring excitement, merriment and pure joy. Sit inside and witness up close the artistry of conductor Seiji Ozawa; or sit back on the vast expanse of lawn, sip your wine, watch the stars and satellites in the clear sky overhead, and just listen to these masters make music.

There are those who argue that Tanglewood is too crowded, too expensive, too predictable and too lax in its standards for music making or music listening. It *can* be ironic to find oneself in the open Berkshire countryside stuck in a Tanglewood traffic jam. It *can* seem strange to pay Broadway prices for close-up seats at a concert in an open shed with an earthen floor, chilly evening air and the

Portaging music through Tanglewood's parklike setting.

occasional barn swallow flying through. It is easy guesswork to say there will be Beethoven and Mozart programs every summer. And it is easy to fault the musical sound both in the Shed and outside when one applies the tests of enclosed concert hall acoustics or home stereo fidelity.

Tanglewood is easy to criticize, yet there is a powerful, positive feeling among musicians, students and concertgoers alike. Tanglewood lovers believe that the beauty of the composers' works and of many performances here, and the sheer fun of seeing and hearing all of this in the great outdoors far outweigh any objections. We join in that good feeling and recommend Tanglewood as a quintessential Berkshire entertainment.

Tanglewood started out as the Berkshire Music Festival in the summer of 1934. The New York Philharmonic was seeking a pastoral setting in which to perform, and with the help of Gertrude Robinson Smith of Stockbridge, the seeds of a music festival in Berkshire were planted.

Within weeks, Smith had galvanized the wealthy and powerful of Berkshire County, ultimately transforming a horse ring on a Stockbridge farm into a makeshift concert arena. With the stage set, 65 members of the New York Philharmonic were bused from Manhattan to the mountains and lodged in the area's hotels.

Although the concert series was a sound success and repeated the following summer, the New York orchestra withdrew. But Gertrude Robinson Smith was now in love with the idea of symphonic music resounding through the hills, and she quickly shifted her attentions to Serge Koussevitzky, the Russian-born conductor of the Boston Symphony Orchestra. Koussevitzky was wooed and won. The BSO conductor and his orchestra signed on for a series of three concerts on a single August weekend in 1936.

The popularity of this series was immense, with nearly 15,000 people attending. And in the fall of that year, the Tappan family gave the BSO a permanent summer home in the Berkshires, their Tanglewood estate on the Stockbridge-Lenox border. For the first two summers, concerts were held in a large canvas tent, but during one 1937 program, a torrential thunderstorm not only drowned out Wagner's *The Ride of the Valkyries*, but also leaked through, dampening instruments, musicians and audience alike. During intermission, with the roaring rain still playing above and dripping below, Gertrude Robinson Smith began an impromptu fund-raising drive for the creation of a permanent structure, a "music pavilion." Before the storm had let up enough to allow the concert to resume, pledges totaling $30,000 had been made.

By the following summer, through the combined architectural efforts of the distinguished architect, Eliel Saarinen, and Stockbridge engineer, Joseph Franz, the Shed was a reality. Classical music had a permanent home in the Berkshires. Sensing the opportunity and the ideal setting to establish a powerful school for musicians, Koussevitzky set to work convincing the orchestra's trustees; and by 1940, Tanglewood was not only the site of the Shed and glorious summer concerts, but also of the Berkshire Music Center for advanced musicians.

Tanglewood's First

At Tanglewood's first concert, with ominous threats of World War II coming daily from Europe, maestro Serge Koussevitzky gave the following explanation for his choice of music: "I have selected Beethoven's Ninth Symphony not only because it is the greatest masterpiece in musical literature, but because I wanted to hear the voice of Tanglewood singing Schiller's words, calling all nations to the brotherhood of man."

Koussevitzky assembled an extraordinary faculty for the Center: great teachers and masters of instrumental performance, composition and singing. And for the school's opening ceremony, Randall Thompson wrote his haunting *Alleluia* for unaccompanied chorus, a work that arrived just in time to be performed. *Alleluia* left such a lasting impression that it has been performed as the school's traditional opening music each summer since. By 1941, construction was complete on the Theatre-Concert Hall, the Chamber Music Hall, and several small studios. The Berkshire Music Center had facilities, a faculty and a growing student body. Meanwhile, attendance at the Festival had climbed to nearly 100,000 for the summer concerts.

The school — now called the Tanglewood Music Center — goes well beyond the sheer technique that can be learned with private teachers. At the Tanglewood Center, the emphasis is on making music, in ensemble performance, developing chamber music artistry with a group of talented fellow musicians under the tutelage of a master.

Each summer, the Tanglewood Music Center Orchestra is recreated from that year's crop of students; for their weekly concerts, this impressive group is usually led by a student conductor, but sometimes by the likes of Seiji Ozawa or Kurt Masur. So significant is this Tanglewood education that upwards of 20 per cent of the members of America's major orchestras count themselves among Tanglewood Music Center alumni. Leonard Bernstein was a graduate, as is

Zubin Mehta and Seiji Ozawa. Students come from around the world. Aaron Copland, dean of American composers, once directed the school and taught here.

Tanglewood itself — the Music Festival, that is — has evolved into a performance center of major proportions. With an annual summer attendance now of some 300,000 visitors, it has become a musical mecca. In addition to the regular Boston Symphony Orchestra concerts, Tanglewood presents weekly chamber music concerts in the smaller sheds, Prelude Concerts (Friday nights), and Open Rehearsals (Saturday mornings), the annual Festival of Contemporary Music, and almost daily concerts by gifted young musicians at the Music Center. Some student concerts are free. The Boston Pops comes to play as well. If you're staying in the Berkshires for

Up until his last summer on earth, the late maestro Leonard Bernstein continued to share his musical insights at Tanglewood.

a month or more and want to take in Tanglewood music frequently, join the "Friends of Tanglewood" and enjoy ticket price reductions and other privileges.

It seems that Tanglewood always has something to celebrate. In 1988, it was a gala music party for Maestro Leonard Bernstein's 70th birthday and the 50th anniversary of Tanglewood itself. And in '89, the celebrations continued, with a concert called "The French Connection," commemorating the 200th anniversary of the French Revolution. On Bastille Day, Friday, July 14, Seiji Ozawa led the BSO in a program that included "La Marseillaise" as arranged by Berlioz, and Offenbach's "Gaieté Parisienne."

A typical Tanglewood season lasts eight weeks, is preceded by a chamber music week and followed by two jazz dates (featuring such artists as Ray Charles, Ella Fitzgerald and the Modern Jazz Quartet). Distinguished guest artists returning to Tanglewood to appear with the BSO often include the likes of pianists Emanuel Ax, Jorge Bolet, Rudolf Firkusny, Peter Serkin, Mitsuko Uchida and André Watts; violinists Cho-Liang Lin, Midori, Itzhak Perlman, Frank Peter Zimmermann and Pinchas Zukerman; flutist James Galway; cellist Yo-Yo Ma; and vocalists Maria

Ewing and Jessye Norman.

The summer season is capped each year by "Tanglewood on Parade," an amazingly varied musical melange lasting some 10 hours and climaxing with booming cannon shots and fireworks.

Where to Sit at Tanglewood

If you plan to picnic at Tanglewood, it's best to arrive an hour or so in advance of concert time. Besides allowing time to eat before listening, arriving early affords a greater choice of spaces on the lawn, an important factor if you're to hear the music clearly. Although Tanglewood's amplification system is excellent and facilitates good listening from almost any lawn position, in our experience, places about 25 yards beyond the Shed-mounted speakers provide the very best lawn listening. Inside the Shed, the last series of back rows are good only for saying you were there, in our opinion, allowing only the faintest of distant orchestra views and suffering greatly from much-diminished sound. At the optimum speaker sites on the lawn, the sound is far superior.

If you're not picnicking and can afford to indulge, buy your way forward into the good seats where the sound is rich, sometimes robust and sometimes delicate, and where you can really see classical music in the making. The smaller shed, known as the Concert Theatre, has a lawn of its own; inside, the sound is quite uniformly good, but seating is very tight on stiff metal chairs.

Regardless of where you sit, if time allows, take a walk in Tanglewood's beautifully groomed boxwood gardens. As the sun sets, on a clear day, you can see the hills in three states.

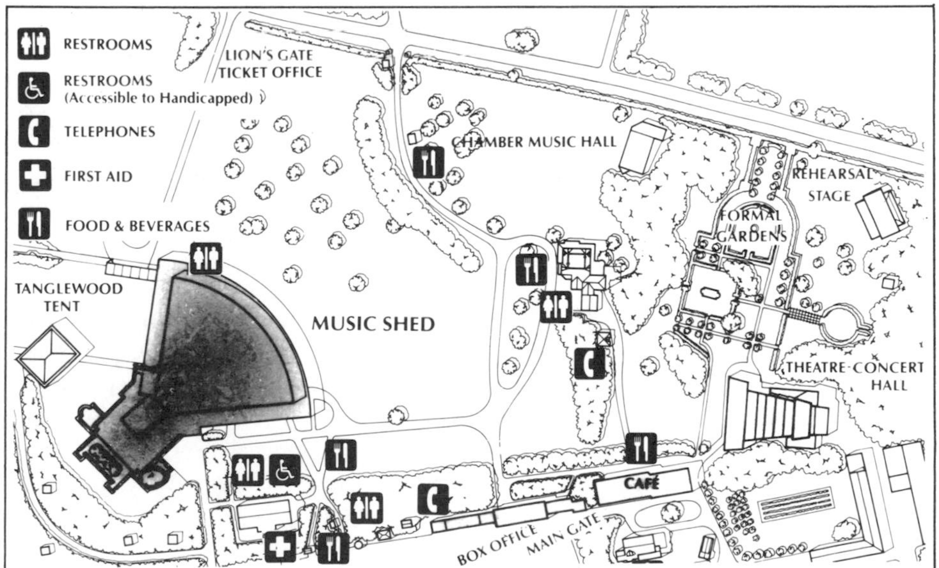

Barbara Peterson, courtesy of the Boston Symphony Orchestra, Inc.

SOUTH MOUNTAIN CONCERTS
442-2106.
Box 23, Pittsfield, MA 01202.
On Rtes. 7 & 20, about 1 mi. S. of Pittsfield Center.
Season: Mid-Aug.-early Oct.
Tickets: Prices vary each concert $15-$18.

It's certainly appropriate that South Mountain's concert hall in Pittsfield is called the Temple. Built in 1918, this Colonial-style Temple of Music was the gift of Mrs. Elizabeth Sprague, created to house the concerts of the Berkshire String Quartet. The acoustically splendid 500-seat auditorium, listed on the National Register of Historic Places, is set gracefully on its wooded South Mountain slope.

South Mountain has for many years presented internationally renowned artists, as well as lesser-known greats. Among the standout performers at The Temple have been Leonard Bernstein, Alexander Schneider, Leontyne Price, and Rudolf Serkin. The 1989 season opened with a piano recital by Lydia Artymiw, and followed with thoroughly enchanting afternoons of performance by the Beaux Arts Trio, the New World String Quartet, the Juilliard String Quartet, and finally, the Emerson String Quartet.

South Mountain Concerts frequently sell out — be sure to call ahead. Unlike Tanglewood where watching the stars or basking in the sunshine may substitute for close listening to the music, South Mountain's more limited season and number of concerts are designed for the serious music lover only.

On stage at South Moutain.

Clemens Kalischer.

ASTON MAGNA
528-3595.
Box 28, Gt. Barrington, MA 01230.
In St. James Church, just S. of the town hall.
Season: July only.
Tickets: $12.50 single, $30 for all 3 concerts.

There's a great deal of historic preservation going on in the Berkshires, and none more artistic than the renaissance of baroque chamber music by Aston Magna. Offering unique cross-disciplinary educational programs for professional musicians and a short run of superb summer concerts, Aston Magna has specialized in 17th-and 18th-century music, always played on period instruments or reproductions. Hear Bach as you might never have before, possibly with festival director John Hsu playing viola da gamba, Stanley Ritchie on violin, Lionel Party, harpsichord. Aston Magna concerts produce musical sounds you are unlikely to have encountered anywhere else: music made on the oboe d'amore, a valveless horn, or on the theorbo, a long-necked cousin of the lute.

Aston Magna's performances interpret the music as much as possible as the composer intended, hence the faithfulness to original instruments. Besides the consummate artistry of the music specialists assembled by this festival each summer, the Aston Magna concerts and lectures add something more: a palpable feeling for the aesthetic of the era which produced such beautiful music. Participants study the temperament and cultural milieu of the baroque age and then make music that is buoyed with the period's sensibility as well.

Said *New York Times* critic, John Rockwell: "The music was dispatched with conscientiousness and care . . . and the spirit of the Aston Magna enterprise commands almost unreserved praise." Richard Dyer, in *The Boston Globe*, went even further: "Aston Magna has become America's preeminent summer early-music event . . . a festival that is out on the cutting edge of its art."

The *New Yorker's* Andrew Porter has given this festival several reviews, noting that "At Aston Magna, much time is spent considering what the music meant to the men who wrote it and those who first heard it . . ." Aston Magna's annual Berkshire festival usually features the chamber music of Bach, Handel, Haydn and Mozart, and concerts are held in the old-world splendor of St. James Church, in Great Barrington. Raved the *Hartford Courant*: "No committed music lover should miss the opportunity to hear this splendid ensemble."

L'ORCHESTRA
528-1872.
Box 828, Gt. Barrington 01230.
292 Main St., Gt. Barrington.
Season: Oct.-June.
Concerts: 7.
Tickets: $10, $15, $20.

"Music is a tremendous spiritual, emotional and psychological source for people; I want to make it available to everyone," says L'Orchestra founder, music director and conductor, David Barg. As a flutist, Barg appeared with the Bolshoi and Kirov Ballets on their American tours, and performed at Carnegie Hall, Lincoln Center and the Kennedy Center as well. But this fine soloist had even greater ambitions —he wanted to lead an orchestra in every way, making decisions about concert halls, programs, musicians, and ultimately, about the way the music is played.

Since 1987, to the delight of thousands, Barg has been making that dream come true. Establishing a dedicated core of Manhattan School of Music (MSM) graduates, he formed the corps of L'Orchestra, often adding distinguished soloists such as pianist Malcolm Frager, and young violin virtuoso Benny Kim. After experimenting with the Berkshire Performing Arts Center and the Cranwell Opera House as their concert home, L'Orchestra has now settled into the venerable Mahaiwe, a space that nicely complements their sound. Programs are rich in the classics, often thematic, and occasionally eclectic.

A recent opening concert was an all- Beethoven affair, with Benny Kim soloing, and was subsequently re-broadcast on Warner Cable TV. Said *The Berkshire Eagle's* critic Justin Kagan: "Mr. Kim's ornamentation was quite beautifully and stylishly executed. Overall, this concert created an idiosyncratic, friendly and impressive atmosphere. The playing was basically first-rate, and often superior, a nice harbinger of things to come from this ever-tightening ensemble."

For their finale of a recent season, L'Orchestra played a program of Mendelssohn, Haydn and Beethoven. "I know that classical music performed spiritedly can be an illuminating experience," says Maestro Barg. If you listen to L'Orchestra, you'll know it too.

Founder–conductor David Barg leads L'Orchestra with an impassioned style.

Arthur Gerstein.

NORFOLK CHAMBER MUSIC FESTIVAL
203-542-5537; 203-432-1966 off season.
During season: Norfolk, CT 06058; off season: 96 Wall St., New Haven, CT 06520.
Rtes. 44 & 272, in Norfolk.
Season: Mid-June – Mid-Aug.
Tickets: $6 to $16. Subscription for 5 concerts $22 to $68.

From mid-June to early August at Norfolk, visiting virtuosos perform regularly, among them the Tokyo String Quartet and the Vermeer Quartet. Orchestral and choral works are also featured. Concurrent with this series of concerts, Yale's Summer School of Music runs a program of classes for its students and regularly schedules recitals by young professional musicians — recitals which are open to the public free of charge (currently on Thursday evenings and Saturday mornings).

The setting is superb. Arrive early, and you can picnic on the grounds of the elegant 75-acre estate on which the music center has grown. Norfolk's Music Shed is enclosed and beautifully crafted of acoustically resonant hardwoods. Some balcony seats along the sides may pose a viewing problem, but the sound is good everywhere, and the ticket prices are somewhat lower than at Berkshire County's more widely known music events.

The 1990 season marked the 50th anniversary of the festival and school, with Friday and Saturday concerts preceded by informal brass quintet recitals. In the southern foothills of the Berkshires, Norfolk is a quiet alternative to the more crowded Tanglewood, offering chamber music at its finest.

MUSIC MOUNTAIN
203-824-7126.
Falls Village, CT 06031.
On Music Mountain Rd., off Rte.7 opposite Housatonic Valley High School.
Season: Mid-June to Labor Day.
Tickets: $10.

Founded in 1930 by Chicago Symphony concert master Jacques Gordon, Music Mountain is the oldest continuing chamber music festival in America. In the acoustically excellent, 325-seat Gordon Hall, set on a woody hilltop, concerts are given by the resident summer group, the Manhattan String Quartet, and by visiting guest artists.

BERKSHIRE PERFORMING ARTS CENTER
637-4718; or Ticketron 800-382-8080.
Box 1989, Lenox, MA. 01240.
40 Kemble St., Lenox.
Season: June-Sept.
Tickets: $15 to $25.

Since the Bible Speaks flew south, the transformed estate on the outskirts of Lenox has been in flux. One of the most exciting developments of the property has been the Berkshire Performing Arts Center (BPAC), presenting a line-up of popular musical talent unmatched by any other venue in the area. In an immaculate hall with irregular acoustics, BPAC offers a summer-long series of musical legends that includes such artists as: Chick Corea, Pat Metheny, John McLaughlin, Laura Nyro, Tom Chapin, Judy Collins, The Nylons, Toots and the Mytals, Emmylou Harris, the Bobs, Stanley Jordan, David Bromberg, Paul Winter, James Cotton and Shadowfax, among others. These concerts are a real thrill — from the extraordinary jazz fluidity of guitarist Stanley Jordan to the jump-to-your-feet good-time sounds of reggae masters Toots and the Mytals, from the high-wire vocal acrobatics of an a capella quartet, The Nylons, to the moody passions of folk star Judy Collins.

For kids, BPAC offers regular Sunday afternoon puppet shows by the Robbins-Zust Family. And we're talking major league marionettes, performing the classics *(Three Little Pigs, Jack in the Beanstalk)*, with power, pathos, and humor.

BPAC is the new kid on the block, and has had their share of production glitches. But they bring to the Berkshires a season of inspiring jazz, pop, folk, blues, ethnic, classical and new music that will resound through these hills forever. We can only say: "Encore! Encore!"

OTHER MUSIC

Astonishingly, there is much, much more music in the Berkshires: choral music, lyric theater, opera, jazz, "world" music, other chamber concerts and folk music series.

In ***South County***, the ***Berkshire Bach Society***, although in existence for only a short time has garnered enthusiastic community support, with an attendance of 400 at the opening concert in November, 1990. Dedicated to the rediscovery of the largely unknown cantatas of Bach, the society will offer lecture series at the Albert Schweitzer Center in Great Barrington and performances, primarily at St. James Episcopal Church, throughout the year. Each summer brings the ***Berkshire Choral Festival***, a five-concert celebration featuring 200 voices, the Springfield Symphony, powerful soloists and conductors, all at one of the loveliest preparatory schools in New England, the Berkshire School (Rte. 41, Sheffield; 229-3522). ***Simon's Rock College of Bard*** (Alford Rd., Great Barrington; 528-0771) is the liveliest promoter of professional music in South County, with various events during the academic year under the name of ***South Berkshire Concerts*** — such as an all-Russian program featuring important but rarely heard chamber works by Prokofiev and Stravinsky. Other concerts at the Simon's Rock's ARC (barn-theatre) have featured special performances by Hot Tuna guitarist Jorma Kaukonen, and by the ecstatic Indian sitar master, Jamaluddin Bhartiya. ***The Curtisville Consortium*** takes its name from the hamlet of Interlaken in Stockbridge, which was originally settled as Curtisville. The Consortium is a group of Boston Symphony musicians and guest artists who present a series of concerts each summer at the Congregational Church in Interlaken.

In ***Central County***, ***Stockbridge Chamber Concerts*** (449-8240) changed its venue once again, playing the summer season at Searles Castle, Great Barrington. Chamber music can also be enjoyed at the ***Commonwealth Chamber Music Series*** (637-0299) in Stockbridge, at the First Congregational Church. And more chamber music is the feature of the ***Richmond Performance Series*** at the Richmond Congregational Church, Rte.41. Each of these chamber music series features professional symphony orchestra veterans, making intimate music in special settings. Also quite special is a summer series of concerts held at the ***DeSisto Estate*** (443-1138), Rte. 183, Stockbridge. The new 60-member ***Pittsfield Symphony Orchestra*** (442-0934) gets especially active in the winter, and recently gave several concerts at the First Methodist Church, in Pittsfield. ***Berkshire Community College*** (499-4660; West St., Pittsfield) offers a wide range of concerts, and the ***Berkshire Museum's Winter/Spring Concerts*** are described under the museum (p. 107). ***Berkshire Opera Company*** (243-1343) continued its winning ways, capping a recent successful season with performances of Rossini's comic masterpiece *The Barber of Seville*, sung in English at the Crosby School, Pittsfield.

In ***North County***, ***Williams College*** (597-3131) alone offers enough music to keep anyone humming, and their season kicks into high gear right after Tanglewood finishes. Among recent offerings have been performances by the ***Williams Choral Society*** at Chapin Hall (597-3146); modern songs by visiting professor and pianist Robert Suderburg with his wife, soprano Elizabeth Suderburg, at Bernhard Hall; concerts of African music by the Williams African Ensemble, with special guests Obo Addy and Kukrudu; a piano recital by the exciting Rudolf Firkusny; traditional and contemporary jazz concerts by the Williams Jazz Ensemble; as well as concerts by the classical Williams Trio and the au courant Group for Twentieth Century Music. Also playing frequently in the Williamstown area is the ***Berkshire Symphony***, an 80-member North County orchestra led by new conductor Ronald L. Feldman. The ***Clark Art Institute*** features major musical performances as well, most recently a concert of Russian piano music by the accomplished Peter Orth; see the entry for the museum, p. 109.

Just ***Outside the County***, in the Berkshire hilltown of Charlemont (Rte. 2, Franklin County), the ***Mohawk Trail Concerts*** presents a season of informal classical concerts at the Federated Church. In nearby Columbia County, NY,

Clarion Concerts (518-325-3837) holds a series of "Leaf Peeper" concerts in the fall, one in the Chapel of the Darrow School at the Mount Lebanon Shaker Village and four others at the Hudson Middle School, Hudson. In adjacent Spencertown, NY, the ***Spencertown Academy Society Chamber Music Concerts*** (518-392-3693; Box 80, Spencertown, NY 12165) are among the Berkshire region's neatest. *The Berkshire Eagle* said, "Acoustically the hall is a little gem, and each featured artist, cognizant of these attractive surroundings, radiates a feeling of 'I am happy to be performing here.' It is no wonder that one feels privileged to attend concerts in an atmosphere where the rating scale starts with 'excellent'." In the Spencertown Folk Series, at the same site, singer Pete Seeger recently gave one of his rousing performances.

The Pillow Music Series

Jacob's Pillow is America's dance "hub and Mecca," said *Time Magazine.* Yet beyond this richness in dance, the Pillow hosts a series of popular Music Concerts, featuring jazz and gospel. Weather permitting, the back of the stage at the Ted Shawn Theatre is opened, blending outside with in.

NIGHTLIFE

When the sun sets on Berkshire, what was quiet becomes quieter — except at the dozens of clubs across the county. From videotheques to cabarets, from hard rock to softly sung madrigals, nightlife in the Berkshires will satisfy most and truly please many. Here are the clubs, together with a few bands and individuals who've performed recently. Check the local papers for current listings.

Starting in ***South County***, in Sheffield, we saw David Bowie at the ***Sheffield Pub*** (229-8880; Rte. 7), a place which frequently shows live rock concerts, videos and "rockumentary" films on their many video monitors. In Egremont, the ***Egremont Country Club*** (528-4222; Rte. 23), has a fairly irregular schedule of good live bands up in the clubhouse, where you, too, are invited to shake your stuff. In Great Barrington, ***Martin's*** (528-5455; 49 Railroad St.) occasionally features live music on Friday and/or Saturday nights, leaning towards soft-singing acoustic players. The ***Tahiti*** (528-4255; on Rte. 7, next to the Cove Bowling Lanes), sometimes gets down and dirty, with the likes of Second Offense. Out in Southfield, at the delicious ***Boiler Room Cafe*** (229-3105; behind the Buggy Whip Factory), occasional evening fare varies from poets reading their works to a Delta bluesman twanging his steel guitar. Up the road in Stockbridge, the ***Lion's Den***, under the Red Lion Inn (298-5545; see p. 45), presents almost nightly live entertainment of high quality, such as folksinger David Grover. On a hot night, the subterranean Lion's Den is thick with music, cigarette smoke, laughter, banter and dish clatter, each apparently competing for center stage. Around the corner, at ***Michael's*** (298-3530; Elm St.) occasional live bands liven the otherwise staid Stockbridge soundscape. Over in West Stockbridge, the ***Shaker Mill Tavern*** (232-8565; Rtes.

102 and 41) occasionally brings in a DJ and gets the joint jumpin'. ***Oak n' Spruce*** (243-3500; South Lee), often features live pop music in their Bear Tree on Saturday nights. And over in East Lee, the ***Belden Tavern*** (243-4660; Rte.20) hosted Frank Miller and His Orchestra on recent Saturday nights, featuring ballroom dancing, big band, jazz and swing.

In *Central County*, the new ***Lenox 218*** restaurant (637-4218; 218 Main St., Lenox) is often graced with Marge Fick at the piano on Friday and Saturday evenings. ***All Seasons Lounge*** (637-4244, Rte. 7, Lenox) is the unlikely setting for lots of fun, with music nightly, a live jazz duo and dancing on weekends. Further down the road, ***Brannigan's*** (443-6223, Rte 7, Pittsfield) features the area's top bands, including Arlo Guthrie's back-up band, Shenendoah.

For lovers of folk and down-home country music, ***Bonny Rigg Inn*** (623-8784; in Becket on Jacobs Ladder Rd.) frequently can stir something up, as can Pittsfield's ***Itam Lodge*** (Waubeek Rd.). But the hottest club for down-home music is the ***Home Club*** (655-2206; up on Rte. 8, Hinsdale) where solid touring acts are booked, where you can see Gloria Curtis and the Country Classics, Easy Livin', and even Box Car Willie.

In Pittsfield itself, the mood is mostly upbeat. ***Jay's*** (442-0767; 1220 North St.) is one of the hotter new clubs, booking bands like Leon Savage, offering frequent comedy and a massive infusion of videos. Also new is the ***Misty Moonlight Diner*** (442-0028; 505 East St.), which offers occasional dancing, with a DJ to guide the mood. Mellowest of the clubs is probably ***La Cocina*** (499-4027; Wahconah St.). Though the fine musicians, such as the Brave Brothers, provide dynamic listening, the crowd can occasionally eclipse the performers. At the lofty ***Top of the Hilton Lounge*** (499-2000; Berkshire Hilton Inn, Berkshire Common), disc jockey Marc Denning keeps things spinning on weekend nights, while folksinger Ronnie Morris handles an occasional weekday evening.

Up the mountain, in the town of Washington, lie two of the county's most spacious rock clubs, ***Woody's Roadhouse*** (623-8302), and ***Bucksteep Manor*** (623-5535; off Washington Mountain Rd.). Woody's is vast; the rock music is driving,

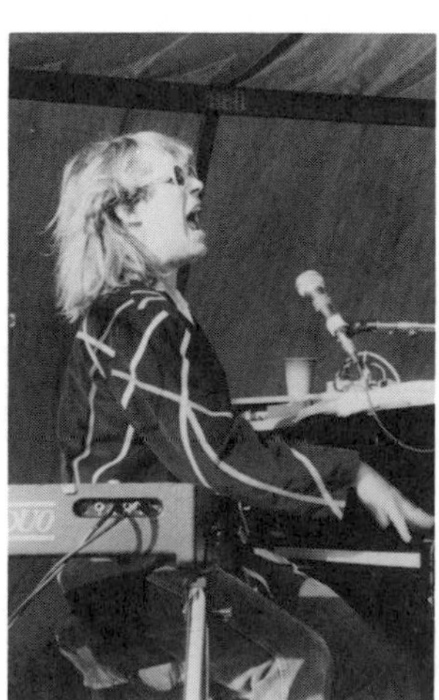

NRBQ's Terry Adams lets loose at Bucksteep Manor.

the crowds youngish. Bucksteep has a motley bunch of bands pass through their lofty music barn, from the clean-cut, good-time music of the Shy Americans to the truly folksy down-home rhythms of Burnt Bacon and the Homefries, from the electricity of The Generators to the obviously industrial strength sound of Vast Ed and the Fabulous Heavyweights. Out in Dalton, the ***Hard Hat Bar and Grill*** (684-9787; 26 Daly Ave.) books some wicked acts, recently offering Bruce Hayes and Wildlife.

In ***North County***, the ***Blarney Room*** at Brodie Mountain (443-4752; Rte 7, New Ashford) and ***Kelly's Irish Pub*** both present live music, such as Reception, and the Pickwell Brothers. Next mountain over, at Jiminy Peak, ***Drummond's Restaurant*** (445-5500; Jiminy Peak, Hancock) offers live jazz piano and the sound of Steve Murray's Little Big Band, on weekend evenings. ***The Springs*** (458-3465; Rte. 7, New Ashford) offers a pianist at the grand piano, on Fridays and Saturdays. Up Williamstown way, the old-sounding but new-feeling ***Williams Inn*** (458-9371; Main St., Williamstown) recently hosted Walt Lehman and his band, playing jazz. ***The Orchards*** (458-9611; Rte. 2) may continue to feature dinner theater and cabaret (see p. 65). And during the summer, the finest late evening entertainment in the county can be found at various Williamstown restaurants in the form of the ***Williamstown Theatre Festival Cabaret*** (597-3400), a combination of theater apprentices, students and current WTF stars. Don't be too shocked if you see Dick Cavett singing and dancing on stage a few feet from your table.

Just ***Outside the County***, over in Northampton, the ***Iron Horse*** (584-0610; 20 Center St.) presents the region's best and most regular folk and jazz, offering concerts with such local greats as blues guitarist Rory Block, and jazz legend, Wynton Marsalis.

THEATER

WILLIAMSTOWN THEATRE FESTIVAL
597-3400.
Box 517, Williamstown, MA 01267.
1000 Main St.
Season: Summer only.
Tickets: $8 to $21.

"Miracles every summer since 1955," raved *The Boston Globe*, and even without founding director Nikos Psacharopoulos, the miracles continue. The stars come out on Berkshire summer nights, and nowhere are they brighter than on stage at the Williamstown Theatre Festival. Here in a typical show you'll find the likes of Broadway and Hollywood luminaries Marsha Mason, Dick Cavett, Blythe Danner, Edward Herrmann, Richard Thomas, and Christopher Reeve — all performing live in the region's most sophisticated straw-hat theater.

Not long ago, *People* Magazine put it this way: "The showbiz capital of the U.S. may, for once, be on neither coast. The Williamstown Theatre Festival could boast the most powerful concentration of acting talent any place this summer."

For three decades, under the bold and creative direction of Nikos

Psacharopoulos, WTF provided a wide range of theatrical experience for audiences in the Berkshires. Since his death in 1989, the artistic vacuum that was part of his legacy has been amply filled, first by associates Austin Pendleton and Peter Hunt, then by Hunt alone.

A recent summer at WTF opened with an adaptation of Stephen Vincent Benet's epic poem, "John Brown's Body," starring Christopher Reeve. Wrote *NY Times* critic Mel Gussow: "*John Brown's Body* begins the company's 35th season on a note of eloquence." An eloquence that saturated the summer, being followed by *Henry IV, I, and II* (directed by Austin Pendleton); Tennessee Williams' *The Rose Tattoo*; and finally, Brecht's *Mother Courage*, starring Academy Award winner Olympia Dukakis. Each summer, in addition to mainstage, full-scale productions with first-rate sets and costumes, WTF offers other more intimate theater experiences. Late night musical cabaret, at the Williams Inn, serves as a showcase for the abundant young talent in the Second Company, and provides surprise cameo appearances by celebrities like Dick Cavett, inveterate songster and raconteur. There are Second Company plays, too, independent of the main stage. And for the naturalist in you, WTF offers the Free Theatre, outdoors in a meadow at the Buxton School. Here's a rare opportunity for a free theatrical picnic party, for you, your family and friends. You supply the lunch, WTF will supply the pastoral setting and complimentary, first-rate theater.

On Sunday afternoons, at the nearby, elegant Clark Art Institute, WTF presents a series of special events — poetry readings, literary adaptations and one-person shows. A typical WTF Sunday saw Blythe Danner and Frank Langella reading from the works of Zelda and F. Scott Fitzgerald. It's no mistake then that *Newsweek* ranked WTF as "the best of all American summer theaters," with "the cream of America's acting crop."

Nikos, Nikos, Where Art Thou?

Born in Athens, Nikos Psacharopoulos began producing theater when he was 15, came to America at 20, studied at Oberlin, then Yale, and blossomed into an immense talent by the time he came to the Berkshires, at age 27. Through his enormous charm, wit and vitality, Nikos staged great, moving dramas, and convinced powerful players to journey to Williamstown to perform. "Interesting plays, well done," was Nikos' formula, and he chose the works of playwrights such as Tennessee Williams, Ibsen, Shaw and Chekhov, attracting such major talent as Lee Grant, Frank Langella, Christopher Walken, and Joanne Woodward. A perfectionist by nature, Nikos wasn't always easy to work with, but he often undercut his temper with humor, as in the stage direction he once shouted: "You crissed when you should have crossed!" Whatever the means, the results were undeniable. Said Williamstown resident, stage and film star Christopher Reeve, a 20-year veteran of work with the director: "Nikos has done what they couldn't do in Brooklyn or Washington or at Lincoln Center. He has managed to achieve a national theater."

Maria Tucci and recent Tony Award winner James Naughton in WTF's production of "The Rose Tattoo."

T. Charles Erickson, courtesy Williamstown Theatre Festival.

SHAKESPEARE & COMPANY AT THE MOUNT
637-3353-box office;
637-1197 off season.
The Mount, Plunkett St.
Lenox, MA 01240.
On Plunket St. in Lenox, near southern jct. of Rtes. 7 & 7A.
Season: Summer only.
Tickets: $15 to $22.

Shakespeare is alive and well in the Berkshires, alive, that is, on stage in Lenox, at Edith Wharton's palatial estate, the Mount (see p. 95). A finer setting for the Bard's plays you could not imagine. Shakespeare & Company has made splendid use of the Mount's rolling lawn, performing most of their plays outdoors on a stage built in a glade against the lovely stone wall of a rose garden. Seating is either on your own blanket or on the company's low-slung aluminum chairs. Everyone's a groundling at these plays, and nearly everyone goes home elated, so energetic are the productions.

Under the powerful artistic guidance of English actor-director Tina Packer and her associate, Scottish vocal maestro Kristin Linklater, Shakespeare & Company has brought new light, feeling and clarity to Shakespeare's plays, making the works much more accessible to many people. The company does not cast or rehearse shows hurriedly. An arduous, continuous and multifaceted training process is the source for each play these actors present. By merging a perceptive British approach to the intricate nuances of Shakespeare with the emotional and physical directness of the best American acting, the Elizabethan texts are communicated with restored impact. Sit before these classic plays, and these players will make you understand words you never knew, scenes you never could fathom.

Frank Rich wrote in a *New York Times* review: "In the *Twelfth Night* I saw, their love of language was backed up by solid achievement. This was a verbally lucid and athletic production of the play. The actors' enthusiasm for their playwright is never less than infectious."

Part of that infectious quality is the actors' ability to treat the audience as their alter ego, always privy to secrets of the drama. The plays are staged all around the seating area; intimacy is inevitable, with stage and lighting design creating magical effects.

The company's inspired clowning is infectious, too. Says Tina Packer: "The function of the clowns is of the utmost importance in Shakespeare's plays. The influence of *comedia del arte* on Elizabethan theatre, with its knockabout and improvised humor, cannot be overemphasized. Because of the inordinate amount of 'seriousness' that has been attached to the 'Bard,' much of the sheer joy and fun of Shakespeare has been lost for modern audiences." Not so at the Mount where you're in for a good time.

The effervescent Karen Allen (center) sparkled through the Mount's woodland stage in "As You Like It."

Courtesy of Shakespeare & Company.

Besides their regular summer performances of Shakespeare, the company has a Schools Program in which a team of touring actors performs the plays and directs students in doing the same. And every winter, although not in the Berkshires, the company offers an intensive acting workshop, a 60-hour-per-week training in voice, dance, mask, sound, movement, combat, Shakespearean text, the role of the unconscious, actor-audience interaction, and First Folio analysis.

The company has toured, for performances and workshops, to Denver, Toronto and other cities. Under the aegis of Joe Papp's New York Shakespeare Festival, they have also taken productions from the Mount to Brooklyn's Prospect Park.

In our opinion, Shakespeare & Company is a "must see" for locals and visitors alike.

BERKSHIRE THEATRE FESTIVAL
298-5576; 298-5536

In 1887, architect Stanford White completed his design for the Stockbridge Casino Company, created for the "establishment and maintenance of a

off season.
Box 797, Stockbridge, MA 01262.
East Main St., Rte. 102, Stockbridge.
Season: Summer only.
Tickets: Main Stage, $10 to $25; Unicorn Theatre, $10, Children's Theatre, $2.50; students & senior citizens, 15% discount.
Gift shop.

place for a reading room, library and social meeting." Forty years later, when the structure had fallen into disuse, it was purchased by Mabel Choate, daughter of Ambassador Joseph H. Choate of Stockbridge. Miss Choate gave the building to the Three Arts Society which in turn moved the Casino to its present site at the foot of Yale Hill, then rented it to Alexander Kirkland and F. Cowles Strickland. In cooperation with a group of Yale Drama School students, Kirkland and Strickland opened the Berkshire Playhouse in 1928.

Since that time, the Berkshire Playhouse, later renamed Berkshire Theatre Festival, has fostered the development and presentation of American drama. Major works by nearly every American playwright of note have been performed here, including plays by Lillian Hellmann, Tennessee Williams, Eugene O'Neill and Thornton Wilder. The playhouse produced Wilder's *Our Town* and *The Skin of Our Teeth*, with Wilder himself playing featured roles.

The Berkshire Theatre Festival, designed as the Stockbridge Casino by Stanford White.

In the summer of 1930, a budding actress named Katherine Hepburn came to Stockbridge to further her training at the Berkshire Playhouse. She first appeared in Barrie's *The Admirable Crichton*, and then was given the lead in a play called *A Romantic Young Lady.*

Other players arrived in Stockbridge already closer to stardom. Ethel Barrymore, James Cagney, Tallulah Bankhead, Ruth Gordon, Gene Hackman, Anne Bancroft, Dustin Hoffman, Al Pacino, Frank Langella and Joanne Woodward are among the many prominent actors and actresses who have played the Berkshire Theatre Festival.

A recent season saw *Lute Song*, an adaptation of a Chinese classic, directed and choreographed by Marge Champion; *Tête-à-Tête*, a witty portrait of the relationship between Simone de Beauvoir and Jean Paul Sartre; *The Middle Ages*, A.R. Gurney's romantic interlude with a modern-day Robin Hood and his reluctant Maid Marian; and finally, Harold Pinter's *Betrayal*, a journey on the knife edge of disenchantment, following a love affair in reverse. Under the artistic direction of Richard Dunlap, this was a summer of strong theater, with lots of laughs, often undercut by the realities of life.

The last two decades have been a period of growth and refocusing for BTF. In the spring of 1976, the building was entered on the National Register of Historic Places. Since then, gradual refurbishment has continued.

The Theatre Festival has expanded its educational and rehearsal facilities, principally upon the gift of the Lavan Center (formerly Beaupré Art School), a few miles north of the playhouse. Interns and apprentices live at the center and rehearse there, while pursuing a program of classes in acting, voice, movement and design.

BTF also features shows at its 100-seat Unicorn Theatre, a showcase for younger artists. For the local community, BTF has several outreach programs, offering discount tickets to the elderly and dramatic production of prize-winning plays written by local grade schoolers.

BERKSHIRE PUBLIC THEATRE
445-4634 & 445-4631.
Box 860, Pittsfield, MA 01202.
30 Union St., in the center of town.
Season: Year-round.
Tickets: $9 to $16, students & senior citizens $2 off.
Gift shop.

A theatrical powerhouse of local dramatic talent, The Berkshire Public Theatre has quickly evolved toward its goal of being the county's only year-round, regional repertory theater. And so it looks like artistic director Frank Bessel's dream will come true.

Frank Bessel likes to call his theater "The Public" with a nod to Joe Papp in New York. Under Bessel's leadership, BPT has always attracted talent, and of late, the theater has won financial support as well. In the grand old Union Square Vaudeville Theatre, opened in 1912, and recently purchased for the BPT

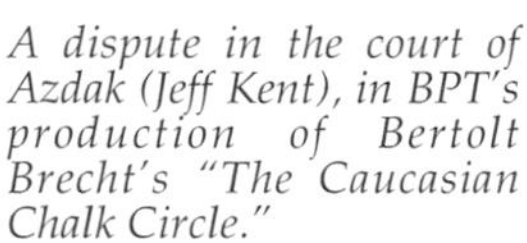

A dispute in the court of Azdak (Jeff Kent), in BPT's production of Bertolt Brecht's "The Caucasian Chalk Circle."

Everidge Productions, courtesy of the Berkshire Public Theatre.

by the city, Bessel's group has a wonderful work-play space, a space they're restoring, expanding and sharing.

Such local artists as the Berkshire Lyric Theatre, Mixed Company, the Robbins-Zust Family Marionettes and the Olga Dunn Dance Company have all used the BPT stage to good effect.

Theatrically, Bessel's company has evolved tremendously over the years. Early on, in another space, they recreated the magical moods of Dylan Thomas' *Under Milkwood*; there have been outdoor spectacles at Wahconah Park Stadium, including *Jesus Christ Superstar* in 1981 and *Hair* in 1982; *Moby Dick, On Stage* was presented in Herman Melville's pasture at his home, Arrowhead. Performances in a recent fall season included: *Remember My Name*, a searing patchwork of impressions from the AIDS quilt members; *The Haunted Theatre*, some good, clean horrifying fun; and a musical revue by Tommy DeFrantz.

Whatever one thinks of individual shows at the Berkshire Public Theatre, it's hard not to applaud the general enterprise. For bringing powerful year-round theater to the Berkshires, Frank Bessel and friends deserve a heart-felt Bravo!

MUSIC THEATRE GROUP/LENOX ARTS CENTER
298-3400; 212-924-3108 off season.
During season: Box 128, Stockbridge, MA 01262.
Off season: 735 Washington St., New York, NY 10014.
From Stockbridge: W. on Rte. 102, right on Rte. 183 N., right at Congregational Church sign, turn left on Willard Hill Rd.
From Lenox: S. on Rte. 183, 4 1/2 mi., left at Congregational Church sign & follow as above.
Closed Sept.-Mid-June.
Tickets: $15 to $20.

For their innovative and penetrating explorations of music-theater, the Music Theatre Group/Lenox Arts Center has won 20 Obie awards in New York, and they bring to the Berkshires a world-class adventure for all lovers of music and drama. Under the leadership of producing director Lyn Austin, the group has tackled difficult, esoteric works and created ones that are close to sublime.

"The Music-Theatre Group blazes trails...," raved The Boston Globe, and in a recent summer, they presented two dramas and three readings. *Paradise for the Worried*, a witty look at the manners and mores of pre-WW I society, was good fun, and called by *The New York Times* "dazzingly distinctive." And *Legacy* was a haunting reminiscence of country life, as described by Breece D'J Pancake, a writer who Joyce Carol Oates has compared to Hemingway. Three other literate evenings heard poetess Honor Moore reading from her work, actress Kathryn Walker reading from a William Alfred anthology, as well as an evening of readings from the works of Hawthorne, Melville and other Berkshire writers.

Productions are staged at the classically Victorian 100-seat Citizen's Hall, which crowns a hilltop in the Interlaken section of Stockbridge. Theater here is minimally staged; the emphasis is more on script and musical development, as many of these works prepare for a New York run.

Said *The New York Times*: "The Music-Theatre Group/Lenox Arts Center has produced one of the most innovative and original bodies of work in American theatre."

OTHER THEATER

There are more than a dozen other theater companies scattered about the Berkshire Hills.

In South County, the biggest little theater in the world is ***Mixed Company*** (528-2320; at the Granary, 37 Rosseter St., Great Barrington), where fall-off-your-seat comedy alternates with moving drama. Under the direction of Joan Ackermann and Gillian Seidl, Mixed Company has built a solid following, and there is often competition for the theater's few dozen seats. Ackermann's award-winning *Zara Spook and Other Lures* premiered here, as did her droll *Bed and Breakfast*, in which she played an addled Mrs. Digby. The company has settled into an annual presentation of Ackermann's Christmas fable for the stressed-out *Yonder Peasant*, and occasionally they feature New York revivals, like *Greater Tuna*, a laugh-till-you-cry look at the foibles of the Greater Tuna, Texas radio listening area. More fun than a barrel of monkeys. And with considerably greater charm, too.

Central County's theater scene has never been livelier. ***The Berkshire Community College Players*** regularly stage productions at BCC (499-0886; West St., Pittsfield) and the Berkshire Museum (443-7171; 39 South St., Pittsfield) sometimes hosts touring and local theater groups. ***The Town Players*** (443-9279) also occasionally perform at either BCC or the Berkshire Museum, and in a recent season, they presented *I'm Not Rappaport.*

North County is especially theatrical. Besides the Williamstown Theatre Festival, Williamstown has five other theater companies, loosely grouped in a consortium called ***Summer Stages***. These include the Berkshire Ensemble for Theatre Arts; Calliope Theatre Company; the Starlight Stage Youth Theatre; Thespis; and the Springstreet Ensemble Theatre. ***Berkshire Ensemble for Theatre Arts*** (458-9441) has recently staged a New Music Theatre Festival, at the Clark, and a cabaret based on Studs Terkel's *Working*, at the Williams College Faculty Club. ***Calliope Theatre Company*** (458-9161) was founded by four local female playwrights, and continues to offer innovative drama, most recently, *Droga the Dragon*, a fantasy adventure staged in the woods behind the Clark. The ***Starlight Stage Youth Company*** (458-4273), features young area residents who perform at the First Congregational Church. ***Thespis*** (458-8266),is a local non-Equity company that also performs at the Clark, recently staging Kurt Vonnegut's *Happy Birthday, Wanda June*. ***The Springstreet Ensemble Theatre*** is aimed at experimental drama, questing unusual plays and different interpretations of familiar ones, performing at the Log, on Spring Street.

After such a busy summer season of theater, the fall-winter slack is picked up by ***Williamstheatre***, the Williams College theatre group (597-2342; Adams Memorial Theatre), producing impressive revivals of plays by the likes of Brecht and Becket; and by the drama department at ***North Adams State College*** (664-4511), whose fare recently ran from Ibsen to Rogers and Hammerstein. Finally, the ***Williamstown Community Theatre*** (458-5833) performs two or three productions a year, an annual cabaret, a freebie at the Clark, one-act plays and an occasional radio play.

Outside the County, in neighboring Chatham, New York, just west of Central Berkshire, the ***Mac-Haydn Theatre*** (518-392-9292; Rte. 203), has been offering 15-week-long summer seasons of robust Broadway musicals since 1969. Productions are staged in the round, and their high-energy casts are guaranteed to deliver a supercharge of musical theater. Less than truly sophisticated and a bit out of the way, but usually a whole lot of fun. ***Proctor's***, in Schenectady (518-346-6204), the ***Egg*** in Albany (518-443-5111), and ***StageWest*** in Springfield (781-2340) all provide top-quality theatrical experiences, expanding the Berkshire options even further.

SEASONAL EVENTS

There are a number of special Berkshire events tuned to the weather, and somehow the Berkshire year wouldn't unfold properly without them.

The two-man saw competition at the Tyringham Fair.

Berkshire Crafts Fair is a mid-August event, held at Monument Mountain Regional High School (528-3346; Rte. 7, between Stockbridge and Great Barrington). Top local and regional craftspeople offer their extraordinary creations.

A Christmas Carol by Charles Dickens has been read for many a Christmas now; and for some years, there's been a live reading at the Stockbridge Library. Usually a week or two before Christmas, this little-publicized event is worth watching for. The Berkshire Theatre Festival often has a hand in the casting of indigenous Scrooges and Tiny Tims. Outstanding dramatizations of the story are staged annually by the Berkshire Public Theatre, in Pittsfield. And God Bless You, one and all.

Downtown Days on a weekend in July in Pittsfield brings you the grand Ethnic Fair, a classic car show, historic exhibits, and a gang of children's activities. Pittsfield's 1991 centennial celebration makes it even bigger, better and brighter.

Downtown, Live! regales midday visitors in Pittsfield with live concerts from the end of June to the end of August every Friday at noon on the steps of the city hall. Sponsored by Pittsfield Central, which is made up of the Downtown

Business Association and several other groups, the concerts feature every kind of music, from Dixieland to rock, blues, folk, and jazz.

Fireworks over Stockbridge Bowl are spectacular because of echoes from the hills. The biggest bangs and most colorful starbursts come from Tanglewood, on the Fourth of July, and following the 1812 Overture at the end of "Tanglewood on Parade" which closes the BSO Berkshire season in late August.

The Great Barrington Fair provides every camp-and nostalgia-lover a chance to step out of time and become a bit player in the carny drama of yesteryear. Fascinating agricultural exhibits, a restored fair grounds and renewed horse racing make this fair a highlight of the harvest season.

Greylock Rambles are hikes and climbs to and around the lofty top of Mt. Greylock in North County. Sponsored by the Appalachian Mountain Club and the Williams College Outing Club, the walks are often narrated by well-informed guides. Best time to go? Fall foliage, of course.

Harvest Festival at the Berkshire Garden Center (recently renamed the Berkshire Botanical Garden), Stockbridge (see p. 245) is a fall event packed with seasonal goodies such as cider and doughnuts, apples and pumpkins, crafts and workshops, haywagon and fire engine rides, plants and seeds, and mayhem of all sorts appealing to children and grownups of every persuasion.

The Great Josh Billings RunAground is likely Berkshire's greatest one-day party, an athletic extravaganza that involves thousands of participants and many more admiring, supportive spectators. This late September biking-canoeing-running triathalon takes its name from Lanesborough's Henry Wheeler Shaw, a 19th-century inveterate prankster, who fashioned something of a career for himself as a humorist, under the pen name of Josh Billings. "If a fellow gets to going down hill, it seems as if everything were greased for the occasion," wrote Billings (more or less); and every fall at the RunAground the bike racers, shooting down that last hill on Rte. 183 to Stockbridge Bowl, prove how right old Josh was.

One of Billings' greatest fans was President Abraham Lincoln, who once interrupted a cabinet meeting to read aloud the humorist's "Essay on the Mule." Tickled beyond reason, Lincoln remarked, "Next to William Shakespeare, Josh Billings is the greatest judge of human nature the world has ever seen." Farfetched? One critic saw in Josh, "Aesop and Ben Franklin, condensed and abridged." And as you bike your butt off from Great Barrington, or paddle your back out around Stockbridge Bowl, or run yourself ragged climbing up to Tanglewood, or as you do all three as some "Iron Men" and "Iron Women" do, or as you watch a friend in the race, remember the words of Josh Billings: "Be sure you are right, then go ahead; but in case of doubt, go ahead anyway." After the race, there's a huge party at Tanglewood with food, drink, dancing and Berkshire camaraderie.

The Monument Mountain Author Climb is a literary event commemorating the August day in 1851 when Melville, Hawthorne, Holmes and friends scaled the Great Barrington peak. They imbibed a good deal of champagne, weathered a thunderstorm, read William Cullen Bryant's poem about the Indian maiden who threw herself in sorrow from the top, and began a lasting friendship. Watch *The Berkshire Eagle* in late July for an announcement.

Naumkeag at Christmas is extra-special, because that's when the Choates' Christmas decorations are taken out and the house is made to look ever so festive. The historic home in Stockbridge (see p. 97) offers this opportunity to the public on an irregular basis.

Summerfest in Great Barrington has become a highlight on South County's early summer schedule. Held on a Saturday evening in mid-June, the last edition was the most successful ever, raising thousands of dollars for Hospice of South Berkshire, and raising the spirits of thousands who attended. With the entire downtown closed off to motor traffic, locals and visitors have a grand old time — listening to music, watching dance or magic, admiring the classic cars, or gnoshing on various snack foods. Dozens of performers, from the Olga Dunn Dancers to the Bluestars contribute their time and talent, making this a community celebration of unqualified good cheer.

The Tea Ceremony at Great Barrington Pottery is a moving meditation, a highly stylized form of social communion for both the Tea Mistress and those she serves. Enter the *Chashitsu* (Japanese Ceremonial Teahouse and Formal Garden) at Richard Bennett's Great Barrington Pottery (see p. 269), and you'll be taken back in time to 14th-century Japan. Leading with the concept of *wabi* – quiet simplicity – both the building and the slow-moving ceremony gently harmonize you. Bow, as you must, to enter the ceremonial washing area, and follow the Tea Guide's instruction in the proper ritual cleansing. Then follow her, bowing, through the low door into the teahouse itself, a structure four-and-a-half *tatami* mats in size. In the *tokonoma*, or ceremonial alcove, observe the calligraphy, and below it, note the grace, elegance and appropriateness of the flower arrangement, a bouquet the Tea Mistress has made especially to meet the mood of this day. Then observe the silent power of the Tea Mistress, for whom serving tea is "The Way." The menu may be limited, but the Tea Ceremony at Great Barrington Pottery offers the most gracious service in the Berkshires.

VIDEO RENTALS

South County

Alice in Videoland (528-4451; 301 Stockbridge Rd. [Rte. 7], Gt. Barrington).
Impoco's (528-9162; 54 State Rd. [Rte. 7], Gt. Barrington).
Video File (243-0468; 60 Main St., Lee).
Video Shed (243-0743; 152 W. Park St., Lee).
West Stockbridge Video (232-7851; Main St., W. Stockbridge).

Central County

Action Video (499-4208; 44 S. Main St. [Rte. 7], Lanesborough).
East Street Video (443-2000; 10 Lyman, Pittsfield).
Either/Or Bookstore (499-1705; 122 North St., Pittsfield).
Master Darkroom and Video (443-9763; 758 Tyler St., Pittsfield. 499-7989; 89 W. Housatonic St., Pittsfield).
Plaza Video (443-0943; 444 W. Housatonic St., Pittsfield).
Pontoosuc Video (445-7525; S. Main St., Lanesborough).
Variety Video (637-2046; Housatonic St., Lenox).
Video Studio 12 (447-7595; 180 Elm St., Pittsfield).

North County

Adams Video (663-5440; 85 Main St., N. Adams).
Adventure Land Video (662-2896; North Adams Plaza, N. Adams).
A and T Video Rental (458-5503; 406 Main St., Williamstown).
Sound Investment (743-4919; 83 Park St., Adams).
The Wholesale Connection (663-8953; 746 State Rd., N. Adams).

CHAPTER FIVE
Pleasing the Palate
RESTAURANTS AND FOOD PURVEYORS

Luncheon on Mom's new riverside deck.

As "The Inland Newport" of the Gilded Age, Berkshire would need its complement of *haute cuisine* dining rooms and gourmet purveyors. Today, some of the county's best restaurants are found in the "cottages" of that era, at Orleton, now called the Gateways, and at Blantyre and Wheatleigh. But there is great dining in more humble Berkshire settings, too, in pre-Revolutionary farmhouses, old mills and inns.

The number of restaurants in the county is vast — upwards of 200. There are dozens of specialty food suppliers, too, engaging alternatives to supermarkets. We concentrated on the establishments we found most interesting and most successful. An old adage says: *De gustibus non disputandum* — there is no accounting for taste, and our travels surely confirmed this. We've made every effort to account for the idiosyncrasies of various palates. Our research team included a lover of spicy dishes, one who likes little seasoning, people with differing tastes. In the spirit of candid reporting, we hope you'll agree the risks of critical judgment are worth taking. From our gourmet tour, we have assembled an honest guide to Berkshire eateries and food suppliers, one that steers you right past the chaff to the wheat.

A dining experience has many dimensions. The food, of course, is primary, and must be skillfully prepared from the freshest, best quality ingredients available. The menu ought to be imaginative, a reminder that we're dining out. Presentation is important, too, not only in service but in the arrangement of individual plates. Just as aroma is essential to taste, so too is an appetizing appearance.

Ambiance is critical as well; for if you're not comfortable during a meal, even good food won't sit well. Here a restaurateur needs to pay attention to the feelings evoked by architecture, decor, seating arrangements, table settings and formality of service. Background music is a key issue but is often mistakenly left to an anonymous DJ or, worse, to Muzak.

Good service is a critical craft. Besides being well groomed and cheerful, a good waiter or waitress must be swift of foot and deft of hand. He or she must be attentive without being intrusive, perfectly knowledgeable about the restaurant's fare, and friendly only to the degree asked for. An effective waiter is a master of timing, delicately balancing the chef's need to cook many dishes simultaneously with the customers' need for the meal to proceed at *their* pace.

We found it equally easy in Berkshire to spend $5 or $25 for a meal, and in several instances would prefer the bargain food and the service and ambiance that came with it. Remember: we designate each restaurant with a price code, signifying the approximate cost of a meal, including appetizer, entrée and dessert, but not cocktails, wine, tax or tip. Restaurants with a *prix fixe* menu are noted accordingly.

Reviews are organized first by section of the county, then alphabetically by town, then by restaurant name. Food purveyors are grouped alphabetically by type, then by name of establishment. Every entry appears in the general Index too.

Bon appetit!

Dining Price Codes

Inexpensive	up to $15
Moderate	$15 - $20
Expensive	$20 - $30
Very Expensive	over $30

Credit Cards

AE - American Express
CB - Carte Blanche
D - Discover
DC - Diner's Club
MC - MasterCard
V - Visa

Meals

B - Breakfast
L - Lunch
SB - Sunday Brunch
D - Dinner

RESTAURANTS SOUTH COUNTY

North Egremont

ELM COURT INN
528-0325.
Rte. 71, N. Egremont.
Closed: Mon.-Tues. in winter.
Price: Expensive.
Cuisine: Continental.

The Elm Court has changed hands, and what had been a very fine restaurant is even better. New hosts Urs and Glee Bieri continue the Elm Court's Swiss tradition, bringing a polish and imagination that lifts the dining experience to great heights. In the pleasantly redecorated dining rooms, there's

Serving: D.
Credit Cards: MC, V.
Reservations: Recommended.
Special Features: Fireplaces.

candlelight on the table, a crackling fire in the nearby fireplace.

Glee is from Connecticut, and she handles the dining room, ensuring her guests' good times. Urs is Swiss, and before coming to the Berkshires, he was executive chef at the United Nations, overseeing an international feast that had to satisfy thousands of discriminating diners daily. At the Elm Court, he's able to concentrate his substantial culinary talents on far fewer meals, and the results are extraordinary. Complimentary crackers and *pâté* start the meal on a promising note. A freshly baked, still warm loaf follows, continuing the appeal. Both black bean soup and French onion soup are superior, as is chef Bieri's salad. The onion soup features a first-class Gruyère lid; the salad, a lively mix of endive, watercress, celeriac, romaine and radichio, dressed with a delicious creamy herb dressing.

The Elm Court's wine list offers a nice range of French, Swiss, German, Italian and California bottles, at surprisingly affordable prices. Many good wines are priced around $15, with some of the best up around $100. Service is superior - from wine uncorking and icing to table crumbing and meal timing - and our waitress could confidently tell us just what was in the filet of sole's sauce. A light *hollandaise* with diced tomatoes and herbs was the answer, and it made this very subtle fish leap off the plate in taste. Veal *Picatta* with *Risotto* and Filet Goulash *Forestière* was also excellent, the goulash made with the tenderest filet mignon. The very fresh broccoli and carrots as well as the superior Swiss *rosti* made vegetable eating a pure pleasure. And the outstanding, artful presentation of each plate enhanced their complete appeal.

The menu changes daily at Elm Court, but truly awesome desserts are standard fare here. The whipped cream served on most of these is about the finest we've tasted — stiff, rich and only slightly sweetened. Pear Tarte is at once hearty and delicate, with a thick, cakey crust. The *Mont Blanc*, a small mountain of meringue and chocolate ice cream, is encased in a nest of chestnut purée, topped with a pinnacle of whipped cream and surrounded by swirls of fresh raspberry sauce. The regulars who were dining near us, however, wouldn't even consider it, the Chocolate *Mousse* Cake being a part of their frequent nights out at Elm Court. A nice touch, the dessert menu also offers eight cognacs, two armagnacs, two ports and four cordials. No wonder you'll have to call the Elm Court for a reservation on weekend and holiday nights.

South Egremont

THE EGREMONT INN
528-2111.
Old Sheffield Rd., S. Egremont.
On side street off Rte. 23 in center of village.
Closed: Mon.-Tues.
Price: Moderate to expensive.

Since 1780, the Egremont Inn has welcomed travelers, offering charming, tidy rooms and hearty fare. In its latest incarnation, under the stewardship of innkeeper John Black, the inn is bedecked with a fresh paint job, a dash of elegance, and a personable new host. Dining here has an old-fashioned, village-pub atmosphere matched by precious few other Berkshire restaurants. Proceed at your own pace —

Cuisine: American.
Serving: SB, D.
Credit Cards: DC, MC, V.

stop at the long woody bar and have a drink; there's usually somebody interesting to meet, and there's always the dart board nearby, to measure your shot before and after dinner.

Your meal could happen in the tavern room, or in one of the four dining rooms adjoining. If it's a cool night, you'll almost certainly find yourself beside one of the inn's many crackling hearths. On your table will be fine linens, china, crystal, candlelight and a seasonal bouquet. With the convivial bar life spilling into the dining rooms, and intelligent, assured service, you're likely to feel comfortable and cared for here. From a wine list nicely illustrated with the bottles' labels, we chose an Argentine cabernet sauvignon, from an Andean vineyard (Mendoza). This 1985 vintage proved to be as full bodied and robust as its French cousins. Alas, our dinners themselves proved uneven on a recent outing, with several dishes failing to satisfy because of unmarried ingredients. One entrée, however, showed the capability of the inn's new chef — Duck with Port, Ginger, Pear Sauce. This was superb, a medley of flavors in unusual and delicious counterpoint.

In warm weather, the inn serves a Sunday brunch out on its curved porch, and the meals we've enjoyed out there have given us the sure feeling that all's right with the world.

THE GASLIGHT STORE
528-0870.
Rte. 23, S. Egremont.
Price: Inexpensive.
Cuisine: American.
Serving: B, L, SB; D (Fri. & Sat).

Though the Gaslight has spruced itself up, it's still one of the quaintest, old-time country cafes in the Berkshires. Tablecloths are still checkered, penny candy's holding steady at a penny, and the early-morning blueberry pancakes continue to satisfy the ravenous. For lunch, there are burgers and sandwiches of several varieties, and best of all, the Gaslight serves essential brews like egg cream and root beer float.

JOHN ANDREW'S
528-3469.
Rte. 23, S. Egremont.
W. of village 2.5 mi.
Price: Moderate.
Closed: Wed. in winter.
Cuisine: American.
Serving: D, Sat. brunch.
Credit Cards: MC, V.
Reservations: Recommended.
Special Features: Terrace dining; Fireplace.

Another star is rising in Berkshire's culinary constellation! Dan Smith, and his wife, Susan, have taken over Sebastian's and, with appropriate reverence for such a legacy, have transformed a fine restaurant into an even finer one. Sip a drink in the sleek, modern bar or at the windowed alcove nearby. Either way, the mood is sophisticated and relaxing. Then choose your dining room: either the polished main room or the glassed-in porch out back. From the porch, lovely vistas of the restaurant's back yard are part of the menu.

With recent stints at the Ragamont Inn in Salisbury, Connecticut, and then as chef at Sebastian's, Dan comes to his new challenge well prepared. His menu at John Andrew's is as appealing as it is savory. Appetizers range from Chilled Oysters, Shallots and Balsamic Vinegar to a mouth-watering Eggplant and Roasted Garlic Terrine.

Cured Salmon served on Corn Crêpes with Sour Cream and Chives was a splendid counterpoint of tastes, the smoky salmon, slightly sweet crêpe (closer to a fritter, really), sour cream and chives delighting different parts of the palate and pleasing nearly every taste bud. Salads were nearly as successful and creative, with absolutely fresh greens.

Pastas are quite fine here, especially Fresh Basil Spaghetti, Clams, Fresh Tomatoes, Garlic and Olive Oil; and Ravioli of Blue Crab with Fresh Chervil and Sauvignon Blanc Sauce. Since half-orders of the pasta are available, they make an intriguing side dish. But the entrées are so ample, you may want to move right along to the main course, one of whose hallmarks is stunning presentation. On oversize, black plates, each entrée and its accompanying vegetables (often snow peas and asparagus) are artfully and dramatically arranged. Chef Smith has a fine hand with his seasonings, and each entree is redolent with his sensitivity. Grilled Shrimp, Buckwheat Pasta and Tomato Sauce here is as pretty as it is tasty; the Cured Loin of Pork, Grain Mustard, Pinot Noir Sauce is meaty, succulent, and sassy. Roast Duck with Ginger and Lingonberry Sauce is suitably rich, wonderfully tart and sweet simultaneously. The accompanying wild rice is first class, the entrée altogether hearty yet delicate.

Desserts at John Andrew's are simple but satisfying. Raspberry-Blueberry Pie is a standout. We found the wine list well rounded, service attentive, and ambiance convivial. Elegant floral arrangements by Catherine Brumley add an extra note of sophistication and beauty. From sideboard to table, John Andrews has arrived in style.

MOM'S
528-2414.
Rte. 23, S. Egremont.
Price: Inexpensive.
Cuisine: American & Italian.
Serving: B, D, L.
Credit Cards: None.

Despite novelist Nelson Algren's recommendation that you "Never eat in a place called `Mom's,' " this one is holding the course. It's a brookside, woody dining room (with a nifty deck over the water), serving breakfast and lunch all day long and dinners on many nights. The restaurant has changed owners but continues to provide satisfying, simple food. Mom's has one of the few open kitchens in the county, with the pots and pans hanging from a wheel above. Omelets such as the Feta and Tomato are excellent; sandwiches are meaty and flavorful. Side dishes such as homefries are outstanding, neatly served with bits of fresh scallion on top. Homemade baked goods, such as the raspberry pie, have diners cooing. Just like Mom's!

THE OLD MILL
528-1421.
Rte. 23, S. Egremont.
Closed: Mon. in winter.
Price: Moderate to expensive.
Cuisine: American.
Serving: D.
Credit Cards: AE, CB, DC, MC, V.
Reservations: Recom-

In the beautifully restored 1797 grist mill at the center of South Egremont, Britisher Terry Moore and his wife, Julie, run the Old Mill, one of southern Berkshire's most popular dining spots. Look inside the Old Mill, and you'll understand why. With its 18th-century proportions, its simple exposed beam construction, and the artistry of its decor, the Old Mill welcomes you, offering elegance without pretension. Its classy old bar serves as comfortable accommoda-

Grace and simplicity at the Old Mill.

mended for parties of 5 or more.
Special Features: Private dining room; Fireplaces.

tion for those awaiting dining room tables, and for the many who prefer the bar's more intimate seating and simpler fare.

The main dining room was once the mill's blacksmith shop, and the anvil's massive stone foundation still sits surrounded by centuries-old wide-board flooring. Both this flooring and the white stucco walls bear a few, very sparing painted stencils. The walls are further hung with the Mill's collection of antique food choppers and sauerkraut shredders. Stunning floral arrangements by Barbara Bockbrader complement this gentle, beautiful interior. Happily, both staff and cuisine match the splendid ambiance. Waiters, waitresses and young buspersons all wear neckties, some looking more from the British Berkshires than the American; service is friendly, attentive, and intelligent.

The Old Mill's menu is simple by *haute cuisine* standards, but therein lies its winning way. Many entrées are broiled; sauces are sparing. Using ingredients such as the fresh imported Norwegian salmon and Dover sole that the Mill's purveyor has flown in thrice weekly, the kitchen consistently turns out first-class meals. Entrées of note on a recent night included smoked pork chops with red cabbage, and a sautéed shrimp with artichokes and mushrooms. Desserts are memorable, and the *profiteroles au chocolat* are surely the best for many miles around. These tiny ice-cream-filled puff pastries tend to disappear quickly from your plate, occasionally inciting wicked contemplations of seconds.

THE WEATHERVANE INN
528-9580.
Rte. 23, S. Egremont.
Price: Expensive.
Cuisine: International.
Serving: D.
Credit Cards: DC, MC, V.
Reservations: Recommended.
Special Features: Private dining room.

This may be a cozy New England inn, but prepare yourself for a worldwide culinary adventure! With the kitchen under the direction of Burmese-born Olena Rajan Murphy, the Weathervane takes a giant leap into heavenly cuisine.

"Discipline, organization, tenacity, and a respect for ingredients," these are the virtues Olena's mother instilled in her, the chef says. "We don't have cookbooks in Burma," Olena explains. "Everything I serve I learned to cook from my mother." So it's

Mom's home cooking, Burmese style, that you'll dine on at the Weathervane. But it's also a precocious daughter's culinary explorations that you'll taste here, as Olena offers dishes that range from Louisiana Catfish Sautée to Panfried Quail with Guava and Passion Fruit Compote; from Peruvian Fish Chowder to Grilled Bluefin Tuna with Sesame Creme and Marinated Daikon. More "conventional" fare, such as Chicken Egremont (with Boursin and Fresh Spinach) and Smoked Pork Chop with Brandied Apple Slices is also offered, and even these manage to convey new and delicious flavors.

Chef Olena Rajan Murphy introduces one of her international feasts, at the Weathervane.

Olena cooks with her mother's four culinary virtues, and she cooks with love and passion as well. For a Burmese feast we attended, the first of many such special International Dinners, Olena spent days shopping, combing specialty grocery stores and food purveyors in New York and Boston. The result was *Mya-Ma*, an 11-course Burmese blowout that took dozens of lucky diners into new territories of taste. Subsequent extravaganzas here have explored the delights of Middle Eastern and other Southeast Asian cooking. We suggest you call ahead for a schedule of special dinners.

The Weathervane — for a taste of the world at its most wonderful.

WINDFLOWER INN
528-2720.
Rte. 23, Gt. Barrington.
Price: Expensive-*Prix fixe*.
Cuisine: Eclectic.
Serving: D.
Credit Cards: None.
Reservations: Required.
Special Features: Non-smoking area; Outdoor dining; Fireplace.

When you call for reservations at Windflower (as you must), they'll tell you right out they accept no credit cards and there's no smoking in the dining room. Their most recent policy has you calling by noon to hear that evening's selection of entrées, from which you're expected to choose, on the spot. As convenient as this is for the kitchen, it allows little flexibility in your party. Despite these restrictions, quite a good meal awaits you at the Windflower. The atmosphere is country casual, the pace unhurried.

A recent evening menu featured an appealing Herbed Brie in Phylo or Potato Leek Soup as starters, both of which hit the mark. One of the best house salads in Berkshire followed, a super fresh mix of red leaf lettuce, carefully chopped red pepper and cucumber, a generous sprinkling of feta cheese, and a fine vinaigrette. Three entrées were offered: Veal Marsala, Shrimp *Provençale* and Duck in Plum Sauce. The duck made a superior meal, and a nearby diner, a New York magistrate, judged it finer than any of the dozens he'd sampled in the Big Apple. Neither gamy nor fat, this duck's crispy skin was deliciously glazed with a thick and sweet yet tart sauce. The wild rice and asparagus accompanying the entrées was well cooked all right, but retained little taste to counterpoint the fish or meat.

Fingerbowls preceded dessert, a welcome respite from eating. The desserts themselves were deadly: a multi-flavored ice cream cake laced with a liqueur, and a multi-layered torte with several different jams.

After your meal at Windflower, you might adjourn to the living room to chat or just sit by the fire and digest. On your way out, look over the inn's guest book where the micro-stories and thanks of scores of pleased guests are inscribed. Perhaps you'll add your own.

Great Barrington

CASTLE STREET CAFE
528-5244.
10 Castle St., Gt. Barrington.
Closed: Tues.
Price: Moderate to expensive
Cuisine: American, French, Italian.
Serving: D.
Credit Cards: D, MC, V.
Special Features: Cruvinet wine bar.

A new gem in Great Barrington's crown! Chef-owner Michael Ballon has transformed a previously jinxed restaurant space into one of the liveliest and most consistently satisfying eating establishments in Berkshire. The decor is straightforward upscale bistro with *de rigeur* exposed brick walls, white linen tablecloths, fresh flowers and a handsome, inviting bar at the back of the dining room — a great spot for a cool drink late on a summer's night or a hot toddy after the movies at the nearby Mahaiwe. The bar is equipped with a *cruvinet* to keep several special wines fresh even though opened: a nice touch for diners who may want only a glassful but who want something better than standard restaurant house wine. Table service is top-notch — attentive, well informed and prompt. Unlike many other sophisticated restaurants which turn away the dessert and coffee crowd, Castle Street treats everyone with the same warmth and welcome.

A principal ingredient of chef Ballon's excellence is his reliance on the best local suppliers for everything fresh — from goat cheese to French bread to produce. The menu tips its hat to these Berkshire provisioners by listing them prominently, a friendly custom we'd like to see more often. Even on busy nights, the Castle Street chefs find time to schmooze with the crowd, affording diners the opportunity to ask about certain dishes or offer a word of praise. There is much here to applaud.

The eclectic menu combines French, Italian and American influences, sometimes in traditional dishes like *Cassoulet* (from southwestern France) and sometimes in more adventurous dishes like Eggplant *Roulade*, stuffed with three cheeses, an entrée one might associate with the new cuisine from California. Flavor, color, aroma and all-around zestiness characterize the cooking here.

Vegetarians and carnivores alike have a good range of choices. On our many visits we have enjoyed entrées such as perfect *Fettucine Alfredo*; the Three-Cheese Eggplant *Roulade* with a pungent tomato sauce inside; and pasta with wonderfully fresh jumbo shrimp. Some of the side dishes — the Zuchini Fritters and the Sautéed Broccoli — even outdo the entrées.

The dessert list proves again that less is more. Avoiding the temptation to dazzle its patrons with a long list of desserts, Castle Street offers a modest array of uniformly excellent sweet treats. Consider the Chocolate *Mousse*, which *Newsday* declared "the world's best." But you might also try one of our favorites, humbler but possibly more satisfying: Castle Street's Apple Crisp.

Castle Street is not inexpensive, but we've always felt it to be a great value, extremely fine fare for a fair price. For its superior food, reasonable prices, and extraordinarily convivial atmosphere, Castle Street rates as one of Berkshire's very best.

Chef Michael Ballon chatting with diners at his Castle Street Cafe.

D & J'S AMERICAN GRILLE
528-3201.
11 Stockbridge Rd., Gt. Barrington.
Price: Inexpensive.
Cuisine: American.
Serving: L, D.

A while back, the prestigious *Food & Wine* magazine rambled through these parts, dining and drinking. When they recovered, they reported on only a handful of Berkshire restaurants, D & J's among them. Wrote their critic: "The Southern-fried chicken is just about the best I've had north of the Mason-Dixon, as were the biscuits, the baby back ribs and the barbecued pork sandwhich. Desserts are no less satisfying; in fact, the apple crisp, baked with Granny Smiths and topped with homemade cream, would put anybody's grandmother to shame."

D & J's says they provide "The Real Food Experience," and indeed, they'd better, serving as they do out of an only moderately remodeled Dairy Queen. There is a beautiful antique patchwork quilt on one wall, and some nice Maxfield Parrish prints on another, but the ambiance is still strictly luncheonette. If you like formal, gracious settings for your meal, stay in your car and head on down the road. If you like delicious sandwiches, perfectly done French fries, flavorful baked beans, dynamite ribs and chicken and a host of other yummy offerings, pull in at D & J's. You'll walk out with a smile, guaranteed.

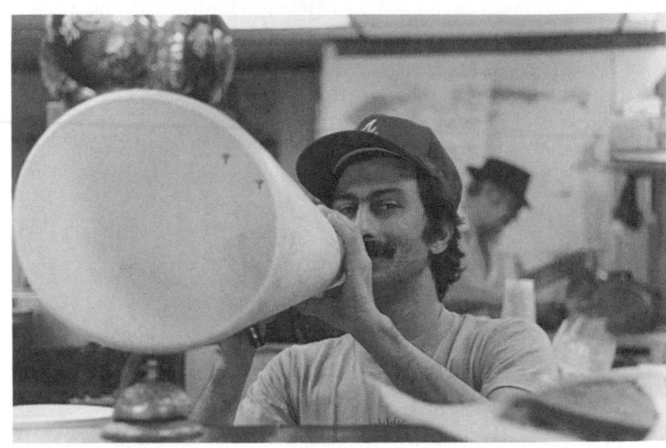

Owner/maestro Frank Tortoriello calls 'em out at the Deli.

THE DELI
528-1482.
345 Main St., Gt. Barrington.
Price: Inexpensive.
Cuisine: American.
Serving: B, L.

New Deli! No, not India, the Deli has moved just down the block, but where else could you have lunch with Ex-Gov. Dukakis, Perry Como, Tex Ritter, Gilda Radner, Dr. Johnny Fever, Jacques Cousteau, Zonker Harris, Mrs. Emma Peel, Bebe Rebozo, Groucho, Zeppo, and Carlos Castenada? Only at the Deli, where the delicious sandwich makings named after these luminaries actually appear between two slices of bread, in a pita, or between bagel halves. The sandwiches are huge (for a lighter lunch, they'll make you a half). Soups are delicious, juice combos quenching, everything tasty-fresh. Owner and chief sandwich artist Frank Tortoriello and his fun-loving staff create an air of summer camp all year long, serving up almost any sandwich you can imagine and many you never would. Bored or feeling a little nutty? Take out a Winter Sheik: cream cheese, walnuts and honey on a bagel. Perhaps you're more in the mood for a sandwich named after that famous actor, Avocado Montalban, a delicious layering of tuna, avocado, sprouts, tomatoes and melted cheese. In or out of office, "Dukakis" here will always be "Ex-Gov." — cold turkey, hot pastrami and onions.

If you're up early — hunting, fishing, photographing, or leftover from the night before — breakfast starts here at 5:30 a.m., with omelets like the Cisco Kid, Eve Arden, Ken Kesey (Muenster and onions) and Miss Piggy rolling off Frank's pan till 10.

Looking for guitar lessons, a '58 Cadillac convertible, a pen and ink drawing of your house, or a massage? Check the Deli's wall-sized bulletin board for these and other necessaries. If it's not there, you didn't need it in the first place.

DOS AMIGOS
528-0084.
250 Stockbridge Rd. (Rte.7), Gt. Barrington.
Price: Inexpensive.
Cuisine: Mexican.
Serving: L. D.
Credit Cards: MC, V.
Reservations: Preferred for groups of six or more.
Special Features: Vegetarian dishes; Children's menu/highchairs; Entertainment.

Few cuisines inspire more impassioned loyalty than Mexican. We wouldn't try to defend our preference of Great Barrington's Dos Amigos over Pittsfield's La Cocina. A purist would say that neither of these fine eateries is exclusively a Mexican restaurant at all, and reluctantly we would have to agree. But this is New England, not Mexico City.

Dos Amigos offers a pleasant informal setting — bright colors and souvenirs from the border towns bestow an infectious cheer. The distinguishing characteristic of Dos Amigos food is the abundance of fresh ingredients. The Special *Taco* is an enormous flour *tortilla* overfilled with lettuce, tomatoes, freshly grated cheese, beans, chicken or beef, and *salsa*. The beef is particularly recommended; it is given a long slow roast and is served shredded, not ground. *Enchiladas* and especially the *enchilada* sauce are both made very well here. The selection of fillings ranges from cheese and onion — a favorite — to beef and *jalapeño* for the more iron-clad *aficionado*. A word about the heat: they will make it hot, but to get it really hot, you must in graphic terms convey to the chef just how much importance you attach to self-immolation. On this score, it's a pity that whole *jalapeños* are not served as a garnish.

To complement — or to extinguish — your meal, various Mexican beers, wines and bar drinks are available. A large Margarita is served in a glass the size of a bird bath, and specialty coffees are available as post-prandials.

[**NOTE: Hickory Bill's Bar-B-Que** was planning a move to Great Barrington as this book went to press. See review under Pittsfield, in Central County.]

JODI'S COUNTRY COOKERY
528-6064.
327 Stockbridge Rd., Gt. Barrington.
Price: Inexpensive to Moderate.
Cuisine: Italian.
Serving: B, L, D, SB.
Credit Cards: MC, V.
Reservations: Recommended.

In an abandoned, unassuming country house — which had lost its charm of yesteryear when the state highway was a quieter road — Steven and Jodi Amoruso and their partner, Carole Altman, have created a surprisingly lively eatery, serving breakfast, brunch, lunch and dinner. If a crowd of cars in the parking lot and a steady flow of customers seated on the front porch, in good weather, are any indication of success, this new place has hit the mark. Compared to many other Berkshire dining spots, Jodi's location lacks all charm: the view includes a car dealership, a liquor store and a shopping plaza parking lot. Inside, however, Jodi's provides a bright and rustic atmosphere, with colorful original art (for sale) gracing the walls.

Reasonable, moderate prices no doubt explain Jodi's popularity. The menu tilts slightly toward Italy (the Amorusos grew up in the Italian restaurant business in New York), but it's mostly generic American. On one of our visits we gave high praise to a seafood ragout, actually a thick soup with a tomato base and zesty croutons. But the meal slid quickly downhill from this auspicious beginning. The chili cried out for seasoning; its sidesaddle slice of cornbread set a new standard for blandness. One of the day's specials, Sausage and Chicken Stir Fry, was like a failed liftoff by NASA: lots of anticipation, a good-looking presentation, but no oomph. We suspected the chicken had been frozen one too many times, or possibly steamed too long before hitting the wok. Dessert selections looked tempting and revealed a decided prejudice for chocolate. Service was antic and careless, albeit cheerful.

LA TOMATE
528-3003.
293 Main St., Gt. Barrington.
Closed: Mon. & Tues. in winter.
Price: Moderate.
Cuisine: French.
Serving: L, D.
Credit Cards: AE, MC, V.

Berkshire has long needed a French bistro, a Gallic dining room which blends an informal setting with serious cuisine. Chef Jean Claude Vierne originally opened on Railroad Street at the site of the former Noodles, but within a year has found it necessary to move to larger quarters. La Tomate is proving to be one of South County's hot spots.

Vierne comes well seasoned, having cooked at such chic New York restaurants as La Colombe d'Or and La Cote Basque, then having started as chef at Castle Street Cafe in Gt. Barrington. In mid-1990 Vierne realized most every talented chef's dream — a restaurant of his own.

At very modest prices, La Tomate serves authentic French dishes, some of which can surely transport you back to the Old Country, specifically to Provence. As an appetizer, *Moule du Midi* is a standout, mixing fresh mussels with tomato, white wine and garlic. Salads, such as *Epinard aux Lardon*, are close to divine, this one combining spinach, bacon, and goat cheese vinaigrette. Pasta dishes here are the real bargain; their taste more subtle. *Rigatoni Saucisse et Sauge* (sausage, spinach and sage in a creamed demi-glacé sauce) is downright delicate, but *Linguine a L'Epice* (spicy pasta, chicken breast, eggplant and pepper, tomatoes in an *Espagnole* sauce) we found disappointingly under-seasoned.

Among the entrees, at least one bowl of Vierne's *bouillabaise* ought to be ordered for your table. This Mediterranean specialty calls together mussels and clams, fish filets, saffron and herbs. *La Tomate* offered a rather timid *Aioli* sauce on the side for dipping our French bread. At once hearty and refined, the *bouillabaise* is one fish stew that lingers on the palate and in the memory. Other tempting main courses include *Sauté du Bateau* (scallops, shrimp and lobster in a Cardinal sauce); two chicken dishes; and a very French *entrecote.*

Desserts run from predictable and none-too-spectacular Créme Caramel and *Mousse au Chocolat* to a superior *Tarte aux Fruit* and an excellent Pudding *au Pain.*

A welcome addition to the list of satisfying Berkshire restaurants. Vive La Tomate!

MARTIN'S
528-5455.
49 Railroad St., Gt. Barrington.
Closed: Wed. in winter.
Price: Inexpensive.
Cuisine: American.
Serving: B, L.
Credit Cards: None.

The restaurant space at the top of Railroad Street seems to have been jinxed these last few years, and we've seen several pleasant eateries come and go. Now Martin Lewis appears to have broken through, bringing an eclectic menu to the masses and packing them in daily. After a stint at the prestigious Old Inn on the Green, Martin felt that age-old longing to do his own thing, and many of us are mighty glad he did. In his cozy, bright dining room, Martin has brought an extremely cheery staff to serve just the food his customers have asked for. Breakfast is served here all day long, and the omelets are outstanding. Choose from ones made with smoked salmon and cream cheese, Brie, spinach and cheddar, or make one up yourself. Or how about some apple pancakes for a fun way to start your day? For lunch, there are burgers in many styles, including the Berkshire Cheeseburger (mushrooms, onions, tomatoes and peppers). Sandwiches, salads and soups are also well represented, as are daily specials such as Beef Bourguignon.

Beverages available include Heinekin, Rolling Rock, Perrier, juices, and herbal teas. Though we've rarely made it to dessert, there are many fine selections to choose from, and recently we sampled a rather special poppyseed cake and a whiskey chocolate cake.

Best of all, Martin's has attracted an extraordinarily convivial crowd. There are crayons supplied with each table, allowing kids of all ages to make merry, coloring their paper placemats just the way they want. Martin's is open Saturday nights for dinner, with candles on the tables and soft, live music in the background. A good thing keeps getting even better.

THE PAINTED LADY
528-1662.
785 Main St., Gt. Barrington.
Closed: Wed.; Nov. 1-June 1.
Price: Moderate.
Cuisine: Northern Italian, Continental.
Serving: D.
Credit Cards: MC, V.
Reservations: Recommended.
Special Features: Vegetarian dishes.

"Painted Ladies" are San Francisco's colorful old Victorian houses, and chef Jimmy De Mayo established the Berkshire's first, then sold it to Julie and Dan Harris. Dan mans the kitchen, while Julie works the crowd. Together, and with a little help from their friends, theirs is one the the liveliest, finest Italian restaurants in the region. A nice mix of California, French and Italian wines is offered, at moderate prices. A complimentary *hors d'oeuvre* of *ceci* beans in a garlic vinaigrette, and fine, fresh little loaves of Italian bread seduced us into feeling we were in the right place, at the right time. The Eggplant Crêpe with capers, whole olives and *mozzarella* convinced us. All that followed — the Chicken *Prosciutto*, the Baked Stuffed Trout, the Roast Duckling with Apricot Sauce, the *Ossobuco*, and the Chicken Florentine — furthered our delight, making the Painted Lady clearly one of Berkshire's best dining values. Desserts were first class, with one small mountain of pastry and ice cream registering an impressive 8.5 on the *profiterole* scale.

PANDA WEST
528-5330.
300 State Rd., Gt. Barrington.
Price: Inexpensive to Moderate.
Cuisine: Hunan, Szechuan, Mandarin, Cantonese.
Serving: L, D.
Credit Cards: MC, V.

Panda-monium Reigns! Berkshire Inundated With Good Chinese! Fortune cookie say: Heaven come to Earth!

First there were no Chinese restaurants in Berkshire, then there were only ersatz Chinese, now there are three Pandas, rare species thriving in Berkshire Hills! All serve *Peking, Hunan, Szechuan, Shanghai* and Cantonese specialties — magic meeting places for Chinese regional cuisine. With its expansive, woody dining room, the Great Barrington Panda is our favorite, though the menus of all three are nearly identical and always well prepared. Service is superb, and no MSG thank you, just fine ingredients, fabulous sauces, exuberant combinations. Among our favorites are Tangerine Chicken and Prawn Amazing.

Steamed dumplings at Panda West.

THORNEWOOD INN
528-3828.
Stockbridge Rd., Gt. Barrington.
Closed: Tues. (summer); Mon.-Tues. (winter).
Price: Moderate to expensive.
Cuisine: Country Continental.
Serving: D.
Credit Cards: AE, D, MC, V.
Reservations: Preferred.
Special Features: Vegetarian dishes.

Terry and David Thorne have taken an old farmhouse on the southern slope of Monument Mountain and transformed it into a rather remarkable restaurant-inn. With the feel of a well-decorated British B&B, replete with tiny bar, the Thornewood is strong on charm. Here is that rare dining room where we actually admired several of the original oil paintings nicely hung and lit on the walls.

The menu is surprising — at once ambitious, creative, and delicious-sounding. An appetizer of *Vol-au-vent Langostinos* — baby lobster tails encased in puff pastry, served in an asparagus and champagne cream sauce — was at least excellent, maybe better. New England Crab Cakes topped with Béarnaise sauce were fine, the sauce a trifle thin. Roast Tenderloin of Pork in Apple Gravy was the weakest offering, and it was nonetheless quite good, though the meat could have been more tender and flavorful, the sauce more appley. A Pocket Steak — a butterflied New York sirloin filled with a scallop, shrimp and crabmeat stuffing — was extraordinary, the steak perfectly juicy, the shrimp and scallops unquestionably fresh, and the crabmeat stuffing as satisfying as anything grandma makes for Thanksgiving. A rice medley presented a true medley of flavors, and a twice-baked potato came out as a splendid blend of sour cream, chives, and potato decoratively squeezed back into its skin and lightly browned. Artfully placed radish florettes and bicolored orange slices (one half of one side dusted with paprika, the other half of the other side dusted with chives) adorned our plates. Though we thought one of the salad dressings could have benefited greatly from the use of fresh scallions, almost every other culinary detail was well executed. And despite several unappealing maraschino cherry halves atop the pineapple upsidedown cake, the finale was a memorably sweet and dewy conclusion that left us murmuring contentedly.

20 RAILROAD STREET
528-9345.
20 Railroad St., Gt. Barrington.
Price: Inexpensive.
Cuisine: American.
Serving: SB, L, D.
Credit Cards: MC, V.
Special Features: Open late.
Handicap. Access: Yes.

Born in 1977, 20 Railroad Street continues to be a great spot for food, spirits and conversation. This is the restaurant that launched the Railroad Street revival. With its tall brick dining room, 20 Railroad is first and foremost convivial. Here you'll share dining space with jovial families, cooing couples, young and old, as well as softball teams and ski patrol squadrons. You'll hear about divorces and deals, patients and quarterbacks. In story or in person, most of southern Berkshire has been in 20 Railroad.

The tables are wood, the lighting low, the mood classic, laid-back Berkshire without the frills. But 20 Railroad didn't build its popularity on good vibes alone; a bar could, but a restaurant could not. From the outset, 20 Railroad has served good food — solid fare at people's prices. Since other restaurants have joined the Railroad Street renaissance, this good restaurant has gotten even better, broadening its menu, always serving half-a-dozen dinner specials that extend the range further.

For lunch, dinner or whenever, 20 Railroad's starters, salads, sandwiches and burgers are legendary for their consistent ability to satisfy, without denting even a thin wallet. Unusual starters include the Plowman's Snack, a combination of Brie, *sopresotta* sausage and French bread; and hot and spicy chicken wings marinated in soy, ginger, sherry and garlic. Salads run the garden gamut from spinach to chef, from Greek to Caesar.

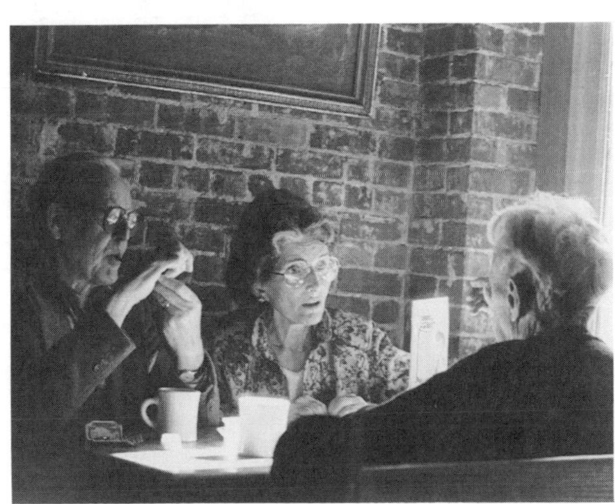

Enjoying midday coffee in a sunny booth at 20 Railroad Street.

Pocket sandwiches are outstanding, with the vegetarian side pocket — lettuce, fresh veggies and blue cheese in a *pita* all "smothered under melted swiss cheese" — being among our favorites. More than a dozen different burgers and an equal number of sandwiches fill out Railroad Street's printed menu.

On the chalkboard, specials usually include soups, a variety of meaty entrées and sometimes a vegetarian dish. Service is efficient and always friendly. Once touted by *The Boston Phoenix* as "The Best Bar in the Berkshires," 20 Railroad Street is not doing too badly in the restaurant department either. "Famous since 1977," and famous into the future.

> The 28-foot-long bar dominating 20 Railroad Street was built in New York City, in 1883, and was moved to Great Barrington in 1919. Originally, the bar was named "Mahogany Ridge," deriving its name from an inside joke among some regulars. When asked by their waiting wives where they had been, their usual reply was, "Oh, we hunted the state forest in the morning and posted `Mahogany Ridge' in the afternoon." During the '20s, through the end of Prohibition, the bar served as one of the area's speakeasies. Maybe that's why the talk comes so easy at 20 Railroad.

A young gourmet places her order at Embree's.

Housatonic

EMBREE'S
274-3476.
Main St., Housatonic.
On Main St., midway between Rtes. 41 & 183.
Closed: Mon.-Wed. in winter.
Price: Moderate to expensive.
Cuisine: Italian.
Serving: SB, D.
Credit Cards: MC, V.
Reservations: Required on weekends.
Special Features: Vegetarian dishes.

In the expansive, lofty space that once served as the company store for the Housatonic mills, former theatrical set painter Jay Embree has created a spacious, dramatic dining room. Mauve walls, polished hardwood floors, comfy Windsor chairs, small fica trees and hand-carved Indonesian miniature fruit trees — such design details immediately relax and please. And the food created by Embree's sister, chef Joan Spence, is a perfect complement to the lovely setting.

When we visited, the menu was rife with delicious choices, among them: Pot Roast, the old fashioned way; Shrimp and Tenderloin of Beef Kabob; *Manicotti Crespelles; Tofu Szechuan;* Poached Mussels; and Cajun Catfish. *Babotie* at Embree's is a spicy curried ground lamb, served with custard and chutney. Vegetables served with the entrées continue in Embree's tradition of excellence, adding the satisfaction of real herbed mashed potatoes, moderately chunky with bits of skin, and dill-glazed carrots. Pies are almost too much, with apple, pumpkin and banana cream tempting even the already-stuffed diner.

We predict Embree's will someday be known as the restaurant that put sleepy Housatonic back on the map.

Lee

CYGNET'S AT THE BLACK SWAN INN
243-2700, 800 876-SWAN.
Rte. 20 W., Lee.
At Laurel Lake, N. of Lee.
Closed: Tues.
Price: Moderate.
Cuisine: Country-style American.
Serving: L, D; winter: D.
Credit Cards: AE, CB, DC, MC, V.
Special Features: Atrium restaurant overlooking Laurel Lake.

In their atrium dining room overlooking Laurel Lake, the Black Swan Inn provides a dining experience with unexpected pleasures. Besides the felicitous setting, the restaurant offers an impressive Continental menu with wine list to match. This surprisingly serious collection features a broad range of French, American, German, Italian, Australian and Hungarian wines from $15 to $225, as well as dessert wines.

Chef John Allen and his staff turn out truly fine food, from a juicy New York sirloin steak to some of the finest authentic Hungarian *Gulyas* with Homemade *Spaetzle* we've ever eaten. A seafood chowder, which included healthy bits of lobster, was satisfying in every respect. *Cerapcic* — mildly spicy, handmade, skinless grilled sausages — disappointingly tasted like a fine hamburger in little hot dog form. Vegetables were uniformly lively, cooked *al dente*, maximizing their goodness. Shrimp and Scallops *Cilantro* was highlighted by very fresh shellfish and sassy lemongrass on a bed of angel hair pasta. Desserts were right up there, and a lemon tart with raspberry sauce, a single sliced strawberry and real whipped cream made a grand way to go out.

JOE'S DINER
243-9756.
63 Center St., Lee.
At corner of Center & Main Sts.
Closed: Sun.
Price: Inexpensive.
Cuisine: American.
Serving: B, L, D.

Enter the Twilight Zone, the twilight of anybody's years, where time has stood still and isn't waiting for anything, where things *are* just as they were and just as they will be. Enter Joe's Diner, still bustling with the vigor of the 1940s, the kind of diner that still stocks packets of Red Man Chewing Tobacco right next to buckets of lifetime-guarantee combs.

But it's not the funkiness or even the old-time prices that keeps Joe's jammed most of the day and night. Joe Sorrentino serves good food. With the help of many other assorted Sorrentinos and friends, this ex-Army cook will happily serve you "breakfast at dinner, or dinner at breakfast," any way you like it. Joe creates a special each day, and many regulars are attuned to his menu. "We'll go through a whole hip of beef every Monday, 120 pounds of corned beef every Thursday," says Joe. If you're serious about taking in one of Joe's specials (like a roast beef dinner, with vegetable, potato and bread for four bucks), you'd better arrive early. We came on corned beef night recently and watched the last of the 120 pounds disappear quickly, leaving many disappointed latecomers.

"What time is your reservation for?" asked the cheerful chief Sorrentino, eyeing his new customers amidst the legions.

"Whenever you can take us," replied the eager diner.

"Would you like the dining room," asked Joe, standing in his one-room diner, "or the counter."

"That'd be fine," said the customer, knowing he'd have to wait a few minutes for either.

"This is Gene Shalit's favorite seat," said an elderly lady, brimming with pride from the corner.

That's who you'll dine with at Joe's: everybody. With media personalities and housewives, construction workers and psychiatrists, movie stars and lads on the lam, *haute cuisine* chefs and folks who never cook, antique dealers and antique people, kids and ultrasophisticates, locals, foreigners, and every kind in between.

Owner Joe Sorrentino works the crowd at Joe's.

MORGAN HOUSE
243-0181.
33 Main St., Lee.
Price: Moderate to expensive.
Cuisine: Continental.
Serving: L, D.
Credit Cards: AE, CB, D, DC, MC, V.
Reservations: Recommended.

"A cozy and authentic stagecoach inn featuring superb New England fare," says the Morgan House brochure, and though this 1853 institution satisfies its first claim, its New England fare is far from superb. Their ambitious menu is dotted with cute hearts, each heart indicating an entrée that can be prepared without margarine or wine. We can't make any suggestions, even to those of you on a restricted diet, as this kitchen's fare even with wine and margarine is far from its intention. Many fancy dishes, such as Scallops *Florentine en Croute*, seemed like precooked reheats, the scallops in particular being slimy and unappetizing. On Friday nights, Morgan House offers a huge buffet, with the likes of lasagna, stuffed chicken breast and roast beef. The lasagna was cold, the chicken breast okay by airlines food standards, and the roast beef just too, too rare.

At a quarter the price, Joe's Diner does better.

THE PLACE
243-4465.
51 Park St., Lee.
Closed: Sun.-Mon. in winter.
Price: Moderate.
Cuisine: Eclectic.
Serving: D.
Credit Cards: AE, MC, V.
Special Features: Vegetarian dishes.

The Place calls itself "A Berkshire Experience," and in many ways, it fills that bill. Innkeepers Richard Rice and Charles Petrie, and chef Charles Kemper provide a sophisticated country feel, with food to match. On cooler nights, the cozy bar glows with the warmth and aroma of a wood fire in the brick fireplace. Service is friendly, knowledgeable, attentive, and accommodating.

From their recent Harvest Menu, many intriguing possibilities were suggested. Appetizers included two shellfish dishes: *Malpeque* Oysters on the Half-shell and *Escargo*t in Puff Pastry. We opted instead for lighter starters: Sweet Potato and Apple Fritters, and Peasant Bread (Italian bread topped with olive oil, garlic, sun-dried tomatoes and *mozzarella*, then finished under the broiler). The Place was off to a very strong start — both these appetizers were excellent. Cheddar Cheese Soup with Cob-Smoked Bacon was fine, but Manhattan Clam Chowder was merely good. Special for the night was Goose for Four, an enticement to be sure. Instead, we sampled two pasta dishes and two fish entrees: Vegetable Lasagna with Three Cheeses; Spinach *Fettuccini Carbonar*a; Grilled Swordfish Steak and Sautéed Tiger Shrimp-*Sauce Piquante.* Both pastas were fine, the lasagna being especially memorable for its layer of smoked Gruyère cheese. Sadly, the fish floundered. How fresh was this fish? It's hard to say. But both the swordfish and the shrimp tasted as if they'd been frozen at one stage of their journey to the plate. Amazingly, the wild rice on which the shrimp lay was the worst we'd ever tasted, being at once bland and chalky. Desserts were back on course, with a fine, nutty and none-too-sweet pecan pie topped by fresh, vanilla-laced whipped cream. To accompany your meal, the Place offers an admirable list of international wines at very reasonable prices. In Lee, the place is *the* Place.

SULLIVAN STATION
243-2082.
Railroad St., Lee.
Price: Inexpensive to moderate.
Cuisine: New England.
Serving: SB, L, D.
Credit Cards: MC, V.
Reservations: Accepted.
Special Features: Converted 19th-century train station.

We've always enjoyed the wood paneled interior of this converted 19th-century railway station, tastefully decorated with railroad maps and memorabilia. Now the food is good, too, making the Station a smart stop for soups, salads, burgers, sandwiches and quiches. Juicy burgers are served with a generous salad and twice-fried home fries — making for a filling, satisfying plate. There are daily specials, friendly waitresses, and a folksy bar near the entry. Altogether, Sullivan Station is right on time.

South Lee

FEDERAL HOUSE
243-1824.
Main St., Rte. 102, S. Lee.
1 1/2 mi. E. of Stockbridge.
Closed: Mon.

Robin Slocum and Ken Almgren met when they were working at the well-known Stonehenge restaurant in Ridgefield, Connecticut, and since that time, they married and opened the Federal House,

Candlelight and flowers set the tone for dining at the Federal House.

Price: Expensive.
Cuisine: Continental.
Credit Cards: AE, MC, V.
Reservations: Recommended.
Special Features: Fireplaces.

with Ken as chef. The atmosphere at their restaurant is elegant and European, with white linens, heavy silver and fresh flowers adorning every candlelit table. More than likely, a fire will be crackling in the hearth of the tall, stately dining room, welcoming you on a crisp evening.

After a drink in the intimate bar, approach the table with anticipation, for we've never had less than a superior meal here. For starters, recent offerings included Seared Yellowfin Tuna with Horseradish & Soy Sauce; Smoked Duckling with Fresh Peach Chutney; and an intriguing Terrine of Rabbit with Lingonberry Sauce.

A simple green salad is highlighted by an absolutely first-class vinaigrette. The wine list at Federal House is excellent, strong in French vintages, with Bordeaux from $15 to $130 and Burgundies from about $25 to $75.

Recent entrées included *Quenelles* of Chicken, Cognac and Fresh Basil; Sautéed *Tournedos* with Armagnac & Mustard Butter; and Filet of Beef *Grille,* Five Peppercorn Sauce. Also featured as entrees for two are *Chateaubriand Bouquetiere* and Roast Rack of Lamb *Provençale.*

Chef Almgren started his career as a pastry apprentice, later working at the Windows on the World; and at dessert time his great skills with sweets and cakes come forth. He is justly well known for his apple fritter: feathery fruity pancakes in a sauce of ice cream, stiff whipped cream and kirsch. This is a symphonic creation, and at least one for the table ought to be ordered to cap a Federal House feast. His *profiteroles* are nearly as good, and even if you no longer have any hunger, these ice cream puffs make an exceptionally satisfying conclusion.

Tomorrow, you'll consider the calories.

HOPLANDS
243-4414.
Rte. 102, S. Lee.

In a beautiful brick inn, built around 1803, Hoplands embraces you with antique ambiance. At the handsome bar, a gargantuan bowl of popcorn can

1 mi. E. of Stockbridge.
Closed: Mon.-Tues. in winter.
Price: Inexpensive.
Cuisine: American.
Serving: SB, L, D.

take the edge off any appetite, or provide good munchies if you're just drinking. On the walls: antique maps of Berkshire, town maps, showing Stockbridge and Lee the way they used to be, when the township of Hoplands lay between them. The light is soft amber, the mood mellow. Here's a restaurant and bar that feels mighty close to an old-time Berkshire tavern, a place where you can park your steed, pull up a chair and set a spell. And with beers like Samuel Smith's Pale Ale, Kirin, Guiness Extra Stout, and Corona available, you just might want to sip while you sit.

Then again, there already might be too much hop afloat at Hoplands. For the menu is crowded with such fare as Hopburgers (like a tasty Canadian Bacon Swissburger), a Hopdog (fried in their special batter), and a Chili Hopdog (topped with chili and Vermont cheddar). Hopplates include Chicken Pot Pie and Pasta Hopfredo. Well, no matter. The food's good, the ambiance (on both floors) is great, the tab, quite modest. French fries are curly style, and tend to disappear rather quickly. The Joshua Slocum is a fried fish sandwich, named after the first man to sail around the world alone.

There are other fish stories at Hoplands, and other sagas of singlehanded sailing. There are stories of kids and grandparents, stories in code and stories told right out. Jokes, anecdotes and puns. Lies, whoppers and plain tall tales. Good ones, bad ones and lots in between. And always at Hoplands, there's room for yours or mine.

New Marlborough

THE HILLSIDE
528-3123.
Rte. 57, New Marlborough.
Closed: Mon.; Mon. & Tues. in winter.
Price: Moderate.
Cuisine: Continental.
Credit Cards: MC, V.
Serving: D.
Reservations: Recommended.
Special Features: Outdoor dining; Fireplace.

The front cover of the Hillside's menu shows a young Swiss couple holding hands, gazing fondly into each other's eyes. Appropriately, the Hillside dining room is one of the most romantic in the Berkshires. Simple Swiss elegance is in evidence everywhere, from the pale blue table linen and its matching artfully folded napkins, to the fresh-cut flowers, from the rubbed honey-colored woodwork to the exceptionally flattering candlelight. Waitresses are dressed in dirndl and apron; service is first-rate. This is not a stuffy atmosphere or one even tinged with pretension; rather, the air in the Hillside is one of casual conviviality.

Hillside's Onion Soup is still among the Berkshire's best. Melon and *prosciutto* makes a pretty plate, the honeydew carefully cut into wedges and arrayed in offset. The melon is sweet and perfectly ripe; the *prosciutto*, gamy, even tangy. Salad ensues, featuring alfalfa sprouts — another surprise in a European-flavored restaurant — and slices of golden bell pepper. This newly popular pepper is far sweeter than its red or green cousins and lends real excitement to greens.

Entrées at the Hillside are strictly meat, fish and fowl, with the accent on excellent ingredients and preparation. The menu features many veal dishes that are as fine in flavor as they are tender. Excellent duck *flambé* is gamy and not fatty, though the orange sauce that comes on the side is far too sweet.

Desserts are special. Cheesecake is light and not too sugary, its topping of fresh strawberries showing off their natural sweetness. Chocolate crêpe filled with chocolate ice cream and topped with chocolate sauce is a semi-sweet winner at every layer and in combination. Coffee is excellent; *espresso* arriving in a stately demitasse with its own *espresso* pot for a second cup, covered with its own blue linen *espresso* cozy.

Up on a hill in the Hartsville section of New Marlboro, there's Continental excellence at the Hillside.

A candlelit mantel at the Old Inn on the Green.

OLD INN ON THE GREEN
229-3131.
Rte. 57 (6 mi. E. of Rte. 23) New Marlborough.
Closed: Mon.-Thurs. winter only.
Price: Weekday, Moderate to expensive. Weekends: Very expensive, Prix-Fixe.
Cuisine: French, American.
Serving: D.
Credit Cards: None.
Reservations: Required.
Special Features: Intimate candlelit dining rooms, fireplaces, outdoor patio.

It's hard to improve on near perfection, but the Old Inn has done it. Innkeepers Miller and Wagstaff have astute instincts for putting the emphasis right where it belongs. Their restoration of an 18th-century stagecoach stop includes preservation of several kinks and quirks in the old building: uneven wide floorboards, less than perfect wainscotting, relined but still finicky fireplaces. In the structure or on your table, you will find no synthetic substances here. The whipped cream is the real stuff. The outstanding French bread is baked on the premises. There is no Muzak.

There is, however, the enchanting glow of candlelight — and no other light — in all four dining rooms and in the bar. And there is now a charming backyard extension of the bar (a patio and awning) for warm weather *alfresco* drinks and less formal weekday dining. The Old Inn strikes a rare chord: you can dine here dressed in your finest finery or in sportsclothes and feel equally welcome and comfortable. What's more, there are fireside tables and dining alcoves that surely win the prize for "most romantic dinner spots in Berkshire."

After years of French experience, chef David Lawson came to the inn mid-1989, quickly establishing a positive reputation. The inn's fixed price menu (announced via mailing list, a season in advance) still consists of essentially one set meal each night. With advance notice, vegetarians and fish eaters can be accommodated when the entrée is meat. Chef Lawson ranges freely from Continental to American regional cuisine, with equally wonderful results. His plate presentations are stunning displays of color and design. Concluding matters, Leslie Miller's desserts are divine. And partner Brad Wagstaff maintains a well thought out, high-quality wine cellar. Serious diners: get on the Old Inn's mailing list.

FRIDAY, JUNE 29
An Evening with Joshua Wesson: Wine Consultant, Editor, *Wine & Food Companion*, and author, "Red Wine with Fish."

A Tasting Dinner focusing on the art of successfully matching wine with food.

Parchment Baked Scallops with Ginger and Saffron Oil
Marinated Roast Quail with Szechuan Pepper and Honey
Grilled Whole Sirloin of Beef with Port Braised Shallots
New Potatoes Cooked in Coals
Zucchini Stuffed with Vegetable Brunoise
Peach Tarte Tatin with Caramel Sauce

Regional French and American wines selectively chosen by Joshua Wesson to match the Tasting Menu.

Prix-fixe Supplement: $30 per person.

A winetasting dinner menu from the Old Inn on the Green.

There is impressive diversity here. A recent menu featured mouth-watering homemade Chicken Sausage in a Truffled Madeira Sauce, as light as a *quenelle*; then Filet of Sole with Red Beet Butter, a dramatic taste and visual sensation. The Sautéed Spinach with Garlic would turn even a spinach-hater into Popeye: you could eat it all day, everyday. The meal finished with a Lemon and Lime Sorbet (a study in cool subtlety) and *Espresso* Cheesecake (fasten your seatbelts).

The Old Inn is a Berkshire treasure.

Sheffield

STAGECOACH HILL INN
229-8585.
Rte. 41, Sheffield.
On Rte. 41, several mi. N. of Lakeville, CT.
Closed: Wed. (May-Nov.) Tues.-Wed.(winter) & 3 wks. in Mar.
Price: Moderate.

The 18th-century pub here has Watney's on draft, Smith's Taddy Porter in bottles, and can serve up a lager and lime without question. Well-cushioned couches provide luxurious seating in one cozy nook of this rustic saloon. Should you settle in for a drink before dinner, you may find yourself lingering longer than anticipated, especially if a winter's fire is crackling in the doublesided hearth. Under the direction of

Cuisine: English, Italian.
Serving: D.
Credit Cards: AE, DC, MC, V.
Reservations: Recommended.
Special Features: Outdoor dining; Private dining room; Fireplace.

John Pedretti and his English wife, Ann, Stagecoach Hill maintains its British flavor throughout, from the London street signs in the bar, to the hunting prints and portraits of the Royal Family on the walls, from the slightly dowdy character of its dining room to its steak and kidney pie.

On Saturdays, Stagecoach Hill serves traditional English roast beef and Yorkshire pudding. During the rest of the week, entrées consist of steaks, chops, fish and fowl. Grilled salmon is succulent, firm and delicious. Steak and kidney pie tastes authentically British.

A coach stop since the early 1800s, Stagecoach Hill Inn continues to serve "Fine Victuals and Ardent Spirits." For English fare in the Berkshire Hills, tie up your horses here and have a pint, a chat and a kidney pie.

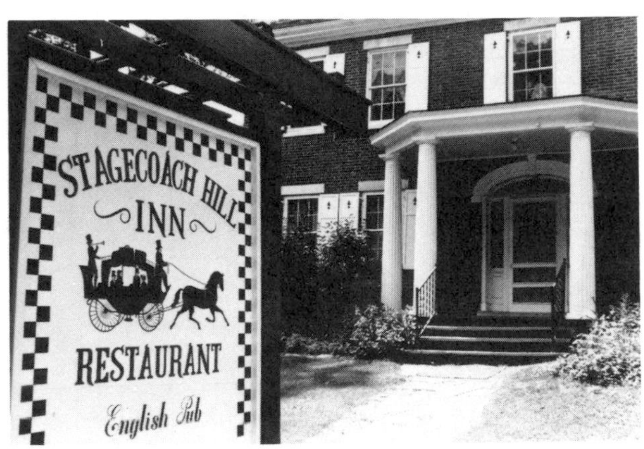

Southfield

BOILER ROOM CAFE
229-3105.
Southfield.
Behind the Buggy Whip Factory, Southfield.
Closed: Tues.-Wed.; Mar. 15-Apr. 15.
Price: Expensive.
Cuisine: European, American.
Serving: L, D.
Credit Cards: None.
Special Features: Frequent live music.

Michelle Miller founded the extraordinary bakery, Suchele, in Lenox, helped found the extraordinary restaurant, the Old Inn on the Green, in New Marlborough, and has established her own place in sleepy Southfield — cooking, baking and managing the delightful Boiler Room Cafe. Hers is an intimate, candlelit restaurant with a distinctive personality. Musicians, either jazz, folk or classical, often accompany Boiler Room dinners, enriching an already pleasing atmosphere. The restaurateur presides warmly over her small dining room, making sure her guests are enjoying themselves. Service is exemplary: friendly, knowledgeable, and deft at tableside.

The fare is even better. To start with, there's

Michelle's crusty, chewy French bread, possibly our pick for the best in the Berkshires. Among the delights we have sampled are appetizers such as a slightly warm Cheddar and Cumin Pie, with beet salad; and Fried Oysters with Cornbread. The cheddar and cumin pie is memorable, seasoned to perfection, its crust, flaky yet substantial; the fried oysters we rate about the finest we've tasted, with just the right ratio of tasty breading to squishy delicious oyster. The Boiler Room's brief wine list offers an interesting array of Spanish, Italian and French wines, with an American chardonnay looking a bit lonely.

On our visit the vegetable accompaniments to the entrées were a moist, roasted sweet potato, and slightly undercooked green beans, by now a *nouvelle* tradition we don't completely admire. *Polenta* was unexceptional as a main dish, but panfried Pecan Breaded Trout and Marinated Angus Sirloin with Spicy Red Wine and Tomato Sauce were both very fine, the steak smothered with a saucy mix that included olives, raisins and onions. Desserts at the Boiler Room are duly devastating. Among the Pear Cranberry Pie, Apple Walnut Crumb Pie, *Gâteau au Chocolat* and Orange Tart, our already satisfied taste buds rang up several perfect scores.

Stockbridge

THE CAFE
298-4461.
Off Main St., (in the Mews), Stockbridge.
Closed: Tues. during winter.
Price: Inexpensive.
Cuisine: American.
Serving: B, L.; D (June-Sept.).
Credit Cards: None.

The Cafe has settled in, enclosing its porch in a skylit, woody atrium, and expanding its menu. In a village somewhat given to hype, this place is refreshingly plain and simple. Breakfast is something of an event, with offerings such as Eggs Florentine and "Not Just French Toast," a heavenly layering of cream cheese and orange marmalade between two slices of *challah* French toast. And lunch keeps pace: Mesquite Grilled Chicken Breast Sandwich, Cajun Burgers, and Hawaiian Chicken Salad are all well prepared. There's beer on tap or in the bottle and wine by the glass. The Cafe overlooks the Red Lion Inn's garden, one of the best views in Stockbridge.

GHINGA
298-4490.
Rte. 7, Stockbridge.
At Stockbridge Station, S. of village.
Closed: Mon.-Wed. (winter & spring).
Price: Moderate to expensive.
Cuisine: Japanese macrobiotic.
Credit Cards: AE, D, MC, V.
Reservations: Recommended.

Michio and Aveline Kushi are known worldwide as leaders of the macrobiotic movement. Based in Boston for many years, they recently purchased a 600-acre spread in Becket and opened Ghinga, a Japanese macrobiotic restaurant, at the Stockbridge Station.

The Station had its origins in 19th-century England, in the mind of Stockbridge-resident Ambassador Joseph Choate. Thinking fondly of his distant hometown and the frequent trains trips from New York he and his wealthy friends would make, he realized the town needed a new station. Solution?

Special Features: Open late; Vegetarian dishes.

Choate had Stanford White design one. This gracefully proportioned 1893 English Gothic Revival building, with its blue dolomite walls and an American shingle roof, is now Ghinga.

For lovers of things Japanese, there are many treats here. For *sushi* fans, this is undoubtedly the place in the Berkshires, offering a *sushi* menu more far ranging than most big city *sushi* bars. For those who eat a vegetarian or macrobiotic diet, Ghinga is incomparable.

Ghinga is thoroughly macrobiotic, thoroughly Japanese. Food is meticulously prepared; the *sushi* (raw fish) alone is well worth a visit. Behind a glass case holding fresh fish fillets, Ghinga's *sushi* chef skillfully thin-slices the fresh seafood, then deftly arranges it on little wooden platters. Available are *sushi* such as sea bass, sea trout, tilefish, tuna, *toro* (tuna belly), yellowtail, sea urchin, shrimp, scallop, salmon, salmon roe, squid, octopus, mackerel, horse clam, halibut, fresh water eel, and flying fish roe. The *wasabi* (green horseradish) that accompanies these delectable *sushi* is sassy in the extreme and often compels a friend to exuberantly rub the green hot sauce on her gums, claiming she has found God.

Cooked food at Ghinga is decidedly less spicy, and in fact, though distinctly Japanese, is occasionally bland by conventional tastes. This surely is the macrobiotic dimension of Ghinga, but lively dipping sauces are frequently provided for entrées. *Tempura* is outstanding by any standards, featuring lightly battered and deep-fried onion, shrimp, carrot, pepper, and squash. But *soba* (noodle) and *miso* soup are occasionally flat, even with the addition of *tamari*. Broiled scrod with its dipping sauce is far better, and the salads are outstanding for freshness, taste and dressing.

Outstanding sugar-free desserts by Laura Magis make a sensational, guilt-free close to a wholesome, fine meal. Besides her incredible fruit pies (sweetened with barley malt or maple syrup), we especially love her Pear Crunch.

Besides hot *saki*, Ghinga serves Suntory beer, Metbrau all natural draft, several French wines, Anchor Steam beer from San Francisco, Samuel Smith's Oatmeal Stout, and MacAndrew's Scotch Ale. Every once in a while, they host the Bluestars or other musicians for a night of beer and boogie.

Who said those macrobiotics don't know how to have a good time?

Sushi and conversation at Ghinga.

MICHAEL'S
298-3530.
Elm St., Stockbridge.
Price: Moderate to expensive.
Cuisine: American, Italian.
Serving: L, D.
Credit Cards: AE, CB, DC, MC, V.
Special Features: Late night menu.

Michael's cavalierly calls itself "The Restaurant for Everybody," and though we'd take some exception to that, their range is indeed wide, from pulsing, oversized MTV in the back room, to a quiet country tearoom in the front, from burgers and sandwiches to *chateaubriand* for two. Michael's features an extensive menu of northern Italian cuisine. In a place like the Berkshires where most kitchens close early, Michael's is one of the few late-night eateries that can serve up a moist piece of carrot cake with honey cream-cheese icing at 1 a.m. Michael's is also recommended for viewing televised sporting events, and watching fish (in two aquariums, the first of which holds an adorable miniature hammerhead shark).

MIDGE'S
298-3040.
Elm St., Stockbridge.

Possibly unremarkable in any other locale, Midge's offers relief from the pervasive Stockbridge preciousness. By serving good soups and sandwiches at reasonable prices, this hole in the wall champions the ordinary in us all, providing sustenance to the people. If you're a people, you might want to head down the alley for some real food at Midge's.

THE RED LION INN
298-5545.
Main St., Stockbridge.
Price: Expensive
Cuisine: Traditional American.
Serving: B, L, D.
Credit Cards: AE, DC, MC, V.
Reservations: Recommended.
Handicap. Access: Yes.

Some restaurants bring you a few rolls with your meal; some even offer a freshly baked small loaf. The Red Lion Inn has a bread boy who carries a trayful of fresh slices of three different breads: whole wheat dill, Irish soda, and (too sweet) lemon bread. Then they bring you the hot rolls. Such is the bounty of the Red Lion, and as the bread goes, so goes the whole meal.

Choices abound. Where would you like to dine — in the cozy tavern; in the quaint formal dining rooms; or, during summertime, out in the flower-decked garden? The main dining room requires jacket and tie for gents, seating guests in a 19th-century, chandelier-lit space dotted with dozens of antique teapots, the collection of a former owner, Mrs. Plumb. Widow Bingham Tavern, by contrast, is dimly lit, rough-hewn and intimate, with one especially cozy alcove you can reserve; and there is no dress code here. A similar policy applies to the rear porch and shaded garden, one of the loveliest, most pleasant outdoor restaurant settings in Berkshire.

But before the bread, before you sit down to dine, if time and weather allow, have a cocktail out on the legendary front porch at the Red Lion, and drink in some old-world feeling. This is the most seasoned porch in the Berkshires and has seen more rocking and more rockers than all others combined. Before its columned, flowery majesty, all the Berkshires pass, as if in an updated Norman Rockwell painting. Sit there long enough and perhaps you too will become part of the tableau.

Rock vigorously; prepare for the feast to come. The Red Lion's kitchens serve only the freshest, highest quality foods, carefully prepared by chef Steven Mongeon. The menu is traditional New England fare — solid, with steaks, fish and poultry. A vegetarian plate is available, but not worth a detour. Appetizers are traditional, relying more on fine raw ingredients than culinary skill or inventiveness.

Entrée portions are more than ample, sometimes bordering on huge. Lamb chops are an inch-and-a-half thick. The meat is consistently succulent, cooked to order, and delicious. Duckling comes with a cranberry demi-glaze, and nearly crowds its wild rice and green beans off the plate, so generous is the portion.

If you're person enough, proceed to the desserts, considering among others the bread pudding, Indian pudding, pecan ball covered with butterscotch sauce or pecan pie. You'll never leave that Lion hungry.

"Back of the Bank," the Red Lion's magical outdoor bar.

The Red Lion also serves breakfast (an elegant bargain), lunch, various in-between-meals, snacks and, in summer, a most welcome light, late-night menu. The inn's lively, music-filled tavern downstairs, the Lion's Den, offers tasty sandwiches and desserts. When the inn is busy, breakfast may be restricted to lodgers; be sure to phone ahead. Watch for special holiday and Sunday dinner menus announced in *The Berkshire Eagle*. Whatever the day, service is exemplary throughout the Red Lion, a bright, attentive enthusiasm that never becomes intrusive.

West Stockbridge

SHAKER MILL TAVERN
232-8565.
Rte. 102, W. Stockbridge.
Price: Moderate.
Cuisine: American &

Calling itself "A Classic American Tavern," Shaker Mill Tavern will chill, grill, bake, sizzle or broil it to get it just the way you like it. What was a lively place has gotten livelier; and good food has

Italian.
Credit Cards: AE, MC, V.
Reservations: Recommended on wkends.
Special Features: Outdoor dining; Private dining rooms; Fireplaces.

gotten even better. Besides a vast selection of sandwiches, burgers, tidbits, soups, salads, pasta, kabobs, and...pizzas(!), Shaker Mill has one of the most effervescent beer lists in the Berkshires, including: Samuel Smith's Pale Ale (England); Pinkus Original Weizen (West Germany); Aass Pilsner (Norway); and John Courage Draft (England).

In its expansive, woody dining rooms, Shaker Mill continues to please.

TRUC ORIENT EXPRESS
232-4204.
Harris St., W. Stockbridge.
One block off Main St. (Rte. 102), over Williams River.
Closed: Mon.; Nov.-May.
Price: Moderate to expensive.
Cuisine: Vietnamese.
Serving: L, D.
Credit Cards: AE, MC, V.
Reservations: Recommended.
Special Features: Vegetarian dishes; Outdoor dining.

"Truc," as it's called, is one of the most appealing of Berkshire restaurants. As soon as you enter the building, you will see that owners Luy Nguyen and Trai Duong have dedicated themselves to quality and artistry. The delicate aromas from the open kitchen arouse the appetite, while the the clean white walls, exposed wood, soft indirect lighting, rattan furniture and various *objets d'art* create an atmosphere that is gracious and welcoming . . . and a welcome relief from pervasive New Englandiana. Here you can have fun pretending you're somewhere in exotic Southeast Asia, sitting back in some of the best cushioned chairs in Berkshire.

A word to the wise: abandon caution. In selecting items from this generally Vietnamese menu, it is best to experiment. Ask the waiter for his recommendations, or give the chef free rein, specifying only the principal ingredient you want and the amount you're willing to spend. In this manner, the only weakness of Truc's menu — its bland Americanized alternatives for the timid — may be confidently avoided.

Of the appetizers, the best we have tried is the Truc special shrimp roll, a triangular package of crabmeat, pork, vegetables and shrimp, served with a garnish of ruby red lettuce and a spicy sweet-and-sour Vietnamese dipping sauce.

Two fine entrées at Truc are the Sweet and Sour Fish and the *Nahtrang* Pork Barbecue. The fish is a pleasant discovery: deep-fried flounder in a light, crisp batter, dressed in a sauce that is neither too sweet nor too sour. The absence of red dye is greatly appreciated and underscores the importance attached in this cuisine to ingredients that are fresh and to cooking techniques accentuating this freshness. The barbecued pork is ground, slightly spiced, and seared on a bamboo skewer over an open flame. This is a good hearty entrée, with plenty of pork, and many diners will certainly appreciate the chef's attempts to satisfy the lusty American appetite.

One of the great surprises at Truc Orient Express is the dessert course. Although these items do not play a major role in a Vietnamese meal, we have found both the *créme caramel* and lemon *mousse* pleasing if untraditional.

For an extraordinarily comfortable and gracious gourmet Vietnamese meal, Truc's the only game in town.

THE WILLIAMSVILLE INN
274-6118.
Rte. 41, W. Stockbridge.
About 10 mi. N. of Gt. Barrington, in hamlet of Williamsville.
Closed: Mon.-Wed. in winter.
Price: Expensive.
Cuisine: Country French.
Serving: D.
Credit Cards: MC, V.
Reservations: Requested.
Handicap. Access: Yes.
Special Features: Fireplace.

If past is prologue, the new incarnation of the Williamsville Inn is bound to delight. Under several previous managements and their respective chefs, we have had some of our best meals in the Berkshires at this irresistibly charming restaurant. As we went to press, Williamsville had recently changed hands again; the new chef is Stephen Daoust. Do keep your eyes on this place. Summer or winter, perhaps winter especially when the great stone hearth cheefully warms the main dining room, Williamsville's early New England ambience is delicious.

RESTAURANTS CENTRAL COUNTY

ANTONIO'S
637-9894, 637-1050.
15 Franklin St.
Closed: Tues.
Price: Moderate.
Cuisine: Italian.
Serving: D.
Credit Cards: AE, MC, V.
Reservations: Recommended.
Special Features: Children's menu; Vegetarian dishes.
Handicap. access: Yes.

If you're looking for gourmet Italian, keep looking. But if you're looking for satisfying, family-style pastas in a nondescript setting, Antonio's may be just your ticket. Repeated samplings of this restaurant's meaty entrees have left some of us wondering, some of us determined never to return. The bread and butter, however, has been consistent: atrocious. Surprisingly, pasta is well-prepared here: an angel hair with white clam sauce is quite fine. A linguine with tomato sauce is also generally good. Keep it simple at Antonio's — stick with the pastas and you'll walk out humming.

APPLE TREE INN
637-1477.
224 West St.
On Rte. 183, S. of Tanglewood main gate.
Closed: Mon.-Wed.
Price: Expensive.
Cuisine: Continental.
Serving: SB, L, D.
Credit Cards: AE, DC, MC, V.
Reservations: Recommended.
Handicap. access: Yes.

Up above Tanglewood, looking over Lake Mahkeenac and all of southern Berkshire, the Apple Tree Inn sits majestic. As you approach, up the long steep drive, through a lane of apple trees, you rightly feel you're about to dine in a place close to the heavens. The daytime views are among Berkshire's best. In summer, it's usually cool and breezy. We once visited Apple Tree in the fall, and as we walked past crates of windfall apples, the aromas from the kitchen wafted by, blending with the scent of ripened fruit.

We have fond memories of this place when it was Alice's Restaurant (actually "Alice's at Avaloch," years after the original "Alice's"). The octagonal dining room, set as it is into the southern slope, delivers daytime vistas that are powerfully distracting from food, friends or conversation. By night, hundreds of tiny "starlights" glow from the ceiling.

Alas, on more than one visit, we have found the Apple Tree menu too ambitious and surprisingly mediocre in execution. Nonetheless, the setting is so special....

BLANTYRE
637-3556 (Winter: 298-3806).
Off Rte. 20, several mi. NW of Lee.
Closed: Nov. 1-May 31.
Price: Very expensive-Prix Fixe.
Cuisine: French.
Serving: D.
Credit Cards: AE, MC, V.
Reservations: Required.
Special Features: Fireplaces, private dining room.
Handicap. access: Yes.

Blantyre is a true representation of Berkshire life as it was lived in the Gilded Age. Motoring up the castle's gently curving drive, you pass acres of closely cropped lawn; the grace of nobility surrounds you. Enter the expansive Tudor manor hall and that feeling will amplify as the paintings, antiques, carpets, houseplants and even the array of coffee table magazines all tell you this is the realm of the rich. Blantyre, the house, is baronial. Read the story of its builders and its style in *Lodging*, Chapter Three.

Dinner here is decidedly theatrical. To start with, the tuxedo-attired *maitre d'* offers drinks (serve-yourself-style at the open rolling bar) for which you sign. On a couch that had room for an entire retinue, we sat, drank our cocktails, ate *hors d'oeuvres* and watched the fire crackle in a hearth so broad it took four-foot logs. Properly intoxicated now with opulence, we received the most elegant menu and wine list in the Berkshires — leather portfolios, lined with green moire silk, the offerings magnificently lettered in emerald green calligraphy.

Harp music before dinner, at Blantyre.

The wine cellar at Blantrye is spectacular. A tremendous range of the best vintages from France, Italy, Germany and California give choices for even the most particular of oenophiles. Under the *prix fixe* scheme, chef Steven Taub's fall menu proposed many delights. For soups: Light Shellfish Chowder and *Velouté* of Pumpkin and Leeks. For appetizers, a choice of five: Game Sausage with Pineapple Sage and Fresh *Spaetzle*; Warm Lobster Salad on Sautéed Snow Peas and Mushrooms with a Lobster Vinaigrette; Grilled Confit of Duck with a Garlic Custard and a *Hoisin Demiglacé* Sauce; Ravioli of Lamb and Fennel with a Goats' Cheese Sauce; and a Salad of Saffron Glass Noodles with Cold Grilled Jumbo Shrimp and Slivered Smoked Pork. These were major league choices, for sure, but both the ingredients and seasoning didn't quite match up to the titles.

To clear the palate, the next course recently served at Blantyre was a lemon sage *sorbet*. This was culinary brilliance — at once tart, slightly sweet, herby, and surely palate cleansing. Among the half dozen entrees offered, we enjoyed both our Venison with a Turnip *Mousse* and Port Wine Sauce, and the Salmon on a Bed of *Brunoise* Vegetables with a Balsamic Vinegar Sauce. Astoundingly, though, an elegant little plate of nouvelle miniature vegetables was totally tasteless. We didn't let it bother us, and proceeded happily to delicious desserts, including a superb *tarte tartlin* with *crème fraiche*.

Service through all five courses was assured and knowledgeable, formally correct but still somehow friendly. Coffee was served in the drawing room, and it was there we renewed our vows of allegiance to Blantyre.

BRUSHWOOD CHEF
637-2711, 800-244-CHEF.
Brushwood Farm (Rtes. 7 & 20).
Closed: Wed.
Price: Moderate.
Cuisine: European.
Serving: SB, L, D.
Credit Cards: MC, V.
Reservations: Recommended.

With hardly a change of costume, Paolo's Auberge has become Brushwood Chef. By first accounts, this may become one of the area's better restaurants. While the name "Brushwood Farm" dates from 1915, the front section of this attractive, rambling building is actually one of the oldest houses in Lenox, reaching back to the 1750s. There is a comfortable mix of the Colonial and the Victorian styles here. Both dining rooms have large fireplaces. The Brushwood name comes from the Godwin family, who used the property as a Berkshire summer residence (they were newspaper publishers in New York); and they were connected by marriage to William Cullen Bryant, the prominent Berkshire poet of the early 19th century.

The menu is perhaps a bit ambitious, offering a range of dishes from Continental to Cajun to Vegetarian. We doubt that a restaurant can be all things to all people. But we dined satisfactorily, beginning with a deceptively subtle chicken liver pâté, zesty and fresh. The Cream of Mustard soup got an A+ for its full-bodied chicken stock base and its texture, almost reaching the delirious heights of a sauce *velouté*. Just as good was a *Ragout* of Herbal Mushrooms in a homemade Puff Pastry, a little meal in itself. For entrees we enjoyed Scallops *Provençal* and Veal in *Morille* Sauce. The shellfish were succulent and fresh, but not truly memorable. Nor was the veal dish, despite its successful brown sauce and its generous supply of wild mushrooms. Vegetables were well prepared but odd in their combinations: snow peas, brussels sprouts, wedges of spongy spinach souffle. Simpler would have been better.

Though the coffee itself was so-so, the coffee service was unique. Our waiter brought out a marvelous antique pewter pot to pour from, and a second cup was worth the wait just to see the pot again. For dessert, a somewhat too moist *Linzer Torte* was, nonetheless, accompanied by fresh whipped cream and a sprig of spearmint, a welcome hint of spring on a damp winter's night.

CAFE LUCIA
637-2640.
90 Church St.
Closed: Sun. & Mon. during winter.
Price: Moderate to expensive.
Cuisine: Italian.
Serving: D.
Credit Cards: AE, CB, DC, MC, V.
Reservations: Recommended.
Special Features: Vegetarian dishes; Outdoor dining.

From the sleekly remodeled house that was once art-dealer Honey Sharp's gallery-restaurant, Dianne and Jim Lucie have created Cafe Lucia, serving sophisticated, freshly prepared Italian specialties. In mild weather, their shaded deck, under the awning or under the trees, is very popular; on weekends especially, you may have to wait a few minutes for a table.

Lucia currently serves dinner only, a limited selection of excellently prepared specialties. *Antipasti* include *Carpaccio* (thinly sliced raw beef) with capers and mustard; and roasted peppers and anchovies dressed in olive oil, lemon, garlic and capers. Five *linguini* plates are offered, as is lasagna. Outstanding entrees include *Scallopini di Pollo* (sautéed boneless breast of chicken); *Arrosto di Maiale* (boneless grilled loin of pork); and Lucia's signature dish - *Ossobuco con risotto* (a milk-fed veal shank sautéed, then braised in a veal sauce seasoned with diced carrots, onions, celery and fresh herbs). Helpings are hearty, the fare is filling. Desserts are orchestrated by Dianne, and among our favorites was her deep-dish apple, cinnamon and sour cream pie.

"Cafe Lucia is as good as the Old Country," reported a food critic friend, recently back from Italy.

THE CANDLELIGHT INN
637-1555.
53 Walker St.
Price: Expensive.
Cuisine: Continental.
Serving: SB, L, D.
Credit Cards: AE, CB, DC, MC, V.
Reservations: Recommended.
Special Features: Fireplaces.

The Dutch have a word for it, *gezelligheid* — homeyness taken to its highest power of coziness — and without doubt the Candlelight Inn wins our "Golden Tulip" award for the most *gezellig* dining room in the Berkshires. Our table, with its pewter and flowered china settings and meticulously arranged seasonal flower display, brought us back to one of our favorite Continental inns.

The menu, too, was inspired by the Old World. Appetizers included a very French country *pâté* and a marvelous Italian eggplant sauté with *Prosciutto* and *Fontina* — an exciting counterpoint of tastes. A complimentary sorbet followed, effectively clearing our palates for the next course. Unfortunately, the quality of that next course dropped several notches, especially the Italian Fisherman's Stew which was far too soupy and understated. Desserts restored the mood, especially the Lemon

Mousse Torte and an all-American apple crisp.

Though uneven, the entire meal was served with such unpretentious grace and warmth that we finished feeling quite satisfied. The charm of the Candlelight warms us still.

CHEESECAKE CHARLIE'S
637-9779.
83 Church St.
Price: Inexpensive.
Cuisine: American.
Serving: B, L.
Credit Cards: MC, V.
Reservations: Not accepted.
Special Features: Over 50 varieties of cheesecake.

Charlie's fills a big gap in Lenox, a top-notch breakfast-lunch-coffee-and-dessert kind of place that takes pride in whatever it serves. Breakfast ranges from croissants and fruit to Eggs Benedict. Coffee comes in a dozen blends, including the supremely mellow Costa Rican La Minita, and is supplied fresh roasted from the Berkshire Coffee Roasting Company in Great Barrington. *Cappuccino*, exotic teas including Assam and Keemun, sodas, beers and wine by the glass fill out the drink possibilities. For lunch, Charlie's offers soups, burgers, omelets, pita pockets, sandwiches and salads. The portions are very generous, the quality very evident. A Cheesecake Charlie's Turkey Club Sandwich, made with meat carved off a real bird, lingers in the memory as one of the best in Berkshire, ever. Salads are very fresh, and gargantuan.

For dessert, if you're person enough, Charlie tempts you further, into the rich realm of his cheesecake. Consider some of the inventive cheesecake varieties — Dutch Apple, Brandied Peach Cobbler, Snickers, Heath Bar, Amaretto or Bailey's Irish Cream — they're all made by hand right at Charlie's.

Mecca for cheesecakeaholics, Charlie's has food for all the pilgrims, and for you, too.

CHURCH STREET CAFE
637-2745.
69 Church St.
Price: Moderate.
Cuisine: American.
Serving: L, D.
Credit Cards: MC, V.
Reservations: Recommended.
Special Features: Outdoor dining.

Clayton Hambrick's cooking at Church Street Cafe has been so well received, he and co-owner Linda Forman have expanded their restaurant three times. Church Street's patio is one of the prettiest in the county, and its interior dining rooms resemble art galleries — which they are. With every table candlelit, and classical music playing softly in the background, the restaurant makes for a most comfortable and appealing setting.

The food is even better. In our many years of dining at Church Street, we have never had a meal that was less than excellent. Given their only moderately expensive prices, this restaurant is an uncommonly good bargain. Soups are always imaginative and hearty, salads fresh and prepared with care. The wine list is unpretentious, refreshingly brief and intelligent. Service here is cordial and attentive; and even when Church Street is busy, which is often, meals generally unfold at the customer's preferred pace.

Pecan Chicken with Mustard Sauce is a Hambrick creation so delicious it's hard not to order it when at Church Street. It's the nuttiness and piquancy that stand out. Spicy Shrimp Stir-Fry, which calls for ginger, sesame oil, peppers, garlic and chili paste, is always another winner. Things Southern, like gumbos or New Orleans Shrimp show Hambrick and his well-trained staff at their best.

All Church Street desserts are created in house; each has earned applause. Mocha torte, misnamed but divine, features Heath bars blended into chocolate-and-mocha ice cream, then topped with hot fudge. Swedish cream is a slightly sour, creamy custard under a delicate strawberry sauce.

In a rolling landscape of good restaurants, Church Street Cafe stands out.

CRANWELL
637-1364.
Rte. 20.
Price: Expensive.
Cuisine: Continental.
Serving: D.
Credit Cards: AE, MC, V.
Reservations: Recommended.

Cranwell was originally the "cottage" of John Sloane, built after his brother William had finished his "cottage," Elm Court, just across town. Wyndhurst, as Cranwell was called then, was a formal Tudor estate, with gardens by Frederick Law Olmsted who also designed New York's Central Park. The estate passed through the hands of the Sloane children, then served relatively briefly as a Jesuit order, then as a prep school. Now it's a resort and conference center, and at its heart, is its restaurant.

You'll be served in the Wyndhurst Room, a grand space with ornate, high ceilings, and tall, majestic windows. Tables are lace covered, candlelit and flower decorated, and altogether, the effect is of hushed dignity. Cranwell's menu is imaginative and well prepared, though true culinary greatness is never quite achieved. Appetizers recently included a subtle Wild Mushroom *Terrine* with Morels, *Shitake* and White Button Mushrooms in Chicken *Mousseline* with Herb Vinaigrette; a very satisfying Shrimp and Scallop in Puff Pastry with Tomato *Concasse*, Herbs, and Cream; and Warmed Oysters with *Hollandaise*, Herbs, and Tomato Vinaigrette. Entrees were uniformly fine. *Tournedos* of Beef *Chasseur* with a Sauce of *Shitakes*, Morels, Fresh Tomato and Beef Stock was tender and flavorful. Roasted Half Duckling with Apple and Port Wine Sauce had a crispy exterior, moist and non-fatty meat, with a very pleasing flavor. Roast Rack of Lamb *Au Jus* with Fresh Pear and Apple Chutney was as fine as this delicacy gets, its meat buttery-tender, succulent, and delicious. A vegetable plate of wild rice, steamed broccoli and cauliflower was nicely cooked but a bit understated to our tastes.

Cranwell's Wyndhurst Room has a suitable selection of fine wines to accompany your feast, ranging from $15 California reds to $200 vintage champagne. And desserts keep up the standard, with a recent Strawberry *Tartelette* in particular etching itself deep in memory.

THE GATEWAYS INN
637-2532.
71 Walker St.
Closed: Sun. & Mon. in Winter & Spring.
Price: Expensive to Very Expensive-*Prix Fixe.*
Cuisine: Continental.
Serving: D.

Good news and bad news. First the bad news: master chef Gerhard Schmid is no longer at Gateways, having sold the distinguished inn and restaurant to New York caterer Vito Perulli. Now the good news: with the kitchen under the supervision of Schmid's former sous chef, CIA graduate Jeffrey Niedeck, Gateways continues to offer culinary excel-

Credit Cards: AE, DC, MC, V.
Reservations: Required.
Special Features: Vegetarian dishes; Dress requirements; Outdoor dining; Private dining room; Fireplace.

lence. Only eight restaurants in New England have been awarded a four-star rating by Mobil, and the Gateways continues to be top rated (translated by Mobil as "outstanding — worth a special trip"). Every dimension of dining is elegant at Gateways, from the splendid china and silver to the French-folded damask napkins, from the lively floral centerpieces to the woven silver breadbasket.

In the rather formal dining room of "Orleton," the 1912 mansion built by Harley Proctor of Proctor and Gamble soap fame, you'll be treated like the magnate himself. After a surprisingly flat start with utterly undistinguished complimentary cheese spread and store-bought crackers, meals at the Gateways settle into uncompromising excellence. Appetizers include Duck Salad with Raspberry Vinaigrette, and Lobster and Sweetbread *Crêpes*. Of the five soups offered, both the Baked French Onion and the Lobster and Clam *Bisque* were fine indeed. An ambrosial blend of shellfish in a creamy sherry base, the *bisque* is a soup whose richness is matched by the surety of its tastes.

The Gateways' wine list is suitably impressive, extensive, and expensive. Fine French, German, Italian, American and Australian bottles may be had from about $15 to $200. To go with our meaty entrées on our most recent visit, we ordered a 1982 Napa Valley Syrah, which proved the perfect choice.

Pheasant in a sauce of white grapes, juniper berries, brandy and cream is sensational, an enticing counterpoint of gamy, sweet and creamy. Veal Forest Master, another hit, is loin pieces of veal, sautéed, garnished with *cèpes* and morels. Provincial rack of lamb, one of the restaurant's specialties, is superb. Other entrées are no less tempting. Breast of Chicken Lucullus is a baked chicken breast topped with crawfish, truffles, and *cèpes*, and served with a light honey liqueur sauce. Portions are enormous, the entire pheasant, for instance, obscuring the plate beneath it. Vegetables, including a rice medley, are both pretty and delicious.

A tuxedoed waiter pours wine with panache, at the Gateways.

Though the Gateways is a trifle stiff, it also includes such *nouveau* anomalies as easy-listening music over the house stereo and well-meaning waitresses, who are asked to introduce themselves by name, an awkward ploy we thought had been ridiculed out of existence.

Desserts at Gateways are sumptuous. Viennese Apple Strudel is a divine, old-world pastry, with raisins and walnuts, topped with home-made vanilla ice cream. Grasshopper Pie is awesome: a four-inch tall, wedge-shaped tower of mint ice cream and mint meringue, dressed in fudge sauce.

Hardly missing a beat, Gateways carries on, delivering a dining experience fit for royalty.

LAURA'S SCOTTISH TEA ROOM
637-1060.
Lenox House Country Shops, Rte. 7 & 20.
Price: Inexpensive.
Cuisine: Scottish.
Serving: B, L.
Credit Cards: None.
Reservations: Not accepted.
Special Features: Vegetarian dishes.

You don't have to be Scottish to love Laura's. Though the setting (Lenox House Country Shops) and ambiance (strictly luncheonette) are nothing special, the Scottish fare is delicious. Breakfast is served all day. With your eggs, pancakes or French toast, you can get real Scottish scones and "bangers" (sausage). For lunch, there's official steak and mushroom pie, garnished by several tomato wedges, a leaf of red-tipped lettuce, and a piece of ripe cantaloupe. In every respect, this economical plate is a winner.

Hot cider comes with a floating clove-studded lemon slice. English teas are available in profusion. Desserts are definitely dangerous, and all sweets are made on the premises. Choose from among chocolate truffle cake, raspberry cheesecake, mincemeat tart, Kahlua cheesecake and many others. A complimentary shortbread square accompanies your bill. Laura's will leave you smiling from start to finish.

LENOX HOUSE
637-1341.
Pittsfield-Lenox Rd. (Rtes. 7 & 20).
Just N. of village.
Price: Moderate to Expensive.
Cuisine: Continental.
Serving: L, D.
Credit Cards: AE, CB, DC, MC, V.
Reservations: Recommended.
Special Features: Children's menu; Private dining room; Fireplace.

Lenox House serves busloads (literally) of Berkshire visitors and is one of the few restaurants in the area paying substantial attention to younger diners (with a children's menu). We found some sophisticated touches here, such as table linens and candlelight but found the food unappetizing.

LENOX 218
637-4218.
218 Main St., on Rte. 7A.
Price: Moderate.
Cuisine: New American, Continental.
Serving: L, D.
Credit Cards: AE, DC, MC, V.
Handicap. access: yes.

Chef-owner Jimmy De Mayo has moved, again. After selling his Lenox Candlelight Inn for close to a million dollars, he signed an agreement stipulating that he wouldn't establish another restaurant within ten miles for a period of two years. Almost immediately, he started the Painted Lady, in Great Barrington. When the two years were up, he sold the Painted Lady and opened a new Lenox restaurant, this time in what used to be the Log Cabin.

Teaming up with chefs Steve Shallies and Hugh Pecon, Jr., De Mayo has transformed the rustic old steak house into one of the areas' sleekest dining spots. Lenox 218 makes a statement: "we are interior decorated," with shiny black tables (cloth covered for dinner), comfy black and brass chairs, vaulted ceilings with fans and skylights, and lots of framed prints. Altogether, the feeling is southern California.

Despite a rather unadventurous menu, the food at 218 is close to De Mayo's finest. Soups are hearty and fresh. Cajun trout was fine, but we would have liked it sassier. A chicken pot pie was meaty, its crust flaky as it should be. Dinner entrées included Roast Long Island Duckling with Raspberry Chambord Sauce, Medallions of Veal with *Prosciutto*, Spinach and Cheese, and Broiled Filet of Cajun Catfish, Louisiana Style. Presentation was excellent, with each hot plate appealing in every way.

The restaurant draws business types for luncheon, couples for dinner, and either way, you're in for a sophisticated meal, at a fair price.

PANDA HOUSE
499-0660.
664 Pittsfield-Lenox Rd.
Price: Moderate.
Cuisine: Szechuan, Mandarin, Hunan.
Serving: L, D.
Credit Cards: AE, MC, V.

Though not part of a chain, this Panda very much resembles the others in Berkshire with the same name, except that it's on the strip just south of Pittsfield. Like other local Pandas, the Chinese food is delicious, chock-full of good ingredients that are well prepared. Threatened with extinction elsewhere, Pandas are now thriving in Berkshire.

SEVEN HILLS INN
637-0060.
100 Plunkett St.
Closed: Mon.-Tues. during winter.
Price: Moderate to expensive.
Cuisine: European.
Serving: D.
Credit Cards: AE, MC, V.
Reservations: Required.
Special Features: Fireplace; Vegetarian dishes upon request.
Handicap. access: Limited.

One of the original Berkshire "cottages," Seven Hills Inn beckons with turn-of-the-century grandeur, its stone terrace overlooking manicured gardens, its high-ceilinged dining rooms as elegant as when next-door neighbor Edith Wharton and her weekend guest Henry James dined here. Yet today's dinner guest will have to settle for something less than grandeur — something much closer to pretentiousness.

Our first indication that the era of elegance had vanished came as we waited for our appetizers: at a pause in the piped-in music, a radio announcer delivered a health "up date" on glaucoma that carried through the dining room unabated for several minutes. Had we drifted into a nursing home? Then the food arrived. Something listed as "Mixed Greens with Warm Brie and Garlic Croutons" consisted of an undistinguished salad-bar-quality salad on one side of the plate, a hot slab of less-than-ripe Brie on the other. Silly.

We chose entrées of sautéed chicken breast with shallots and roast loin of pork with honey mustard, expecting them to be the kind of hearty, country inn dishes we could fill up on, but our plates arrived looking like minamalist art. The only treat of the evening was a lovely, sweet and creamy pumpkin bread topped with ginger sauce.

On our way out, we picked up a brochure titled, "The Country Inn Collection" that listed Seven Hills amongst eleven other inns from Maine to Connecticut — the Baron Country Inns. It's a chain, don't you know, complete with an 800 number. Very safe and dependable. Oh Edith! Oh Henry!

THE VILLAGE INN
637-0020.
16 Church St.
Closed: Mon.-Tues.
Price: Expensive.
Cuisine: Regional American.
Serving: B, SB, L, D.
Credit Cards: AE, CB, DC, MC, V.
Reservations: Recommended.
Special Features: Traditional English Tea served every afternoon.

For over 200 years, the Village Inn has glowed at night, and the glow continues. In the soft amber light that pervades this Colonial waystation, you can see the luster of old-world attention. Not a detail is missed, and whether you dine in the dining room or out on the porch, the ambiance will be as cozy as it gets.

With talented chef John Clapper in the kitchen, innkeepers Cliff Rudisill and Ray Wilson have taken their restaurant up another notch. Though our most recent meals at the inn had their shortcomings, they were essentially excellent and we happily polished off every morsel served to us.

From a wine list that encompasses the broadest selection of fine American wines in any Berkshire restaurant, we chose a 1987 Sonoma Cutrer, a supremely smooth and crisp chardonnay. This bottle proved a perfect partner for our entrées that evening, each of which featured fish. Peppered Shrimp in a red butter sauce was lively; Ocean Perch, delicate; and Veal and Shrimp in a butter sauce a splendid counterpoint of richness. Vegetables and salads proved pleasing as well.

Desserts are a serious bit of deliciousness here, and chef Clapper prepares a very fine *Crème Brulée* and an extraordinary *brioche*-based Chocolate Bread Pudding with Brandy Custard Sauce.

Breakfast or Sunday brunch at the Village Inn are special events in themselves. The Harvest Breakfast includes an omelet of your choice or such regional specialties as Yankee Johnnycakes, made with white cornmeal from an authentic Early American recipe. As good as the food can be, the setting is truly wonderful, especially in warm weather when the sun dapples the screened porch, and you dine amidst rocking chairs, houseplants and a view of inn guests reading morning papers out on the lawn.

Into its third century, the Village Inn is still one of the sweetest stopovers on the Berkshire map.

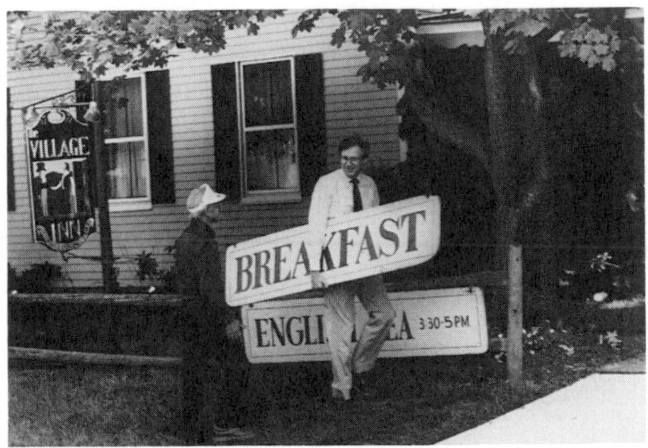

Innkeeper Cliff Rudisill keeps time, from Breakfast to Tea at the Village Inn.

> ***High Tea at The Village Inn***
>
> English Tea is available every afternoon from 2:30 to 4:30, and for such a veddy British affair, there is an assortment of finger sandwiches, homemade scones with preserves and clotted cream, as well as the dessert tray. A choice of select loose teas accompanies this delightfully light repast.
>
> A considerably more elaborate and elegant High Tea is offered on many Sunday afternoons, October through May. On those occasions (be sure to phone for reservations), the event begins in the living room with live chamber music, then proceeds into the dining room for such English afternoon fare as trifle with sherry, creamed mushrooms on toast, Welsh rarebit, or asparagus wrapped in ham with cheese sauce. English teas, of course, are the accompaniment.

WHEATLEIGH
637-0610.
West Hawthorne Rd.
Closed: Tues.
Price: Very Expensive-*Prix Fixe.*
Cuisine: Contemporary French.
Serving: D.
Credit Cards: AE, CB, DC, MC, V.
Reservations: Required.
Special Features: Fireplaces, private dining room.

There are many places in Berkshire where you can look back in history to the Gilded Age, when moneyed men and women built their hilltop "cottages." But precious few of these mansions have maintained their style, and still fewer offer *haute cuisine* dining. Wheatleigh, the grand 19th-century Italian *palazzo* built for the Countess de Heredia, is a "cottage" that is carrying on the tradition, a rare opportunity to experience royal elegance.

Like its country cousin, Blantyre (see p. 171), Wheatleigh has had its share of fine chefs. Now Peter Platt from Chicago has settled into its kitchens, and is turning out what is probably the most refined fare in all the Berkshires.

From concept to provisions, preparation to presentation, Wheatleigh's food is as memorable as dining gets. The wine list is studded with scores of the finest vintages, a list that brought the 1989 Wine Spectator Award of Excellence as one of the most outstanding restaurant wine lists in the world.

From the imaginative list of *hors d'oeuvres*, we selected a Warm Salad of Grilled

Louisiana Shrimp, Sea Scallops, Lobster and Slivered Endives with a Lemon Butter Sauce; Ossetra Caviar, Smoked Salmon and Smoked Trout *Mousse* on a Buckwheat *Blinis;* and an order of *Tagliatelle* Pasta with Fresh White Truffles (at $15 supplementary). The warm sea salad and the smoked fish were extraordinary in every respect; the pasta with truffles faltered, its heavy cream sauce smothering the delicacy of the truffle.

Courtesy Lenox Library.

Entrées were uniformly exceptional. This is as close to culinary art as you're likely to get stateside. Halibut Enrobed in Crimped Potato with Oysters and a Caviar Butter Sauce was a noble dish, indeed. And Grilled *Grenadin* of Tuna on a Bed of Wilted Spinach with Fresh Ginger and Leeks was a symphony of taste and texture. Roasted Loin of Venison with Wild Black Huckleberries was at once gamy and delicate. Vegetables were just right, with an artful squiggle of sweet potato purée leaving us longing for more.

Desserts at Wheatleigh are awesome. We tasted a subtle Poached Pear in Puff Pastry with Chocolate *Mousse* and Caramel Sauce; a hearty Hot Apple Walnut *Tarte* with Cinnamon Ice Cream; Sweetened, *Framboise*-Scented *Chevre* Layered with Raspberries in Delicate Pastry; and a Tasting of Homemade *Sorbets*, featuring Cranberry-Quince, Pear and Passion fruit.

A concluding cognac, and we left Wheatleigh feeling like royalty.

Hancock

DRUMMOND'S
445-5500.
Corey Rd.
At Jiminy Peak ski area.
Price: Moderate.
Cuisine: American, Continental.
Serving: B, L, D.
Credit Cards: AE, DC, MC, V.
Reservations: Recommended.
Special Features: Panoramic mountain setting, Fireplace.

Jiminy Peak skiers and other sportsfolk attracted to this handsome year-round resort are fortunate in having a mountainside restaurant and bar right in their midst. If a clean, fresh look pleases you, you'll enjoy Drummond's atmosphere, which includes a blaze in the charming oversized fieldstone fireplace and entertaining views out to the ski slopes.

An extensive salad bar offers a satisfactory start, but the entrées that follow are uneven. One winner is the *Linguine Carbonara*, perfectly *al dente* pasta with *prosciutto*, peas and garlic in a light buttery cream sauce. Scallops *Provençale*, however, is too shy in the onion, black pepper and garlic departments. Marinated Grilled Chicken Breast is dry, rather bland and without a trace of the promised fresh rosemary.

Drummond's does have a well thought-out wine

list, and we enjoyed a fine Napa chardonnay from Sequoia Grove winery. Yet, even here the restaurant stumbled. The cork was brittle and so, predictably, broke off in the bottle. The menu promised a half-dozen desserts, but our waiter said the chef didn't quite have his act together; not much was available. A Chocolate *Mousse* Cake had a bad case of freezer burn. A dish of lemon and lime sherbet came across as grocery store ice cream. Our coffee, served a good ten minutes before dessert arrived, was cold.

Drummond's is convenient to the excellent skiing here at Jiminy; we recommend it for an *apres* ski drink at least. As for food: if you choose your course carefully, you can have a good run, but basically, it's downhill.

THE HANCOCK INN
738-5873.
On Rte. 43, reachable via Rte. 22 N. of New Lebanon, NY.
Price: Expensive.
Cuisine: Continental.
Serving: D.
Credit Cards: AE, MC, V.
Reservations: Recommended for parties of 5 or more.
Handicap. access: No.

The mellow tenor of the Hancock Inn has a strong appeal. Upon your candlelit, linen-draped table, a series of gourmet delicacies will appear. In the small, claret-colored room (there are two other dining rooms as well), the feeling of intimacy will give you the impression of feasting at home on a grand occasion.

For appetizers, mushroom caps stuffed with duck liver *pâté* are sinfully rich, savory, *al dente* and fresh. *Billi Bi*, a seafood soup, looks surprisingly thin, with nary a trace of solid mussel; but it tastes splendid, a full-bodied and bold broth.

The Hancock was featured on a "Good Morning America" segment; and the more you relax into your meal here, the more you'll sense why a network TV crew might travel this far to cover a restaurant/inn.

Sunflower oatmeal bread is served with every meal, but be warned: it is delicious and filling, occupying precious stomach space. Among the entrées, one of our favorites has always been chicken in a champagne-cream-and-fruit sauce with apples, peaches and mushrooms. Simply extraordinary.

If you're game, the Hancock can take you still further, but be warned here, too: they finish with a bang not a whimper; and every dessert packs enough cholesterol for any adult's daily dose and then some. The inn is an excellent spot, off the beaten path, for a quiet, sumptuous meal.

Pittsfield

DAKOTA
499-7900.
1035 South St.
Price: Moderate.
Cuisine: American.
Serving: D.
Credit Cards: AE, DC, MC, V.
Reservations: Recommended for parties of 5 or more.
Special Features: Fireplace.

Not long ago, Dakota burned down, but you'd never know it. Using the same architectural ingenuity with which he transformed an old Howard Johnson's into an expansive, woody lodge, Dakota owner Tony Perry has rebuilt, replicating his original retrofit. Dakota calls itself a "Berkshire Roadside Restaurant," and with its pine walls, oak floors, raised fieldstone fireplace, mounted deer heads and overhanging birch-bark canoes, the feeling of a grand hunting lodge is successfully communicated — at least inside. Outside you're on the strip. Perry is given to the slightly wacky as well. At crabfest time he rents a huge inflatable crab and perches it on the rooftop, the Berkshire's answer to Godzilla on the Empire State Building. Although the Dakota's rusticity is brand-new, the establishment is spacious and comfortable. Generally well managed and conceived, it has become one of the county's most popular restaurants.

With good reason. We have seen this restaurant operate with clockwork precision (though we have had unexplainable delays here, too). Dakota serves an imaginative, well-prepared menu, featuring mesquite broiling. The Apache Indians have cooked with mesquite for thousands of years; like them, many restaurants and home chefs have found that this hot-burning Southwestern wood seals in juices and imparts a distinctive smoky flavor. At Dakota you can choose plates such as steak kebab and shrimp, salmon, swordfish, and chicken *teriyaki*.

All meals come with huge slabs of freshly baked whole grain bread and salad bar privileges. The restaurant describes its salad bar as "spectacular," and indeed so bountiful is the array, it must be approached with caution. The wine list offers two dozen popular varieties. Desserts are dandy, prices are moderate, and altogether Tony Perry's Dakota is a Berkshire roadside delight.

DEBBIE WONG
499-3538 or 499-3527.
315 Dalton Ave.
Price: Moderate.
Cuisine: American, Chinese, Polynesian.
Serving: L, D.
Reservations: Recommended.
Special Features: Vegetarian dishes; Private dining rooms.

When you're on your way to the latest Spielberg film, or even better, on your way back, sometimes you get a craving. It could be for sweet and sour pork, or spare ribs, or egg rolls with duck sauce and soy sauce and Chinese mustard. Or it could that rare compulsion to order one of those cocktails served in a ceramic deity with a paper parasol in brightly colored dye that runs all over your napkin. It's a craving for the only kind of Chinese food that was available to most Americans in the fifties and sixties. Nostalgia is at work here, and if the mood is right, nostalgia will temporarily suspend every delicious recent memory of *Szechuan* and *Hunan*, of the true *Mandarin* and *Cantonese*. If you're in Pittsfield and the craving hits, enter the time machine at Debbie Wong.

THE DRAGON
442-5594.
1231 W. Housatonic St.
Price: Inexpensive.
Cuisine: Vietnamese.
Serving: D.
Reservations: Not accepted.
Special Features: Vegetarian specialties.

Pittsfield's premier Vietnamese restaurant, Kim Van Huynh's Dragon has moved out of the tin diner taken over by Hickory Bill (see p. 186), and is now located just up the road, a few miles further out of Pittsfield. Though the interior has absolutely no character or charm, the food continues to be authentic, if occasionally oily. Still, when you have a hankering for Shaking Beef, Dragon is the only game in town.

ELIZABETH'S CAFE PIZZERIA
448-8244.
1264 East St.
Across from "the G.E."
Price: Inexpensive.
Credit Cards: None.
Special Features: Specialty pizzas; no smoking

What do you get when you cross the new California cooking with traditional Italian cuisine? When you juxtapose a grim industrial landscape outdoors with a sparkling white and chrome interior, energized by predictable art museum posters from the land of Gauguin and Matisse? When you imbue your staff with pride and enthusiasm and good humor, such as you'd expect to find at home in the kitchen of a family who love to serve food for their friends? You guessed it: Elizabeth's Cafe Pizzeria. Dear old struggling Pittsfield has developed a penchant for sprouting surprisingly engaging restaurants in the most unlikely places. This is one of the best.

The menu is whimsical and teases the diner into the appropriate mood. Even if you've just popped in to pick up a pizza to go, this food experience will be sensuous and a bit theatrical. The nightly specials described so robotically elsewhere are here presented with such verve and conviction you'll want to try them all. One begins with a large hunk of crusty Italian bread, to break or cut, and Elizabeth's authenticity is thus established immediately. The *soupa del journo* we tried — Fresh Tuna in a Tomato-base Broth, with Onions and Risotto — was superb. We thought a good test would be the humble polenta, easy to prepare but usually a study in blandness. One companion, a cookbook reviewer no less, exclaimed, "This is the best polenta I've ever had, bar none." Eavesdropping from the open kitchen, the chef volunteered that night's secret formula (*jalapeño* peppers, black olives and a little milk). The tomato sauce on top which we enjoyed might be a cheese sauce tomorrow, he said.

There are salads and sandwiches, all made with the freshest of ingredients, many of which are on display at the pizza pick-up counter. It's easy to believe in this kind of place. Nothing is hidden, and the work performed is self-evidently a labor of love. But pizza is the *piece de resistance* here, and so we indulged in a "white pie" called Rustica. Elizabeth's offers traditional pizza, with tomato sauce and a host of fresh toppings, going way beyond the predictable pepperoni. The "white pies," however, are their signature statement. We quote from the entertaining menu, a spasm of playfully purple prose: "Imagine yourself a painter; before you lies a canvas of silken dough. It beckons you in some primitive way. 'Come close,' it says. 'Caress me with oils, flavor me with herbs and cheeses, paint me with fresh vegetables. Use me, I am yours.'" Our rating was A+ for the pizza dough and the same for the Rustica's abundant cheese, chopped tomatoes, onions and olives. At $14.00 this is an excellent way to feed a small crowd.

On your way to or from the movies or a shopping trip downtown or at the mall? Find an excuse to roll down East St. and taste a little bit of this local genius.

ENCORE
at the Berkshire Hilton
499-2000.
Berkshire Hilton Inn (Berkshire Common).
Price: Expensive.

For generations, the Hilton name has been synonymous with luxury lodging and dining. But somehow, the Pittsfield facility managed to escape the notice of the Hilton quality-control crew, and our local version seemed tired, the dining rooms indiffer-

Cuisine: American.
Serving: B, L, D.
Credit Cards: AE, DC, MC, V.
Special Features: Children's menu.

ent. Now, with the infusion of much capital and quite a bit of thought, this Hilton is up there with its siblings, offering immaculate rooms and fine meals.

Though the menu we recently tried had a few potholes, such as a disastrous honey poppyseed dressing on one salad, on the whole, everything was well prepared and quite tasty. Encore's decor is reminiscent of what you might expect at the Bankok Hilton — oriental fans serving both as design motif and lighting shades — and since it hasn't a single window, there isn't a clue as to where on earth you're really sitting. No matter. This restaurant serves till 10 p.m. every night of the week, offering the certainty of good food most anytime. The plates even look great, artfully arranged with a curled orange slice acting as accent.

Grilled Shrimp Rolled in Sweetened Coconut was a surprisingly successful appetizer, as was Herbed, Breaded Deep-Fried Brie. The very ripe Brie was served in a neat half-pound wedge, the size you might put out for a small cocktail party. We didn't quibble, and devoured the entire creamy slab. Entrées were uniformly good, though Chicken Joanna (lobster and chicken in a pastry shell) could have used substantially more seasoning. Broiled Swordfish in Lemon Green Pepper Sauce was fresh, and neither over- nor under-cooked. Filet Mignon with *Béarnaise* Sauce was rich, tender and juicy. Other entrées offered ranged from two kinds of duck to rack of lamb, from salmon to veal.

Though quite full and satisfied by now, we nevertheless forced ourselves further — in the name of culinary exploration — and consumed a Raspberry *Torte* with Almond Paste for dessert, finding it quite delicious. Service was well meaning, but occasionally inept. Still, for us, the Berkshire Hilton had arrived, just in time.

GIOVANNI'S RISTORANTE
443-2441.
1331 North St. (Rte. 7 N.).
Price: Moderate.
Cuisine: Italian, American.
Serving: SB, D.
Credit Cards: AE, DC, MC, V.
Reservations: Recommended for parties over 6.
Special Features: Children's menu.
Special Features: Non-smoking area.

After years of passing by this friendly looking place, we decided, one frosty night, to give it a try. Upon entering the rosy brick building, we knew instantly it was an eatery where kids are welcome, evidenced by the fleet of high chairs and baby seats parked in the lobby. One of the larger restaurants in the county, Giovanni's also boasts the biggest collection of plastic plants and plastic Tiffany-like lamps, a forest of plasticity hanging down from a crowded ceiling.

Bread is often a tip-off as to how seriously a restaurant takes itself, and Giovanni's cold, squeezably-soft, tasteless "Italian" bread did nothing to whet our appetites. Although the menu here sounds authentic, the food is far from it. Soups were awful. Imagine onion soup so unappetizing that you wouldn't want to finish it on a cold, windy night, and you have some idea. Salads looked like leftovers from our otherwise appealing antipasto. By now we were no longer in the mood. Service was cheery, but casual. Among the wide range of traditional entrées, we tried Eggplant Parmesan and *Veal Scallopini a la Giovanni*. The veal dish was the best food of the night, served with a tasty light mustard sauce, sautéed mushrooms and green onions. The eggplant, however, tasted like it was made from prefabricated pucks, giving credence to the news delivered by our waitress that the chef had spent the night "cleaning the stove."

HICKORY BILL'S BAR-B-QUE
499-0211
478 W. Housatonic St. .
Closed: Mon.
Price: Inexpensive.
Cuisine: American.
Serving: L, D.
Credit Cards: None.

Hickoy Bill himself, Berkshire's barbecue king.

In the 30's-style tin diner once occupied by the Vietnamese restaurant, Dragon (see p. 183), Oklahoman Bill Ross, Jr. has established an outpost for another fare foreign to the Berkshires: original Texas-style barbecue. With a quarter of the diner taken up by the 15-foot, steel Oyler Barbecue Pit, Hickory Bill's is not long on atmosphere. But the food is so delicious, so authentic, so satisfying, that Bill's instantly became one of our favorites.

Using a method developed in the 1920s by a Mr. Jack Tillman, a Texan known as the "Barbecue King," Hickory Bill seasons the meat, places it in the pit, hot with hickory coals, then bastes it and carefully controls its lengthy cooking. All meats are smoked and cooked at least six hours; many are left in the pit overnight. The result is fantastic — smoky, juicy and tender beef ribs, spareribs, fancy brisket, and chicken, all sold by the pound. As side dishes, Bill serves dynamite collard greens (with bits of brisket), barbecue baked beans and Mexican cornbread (laced with *jalapeño* pepper). Mrs. Evelyn's Sweet Potato Pie for dessert makes a fitting finish, and you'll go out smiling, we promise.

"Wish I had a bigger stomach!" wrote one guest in the guest book. "Awesome!" penned another. With 40s swing music playing softly in the background, and the day's papers (including *The New York Times* and *Investor's Daily*) available, you might find yourself surprisingly at ease in this funky diner, even if you're the Malcolm Forbes type. "Can we eat back here?" asked one guest, nodding to the back room. "Eat anywhere you want!" replied Hickory Bill. "It's your place! I just work here!" [**Note**: As this book went to press, a move to Great Barrington was being planned for Hickory Bill's. Please check with telephone information – 411.]

THE HIGHLAND
442-2457
100 Fenn St.
Closed: Mon.
Price: Inexpensive.
Credit Cards: None.
Reservations: Not accepted.

The Highland has been serving square meals to Pittsfielders since 1936.

"Spaghetti!" answered the owner when we asked him what kind of food his restaurant serves. "Spaghetti and anything from a hamburger to filet mignon." With lots of veal in between and homemade pudding and cream pies to finish.

Ted Williams and other legendary ballplayers hang out here (in oversized photographic form), and if you weren't looking closely, you could easily be in a bar near Fenway Park or Yankee Stadium. Except here, things haven't changed much since the thirties, and old heroes are still news.

The Highland is homey: the food's pretty good, folks are friendly, prices are right.

Over-the-counter trading at the Highland.

LA COCINA
499-4027.
140 Wahconah St.
Across from Wahconah Park.
Price: Inexpensive.
Cuisine: Mexican, American.
Serving: L, D.
Credit Cards: AE, CB, DC, MC, V.
Reservations: Not accepted.

La Cocina is one of the most popular eateries in the whole county. This place has a devoted following who will vehemently defend its reputation against the only other Mexican restaurant in the area, Dos Amigos, in Great Barrington. The debate focuses mainly on the question of Mexican authenticity. La Cocina does offer "the real thing" in menu items such as *chorizo* (Mexican sausage), cactus salad and *ceviche*. However, the basic orientation is Tex-Mex with predictable tortilla dishes predominating.

La Cocina was devastated not long ago by fire, and the owners promised the faithful to rebuild. The new La Cocina has recaptured the dressed-up "hole-in-the-wall" appearance that characterized the original. Even when filled to capacity, the restaurant retains a dark and cozy atmosphere which — along with the festive cuisine, a couple of margaritas and some music — will make even a first-time visitor feel like one of the cognoscenti.

La Cocina's *sangria* is first rate, a blend of wine, fruit juice, triple sec and brandy that quickly puts you in a party mood. Upstairs at La Cocina is a hot night spot, with live music. Across the street on a summer night you'll find the Pittsfield Mets in Wahconah Park.

NICKLEBY'S
At Union Station
499-4193.
34 Depot. St.
Closed: Sun.
Price: Inexpensive to

Pittsfield's Union Station train depot was a grand space, a monument to the great railroad age in Berkshire. Looking out the windows from your table at Nickleby's — located near the site of the demolished train station — all you'll see today is a parking

moderate.
Cuisine: American.
Serving: L, D.
Credit Cards: AE, DC, MC, V.
Special Features: Children's menu.

lot and Amtrak's sad little replacement, a tiny shed. A sign of the times, this had us looking for the train to yesteryear.

Fortunately, Nickleby's, the restaurant, is just fine as it is, a welcome addition to Pittsfield's short list of medium priced eateries with satisfying food. You're likely to find lunchtime Nickleby's lively with shoppers and downtown business people. A meal here can make a North Street shopping expedition quite a bit more cheerful. The chili has a real kick to it, no doubt largely from its toppings which include *jalapeños*, olives and red onions, along with plenty of melted cheese. Warm and tasty *nachos* ride sidesaddle on the dish. A creamy and handsome plate of *julienned* cole slaw, served on a bed of upturned red cabbage, rounds out one meal. The New Orleans Cajun Chicken Sandwich — appropriately spicy — comes on good local rye bread with lettuce and onion. The accompaniment here is a generous helping of crispy, curled French fries.

Of the desserts, we definitely recommend the Kentucky Pie: its crust and filling both laced liberally with rich chocolate chips, the pie is served floating in a white cream sauce swirled with an abstract design you'll swear is in the lovely china itself. Attentive, efficient, and friendly service smooths the way at Nickleby's.

PANDA WEST
499-3991.
90 North St.
Price: Moderate.
Cuisine: Hunan, Szechuan, Mandarin, Cantonese.
Serving: L, D.
Credit Cards: AE, MC, V.

What? Another black and white bear? Actually, this was the first to appear in the Berkshire hills, and it continues to be an outpost of authentic Chinese food. Sure, the atmosphere says "you could be anywhere," but what does it matter when the food's heavenly? Our advice: head for the starred items; hot here is good!

TEO'S HOT DOGS
447-9592.
1410 East St.
Price: Inexpensive.
Credit Cards: None.

Easy to miss, but hard to forget, this newly expanded doggery still wins no prizes for ambiance. Instead, it concentrates on serving cold beer and a genuinely zesty miniature hot dog which you can have topped with "the works," a "chili-sauce/chopped-onions/mustard" combo that may lead to gastrointestinal meltdown unless you're blessed with an industrial-strength stomach. But relax: even strong men posing as restaurant reviewers often eat these little dogs with less than everything on 'em. We do recommend living dangerously, though: order two or three.

Mysteriously, the dogs taste best when ordered through the tiny, screened take-out window. On your way into or out of Pittsfield on the east side, this is a good bet for fast but original food. Dirt cheap, and you won't need reservations or a coat and tie!

TRUFFLES & SUCH
442-01551.
Allendale Shopping Center, (Rtes. 8 & 9).
Price: Moderate to Expensive.
Cuisine: American.
Serving: L, D.
Credit Cards: AE, CB, DC, MC, V.
Reservations: Recommended.

The idea of a good restaurant in a shopping center is a bit hard to swallow, but Truffles & Such goes down smooth, a first-class dining room that succeeds in most of its creative leaps. The setting is minimalist modern (with no art on the walls), sleek tables and chairs, a jazz singer on the sound system. Owners Mike and Irene Maston have created Berkshire's first traditional *nouvelle* restaurant, a new category we're initiating here and now, which includes obligatory raspberry vinaigrette as a featured salad dressing, baked Brie in *phyllo* dough as an appetizer, and goat cheese spread throughout salads and entrées. In addition, such restaurants must make extravagant use of exotic wild mushrooms, not skimp on portions the way *nouvelle nouvelle* restaurants did, and pack a wallop at dessert time.

Truffles & Such fills the bill admirably. A Wild Mushroom Stew, made with oysters, *shitakes*, buttons and new potatoes is an ambrosial meal in itself. A Caribbean Crab Cake, with ginger and green peppercorns, accompanied by spicy avocado *remoulade* and roast pepper sauces, made a pretty plate, but the hot stuff was too timid. Entrées were similarly well conceived, though not always perfectly realized. A Grilled Shrimp on Pasta with *Pignolia* Nuts featured massive quantities of pine nuts, well-cooked pasta, crisply grilled shrimp, and not much taste, yearning as it did for garlic or Parmesan. Chicken Livers with Sliced Green Apples, however, was an exquisite combination prepared to perfection. The menu offers more than a dozen inventive entrées, half-a-dozen salads and an equal number of appetizers.

For lunch, Truffles & Such is equally creative, featuring many of their best dinner salads, soups and appetizers as well as pastas, egg dishes, and unusual sandwiches, such as Sir Wasso's Chicken Sandwich, a broiled chicken breast in orange, soy and sesame marinade on French bread. In addition to wines and beers, there are Australian Hepburn Spa Quenchers, in flavors such as Lemon-Lime-Orange, Apple-Blackcurrant, and Orange Passion Fruit.

Desserts are breathtaking, if occasionally overwhelming. A Kiwi Tart was superb, light, delicate, and at once creamy and fruity. Something called A Potato — a spud-sized lump of brownie dough, marzipan, rum soaked raisins, bittersweet chocolate and slivered almonds — was a bit much. Still, the range of desserts is ambitious indeed, and here's a place where you can indulge in fine Napoleons, Chocolate Hazelnut Tortes, Sour Cream Apple Pie, and Chocolate...Truffles & Such.

RESTAURANTS NORTH COUNTY

Adams

BASCOM LODGE
At the summit of Mt. Greylock.
743-1591 (Winter: 603-466-2721).
Lanesborough.
On top of Mt. Greylock, off Rte. 7 to S. Main St., Lanesborough, then 7 mi. up on Rockwell Rd. to the top. Accessible from N. Adams also.
Closed: Oct. 20-May 15.
Price: Inexpensive.
Cuisine: American.
Serving: B, L, D.
Credit Cards: MC, V.
Reservations: Required.
Special Features: 100-mi. view.
Handicap. access: Yes.

Whether you've climbed on foot, on bike or in your car, this mountaintop restaurant is a welcome stopover. Breakfast and special dinners are the main events, served in the rustic stone and wood lodge. Berry-laden pancakes and herbed scrambled eggs shine in the morning, the weekly barbecue buffets and New England dinners star at night. Whatever the hour, the views are breathtaking, the elevation heady. Reservations are required, and the restaurant is open seasonally, from mid-May til mid-October. Come on up to Berkshire's "Windows on the World."

Hikers at breakfast in Mt. Greylock's Bascom Lodge.

New Ashford

MILL ON THE FLOSS
458-9123.
Rte. 7.
Closed: Mon., Sept.-June.
Price: Expensive.
Cuisine: French.
Serving: D.
Credit Cards: AE, CB, DC, MC, V.
Reservations: Recommended.

Like the magic elixir from which his family takes its name, Maurice Champagne can provide a culinary experience that is elevating and somehow effervescent. The atmosphere at Mill on the Floss is informal, warm and woody with massive rough-hewn beams overhead and pleasing yellow-lighted wall sconces casting a soft glow. The building is over 200 years old, and was moved to its present site in the late 19th century. Candlelight also adds to the ambiance, as does firelight from the brick hearth in colder weather. The highlight of the dining room is, however, its open kitchen. Here, behind a Dutch tile counter and a gleaming array of hanging copper pots, chef Champagne in his tall white *toque* moves artfully, preparing meals before your very eyes (he is featured on the cover of this book). If you've ever worked in a restaurant kitchen, you'll doubly appreciate the beauty of this normally behind-the-scenes performance.

After some complimentary Jarlsberg and cream crackers, fresh French rolls are delivered, delicious, crunchy and hot from the oven. Soups are superb, the split pea, full-bodied yet delicate, the onion soup, bold in broth, with still-firm bread, and perfectly browned *Gruyère* topping. *Escargots* in garlic butter are plump and flavorful. Eggplant *Parmigiana*, served here as an *hors d'oeuvre*, is so outstanding it ought not be passed by.

Entrées are uniformly excellent. Chicken Maurice is a succulent, boneless chicken breast in a light brown sauce, topped with *Béarnaise*. Shrimp and scallop Creole on a bed of rice is piquant and oceanic simultaneously — a totally satisfying, spicy dish. Crispy duckling *à l'orange* is extraordinary, its skin crisp yet chewy, its meat succulent and flavorful with very little fat. The *julienned* vegetables and broccoli with *hollandaise* that accompany these entrées are superb in every respect. Presentation of the entrées is as pleasing to the eye as it is to the palate. The menu also offers Veal *Picatta, Marsala*, or *Cordon Bleu*. Pasta is served with clam, meat (veal with the chef's brown sauce) or *primavera* sauce.

Service is articulate and attentive, the food being delivered with panache. Desserts range from a delicate *Créme Caramel* to a heavier though no less artful *Gâteau de la Maison*. Cold Grand Marnier *Soufflé* with Raspberry Sauce is incredible, an airy confection sprinkled with slivers of almond and covered with fresh raspberry sauce.

Mill on the Floss — a Champagne toast to the Berkshires.

THE SPRINGS
458-3465.
Rte. 7.
Closed: Christmas.
Price: Moderate.
Cuisine: Continental, American.

A very large, apparently very popular and — to some tastes — very good restaurant (winner of a Mobil four-star award). What it lacks in intimacy, it makes up in overstatement of interior design with, for example, the Berkshires' biggest restaurant chandelier!

Serving: L, D.
Credit Cards: AE, CB, DC, MC, V.
Reservations: Recommended.
Handicap. access: Yes.

North Adams

THE FREIGHTYARD PUB
663-6547.
Furnace St.
In Heritage State Park.
Price: Inexpensive.
Cuisine: American.
Serving: L, D.
Credit Cards: AE, MC, V.
Special Features: Fireplace.

One of the few pubs in all of Berkshire, the Freightyard is a two-story brick tavern in a historic district. Though the construction's new, somehow the building manages to lend an antique ambiance, harkening to the 19th century when North Adams was a railroad hub. Both the satisfying food and friendly locals manage to enhance this quality.

A *kielbasa* made locally in Lanesborough, presented with sauerkraut of course, is among the best we've tasted. Chicken *teriyaki*, a dish easy to spoil, comes off quite well. Burgers, soups and sandwiches are the basic fare. A generous, well-stocked salad bar can fill any stomach space left.

When you reach Heritage State Park, consider fueling-up at the Freightyard... before continuing on down the track.

JACK'S HOT DOGS
664-9006.
12 Eagle St.
Off Main St.
Closed: Sun.
Price: Inexpensive.
Serving: B, L.

Premier doggery in North County, Jack's continues a 70-year family tradition by serving outstanding dogs with all the trimmings. Jack's is supplier of the official dog for the North Adams State vs. Williams College hot dog eating contest. As one local put it, "You haven't really been to North Adams 'til you've been to Jack's."

Williamstown

THE CAPTAIN'S TABLE
458-2400.
Cold Spring Rd.
Closed: Tues. in winter.
Price: Moderate.
Cuisine: American.
Serving: D.
Credit Cards: AE, D, MC, V.
Reservations: Recommended.

This is our idea of what a family-style restaurant ought to be. With a long history of successful service, the Captain's Table gets our applause for its competence in a much-maligned category in the restaurant business: standard American Surf and Turf fare for those without gourmet expectations. If you're a nonsmoker, take our suggestion and ask for "a table by the water" when you enter the dining room. You'll end up sitting in a hokey-as-all-get-out blue underwater glow (reflecting off the coral reef wallpaper). But hey, you're in the mountains: how much seaside authenticity did you expect?

Begin at the shrimp and salad bar. Medium-sized shrimp, dozens of 'em, await your pleasure in a large bowl of crushed ice. A zesty cocktail sauce is provided.

The salad bar is moderately extensive, with colorful touches, such as both poppy seeds and sesame seeds to sprinkle on top. A freshly baked loaf of warm white bread (no health food whole grains here...), brought graciously to the table on a cutting board, was thoughtfully accompanied by both butter and margarine.

The appetizer portion of the menu is impressive, but beware, because the entrées to follow come in large servings. We could have stayed firmly on the Turf, choosing from a good list of steaks and chops. Various Italian pasta dishes are also available. We went to the Surf instead. We could have picked out our own live lobster from a chock-full, bubbly tank where the underwater mini-monsters bobbed lugubriously. But the fried oysters, one of that night's specials, got our vote, and we weren't disappointed. The batter was pleasingly light and the flavors quite tasty. From the regular menu we sampled broiled scallops. All the dishes here have straightforward names, and nothing makes you wonder what may have possessed the chef to put this and that together on the same plate. Halleluiah, the scallops were fresh, large and flavorful, moistened by a moderately buttery sauce. An absolutely nondescript baked potato and dish of buttered carrots, just like mom used to serve, added ballast to the main course.

One memorable dessert drew all of our sugar-lusting attention: Super Snickers Chocolate Pie, an apotheosis of gilding the lily in its deft blend of crushed candy bar, plus additional chocolate and peanuts, all on a pastry crust. Service was friendly, quick and polished. It's no mistake that the parking lot at this roadside restaurant is usually almost full.

CHOPSTICKS
458-5750.
412 Main St.
Price: Inexpensive to moderate.
Cuisine: Chinese.
Serving: L, D.
Credit Cards: AE, MC, V.

An old friend has a new home. Chopsticks, Williamstown's major source of Hot and Sour soup, *Moo Shee* Pork, *King-Pao* Chicken and other essentials of life, has moved. Happily, little has changed besides the address. Justin Ahn still presides over the proceedings in a friendly manner, and in the kitchen, Hsiao Lin Juan and his wife, Sheue-Jen, are busy at the *wok.*

Chopstick's menu lists 112 items, most of which are standard in Chinese restaurants. Starred dishes are hot and spicy. For those with asbestos throats and a taste for chili oil, these dishes can be made even hotter on request. Ask for no MSG, and no MSG shall be forthcoming.

There are few surprises here, but the food is well prepared, the sauces special. The atmosphere is pleasant, the service accommodating and there is a full bar with a small wine list. Purists have complained about the quality of the martinis at Chopsticks, and a bottle of Tsing Tao Chinese beer or even a glass of Chinese white wine may be a better choice.

The new location features a Chinese grocery store downstairs. Customers in the area who crave Spicy *Szechuan* Pork or Shrimp *Lo Mein* can now also have them delivered, eliminating those death-defying midwinter trips over icy roads. Chopsticks remains a wellspring of comfort in North County for the many who feel that life without good Chinese food is dry indeed.

COBBLE CAFE
458-5930.
27 Spring St.
Closed: Easter, Thanksgiving, Christmas, New Year's Day.
Price: Inexpensive.
Cuisine: American.
Serving: B, L.
Credit Cards: None.

In the fall of 1990, the Cobble Cafe moved into the prime Spring St. space vacated by Bette's Life and Times — which was surely a candidate for all-time best restaurant name. We visited not long after the opening, and understandably, service was still a bit discombobulated. We had to go through ordering four items on the menu to find one the kitchen could actually provide. Time will no doubt smooth out such speed bumps in the road.

Bette's funkiness has been replaced by a spare, off-white interior, with abstract art enlivening the walls, which makes sense in a town with two dynamite art museums. The menu is lively, too, brief but imaginative, drawing clearly on the new California cooking with its stunning and untraditional juxtapositions of meats, fruits, cheeses and vegetables. We sampled the soup du jour, Farmer's Vegetable, and found it barely a cut above Campbell's, altogether bland and too salty. Oyster crackers, still sealed in plastic, were tossed indifferently on the table.

On another visit we hope to try the cafe's interesting salads (unavailable this time), such as Breast of Duck and Pear, and Shrimp and Grape (served with mixed greens and dill mayonnaise dressing).

The Fissili Pasta with Roasted Garlic and Black Olives (in a marinara sauce with goat cheese atop) made a fine entree, though it was shoved in front of us while we raced to finish our soup. There was no shyness about the garlic, and we say bravo. Cobble Cafe is an easy place to dine as a vegetarian and still find tempting dishes. Carnivores might want to try the Pork Tenderloin with Apples and Raisins (flamed in brandy with a light cream sauce). Our Raspberry Almond Tart for dessert was a handsome affair, but having been snatched only seconds before from the cooler, whatever taste its pastry or fruit might have had were chilled beyond recognition.

We wish this establishment well because its menu is so promising and the location is perfect for townies and visitors to Williamstown. Plans for serving dinner are on the boards, and may, even now, be in effect. But the kitchen and staff can take a tip from the local theater festival: rehearse, rehearse, rehearse.

HOBSON'S CHOICE
458-9101.
157 Water St.
Closed: Sun.
Price: Moderate.
Serving: L.
Credit Cards: MC, V.
Reservations: Recommended.

Back in the 17th century, Thomas Hobson ran a livery stable near Cambridge, England, and always tethered his best horse near the stable door. Travelers wanting to rent a steed were somehow corraled into choosing that horse, "Hobson's Choice." The expression has persisted and is still quite common in England. Leave it to a restaurant in a college town to take a historical allusion and make ironic fun with it.

Today, locals and travelers alike know that Hobson's Choice is a good one for lunch. There's plenty to choose from here. Dark wooden booths line the walls of the restaurant's two rooms, creating a sense of privacy. The friendly, unobtrusive staff makes Hobson's a comfortable place to linger.

Owner Chris Harris describes the cuisine as "eclectic," an accurate term for a luncheon menu that includes *Tempura, Nachos,* Fish N'Chips, Noodles Alfredo and Hot Turkey Sandwiches. Those with curious palates and smaller appetites can make an interesting meal on a combination of appetizers. The sandwich menu includes substantial versions of the classics: Club, Reuben, Corned Beef, and Steak as well as a Hobson Burger Deluxe. You can order half of most of these sandwiches along with some soup for a satisfying lunch.

Hobson's offers homemade soups, and the Onion Soup *Gratinée* is excellent. It never fails to warm, nourish, sustain and inspire.

A comfortable, well-stocked bar includes a nice selection of imported beers and ales plus a modest wine list. Hot Mulled Cider, *Espresso* and *Cappuccino* provide warmth and cheer for the more abstemious.

LE JARDIN
458-8032.
777 Cold Spring Rd.
South of Williamstown.
Closed: Tues. during winter.
Price: Moderate to Expensive.
Cuisine: French.
Serving: D.
Reservations: Recommended.
Special Features: Fireplace; Vegetarian dishes; 3 dining rooms.

High on a hill, lit like a fairy castle, chef Walter Hayn's Le Jardin certainly appeals to the eye as you stroll up its path, past its tranquil pond. Inside, the mood is less elegant, and its qualities as a country inn seem to dominate. Formerly chef at the Springs (New Ashford) and also at Blantyre (Lenox), chef Hayn serves more of a Continental menu than strictly a French one, with a greater emphasis on steaks and chops than on subtlety of sauces.

A favorite among Williams grads, Le Jardin continues to deliver an upscale evening without getting too fussy. Though the menu is in French, it is also in English, and the food generally holds up well in the translation from kitchen to dining room. Gourmets might not want too look or taste too carefully here, as we noted both breads and salads as remarkably undistinguished. But the hearty, homestyle entrées, served with broccoli and cheese, roasted potato and sweet potato, precisely matched the conviviality of the dining room. And besides all their visual appeal, the sole, duck and other entrées proved to be nicely done.

Among the enticing desserts, a particularly sinister one was chosen by a member of our party, our dear friend falling fatally for Death by Chocolate *Gâteau.*

THE ORCHARDS
458-9611.
222 Adams Rd.
Price: Expensive.
Cuisine: American, French.
Serving: B, SB, L, D.
Credit Cards: AE, CB, DC, MC, V.
Reservations: Recommended.
Special Features: Private dining room.

The Orchards is a welcome addition to upscale North County dining, establishing itself as one of Berkshire's better restaurants. Yielding repasts of outstanding graciousness, it has settled its kitchen and service staffs, and the restaurant is now truly outstanding. In its appointments and attention to tableware, the Orchards has few rivals in the county. The tables are lovely, set with pink damask and graceful stemware, German china and Queen Anne flatware, and accented with colorful fresh bouquets. The dining rooms are tall, with walls covered in a

Tea by the fire, after a feast at the Orchards.

Courtesy the Orchards.

green plush velvet; muted lighting is principally from wall sconces. Chairs at the Orchards are undoubtedly the most luxurious in any Berkshire restaurant, splendid Chippendale-style hardwood chairs, generously padded and beautifully upholstered. Sailing ship models in glass cases separate several of the dining rooms, and though the Orchards is new both in business and structure, their dining room has about it the feel of an older metropolitan athletic club, a club for those with substantial resources.

Recent appetizers ranged from an unusual Smoked Duck Breast with Cumberland Sauce to Grilled Blackened Shrimp with *Salsa Cruda.* Under the guidance of chef Kevin Cook, a recent menu offered nine entrées, among them: Sautéed Veal Sweetbreads with Mushroom Thyme Madeira Sauce; Grilled Duck Breast with Orange Hazelnut *Gastrique*; and Grilled *Mahi Mahi* with Fresh Thyme and Roasted Pine Nuts.

For dessert, you're offered the luxurious option of coffee and cakes upstairs in the inn. If your time and mood allow, move up to the cathedral-ceilinged living room and make yourself at home. Sit on the couches, at a coffee or card table — you choose the setting, then choose your delicious dessert. Coffee is poured from a silver pot. The mood of country elegance is complete. [Note: As of this writing, the property was in some financial difficulty with the banks, but was expecting to continue operations.]

PAPPA CHARLIE'S DELI SANDWICH SHOP
458-5969.
28 Spring St.
Price: Inexpensive.
Cuisine: American.
Serving: B, L, D.

Pappa Charlie's has been completely remodeled; and while it's certainly lost its quaint collegiate funk, it still serves good sandwiches and such. If you think you're seeing double when comparing "the Deli" in Great Barrington with this one in Williamstown, well, you are right. We hear there was a great

Special Features: Open late.

deli schism somewhere back in history, with the southern deli forces seceding from the northern ones. Reports are unconfirmed, but we do know this: many of the same crazily named, delicious sandwiches, and elaborately adorned, well-stuffed bagels, are available here and at Barrington's "Deli." Anyone for a bite of a "Bo Derek"? Or an "Avocado Smoothie" (bagel of your choice, spread of cream cheese, slices of avocado: all zapped in the steamer; not exactly *haute cuisine* but still capable of inducing profound satisfaction). There is fine hot and cold cider here too, even homemade root beer; also exotic fruit juice combos (our favorite is strawberry-banana-OJ). The cooler holds one of North County's better arrays of domestic and imported cheeses. Pappa Charlie's is a good place to hang out before or after the movies at Images Cinema, just down the street.

THE RIVER HOUSE
458-4820.
123 Water St. (Rte. 43).
Closed: Mon.
Price: Moderate to expensive.
Cuisine: American.
Serving: L, D.
Credit Cards: AE, MC, V.
Reservations: Recommended.
Special Features: Fireplace.
Handicap. access: Yes.

The River House is one of Williamstown's most popular restaurants and with good reason. The dining rooms are homey, the food well prepared in generous portions, the service exemplary. If you're running late and heading for the theater, there's no better bet for good dining in a hurry. River House can get you in and out in an hour without sacrificing quality or making you feel rushed. Your cheerful waiter will instantly size up the situation, recommend cold appetizers and quickly prepared entrées and in just a couple of minutes, you'll be enjoying *hors d'oeuvres,* with the main courses in preparation.

The River House comes through reliably with its entrées. Baked Stuffed *Scampi* aren't skimpy, nor is the breadcrumb stuffing soggy as is frequently the case. Lamb chops are outstanding, cooked just as ordered — two tender, moist chops. Our own roving fried-onion-ring connoisseur has pronounced the River House rings excellent, not greasy or overbreaded. French fries also hit the mark.

Few things in life are guaranteed, but a good time and good meal are almost a sure bet at The River House.

RESTAURANTS OUTSIDE THE COUNTY

Hillsdale, New York

L'HOSTELLERIE BRESSANE
518-325-3412.
At junction of Rtes. 22 & 23.
Closed: Mon.
Price: Expensive to Very Expensive.

There are many French chefs' associations, so strong is Gallic interest in things culinary. But only two organizations are reserved for the truly elite French chefs, culinary artists celebrated by their clientele, by food critics and by other great French chefs. These are the *Academie Culinaire de France* (limited to fifty chefs in America), and *L'Association des Maîtres*

Cuisine: French.
Serving: D.
Credit Cards: AE, MC, V.
Reservations: Recommended.
Special features: Fireplace, Vegetarian dishes.

Cuisiniérs de France (chef-restaurateurs only; at present numbering 30 in America). The latter organization is presided over by André Soltner, chef-*proprietaire* of New York's Lutece. It is the *Maîtres Cuisiniérs* who present the coveted *Toque D'Argent*, or Chef-of-the-Year Award, a tall chef's hat of silver signifying the admiration of the greatest chefs in France.

Jean Morel, chef-owner of L'Hostellerie Bressane, is a member of both organizations, and winner of the 1985 *Toque D'Argent* (on display at the restaurant).

At L'Hostellerie Bressane, in the sleepy hamlet of Hillsdale, you are likely to be greeted by chef Morel's wife, the directress of the inn; and she will escort you through their cozy 18th-century dining rooms, aglow with candlelight. The redbrick inn was built in 1783 by Parla Foster, who had been an officer in the Revolutionary Army. The Morels have lovingly restored it. Table linens and silver are appropriately fine.

Small French loaves were superior, crusty on the outside, chewy inside, and baked fresh. The wine list at L'Hostellerie features an extraordinary choice of rare bottles. For example, you could order a Chateau Margaux 1955 ($375) or a Mouton Rothschild of the same vintage ($425). Good if not great French wines are also available for around $20.

Chef Morel's range is impressive. For *hors d'oeuvres*, consider his *gâteau de foie blond au coulis de tomate* (chicken liver *soufflé*, with a touch of garlic), light and livery; cold mussels with mustard sauce, a showpiece, a red cabbage leaf acting as a visual center, the sauce a sassy complement to the plump, fresh shellfish. Soups are superb. A *Gratinée Lyonnaise accompagnée des oeufs aux deux alcools* (onion soup with egg yolk, Madeira and cognac) has a symphony of winey flavors supporting the onion.

Entrées include *Aiguilletes* of Duck with Raisins and Sauterne Cream Sauce — slices of duckling breast, an exciting combination of flavor and texture. Trout is exceptionally delicate, and poached salmon studded with red peppercorns is as delicious and rich as that fish gets. Vegetables include fresh *salsify*, imported from Belgium, and sautéed cucumbers, as well as slightly undercooked *riz sauvage* (wild rice). The menu is long and intriguing: there are other top-notch choices.

The extraordinary dessert chocolate *soufflés* must be ordered in advance with your meal. Chef Morel is so masterful at these, it is almost a sin not to partake. For those who can resist this temptation, there is yet another to succumb to: chef Morel makes his own ice cream (in subtle flavors like hazelnut), plus *sorbets, tartes, and mousses.*

After our feasts at L'Hostellerie, we thank chef Morel, we praise him; we feel honored inside and out.

In keeping with his passion to pass on the secrets of great French cooking, master chef Jean Morel teaches cooking classes at his L'Hostellerie Bressane. Courses are usually four days, with a daily schedule that features a 10 a.m. till 2:30 p.m. cooking class, followed by lunch with questions and answers. On Fridays, the class returns to the kitchen at 6:30 p.m. to watch the staff prepare the restaurant dinners. Students may either commute from their own lodging, or stay with the Morels at L'Hostellerie.

SWISS HUTTE
518-325-3333.
Rte. 23.
Price: Expensive.
Cuisine: French, Swiss.
Serving: D.
Credit Cards: MC, V.
Reservations: Recommended.
Special Features: View of ski slopes; Outdoor dining.

The Hutte (pronounced "Hoo'-ta") has been a favorite of friends for many years, so we thought it high time to revisit and perhaps add it to our recommendations. We were thoroughly delighted, and believe you will be, too. From its scenic locale at the base of Catamount ski resort, you can watch skiers in winter, listen to the birds near the deck in summer, or just feel cozy in its woody dining room in spring or fall. Fresh bouquets of flowers adorn each linen-draped table, and brass candle lanterns add a soft glow.

The uncompromising attention to detail carries over from dining room to food, and everything leaving chef Gert Alper's kitchen is delicious in look and taste. Fresh baked rolls and a small tub of firm, sweet butter got us in the mood; an appetizer of *Tortellini* Swiss Hutte sent us soaring. This *Gruyère*-filled pasta was covered with a creamy sauce, garnished with sprinkles of parsley and a tomato puree. Simply symphonic. Onion soup was hearty, with a stringy, *Gruyère* lid that made it difficult to eat, but well worth the effort. Though we would have liked a few more traditionally Swiss entrées to choose from, the *Wienerschnitzel* and Steak *au Poivre* we selected convinced us that this standard Continental menu was just fine, when prepared as well as this. The steak was as fine a peppery rendition as we've tasted, succulent, tender, with a robust sauce. Vegetables here were uniformly excellent, from sweet carrots to cabbage. Swiss *rosti* (potato pancake) was superb.

A note of warning at Swiss Hutte: save room for dessert! Among others, we sampled an incredible raspberry cream pie and a rich, airy, apple puff pastry, both of which featured fresh, whipped cream. Who says you can't have your cake and eat it, too?

New Lebanon, New York

SHUJI'S
518-794-8383.
At junction of Rtes. 20 & 22.
Closed: Mon. in winter.
Price: Moderate to expensive.

The atmosphere at Shuji's combines the Victorian splendor of the Tilden mansion (built by the nephew of the New York governor who lost the U.S. presidency to Rutherford B. Hayes in 1876 by a single electoral vote) with the delicacy of Japanese domestic decor. Step into Shuji's and cross over a footbridge

Cuisine: Japanese.
Serving: D.
Credit Cards: AE, MC, V.
Reservations: Recommended.
Special Features: Tatami rooms: Vegetarian

into a house where the ceilings are inlaid wood, the windows are stained glass or *shoji*-screened and where in four of the mansion's upstairs rooms you must remove your shoes to enjoy the cushioned realm of *tatami*. With authentic pillow chairs to recline upon, even diners unaccustomed to this type of sitting will be comfortable. Two of these *tatami* rooms are for private parties only. Downstairs there is Western-style seating.

Mishiko, chef Shuji's wife, will greet you with welcoming Japanese hospitality. Service is provided by several young American women, one of whom lived in Japan for six years. Our servers (dressed in red kimonos) were well versed, attentive, and graceful in their delivery. Shuji's menu is not only authentic, it is comprehensive and imaginative. You could start with some plum wine or hot *saki*, but you might also like a Samurai Lord (the Far Eastern sour made with Suntory whiskey) or a Black Belt (vodka, kahlua and *saki*). Ashai and Kirin Japanese beers are also available.

In the Tatami Room at Shuji's.

For appetizers, Shuji offers elegant arrangements of *sashimi* (raw fish) and *sushi* (raw fish with rice). Other appetizers include *tempura* (batter-dipped, deep-fried vegetables and fish) and mushroom *teriyaki.*

Several elaborate dinners are offered regularly, among them "King of the Sea" and the "Japanese Gourmet Dinner." The "King" is a melange of lobster, crab, shrimp, scallops, clams and vegetables, all lightly steamed in a seasoned broth. Shuji's vegetables are not only fresh and delicately cooked, but many of the Japanese vegetables are grown especially for the restaurant. The "Gourmet Dinner," delicious as it is, may be misnamed, being better suited to gourmands or possibly *sumo* wrestlers. This gargantuan eight-course marathon begins with *kishikatsu* (batter-dipped, deep-fried crab roll), then smooths out with some miso soup, followed by *sushi*, *yakimono* (steamed clams, chicken, onions, green peppers *en brochette*), *sunomono* salad (a mixture of cucumbers, radish and parsley with an oversugared rice-vinegar dressing). And then come the heavy guns: lobster, *tempura*, and a climactic huge, half-inch-thick Porterhouse steak cooked *teriyaki* style. The *wasabi* (hot green horseradish) that accompanied the superior *sushi* caused at least one of us to experience intimations of immortality. The traditional steaming hot towel at the end of the meal was a heavenly blush.

Fear not, ye dieters and health-conscious ones: for lighter meals, Shuji's also features two delectable vegetarian dinners, one a *tempura* and the other a *teriyaki.* And from the ocean comes Shuji's seafood *misonabe*, a Japanese-style *bouillabaisse* with half a lobster, king crabmeat, shrimp, scallops, *tofu* and vegetables, cooked with a soy-flavored sauce in an earthenware pot.

At dessert time, stick to simpler fare such as artfully served fresh fruit or sherbet. The "Mt. Fuji," a green grape-liqueur shortcake, does not do Shuji or Fuji great honor. Nonetheless, all who leave this restaurant have *"abregato"* (thank you) on their lips.

Other Recommendations

Besides the few outside-the-county restaurants we've reviewed here, several others stand out. Three of these are good bets if you're headed to or from the Berkshires on the south end. ***Charleston*** (517 Warren St., Hudson, NY; 518-828-4990) is John Manikowski and Carole Clarke's new restaurant (they ran the superb Konkapot Restaurant in Mill River), specializing in international cuisine. The setting is simple but gracious, the food extraordinary. The same can be said of the ***Cannery Cafe*** (85 Main St., Canaan, CT; 203-824-7333), an epicenter of Cajun fare. The newly renovated ***White Hart Inn*** (the Village Green, Salisbury, CT; 203-435-0030) is a tastefully revised 19th-century lodging that houses three distinct dining rooms, all quite appealing. The White Hart is under the capable guidance of Terry and Juliet Moore, who also own and operate the justly popular Old Mill restaurant in South Egremont.

A highly recommended Berkshire outpost in the wilds of New York City is ***Miss Ruby's Cafe*** (135 8th Ave., in Chelsea; 212-620-4055), where former Berkshirite Ruth Bronz holds forth from her lively, open kitchen with effusive Southern hospitality. The menu is regional American and it changes every few weeks. The bar is a watering hole for Berkshire people — those happy to be in the city and those wishing they were back up in the hills.

FOOD PURVEYORS

With its traditional down-home farm markets and its sophisticated gourmet emporia, Berkshire now spans the spectrum in specialty food shops. Picnic purveyors are thriving in the county as well, and should you wish to dine *alfresco*, many shops will cleverly outfit you with a basketful of delicacies. There are shops in Berkshire that have been making their own sausages, cider, soda and chocolates for years. Traditional regional products, such as honey and maple syrup, have blossomed. Recently, cheese, pasta and ice cream have joined the growing list of locally made foodstuffs. And for those who want their foods ultrafresh, a *Farm Produce Update* has been published by Berkshire County Cooperative Extension (448-8285), a joint venture with Southern Berkshire Food and Land Council and UMass. The Update is a guide to point-of-origin eggs, milk, cheese, meat, herbs and produce available at southern Berkshire farms.

Bakeries

BAGELS, TOO
499-0119.
166 North St., Pittsfield.

Thirteen kinds of NY bagels made on the premises all day. Cream cheese spreads, lox, specialty coffees and *espresso*. Raved Willard Scott of "The Today Show": "Best bagels outside of NY!"

THE BAKER'S WIFE
528-4623.
312 Main St., Gt. Barrington.
Closed: Tues.

"Just an old-fashioned girl, still baking the old-fashioned way," is her self-description, and the Baker's Wife brings to Berkshire a welcome array of breads and muffins. Breads are baked according to a weekly schedule, and include, among others: Five Grain; Honey Oat; Italian Twist; Korn Rye; San Francisco Sourdough; Seedy Oat; and Wheat Germ. Tasty muffins range from a honey sweetened Ginger-Pumpkin to Sour Cherry-Pecan, from Cranberry- Hazelnut to Blue Cornmeal Blueberry.

BERKSHIRE MOUNTAIN BAKERY
274-3412.
Park St., Rte. 183, Housatonic.
No retail sales on site.

Though Berkshire Mountain doesn't sell retail, look for their traditional sourdough breads in natural food stores both near and far. Richard Bourdon is something of a master breadmaker, and every loaf tastes as terrific as the last.

The peasant bread in particular makes a super picnic loaf, something you can tear at and gnaw on.

THE BREAD BASKET
684-9744.
22 Depot St., Dalton.
Closed: S at. afternoon & Sun. in winter.

Off Main Street, just past Benny's Restaurant, this outfit bakes whole-grain and wheat germ bread, with sourdough rye as a specialty. Also featured are George's delicious breads such as firm textured buttermilk and whole grain with walnuts. George's Bread "The Toast of the Berkshires" — is also available at health food stores and groceries throughout the county.

CEDARS OF LEBANON
743-1791.
131 Columbia St., Adams.
Closed: Sat.

There's no retail outlet here, but look for the Cedars of Lebanon pitas in supermarkets and groceries throughout the area. They're pure, simple and delicious.

CHEESECAKE CHARLIE'S
637-0939.
83 Church St., Lenox.

Cheesecake addicts beware! With 41 tempting flavors to choose from, you could enter this sweet and creamy world, and never come out, neglecting friends and family, shirking responsibilities... Those of you clearly addicted, read no further!

For those with the will power to control their cheesecake intake, meditate on Charlie's Toasted Almond Cheesecake, his Almond Joy, Creamsicle, Peppermint Patty, or Piña Colada Cheesecake. Available in 6" rounds, 9" rounds, sheetcakes and cupcakes, the cheesecake travels well and Charlie will ship it anywhere for you. Send a cheesecake postcard from the Berkshires, or eat one yourself in Charlie's comfortable lunchroom.

CLARKSBURG BREAD COMPANY
458-2251.
37 Spring St., Williamstown.
Closed: Sun.

Courtesy Clarksburg Bread Co.

Hungry in Williamstown? Just follow the aroma of baking bread down Spring Street to the Clarksburg Bread Co. Inside, one case is filled with freshly baked bread: Chunky Cheddar Cheese, Seven Grain, Crusty White, Sourdough Rye and the traditional French *baguettes*. Nearby sit trays of Shortbread, Blondies, Lemon Squares and Date Nut Bars. Some customers love the daily deliberation; for others the choice is clear: bypassing the Gingerbread Wafers and the Walnut Butter Cookies, they head straight for the *Linzer* Snaps. The 17 varieties of bread are produced on a rotating basis according to a printed schedule, with cookies and pastries always available. You can sip tea, coffee, Postum, fruit juice or Snapple soda while you ponder your choices or watch the owners calmly manage their bakery crew. Everything in the shop is baked fresh from scratch daily, and you can really taste the Clarksburg difference.

DAILY BREAD
528-9610.
17 Railroad St., Gt. Barrington.
Closed: Mon.

Give us our Daily Bread! How South County ever did without Daily Bread, Lord only knows, but since they started baking, countless thousands of people have happily relied on them for a supply of real, crusty sourdough French bread and many of life's other necessities. Tradition is carried on in this diminutive shop started by a spiritual commune in the 1970s. This is still surely South County's best source for sticky buns, for orange pinwheels, hazelnut torte, almond crescent cookies and other outrageous goodies.

At Daily Bread, you buy your baked goods right in the bakery (you can see them forming the loaves in the back); baguettes await you in a traditional French bread basket hanging behind the antique cash register. If you have the time, you can sit at one of the three or four tables up front. Coffees and teas are served, as are bakery items fresh out of the oven. Several of the Berkshire's best restaurants buy their breads here. Let us give thanks for our Daily Bread!

SUCHELE BAKERS
637-0939.
31 Housatonic St., Lenox.
Closed: Mon. & Tues.

A happy blend of antique accouterments and up-to-date methods, this bakery is a treat for the eyes, the nose and the palate. Suchele produces breads and European pastries that are rolled out on a giant marble slab right behind the counter. Handsome Victorian stoves and cabinets surround the bakers, who chat with customers as they work. Particular favorites include the sweet sticky buns with currants, the sourdough rolls, the *pain au chocolat*, and the authentic *croissants*, both plain and fancy. A variety of tarts, pies and cakes is always available, and seasonal specialties appear at the appropriate times.

Bottlers of Special Drinks

BERKSHIRE SPRING WATER DISTRIBUTING CO.
229-2086; 800-554-1130.
Norfolk Rd., Southfield.
No retail sales on site.

When Dale Bosworth had the water tested on his newly acquired property near the Berkshire-Connecticut line, his main concern was that it not damage his new white swimming pool. When he realized that he was sitting on top of a huge aquifer of pure spring water, he quickly built a plant on the site and went into business. The spring water, which is bottled just as it bubbles out of the ground, is sold either in 5-gallon bottles delivered to home or office, or in 1- gallon jugs available at supermarkets throughout the county. In either form, it's a refreshing alternative to (many) town waters or to what comes out of most taps!

THE CIDER MILL
663-6951.
800 S. Church St., N. Adams.
Closed: Christmas to Sept.

Owner Charles Ransford purchased the premises 20 years ago as a warehouse for another enterprise, discovered the 150-year-old wooden apple presses inside, and has been in the cider business ever since. The cider-making season "follows the apples" and you can come and watch the process. Inhale the aroma, it's heady. How many apples must an apple picker pick? To produce their average of 2,000 gallons a day, the Cider Mill uses 50,000 bushels of apples each season. In addition, the Ransfords have a complete country store where you can purchase their homemade cider donuts, plain or cinnamon.

GILLY'S HOT VANILLA
637-1515.
Box 1991, Lenox.
No retail sales on site.

A new beverage on the local scene has been created by Joanne Deutch of Lenox, who developed the drink as a result of her allergy to hot chocolate. Sold as a powder, it is mixed with hot water to make a satisfying hot-vanilla drink. Available by the bag at various markets and shops, and served by the cup at local ski areas, tea rooms, bars and restaurants, Gilly's Hot Vanilla is capturing a corner of the sweet-tooth market. It is available at Laura's Scottish Tea Room in Lenox.

SQUEEZE BEVERAGES
743-1410.
190 Howland Ave., Adams.
Closed: Sun.

Berkshire County's answer to the embattled "cola giants," Squeeze Beverages is a feisty local company producing sodas including cola, sarsaparilla, cream, root beer, birch beer and gentian root, as well as mixers and sodas with sugar-free flavors. Exotics include cranberry soda, and "Half and Half" (half grapefruit, half lemon-lime). These refreshingly different drinks are available at **Jaeschke Fruit & Flower Center**, 735 Crane Ave., Pittsfield, MA. 01201.

"Had Your Squeeze Today?"

Butchers

There are several small grocery markets in Berkshire County where in addition to purchasing staples, you can find custom cut meat. In all places listed, there are butchers on hand with whom you can discuss your needs. In several cases, there are excellent house specialties, such as the homemade Polish sausages at **Pleasant St. Market** in Housatonic. Advance ordering can usually assure the availability of unusual or difficult to obtain cuts of meat.

Harry's Supermarket 442-9084; 290 Wahconah St., Pittsfield; Closed: Sun.

Hillsdale Meat Center at Guido's Market 442-8135; 1020 South St., Pittsfield.

Mazzeos Importing Market 448-8323; 479 Fenn St., Pittsfield; Closed: Mon.

Stockbridge Center Market 298-3939; Main St., Stockbridge.

Pleasant St. Market 274-3344; Pleasant St. (on Rte. 183), Housatonic.

Shanahan's Elm St. Market 298-3634; Elm St., Stockbridge.

South End Market 442-6906; 519 South St., Pittsfield.

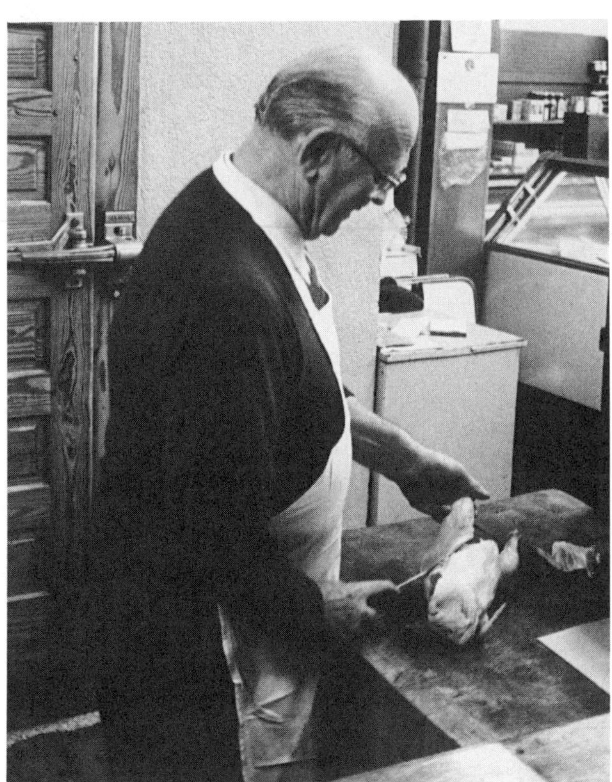

At the cutting block in Pleasant Street Market.

Candy

BOOMER'S OOGIES
443-4857; 800-332-6649.
78 Jefferson Place, Pittsfield.
No retail sales on site.

Just what exactly is an Oogie? Some people say it's a lot like a super moist and chewy cookie...only better. Some people say it's a lot like a very rich and fudgy brownie... only better. And some people say it's a lot like a luscious and sophisticated truffle...only better. But Boomer says the Oogie's beyond the cookie, beyond the brownie, beyond the truffle! Available in Wonderful Walnut, Triple Chocolate and Peppy Mint wherever sinful treats are sold.

CANDYLAND
663-5503.
16 Eagle St., N. Adams.

Candy buttons on paper strips, Mini Red Hots and Mr. Melons, Baby Sugar Daddies, popcorn balls, wax lips and moustaches, candy cigarettes, atomic fireballs and other high-powered sugar fixes.

CATHERINE'S CHOCOLATES
528-2510.
Stockbridge Rd., (Rte. 7), Gt. Barrington.
443-9589.
Berkshire Common,

Mecca for chocoholics, Catherine's will satisfy even the sweetest tooth. In her two shops, all chocolate used is made on the spot from a recipe that has been in Catherine's family since her Uncle Emile first went into the business in New York almost a century ago. The selection of hand-dipped confec-

Pittsfield.
Closed: Sun. (Pittsfield store).

tions includes cordial cherries, colonial creams, apricots, crystallized ginger and oranges, as well as "breakup" chocolate (both bittersweet and white), plus peanut brittle, buttercrunch and nutbark. Not made on the premises but also available are French butter cookies, hard candies, jams, jellies and, for the diet-minded, a variety of stuffed animals. All candies can be purchased by the piece, the pound, or in boxed assortments suitable as gifts. Catherine's has been delighting customers (and their friends) for years by mailing goodies as far away as Singapore. Seasonal specialties are available and special orders are welcome.

GOODIES LTD.
458-3916.
53 Spring St., Williamstown.

Here's the place to go in North County to treat your favorite child, or the child in you. Goodies is a kaleidoscope of color, with lucite bins, filled with jelly beans, hard candies and other bonbons, lining one entire dazzling wall. They have elegant hand-dipped candies, and lollypops, as well as an eclectic (and electric) selection of toys and designer novelty gifts. Goodies will be happy to mail these treats for you (or to you) as the need arises. Upbeat, jazzy, fun!

PINCHES AND POUNDS
442-3270.
Berkshire Mall, Lanesborough.

Ju-Ju's, thin mints, gummy bears, sprinkles, marshmallow bits, chocolate chips and every other kind of candy-by-the-piece imaginable as well as most every type of nut and coffee bean known to mankind.

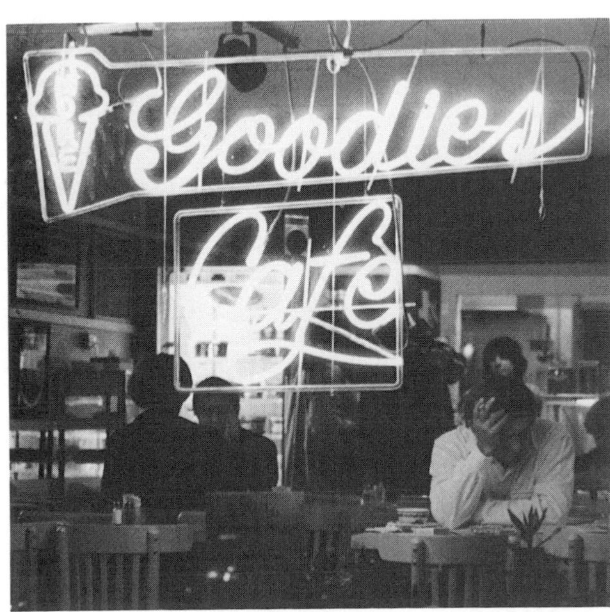

A Coffee Roaster

BERKSHIRE COFFEE ROASTING COMPANY
528-5505.
286 Main St., Gt. Barrington.

How precious is a good cup of coffee! And nowhere in Berkshire will you find more love and attention lavished on the magic bean than at this Great Barrington outpost. Is it true that these are the beans that make the world go 'round? Try a cup of Heather's brew and answer for yourself. Good coffee, it seems to us, is both stimulating and relaxing, a delight to senses of taste and smell, a comma in the run-on sentence of life.

From Africa, South and Central America, Heather imports 100-pound sacks of hand-picked, green coffee beans, the finest money can buy. Then, in a gargantuan, steel and brass coffee roaster, she carefully roasts the beans — lighter for a smoother, more aromatic cup, darker for a stronger, more acidic cup. Either way, she'll sell you beans and blends by the pound, the greatest and most satisfying selection of coffee in the county. And within the shop itself, are art covered walls (most recently hung with the fantastic, painted masks of Embee Bulkley), half a dozen tables, soft classical or country music, and the convivial air of a sophisticated college cafe. What a place to while away a morning or afternoon! With coffees, *cappuccinos, espressos,* hot chocolates and other flavorful exotics to drink, and *biscoti,* cookies and shortbreads to nibble on, your every wish is covered, deliciously.

In Great Barrington, it's the Berkshire Coffee Roasting Company — for that aromatic pick-me-up, or a bag of the freshest beans in Berkshire.

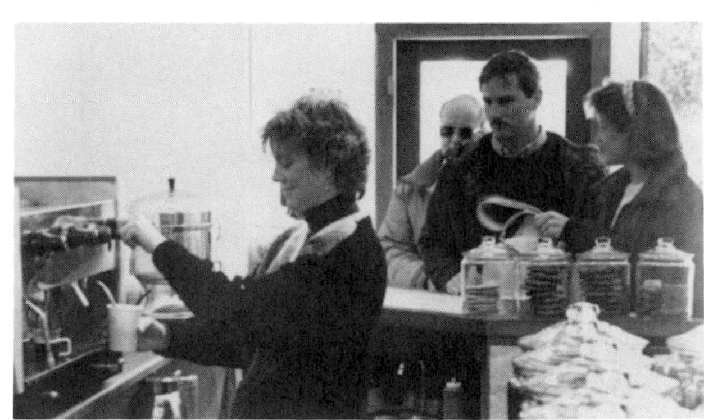

Coffee Queen Heather Austin steam-heats a fragrant cup, at Berkshire Coffee Roasting.

Cold-Water Coffee,
As Served at The Berkshire Coffee Roasting Company

At the Berkshire Coffee Roasting Company, and in a growing number of homes worldwide, coffee is being prepared using the cold water, or toddy method. In this method, ground coffee is allowed to sit in cold water overnight (one pound coffee to two quarts cold water), with the mix filtered through cloth or paper the next morning. The yield is a dark, cold water concentrate, which is then mixed with an equal portion of cold water before heating and serving. This results in a full-bodied, flavorful brew, extremely low in acid. Berkshire Coffee Roasting company sells the Toddy Maker, a rig especially designed for cold water coffee brewing.

In addition to the caterers listed below, many Berkshire restaurants, such as ***Truc Orient Express*** in West Stockbridge; the ***Boiler Room Cafe*** in Southfield; ***Church Street Cafe*** in Lenox; and the ***River House*** in Williamstown also cater. Given some notice, most of the caterers listed below can prepare a suitably delicious picnic for you and your friends to dine under the great Berkshire skylight.

Caterers

MARY L. BAUMAN
229-8784; 528-3770.
Box 245, Sheffield.

New potatoes with caviar and sour cream, lemon chicken skewers, veal and pistachio sausage, orange almond chicken tartlets — these are just a few of the possible *hors d'oeuvres* that Mary can arrange to have passed at your party. Main course options such as *Szechuan sesame* chicken and butterflied leg of lamb marinated in Indian spices are just as imaginative and as delicious. Besides first-class, artfully arranged and imaginative fare, Mary can attend to staff arrangements for up to 325 of your closest friends.

CHEZ VOUS
298-4278.
Box 1162, Stockbridge.
Catering: May 1-Oct.1.

Elegant food, beautifully presented — this is the hallmark of Chez Vous. Chicken Madeira, oriental roast beef, lentil salad plates and wonderful desserts including cakes "for any number and for all occasions" are among their specialties.

CROSBY'S
637-3396.
62 Church St., Lenox.

Our favorite caterer continues to provide absolutely scrumptious food for the finest of parties. The raspberry chicken salad picnic makes a fine traveling companion for supper at the Mount, at Tanglewood or beside some placid pond.

HICKORY BILL'S BAR-B-QUE
499-0211.
478 W. Housatonic St. (Rte.20) Pittsfield.
Closed: Mon.

Hickory Bill's barbecued spareribs bring a taste of Texas to the Berkshires. Smoky, dark and delicious, they're perfect for picnic, parties or regular dinners. Call to order.

TRUFFLES & SUCH
442-0151.
Allendale Shopping Center, Pittsfield.

Mike and Irene Maston cater parties of two or more, with especially creative picnic spreads. Next time you're heading for the hills with a blanket and a friend, consider their sassy Caribbean picnic, with garlic-fried chicken, Frenchtown shrimp and spicy crab cakes.

Condiment Makers

BEAR MEADOW FARM
663-9241.
Moore Rd., Florida.
No retail sales on site.

"This is so good, you should bottle it!" And they did. And we lived happily ever after, enjoying such treats as Cranberry Catsup, Raspberry Vinegar, Peach Jam, Apple Chutney and Hot Pepper Jelly. Available at better groceries, gourmet and specialty shops throughout the county. From the northern farms of Florida, Mass., to the Berkshire flatlands, Bear Meadow is appearing on more and more dining room tables.

SLOAN TAVERN HONEYSUCKLE MUSTARDS
458-4733 or 4947.
Box 169, Williamstown.
No retail sales on site.

"We never leave home without a jar in the car," say Carolyn Umlauf and Michelle Thaisz, creators of these spunky spreads. Available where better condiments are sold. Don't ever say Berkshire can't cut the mustard.

Afternoon milking time for High Lawn's Jersey cows.

A Dairy and a Cheesemaker

HIGH LAWN FARM
243-0672.
Lenox Rd., Lee.
No retail sales on site.

Travel back in time and have your milk arrive at the door clanking in glass bottles, with the cream on the top. Col. Wilde's High Lawn Farm in Lee is every child's fantasy of the dairy farm, where, driving by, you can see the Jersey cows that produce tomorrow morning's milk. The old-fashioned trucks, believe it or not, are still chilled with ice and are driven by a cheerful, chatty group of men who are happy to pass the time of day with their customers. The dairy supplies milk, both pasteurized (creamy on top) and homogenized, as well as heavy, light and all-purpose cream to local stores and restaurants too, though it comes in plastic jugs to these establishments. Arrangements can be made for home delivery, well worth the price for local residents or long-staying visitors.

MONTEREY CHEVRE
528-2138.
Rawson Brook Farm, Box 426, New Marlboro Rd., Monterey.

A delicious example of local initiative and know-how, the Monterey *chèvre* produced by Susan Sellew and Wayne Dunlop is available at many shops in the Berkshires, or you can drive out to Monterey and buy it on the spot. The goats that supply the milk for the cheese are raised on the farm; the acid starter for the cheese comes from France; and the know-how comes from a Quebecois friend. Sold younger and, thus, somewhat milder than imported *chèvre*, the cheese comes plain, with garlic, with chives or with a highly successful seasoning of wild thyme and olive oil.

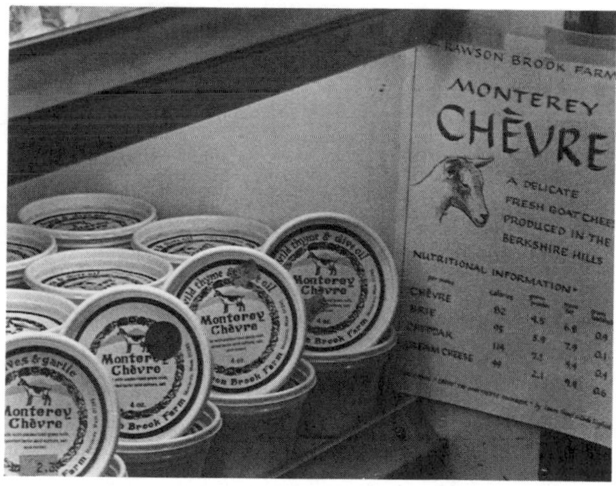

Before the factories, and all this new-fangled fun, Berkshire was first and foremost farms. Still is, if you look anywhere off the beaten track. It's farmers that keep us alive, farmers who grow good things to eat. Below are Berkshire's major farm markets, those that offer a variety of produce, usually on a year-round basis. For the smaller, seasonal farm stands, ones that sell just a few fruits or vegetables in season, consult the previously mentioned *Farm Produce Update.*

Farm Markets

BROAD BROOK FARM PRODUCE
458-3231.
903 Simonds Rd., Williamstown.

Corn and other seasonal produce. Open year round.

CARETAKER FARM
458-4309.
Hancock Rd., Williamstown.

Speaking of her lettuce, organic farmer Elizabeth Smith exclaims: "Our heads are so huge, people come in and say: 'I couldn't possibly eat all this.'" Huge-headed or not, Sam and Elizabeth Smith's organic produce is some of the best around, and their farm stand also sells fine, fresh baked organic bread.

COMMUNITY SUPPORTED AGRICULTURE
528-4374; 528-3253.
Indian Line Farm, Jug End Rd., S. Egremont.
Closed: Sun.

Based near Jug End, this coop sells vegetables year round, and sells shares in their annual harvest.

CORN CRIB
No telephone
Rte. 7, Sheffield.

Burnt to the ground and patched together with the help of community good will, the Corn Crib continues to be an excellent source for fresh fruits and vegetables in South County. The Corn Crib farm not only grows much of the produce it sells, but also serves as a cooperative for other local farmers and growers, particularly of peaches, pears and plums. Can't keep a good farm down!

GUIDO'S FRUIT & PRODUCE
442-9909.
1020 South St., Pittsfield.
At Lenox Town Line.

Guido's owner, Matthew Masiero, has been in the produce business for over a decade, and in addition to overseeing other food purveyors under their roof, Guido's continues to supply central Berkshire County with superior fruit and vegetables. Items such as *shiitake* mushrooms, *radicchio*, *fennel*, *bok choy*, *cilantro*, pomegranates and figs, all of which can be difficult to find elsewhere, are regularly available here. Guido's also now carries a wide-ranging selection of jams, jellies, vinegars, oils, nuts and dried fruits. There are locally produced goods such as Bartlett's cider and Baldwin's vanilla and maple syrup. An extensive line of China Bowl and Joyce Chen Chinese cooking supplies, and a comprehensive array of health foods and new-age cosmetics attests to the scope of Guido's fascinating emporium. For those with a sweet tooth, there is a

Cherry picking at Guido's

reassuringly large supply of ice cream, and bins of Brach's candies. Finally, from the Bookloft in Great Barrington, there is an up-to-date selection of cookbooks. But even that's not the end of it. See "Fish Markets," the next section. For food lovers, Guido's is a good hour's entertainment.

TAFT FARMS
528-1515.
21 Division St., Gt. Barrington.
Corner of Division St. & Rte. 183.

Virtual one-stop shopping for the non-carnivorous, colorful Taft Farms has been supplying South County with the best of fresh produce for decades. In the summer, their own extraordinary vegetables are available including tomatoes, peppers, broccoli, zucchini, cucumbers and potatoes. Taft Farms' crowning achievement though is undoubtedly its late summer harvest of just-picked sweet corn, quite possibly the best in our galaxy. Says Taft farmer Dan Tawczynski: "Our biggest single day we sold almost 26,000 ears here, a few years back. Personally, I like to steam it for about two or three minutes. I cook just the kernels, not the cob. When corn is good, it's really good. When it's not, it's in the supermarket."

They have herbs both fresh and dried from the Wild Thyme Herb Farm in Connecticut. In addition to conventional produce, Taft Farms offers its customers such quasi-exotic delicacies as *radicchio*, pomegranates and kiwi fruit, which are sometimes hard to come by in the nontropical Berkshires. A line of homemade preserves and jellies, labeled "natural," is sold along with fresh-baked goods from the kitchen of a local schoolmarm. Taft Farms is a wonderful place to experience the changing seasons — from the first bedding plants ready for zealous gardeners in the early spring, through the apples, cider and pumpkins that define autumn in New England. There is also a functioning greenhouse where flowering plants can be purchased to help brighten up the winter months. And most recently, Vic's Seafood, a neat little fish market has moved in, making Taft Farms even more nutritionally complete.

TRI-STATE FARMER'S MARKET, Great Barrington

On Sundays, June through October, from 10 a.m. to 3 p.m., at the Great Barrington Fairgrounds, Rte. 7, regional farmers gather to offer their freshest and best.

WILLIAMSTOWN FARMER'S MARKET, Williamstown

Early on Saturday mornings, July through September, local farmers bring their produce to the foot of Spring Street, where it's first come, first served.

A Note for Shitake Mushroom Lovers: Delftree, a local company, cultivates this wild, oriental mushroom on hardwood logs in a 19th-century textile mill in North Adams. They mail their fabulous, fat, tawny exotics all over the U.S., but you can assuage your craving for this delicacy by purchasing the fresh, locally grown article at ***Delftree's Farm Store***, 234 Union St., No. Adams; 800-243-3742. (Also available at Guido's, Rte. 7, south of Pittsfield.)

Fish Markets

CANDEE'S TROUT HATCHERY
528-3397
Warner Rd., S. Egremont.
Evenings, year-round;
Closed: Sun.

Fresh-dressed, antibiotic-free trout, born and raised in the Berkshires. Evenings except Saturdays. Still swimming when you call!

DAY'S CATCH / MOUNTAIN SEAFOOD, INC.
499-FISH (3474); 499-9947.
1020 South St. (Rte. 7) Pittsfield.
At Guido's on the Lenox town line.

The largest variety of shrimp in Berkshire County await you at Michael Hendler's fish market, Day's Catch. An integral part of the Guido's food emporium, Day's Catch has been supplying fresh quality fish, shellfish and live lobsters for over three years, both here and at their shop on Newell St. in Pittsfield. Here's the place to go for a complete line of smoked fish, including smoked salmon, and for imported caviar, as well as prepared dishes like stuffed shrimp or sole, or "seafood spuds." Day's Catch also caters to seafood lovers with everything from platters to real old-fashioned New England clambakes.

VIC'S SEAFOOD
243-1444.
95 Main St., Lee; also at Taft Farms in Gt. Barrington.

Fresh fish, caught by proprietor Vic Hryckvich, Thursday through Saturday only. Also seasonal fruits, vegetables and maple products.

Gourmet Shops

Berkshire's gourmet shops are great for specialty shopping as well as for fine everyday provisions. They're also the starting point for many a delicious picnic.

BEETHOVEN'S
232-7728.
Main St., W. Stockbridge.
Closed: Christmas to Apr.

A charming mixture of cafe, gourmet shop, bakery, picnic source and gift shop, Beethoven's is a great favorite with many musicians who spend the summer at Tanglewood. In the gift section there are lovely baskets with imported candies and antique ribbons — and a nice selection of jewelry. In the bakery department, you'll find delicious cookies, with the house specialty being Proust's favorite . . . homemade *madeleines*. Beethoven's also does some catering, supplying tasty *hors d'oeuvres* and salads for summertime weekend entertaining. This is a shop that will charm everyone from your elderly grandmother to your preschool niece.

GORHAM & NORTON
528-0900.
278 Main St., Gt. Barrington.
Closed: Sun.

Gorham and Norton is a time machine. No electric-eye automatic front door here to whisk you into an overly air-conditioned food warehouse with that disorienting feeling of "this could be anywhere." Here, there's a swinging screen door worn smooth from the hands of faithful patrons. Inside, muted light filters down from a skylight through hanging plants and glows along the walls to illuminate signs from the past proclaiming: "Powders" and "Canned Goods." There is no insidious Muzak, no loudspeaker shopper's specials. Instead, there's an abundance of knowledgeable, personal service, a full line of groceries, imported and domestic cheeses, coffees, candies and a good range of gourmet ingredients. Gorham and Norton's wine selection is surprisingly extensive; and they present a monthly wine tasting, a chatty, informative and informal event.

LA CUISINE
528-5620.
Main St., S. Egremont.
Closed: Mon. (Mar.-Apr.)

Beautifully situated in the living room of an old house (where a friend of ours used to entertain us royally), La Cuisine arrived just as the Gourmet Cottage down the road was closing. Not only was La Cuisine's timing good, but it serves an array of delicacies unavailable for many miles around. Interesting salads are a daily offering, as are pastries such as *rugallah* and leons. Cheeses, *pâtés*, soups and Middle Eastern specialties are the stock in trade, and there are several small tables in the shop should you care to sit for lunch or a snack.

Lavasch, a Syrian flatbread, one of the many locally made food specialties.

NEJAIME'S BAKERY & DELICATESSEN
442-1898.
1020 South St., Pittsfield.
At Guido's on Lenox town line.

This outlying colony of the ever-expanding Nejaime's food empire offers baked goods and choice delicatessen fare. Famous Nejaime's Middle Eastern specialties include *tabouli, hummus, baba ganoush,* and *spanakopita,* all made on the premises. In the Bakery section, in addition to the specialty herb and fruit breads, you'll find fresh *croissants* (with a variety of fillings) and *baklava*. Nejaime's also stocks a good selection of crackers and cheeses including some of the more unusual cheeses such as *raclette, lappi* and *kasseri*. Try their crusty cracker-sheet called *Lavasch* (a Lebanese specialty). If you're still hungry, sample one of their imported *pâtés*. A selection of coffee beans (including green) from White House Coffee is on hand, and you can grind it on the spot in their old-fashioned coffee grinder. Finally, full catering services are available.

THE SLIPPERY BANANA
458-4788.
264 Cole Ave., Williamstown.

A friendly place, with a wide selection of gourmet foods, natural foods in bulk, and fresh produce, the Slippery Banana has moved and expanded. This is the place to go in North County for chocolate chip cookies, *croissants* (fresh-baked daily), New York-style bagels (well . . . almost "New York"; they're from Albany), and products from Clarksburg Bread, a Berkshire bakery.

Bagging some jumbo cashews at the Slippery Banana.

TRUFFLES & SUCH
442-0151.
Allendale Shopping Center, Pittsfield.

Mike and Irene Maston offer their sinfully delicious fare for take-out. Their desserts in particular entice the picnicker or snacker to indulge.

Health Food Shops

AVELINE'S NATURAL FOOD
243-1775.
42 Park St., Lee.
Closed: Sun.

Fresh bread and produce highlight this healthy market, where you can also buy many Japanese foods, cosmetics, teas, juices, health books and magazines.

BERKSHIRE CO-OP MARKET
528-9697.
37 Rosseter St., Gt. Barrington.
Closed: Sun.

The Co-Op Market is a healthy non-profit organization which you can join to get shopping discounts — though a little work may be asked of you. Started by Southern Berkshire Community Action, the Co-Op actively seeks supplies from worker-owned food sources. More of a complete grocery store than many health food stores, it nevertheless leans towards natural foods, cheeses and organic produce. The Co-Op carries a complete line of dairy products including old-fashioned butter in bulk and, for those in the know, fertilized eggs.

The Co-Op's natural food bins.

CLEARWATER NATURAL FOODS
637-2721.
37 Church St., Lenox.
Closed: Sun.

Clearwater must be one of the very few natural food shops with a copying machine for public use. More predictably, they also have, in the dairy case, Upcountry *Seitan*, a local product, and Brown Cow yogurt. In addition to a large selection of whole-grain flours from Arrowhead Mills, there are *bulghur, miso* and other healthy supplies. Clearwater offers an assortment of carob-covered raisins and nuts, and other good-for-you "candy." You can get lunch to go at Clearwater, choosing from a list of soups and sandwiches, many of which feature *tofu* in one of its several guises. You can also indulge in a Haagen Daaz ice cream cone if the sugar spirit moves you. There is a well-stocked section of vitamins, minerals, natural cosmetics and toiletries (including Millcreek products) and an attractive display of natural food books.

CORNUCOPIA NATURAL FOODS
448-8960.
424 North St., Pittsfield.
Closed: Sun.

Theory and practice merge successfully here at Pittsfield's best natural foods outlet. Besides the large selection of books on natural foods and holistic health, the healthiest soups and sandwiches in town are served at the rear of the store. Try the fresh-pressed juices as your "one for the road" (no hangovers, no guilt feelings). The grocery section, though it looks small, is efficiently stocked. Natural vitamins and cosmetics are also in good supply here.

LOCKE, STOCK & BARREL
528-0800.
265 Stockbridge Rd., Gt. Barrington.

Owner Locke Larkin has expanded his healthy selection to fill a remodeled store that is more than twice as big as the old one. Now, in addition to the vast cheese selection, there are huge cases filled with cold cuts, and with fresh fish. There is a wide range of flours, grains, seeds, brown rices, nuts, herbal teas, honeys, yogurts, vinegars, *soy* and *tamari* sauces. Ciders and other juices abound. One whole wall is devoted to frozen health foods, surely the most complete stock in the area. The inviting cheese case offers varieties not usually found in health food emporia: *Brie, St. Andre, Gorgonzola*, and *havarti*, plus some even more unusual types like *ossiago, raclette, Valemoert*, goat gouda and farmers cheese. Locke Stock and Barrel also carries fresh *tofu* and a locally produced food product called Upcountry *Seitan*. Several lines of organic cosmetics, shampoos, vitamins and mineral supplements round out the store's stock. The friendly staff keep merchandise attractively arranged, enhancing your natural foods shopping experience.

PITTSFIELD HEALTH FOOD CENTER
442-5662.
407 North St., Pittsfield.
Closed: Sun.

The less lively of the North Street health-food twins, this one also stocks a wide array of nourishing goodies, though it's heavier into vitamins.

WILD OATS COOPERATIVE
458-8060.
Colonial Shopping Center, (Rte. 2) Williamstown.

Organic and chemical-free foods sold by members of the co-op. Open to the public, member discounts. No need to look further. In north county, they're still sowing their Wild Oats.

A Gourmet Health Food Outlet

ELEANOR & COMPANY
528-9363; 800-762-5436.
Box 809, Gt. Barrington, 01230.

Eleanor Tillinghast has been a summer resident of Mt. Washington all her life, and she's recently started a gourmet health food business based in Great Barrington, providing delicious low-fat, low-sugar, low-salt, low-cholesterol foods to a growing network of hungry consumers. Just by picking up your phone (or by sending in the order blank), you can have UPS scurry to your door with such delicious exotics as: Chukar Dried Bing Cherries; Wax Orchards fruit-sweetened Fudge Sweet; Rainbow Farms canned Rainbow Trout; Buckeye Orzo Mixes; Cinnabar Jamaican Jerk Spice Paste; Pitak authentic Indian Tikka Paste; and Uncle Bum's Romesco Sauce. At their new world headquarters — the Berkshires — Eleanor & Company hopes also to sell retail. Connect with Eleanor for the healthiest gourmet goods this side of heaven.

A Wholesale Food Outlet

WOHRLE'S FOODS INC.
442-1518.
1619 East St., Pittsfield.

A new cash-and-carry section has been added to the Wohrle family's wholesale food business, which was begun in 1921 by John Wohrle, a German immigrant, who made and sold frankfurters and sausages. The retail section offers more than 1,500 foods in refrigerated cases and freezers and on shelves. There are family-sized and larger portions of such items as soups, Swedish meatballs, lasagna, lobster, shrimp, cheeses, marinated chicken breasts, steaks, vegetables, desserts . . . you name it . . . all sold at wholesale prices. Some real bargains here.

Ice Cream Shops

BEV'S HOMEMADE ICE CREAM
637-0371.
38 Housatonic St., Lenox.

An updated, butcher-block version of the old-time ice cream parlor, this is the Central County place to go for ice cream treats. Made daily on the premises, Bev's ice cream comes in a wide range of flavors: from the traditional vanilla, Dutch chocolate and strawberry to the more exotic tastes like ginger or cantaloupe. There is full fountain service, providing sodas, frappes, malteds, floats, sundaes and even egg creams (to keep Big Apple folks from feeling homesick). You can get either pints or quarts of ice cream to go; cakes and pies are also available, to go under the ice cream, *à la mode.*

THE CONE ZONE
243-1132.
Main St., Lee.

A Zen Koan asks: What is the sound of one scoop dripping? This new purveyor may be able to help you find the answer. Serving more than a dozen flavors of Fabulous Phil's ice cream, together with your choice of 15 different toppings, this ice cream shop will take you into the Cone Zone.

Maple sugaring, Berkshire style.

Eleanor Kimberley.

Maple Products

One of the sweetest indigenous products in Berkshire is maple syrup. Trees planted by the Shakers still yield delicious sap every year for the students who tap the trees at the Mt. Lebanon (NY) Shaker Village. And in Berkshire proper, with the cold nights and warm days of March, maple sugaring is still a thriving cottage industry. Trees are tapped, buckets collected, vats boiled...till the precious amber syrup is all that's left. ***Canoe Meadows Wildlife Sanctuary*** (637-0320) in Lenox gives sugaring demonstrations in season, usually on the first three weekends in March. ***Quimby's Sugar House*** (458-5402; Rte. 43, Hancock) holds open house during the last two Sundays in March, beginning at noon. And ***Sunset Farm Maple Products*** (243-3229; Tyringham Rd., Tyringham) has an open sugar house 7 days a week from 9 a.m. to dusk. Besides the farm stands, other sources of local maple products include: ***Gould Farm*** (528-2633; Road Side Store, Rte. 23, Monterey); ***Lone Maple Sugar House*** (258-4706; Rte. 57, Sandisfield); ***Mill Brook Sugar House*** (637-0474; 317 New Lenox Rd., Lenox); ***Monterey Maple*** (528-9385; Hupi Rd., Monterey); (229-8865; Home Rd., Sheffield); ***Swann Farm*** (298-3535; Cherry Hill Rd., Stockbridge); and ***Turner Farm*** (528-5710; Phillips Rd., South Egremont). Flapjack lovers are united: Berkshire's maple is as sappy as a high school infatuation, as syrupy as a teenaged romance, as sweet as puppy love.

Orchards

BARTLETT'S ORCHARDS
698-2559.
Barker Rd., Richmond.

Discover the essence of autumn at Bartlett's, where you can choose from among the freshest apples, including Miltons, McIntoshes and Northern Spys, all grown here on Richmond's rolling hills. Towards the end of September, you can also pick up some fresh-pressed cider (the earlier apple varieties are too tart for cider), and if you're interested, watch the cider press. Bartlett's also carries jams, jellies, honey, maple products and — for the young-at-heart — candied apples (on weekends).

WINDY HILL FARM
298-3217.
Route 7, Gt. Barrington.
Open: Apr.-Oct.

A fine garden shop and nursery where you can also pick your own raspberries and apples in season.

A Pasta Maker

PASTA PRIMA
499-7478.
1020 South St., Pittsfield.
At Guido's on the Lenox town line.

The "Little Italy" of Guido's food emporium is Mason Rose's fresh pasta shop, Pasta Prima. The pasta (plain, spinach, and tomato) is indeed made fresh daily on the premises, and you can actually watch the process if you catch Mason at the controls of the big machine. You can have your pasta cut to order, or it can be purchased in sheets for cutting at home. In addition to the fresh pasta, there is also a complete line of dried pasta from *di Cecco* as well as *tortellini* and *tortelloni* from Pasta and Cheese, in New York. A selection of sauces — (meat, marinara, pesto) also from Pasta and Cheese — is available, as are Parmesan and Romano cheese. *Buono Appetito!*

Pasta Prima: freshest noodle in the Berkshires.

Picnic Baskets

Berkshire seems picture perfect for picnics, providing countless glens, glades, riversides, and well-groomed lawns for *alfresco* dining. And besides the soothing quiet and pastoral splendor, Berkshire picnics offer fabulous entertainment possibilities, such as classical symphony at Tanglewood, classical dance at Jacob's Pillow, and classical drama at the Mount. Given a little notice, almost every firm previously listed under "Caterers" or" Gourmet Shops" can prepare a truly heavenly picnic basket for you, and at many of them, you could put together a sumptuous feast just before picnic time. Below are some additional picnic providers.

Cheesecake Charlie's (637-9779; 83 Church St., Lenox). Special New England Clambake Picnic for Two, includes lobsters, mussels, clams, shrimp, corn on the cob, melon and bread.

Day's Catch at Guido's (499-FISH; Pittsfield-Lenox Rd., Pittsfield). Picnic entrees include whole poached salmon and smoked chicken breast with apricot *cassis* sauce.

Nejaime's Wine Cellars (298-3454; Elm St., Stockbridge. 637-2221; 33 Church St., Lenox. 448-2274; 598 Pittsfield-Lenox Rd., Pittsfield). Smoked salmon, cheeses, venison sausage, cajun sausage and crackers. Picnic boxes.

Samel's Deli (442-5927; 115 Elm St., Pittsfield). Simple Tanglewood boxed lunch includes sandwich, fruit and homemade cookie.

Stockbridge Center Market (298-3939, 298-3930; Main St., Stockbridge). Do-it-yourself and custom picnics include Middle Eastern specialties such as *hummus, tabouli,* and *baba ganoush.*

Pizzerias

When you enter the world of pizza in Berkshire County, you must put aside all memories of crispy, coal-oven-baked crusts topped with *mozzarella* and gutsy homemade sausage in a favorite spot in Little Italy or the North End of Boston. Even recollections of suburban cafes with eighteen-inch steaming pies cut into wedges that you need two hands to hold must be saved for another day.

Pizza in the Berkshires is generally "Greek style," save a few exceptions; and as anywhere, it ranges from good to bad. This pizza is generally smaller (ten to fourteen inches) than Italian pizza and is baked in a pan with a rim instead of on the floor of the oven. So it has a thicker and more bread-like crust (although it is still thinner than Sicilian pizza), and arrives without hollow volcanic blisters on the edges. Greek pizzas generally come with familiar toppings (peppers, pepperoni, onions, etc.), and they can be very good.

One of the highlights of the Berkshire pizza picture is in ***South County*** (Great Barrington) and is aptly enough named ***Manhattan Pizza Company.*** They advertise New York-style pizza, heros, *calzones* and salads. And it's true — the pizzas are big, flat and oozing. They reheat well, and, in a big break with local tradition, they are available by the slice. Also in Great Barrington is the tasty, crustier ***Great Barrington Pizza House*** pizza, and the chewier pizza of the nearby ***Four Brothers*** Pizza Inn. Over in West Stockbridge, pizza *aficionados* no longer have to travel, as the ***Shaker Mill Tavern*** has begun serving pizza and pizza-to-go. In Lee, a town overrun with pizza, three outlets are of particular note: ***Athena's,*** which offers fresh cheesy pies; and the unlikely ***Lee Liquors,*** which produces some of the most delicious crusty pizza in South County. A new entry in the Lee pizza sweepstakes is ***Bill's Restaurant***, a child of the Greek-styled Sophia's.

Berkshire Greek pizza in ***Central County*** can be found on the Pittsfield-Lenox Road at ***Sophia's***, and at the ***Lenox Pizza House*** where the pizza is impressive but the juke box might make you want to take your food home to eat. For those whose pizza cravings must be satisfied by more traditional, more Midwestern or more Continental pies, all is not lost. When you ask year-round natives "where's the best pizza in the Berkshires?" a name that comes up frequently is the ***East Side Cafe*** in Pittsfield. It is essentially a bar with a TV and video games, and they only make pizza Thursday, Friday, Saturday and Sunday evenings from 5:00 p.m. on. Although the pizza doesn't fall into any particular category, it is very good. The pie is small, thin, crisp and tasty. You can order it with hot peppers baked on which is a rare find in the county. This pizza is better eaten at the cafe because, like some fine wines, it doesn't travel well. But our vote for the most innovative and exciting pizza in Berkshire goes to ***Elizabeth's Cafe Pizzeria*** on East St. in Pittsfield (reviewed under "Restaurants"). Their signature "white pies" are extraordinary, the toppings abundant, the ingredients tasty fresh.

In *North County*, the best of the Greek pizza genre is ***Michael's Restaurant and Pizzeria*** in Williamstown — the favorite among Williams College students. Michael's is a small place, not long on charm, but the pizza dough is fresh and comes out crisp. In addition to all of the traditional toppings, you can get a Cape Cod Pizza (seafood, onions, green peppers, mushrooms), Michael's Special (pepperoni, feta cheese, black olives), and for the really daring, the Hawaiian pizza (ham and pineapple). If you're traveling and need your fix in North Adams, look into the ***Pizza House*** on Main Street, where the pies come in 14 varieties and the dough is made fresh daily.

Poultry Farms

BURGNER'S FARM PRODUCTS
445-4704.
Dalton Division Rd., Pittsfield.

A must at holiday time for fresh poultry, Burgner's raises and sells chickens, capons and turkeys; all three may be ordered uncooked, roasted, or stuffed and roasted. The birds come in all sizes, and whatever the numbers around your Thanksgiving table, Burgner's can fill the bill. In addition, they have fresh produce and their own homemade pies, both fruit and poultry. Calling ahead before the holidays is essential.

OTIS POULTRY FARM
269-4438.
Rte. 8, N. Otis.

Turkeys, ducks, geese and chickens, and "custom laid" eggs, in a country store setting that'll take you back in time (also, see p. 287).

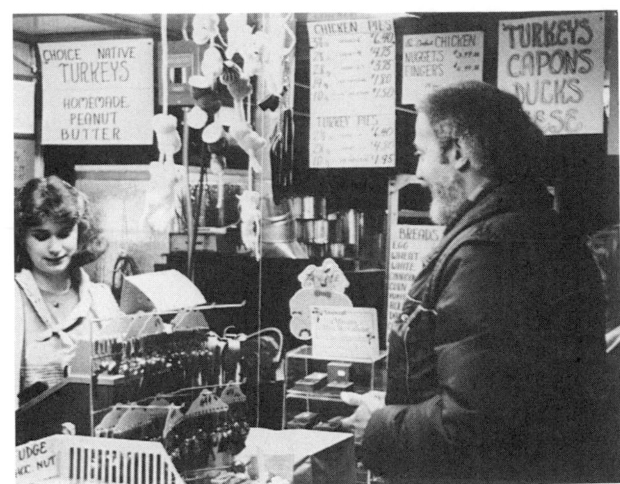

Otis Poultry, a farmstore filled with turkeys, capons, ducks, geese and custom-laid eggs.

Wine And Liquor Stores

When your spirits are low, there are numerous sources of alcoholic beverages throughout Berkshire. Outlanders should note that liquor stores in New England are often called package stores. Several of the large supermarket chains have selections of beer and wine; there are some excellent bargains available here. The shops listed below all carry a good selection of imported wines and beers, in addition to the usual spirits; and several have regular wine tastings. In most cases, the owners are knowledgeable and eager to be of help to the oenophile. Stock up early for the weekend: New England blue laws prohibit the sale of alcoholic beverages on Sunday.

The Buttery 298-5533; Elm St., Stockbridge.

Country Spirits 528-6644; 389 Stockbridge Rd., Great Barrington.

Domaney's 528-0024; 66 Main St., Great Barrington.

Gorham and Norton 528-0900; 278 Main St., Great Barrington.

Lenox Wine Cellar & Cheese Shop 637-2221; Church St., Lenox.

Liquors Inc. 443-4466; 485 Dalton Ave., Pittsfield. The biggest and best for discount wine, beer and spirits.

Liquor Mart 663-3910; State Rd., Adams.

Nejaime's Wine Cellars 448-2274; 598 Pittsfield-Lenox Rd., Pittsfield.

Queensborough Spirits 232-8522; Main St., West Stockbridge.

Spirit Shop 458-3704; 280 Cole Ave., Williamstown.

Stockbridge Wine Cellar 298-3454; Elm St., Stockbridge.

Trotta's Discount Liquors 529-3490; Rte. 23 & S. Main St., Great Barrington.

Val's Pipe & Package Store 743-0962; 7 Columbia St., Adams.

CHAPTER SIX
For the Fun of It
RECREATION

Preparing to dock, at Pittsfield's Pontoosuc.

Berkshire is a sporting landscape, beckoning boaters, hikers, horseback riders, runners, skaters, skiers, swimmers and nearly every other variety of sportsperson. Mountains and trails, lakes and rivers—all the county's topography seems perfect for sport. And there's no doubt about it: Berkshire mountain air is downright invigorating. The ski areas assure groomed winter sport with extensive snowmaking, and in warmer weather, Berkshire's golf courses and tennis courts draw sportspeople from all quarters.

Berkshire also offers many unusual sports, from ballooning to croquet, from polo to soaring. There is now a center for yoga and health arts, with a staff of 150 (Kripalu); a luxury spa with a multi-million-dollar state-of-the-art fitness center and over 50 classes a day to choose from (Canyon Ranch); and two YMCAs offering programs from camping and tennis to aerobics and sailing.

There's baseball both soft and hard, in leagues both amateur and professional, and there are nature centers that offer instruction, creative activities and adventure for explorers of all ages. And for you cave men and women out there, Berkshire offers mysterious caves under the mountains, perfect for dark, dank spelunking fun.

SPORTING GOODS STORES

South County

Four Seasons Sports 528-9061; 645 S. Main St., Gt. Barrington.
Gerry Cosby & Co. 229-6600; Undermountain Rd., Sheffield.

Central County

Arcadian Shop 637-3010; 333 Pittsfield-Lenox Rd., Lenox.
Besse-Clarke Ski & Sporting Goods Shop 499-1090; 273 North St., Pittsfield.
Champs 448-2123; Berkshire Mall, Lanesborough.
Dave's Sporting Goods 442-2960; 1164 North St., Pittsfield.
Dick Moon Sporting Goods 442-8281; 114 Fenn St., Pittsfield.
Klein's All Sports 443-3531; Berkshire Mall, Lanesborough.
Pittsfield Sporting Goods 443-6078; 70 North St., Pittsfield.
Sports Connections 443-4906; 49 North St., Pittsfield.
Sports Inc. 442-1824; Allendale Shopping Ctr., Pittsfield.

North County

Berkshire Outfitters 743-5900; Route 8, Adams.
D & M's Outpost 663-3484; 40 Holden St., N. Adams.
Goff's Sports 458-3605; 15 Spring St., Williamstown.
The Mountain Goat 458-8445; 130 Water St., Williamstown.
Sports Plus 743-4204; Park St., Adams.

BALLOONING

Take off to a world of splendid silence, where the sky doesn't seem the limit, where the wind guides you gently over the Berkshire hilltops. While there is no ballooning outpost in Berkshire County proper, there are two outfits nearby, and on some flights, you'll surely drift over these hills. Both ***Balloon School of Massachusetts*** (245-7013; Dingley Dell, Palmer), and ***American Balloon Works*** (518-766-5111; Kinderhook, NY) can arrange hot-air flights for you. Guaranteed to give you a new perspective on things!

BASEBALL

Professional baseball in the Berkshires began in the 19th century, but it wasn't till the Roaring Twenties that the hardball action was continuous. The Pittsfield Hillies played some admirable ball in the A-level Eastern League, even winning a couple of pennants, but then the Depression came, and baseball went. Through some of the 1940s, the Pittsfield Electrics played to large home crowds, finally being short-circuited by the advent of televised baseball. For 15 years after, the only pro ball in the Berkshires was on TV, featuring the Red Sox. Then, in 1965, a Red Sox farm club came and played at Pittsfield's Wahconah Stadium, and Berkshire baseball reawakened with a bang. The Pittsfield-Berkshire Red Sox played in the AA Class of the Eastern League. Starring George "Boomer" Scott and Reggie Smith (both of whom went on to shine with the Boston Red Sox), the club drew nearly 80,000 fans for the season. The Red Sox farm club moved from the Berkshires in 1976, and it wasn't till 1984 that professional pitches were being thrown again in the county.

Now it's the Pittsfield Mets playing Wahconah, and once again there's an opportunity to watch budding big leaguers in the Berkshires. The fastballs are wicked, homers are truly belted, and the playing field is real dirt (and grass). As a bonus, magic moments, perhaps out of a Norman Rockwell painting, are thrown in for free, as in the evening game delays when the setting sun shines directly in the batter's eyes and the game is temporarily suspended due to sunshine.

The Pittsfield Mets 499-METS; Wahconah Park, 105 Wahconah St., Pittsfield.

A grounder, at the Pittsfield Mets' Wahconah Park.

Softball is rapidly becoming the most popular participatory sport in America, with nearly one out of every ten adults now playing. And in the Berkshires too, softball is played with a passion. Nowhere is the action thicker than at the Berkshire County Softball Complex, a three-field park that sees at least six games a night during the summer. The complex is a not-for-profit corporation headed by banker Jim Bridges and is home to the Berkshire County Slow Pitch Softball League, a 30-team men's league, sponsored by local businesses. Other action at the complex includes a Men's Fall Softball League, a 15-team Women's Slow-pitch League and the 12-team men's General Electric League. To facilitate matters, the complex has a two-story clubhouse with bar and restaurant.

Berkshire County Softball Complex 499-1491; 1789 East St., Pittsfield.

BICYCLING

How sweet is the cycling! From the views, the rolling terrain and the variety of roadways, Berkshire bicycling seems to be custom-made for man and machine.

For racers, there's the ***Josh Billings Run-Aground*** in September, and in October, the ***Berkshire Community College Marathon***, a 14-mile race. In North Adams, the ***Greylock Cycling Club*** sponsors an annual Greylock Hill Climb, a 9.2-mile, decidedly uphill race.

For those who are touring, the back roads are tranquil, the main roads not too scary, and the mountain climbs intriguing. Mountains with roads to their summits make for a fun and challenging day trip, and in the south, the 2,600- foot Mt. Everett is a delight, while in the north, it's the 3,500-foot Greylock that commands premier attention. Climbing is the hard part, elevating you to stunning views available only to people in high places. Descents are exhilarating, but can be dangerous, so be sure to check your brakes before such an outing.

A relatively new species to these hills — the mountain biker — seems to be thriving; 18-speed machines and their smiling power plants are rolling through the picturesque landscape, often leaving the blacktop behind and riding up into the mountains, on hiking trails. Not too steep, not too tortuous, the Berkshire hills beckon those who have enough brawn, coupled with the right machine. Mountain bikers frequently gather at the ***Mountain Goat***, 130 Water St., Williamstown, at 5:30 on Monday evenings, taking to the hills en masse for some "undulating all-terraining." Mountain bikers should remember that the trails, listed under our "Hiking" section (see p. 237), have been established primarily for hikers.

Similarly, cyclists out on the roadways should remember that even on the most remote thoroughfare, cars do come by, do have the right of way, do hurt should you cross paths. It all seems very obvious until you get out there, intoxicated by the pastoral symphony around you, blithely forgetting you're on the road. So: right-hand riding, single file. After dark, the state says you must have a headlight, a red rear reflector, as well as side and pedal reflectors. In traffic, turns require hand signals with the left hand: extended for left turn, raised for right turn, held low for stopping. Helmets are a recommended nuisance, helping, in a crisis, to keep your head together.

An extremely detailed county map is available by mail from the Berkshire County Commissioners (448-8424; Superior Court Building, 76 East St., Pittsfield 01201; $5.85, checks payable to "County of Berkshire").

North Adams' resident Lewis Cuyler is an avid bike rider and a writer as well, and his ***Bike Rides in the Berkshire Hills*** is a fine guide to pedaling through these valleys and over the mountains (see Bibliography).

The critical baton pass, from cyclists to canoeists, at the annual Josh Billings Run-Aground.

BICYCLE DEALERS

South County

Harland B. Foster 528-2100; 15 Bridge St., Gt. Barrington.

Central County

Arcadian Shop 637-3010; Pittsfield-Lenox Rd. (Rte. 7), Lenox.
Ordinary Cycles 442-7225; 251 North St., Pittsfield.
Plaine's Ski & Cycle Center 499-0294; 55 W. Housatonic St., Pittsfield.

North County

The Mountain Goat 458-8445; 130 Water St., Williamstown.
Spokes, Bicycles & Repairs 458-3456; 618 Main St., Williamstown.

BOATING

Berkshire has been called the "American Lake District," and thanks to great glacial activity in its formative stages, the area is indeed blessed with many beautiful bodies of water. Besides the dozens of lakes and "bowls," scores of smaller ponds dot the landscape. For the boating enthusiast, opportunities abound. Here then, are Berkshire's best boating lakes, from ponds suitable only for canoe and rowboat, to grand lakes, where you can go powerboating, water-skiing and sailing.

South County

Benedict Pond Beartown State Forest; 528-0904; Blue Hill Rd., Monterey. Sylvan pond suitable for canoe or rowboat only.
Camp Overflow 269-4036; 5 mi. from Rtes. 8 and 20, in Otis.
Goose Pond Tyringham Rd., Lee. Boat rentals.
Laurel Lake Rte. 20, Lee. Boat rentals.
Lake Garfield Kinne's Grove, Rte. 23, Monterey. Boat rentals.
Otis Reservoir 528-0904; Reservoir Rd., off Rte. 23, Otis. Small powerboats, sunfish and sailboats for rent at the largest of Berkshire's lakes. J&D Marina, 269-4839; and Miller Marine, 269-6358.
Prospect Lake 528-4158; Prospect Lake Rd., N. Egremont. Canoe, paddleboat, rowboat, and sailboard rental and instruction at a private-access family campground and lake.
Sandisfield State Forest 258-4774; West St., Sandisfield.
Stockbridge Bowl Rte. 183, Stockbridge. Free launching sites on one of the county's prettiest lakes, just below Tanglewood.

Central County

Greenwater Pond Pleasant Point, Becket. Boat rentals.
Onota Lake, Pittsfield. Free launching area for motorboats. Good windsurfing. Onota Boat Livery (442-1724; 455 Pecks Rd.) rents small powerboats.
Pittsfield State Forest 442-8992; Cascade St., Pittsfield.
Pontoosuc Lake Rte. 7, Pittsfield. The only place in Berkshire where you can rent a ski boat. U Drive Boat Rentals (442-7020; 1551 North St.) also rents smaller powerboats, sailboats, and jet skis.
Richmond Pond Swamp Rd., Richmond. Boat rentals.

North County

Clarksburg State Forest 664-9030; Middle Rd., Clarksburg.
Hoosac Lake Rte. 8, Cheshire. Boat rentals and launching site.
Privacy Campground 458-3125; Rte. 43, 5 mi. south of junction with Rte. 7, Hancock. Pond for canoeing and rowboating.
Savoy Mountain State Forest Off Rte. 2 in Florida, Rte. 116 in Savoy. North Pond and South Pond are two jewels in the hills, quite remote, rarely busy.

BOWLING

Strike after strike is being bowled in Berkshire, and if you're eager to get in on the action, there are eight locales throughout the county. In ***South County***, head for ***Cove Lanes*** (528-1220; 109 Stockbridge Rd., Gt. Barrington) or ***Lee Bowling Lanes*** 243-0095; Rte. 102, Lee). ***Central County*** offers ***Candle Lanes*** (447-9640; 255 North St., Pittsfield); ***Dalton Community House*** (684-0260; 400 Main St., Dalton); ***Imperial Bowl*** (443-4453; 555 Dalton Ave., Pittsfield); and ***Ken's Bowl*** (499-0733; 495 Dalton Ave., Pittsfield). In ***North County***, bowling's best at ***Mt. Greylock Bowl*** (663-3761; Roberts Dr., N. Adams) and ***Valley Park Inc.*** (664-9715; Curren Hwy., N. Adams).

CAMPS

There's a colorful list of overnight, resident summer camps in the Berkshires — some specializing in sports, some tuned to the arts, some with other enthusiasms. If you or your youngsters are interested in dance or the theater, hiking or canoeing, tennis or gymnastics, dressmaking or computers, Berkshire has a camp for you. Most camps take advantage of the beauty of their natural settings, and for many of them that includes lakes and mountains. Warm days and cool nights make for season-long aquatics and sound sleeping. Berkshire cultural life also enriches campers' time here, with Tanglewood and Jacob's Pillow being two of the more popular side trips.

The Indians were the first campers in the Berkshires, and many of its camps still bear Indian names. In the following list, we give addresses and telephone numbers that will work year-round. "Full program" indicates availability of both arts and sports activities.

South County

Camp Deerwood Director: Zoltan Zantay; 528-2180; Gt. Barrington, MA 01230; Adult; Full program.

Camp Half Moon Directors: Mr. and Mrs. Edward Mann; 528-0940; 400 Main St., Gt. Barrington, MA 01230; Day Camp; Coed, Resident camp, Boys; Full program.

Camp High Rock Director: J.E.F. Craig; 528-1227, summer, 203-367-2267, winter; Mt. Washington, MA 01258; Sessions for boys, coed groups and adults; Full program.

Camp Kingsmont Director: Dr. Richard Rohrbacher; 232-8518; RFD #2, W. Stockbridge, MA 01266; Coed; Nutrition and dietary education program, physical fitness.

Camp Lenox for Boys Directors: Monty and Richard Moss; 243-2223, summer, 718-225-9076, winter; Rte. 8, Lee, MA 01238; Boys; Sports.

Crane Lake Camp Directors: Barbara and Ed Ulanoff; 232-4257, summer, 212-549-8930, winter; 1920 State Line, W. Stockbridge, MA 01266; Coed; Full program.

Eisner Camp Institute Director: Dave Friedman 528-1652, summer, 212-249-0100, ext. 496, winter; Brookside Rd., Gt. Barrington, MA 01230; Coed children's and adult retreats; Full program and Jewish education.

Ralph Schulman, courtesy Camp Mohawk.

Greeting the day, at Camp Mohawk.

Central County

Belvoir Terrace Directors: Nancy Goldberg and Edna Schwartz; 637-0555, summer, 212-580-3398, winter; Cliffwood St., Lenox, MA 01240; Girls; Full program.

Camp Becket Director: Mark Smith; 623-8972, summer, 508-872-1261, winter; Becket, MA 01223; Boys; Full program; Operated by Two-State YMCA.

Camp Danbee Directors: Jim and Marlene O'Neill 655-2727, Summer, 201-316-6660, winter; Peru, MA (Hinsdale, MA P.O., 01235); Girls 7-15; Full program.

Camp Emerson Directors: Addie and Marvin Lien; 655-8123, summer, 914-779-9406, winter; Long View Ave., Hinsdale, MA 01235; Coed 7-15, Full program.

Camp Greylock Director: Bert Margolis; 623-8921, summer, 212-582-1042, winter; Rte. 8, Becket, MA 01233; Boys; Full program.

Camp Lenore-Owaissa Directors: Dorothy and Joseph Langer; 655-2733, summer, 212-338-5785, winter; Hinsdale, MA 01235; Girls; Full program.

Camp Mah-Kee-Nac Directors: Danny and Nancy Metzger; 637-0781, summer, 201-429-8522, winter; Lenox, MA 01240; Boys; Sports.

Camp Romaca Directors: Arnold and Karen Lent; 655-2715, summer, 914-255-8746, winter; Long View Ave., Hinsdale, MA 01235; Girls; Full program.

Camp Taconic Directors: Robert and Barbara Ezrol; 655-2717, summer, 914-762-2820, winter; Hinsdale, MA 01235; Coed; Full program.

Camp Watitoh Directors: Sheldon and Sandy Hoch; 623-8951, summer, 914-428-1894, winter; Center Lake, Becket, MA 01223; Coed; Full program.

Camp Winadu Directors: Arleen and Shelley Weiner; 447-8900, summer, 914-381-5983, winter; Churchill St., Pittsfield, MA 01201; Boys; Full program.

Chimney Corners Camp Director: Susan Frantz; 623-8991, summer, 508-872-1261, winter; Becket, MA 01223; Girls; Full program; Operated by Two-State YMCA.

North County

Camp Mohawk Directors: Ralph and Sue Schulman; 443-9843, summer, 443-5091, winter; Cheshire, MA 01237; Coed; Full program.

CANOEING AND KAYAKING

Besides all of Berkshire's lovely lakes to canoe and kayak, the paddler has several rivers to choose from, with stretches varying from lazy flatwater to rushing rapids. The Housatonic River rises near Pittsfield and flows southward, between the Taconic Range and the Berkshire Plateau, heading for the Atlantic Ocean, near Stratford, Connecticut. Four Berkshire trips down the Housatonic are recommended by the Appalachian Mountain Club: Dalton to Lenox (19 mi.); Lenox to Stockbridge (12 mi.); Stockbridge to Gt. Barrington (13 mi.); and Gt. Barrington to Falls Village, Connecticut (25 mi.). Send for *The AMC River Guide to Massachusetts, Connecticut and Rhode Island* ($9.95, from AMC 5 Joy St., Boston, MA 02108) or ask local booksellers.

In ***South County***, the stretch on the Housatonic from Gt. Barrington to Bartholomew's Cobble in Ashley Falls is classic, lazy river paddling. Canoes can be purchased and rented at Barrington Paddlers (528-6305; 18 Higgins St., Gt. Barrington.)

> Henry Parker Fellows, describing an 1881 canoe trip down the Housatonic through Great Barrington: "The Housatonic is a confirmed coquette, constantly flirting with one mountain range or another, and frequently with several at the same time."

For lovely lake paddling, canoes can be rented at ***Prospect Lake*** (528-4158; Prospect Lake Rd., N. Egremont).

In early April, the West Branch of the Farmington River swells, and the stretch south of Rte. 23, along Rte. 8 in Otis and Sandisfield, is the site of an annual Olympic kayak racing event. In early spring, this stretch is a Class Three rapids and makes for exciting white-water paddling and great viewing.

The challenge of Berkshire whitewater.

William Tague.

Up in ***North County***, the Hoosic River flows northwards, and in those parts, ***Berkshire Outfitters*** (743-5900; Rte. 8, Adams) are the canoe and kayak specialists, renting craft and offering sound advice on the best in area boating.

A Canoe Guide to the Housatonic River: Berkshire County is a nifty little booklet published jointly by the Housatonic River Watershed Association and the Berkshire County Regional Planning Commission. For $3, you get a couple of nice line drawings, a neat history of the river and its flora and fauna, as well as dozens of access points with river descriptions. Highly recommended for any Housatonic paddling; see local booksellers.

CROQUET

In the Berkshires, croquet has had a small, but tenacious group of followers who have fought heated battles on the lawns at the Lenox Club and at J. Gould's, next to Tanglewood. Several clubs were formed in the early 1980s and have constructed tournament-grade lawns in Lenox, Richmond, Sandisfield, Stockbridge and Tyringham. This complex of courts now gives the Berkshires the largest number of croquet lawns in any area of the country.

How does someone who is intrigued by this wicket sport find a way to learn the game and actually play? Local clubs are privately run; so, watch the newspapers for announcements of tournaments open to the public. And, there are two beautiful courts on the grounds of Blantyre, in Lenox, which offers its resident guests the use of imported equipment and lessons by a certified professional, during the season from July to September. See p. 52 for information on Blantyre.

FITNESS FACILITIES

Getting in shape was never so organized. Used to be, you did your work, you had your fun, it kept you in shape. Now, most jobs age us before our time, and Berkshire has joined the growing revolution to reverse that trend. Residential fitness facilities, where you check in and stay awhile, are listed later in this chapter, Canyon Ranch as a "Luxury Spa," Kripalu as a "Yoga Retreat." So you wanna pump a little iron, eh? Have we got a gym for you!

Berkshire Nautilus (499-1217; 205 West St., Pittsfield) Nautilus, stationary bikes, rowing machines, treadmill, StairMaster, whirlpool, sauna, steam, and certified instruction.

Berkshire West (499-4600; Dan Fox Dr.; Pittsfield) Nautilus, stationary bikes, free weights, tennis, racquetball, aerobics, treadmills, nautilus, free-weights, saunas, steam room, hot tub, and certified instruction. Also has a nursery.

Better Bodies (499-7151; 1400 East St., Pittsfield). Polaris and Bodymaster machines, free weights, stationary bikes, rowing machines, sauna, steam, tanning, and certified instruction.

Body Shop Fitness Center (528-2046; 955 S. Main St., Gt. Barrington) Aerobics, Nautilus, free weights, Air-dyne bicycles, Concept II Rowing machines, nutrition consultation, trained staff, showers and dressing rooms.

Eden Hill Recreation Center (298-5222; Congregation of the Marians, Prospect Hill, Stockbridge) Olympic-size heated indoor poor, gym, weight room with Universal machines, ping-pong, billiards, and men and women's sauna. Swimming and aerobic instruction available.

Fitness Express (528-1711; 740 Main St., Gt. Barrington) Aerobics, ballet, karate, myotherapy.

The Fitness Stop (243-3500; Oak 'n' Spruce, Meadow St., S. Lee) Universal equipment, free weights, indoor pool, hot tub, saunas, tennis, basketball, aerobics classes.

Lenox Fitness Center (637-9893; Main St., Lenox) Nautilus, stationary bikes, rowing machines, StairMasters, aerobics, steam rooms, tanning booth, and certified instruction.

FOOTBALL

There are high school games and pick-up touch football games throughout the county, but only in Williamstown will you see spirited collegiate gridiron action. The Williams College Ephmen (named after their school founder, Ephraim Williams), recently outdid themselves, producing the club's first perfect season. In their final clash, a homecoming game with arch-rival Amherst, Williams played sloppy ball for the first quarter, then gained control to prevail.

This is football at its sweetest, where opposing players help each other up after bruising tackles, where the announcer's game call includes such literate descriptions as: "...number 84, levelled by a plethora of Ephmen," or "...number 17, overwhelmed by a veritable deluge of jumbos!"
Williams College Football, Weston Field, Williamstown: 597-2344.

GOLF

In 1895, Joseph Choate, Jr., son of the prominent Stockbridge lawyer, returned from a Canadian trip with three rudimentary golf clubs. Using tomato cans for holes, he made a course in his backyard at Naumkeag, and gave birth to golf in the Berkshires. Three years later, having perfected his swing, Joseph Choate, Jr. won the National Championships with a record low score.

Golf has grown in the Berkshires, and there are now more than a dozen courses county-wide, with hardy sportsfolk teeing up from March through November. Every course and club runs tournaments, and a call or visit to the pro will give you exact dates. Long-distance driving options have expanded, too. First there were wood woods, then metal woods, and now, new for the nineties — developed from Pittsfield-GE engineered resins — Lexan woods, by Thermo Par. And if you just have to hit some in the dark of night, ***Baker's Driving Range & Miniature Golf*** (443-6102: Rte. 7, Lanesborough) keeps its driving range open from 10:00 a.m. till 10:30 p.m.

Practicing at Baker Farm.

GOLF CLUBS

Price Code — Greens Fees	Inexpensive	Moderate	Expensive
	Under $10.00	$10.00 to $15	Over $15

South County

Egremont Country Club 528-4222; Rte. 23, S. Egremont; 18 holes; Par 71; 5,900 yards; Price: Moderate.

Greenock Country Club Pro: Tom McDarby; 243-3323; W. Park St., Lee; 18 holes; Par 70; 5,990 yards; Price: Moderate.

Stockbridge Golf Club Pro: Jim Walker; 298-3423; Main St., Stockbridge; 18 holes; Par 71; 6,294 yards; Price: Expensive; Must be introduced by a member.

Wyantenuck Country Club Pro: Dennis Perrone; 528-3229; Sheffield Rd., Gt. Barrington; 18 holes; Par 70; 6,151 yards; Price: Expensive.

Central County

Bass-Ridge Golf Course 655-2605; Plunkett Ave., Hinsdale; 9 holes; Par 70; 5,164 yards; Price: Inexpensive.

Berkshire Hills Country Club Pro: Bob Dastoli; 442-1451; Benedict Rd., Pittsfield; 18 holes; Par 72; 6,286 yards; Price: Expensive; Must be introduced by a member.

Country Club of Pittsfield Pro: Brad Benson; 447-8504; 639 South St., Pittsfield; 18 holes; Par 70; 6,200 yards; Must be introduced by a member.

Cranwell Golf Course Pro: Geoff Lyons 637-1216 or 637-0441; 55 Lee Rd. (Rte. 20), Lenox; 18 holes; Par 71; 6,225 yards; Price: Moderate.

General Electric Athletic Assoc. Pro: Ed Rossi; 442-5746; 303 Crane Ave., Pittsfield; 9 holes; Par 72; 6,205 yards; Price: Inexpensive.

Pontoosuc Lake Country Club 445-4217; Ridge Ave., Pittsfield; 18 holes; Par 70; 6,305 yards; Price: Inexpensive.

Skyline Country Club Pro: Jim Mitus; 445-5584; 405 S. Main St., Lanesborough; 9 holes; Par 72; 6,643 yards; Price: Inexpensive.

Wahconah Country Club Pro: Paul Daniels; 684-1333; Orchard Rd., Dalton; 18 holes; Par 71; 6,186 yards; Price: Moderate.

North County

Forest Park Country Club 743-3311; Country Club Ave., Adams; 9 holes; Par 68; 5,100 yards; Price: Inexpensive.

North Adams Country Club 664-9011; River Rd., Clarksburg; 9 holes; Par 72; 5,930 yards; Price: Inexpensive to Moderate.

Taconic Golf Club Pro: Rick Pohle; 458-3997; Meacham St., Williamstown; 18 holes; Par 71; 6,575 yards; Price: Expensive.

Waubeeka Springs Golf Links Pro: Bob Thomka; 458-5869; New Ashford Rd. (Rte. 7), Williamstown; 18 holes; Par 72; 6,620 yards; Price: Moderate.

Greylock Glen — Recreational Boon or Boondoggle?

A championship public golf course, cross-country ski trails, ponds, tennis courts, an inn, stores and 850 housing units, set on 1,040 acres of virgin land in Adams — that's the vision of developers, and occasionally the state, whose financial support is a must. What with budget cuts and a very negative review from the Massachusetts Audubon Society, however, Greylock Glen faces an uncertain future. Though the local area certainly could use an economic boost, we'd be happier if they found some other way, and left the land just the way the Maker made it.

HIKING

If you would be happy in Berkshire, you must carry mountains in your brain.

Oliver Wendell Holmes

Massachusetts may be the sixth smallest state in the union, but its forest and park system is the sixth largest. And of the state's quarter-million protected acres, nearly 100,000 are in Berkshire County. With trails along lake and riverside, up hills and steep mountains, the Berkshires offer all types of terrain for anything from an afternoon's jaunt to a full-fledged pack trip. There are 21 state parks in the county, all of which have interesting trails, and the seven Berkshire Nature Centers each have scenic paths. In addition, the Appalachian Trail runs straight up the center of Berkshire County, entering near Bartholomew's Cobble in Ashley Falls and exiting near Clarksburg.

Thou who woulds't see the lovely and the wild
Mingled in harmony on Nature's face,
Ascend our rocky mountains.

From William Cullen Bryant's poem, "Monument Mountain"

Monument Mountain makes an exciting climb in any weather, over giant glacial boulders or up well-marked trails. Most of the cross-country ski trails noted later in this chapter are also excellent hiking trails. Although a compass and maps are advisable for any deep woods hiking, it's comforting to note that in Berkshire County, no matter how wild your surroundings, you are never more than five miles from the nearest paved road. Nevertheless, for hikes of any length, and especially for those taken alone, always notify a friend of your plan and your estimated hour of return.

STATE PARKS IN THE BERKSHIRES

South County

Beartown and East Mtn. State Forest 528-0904; Blue Hill Rd., Monterey; 10,500 acres.

East Mtn. State Reservation 528-0904; Rte. 7, Gt. Barrington.

Mt. Everett State Reservation, Mt. Washington State Forest, Bash Bish Falls 528-0330; East St., Mt. Washington; 3,289 acres.

October Mtn. State Forest 243-1778, 243-9735; Woodland Rd., Lee; 15,710 acres.

Otis State Forest Rte. 23, Otis.

Sandisfield and Cookson State Forest 258-4774; West St., Sandisfield (New Marlboro), 4,378 acres.

Tolland State Forest 269-6002, 269-7268; Rte. 8, Otis; 8,000 acres.

Central County

Mt. Greylock State Reservation 499-4263, 499-4262; Rockwell Rd., Lanesborough; 10,327 acres.

Pittsfield State Forest 442-8992; Cascade St., Pittsfield; 9,695 acres.

Windsor State Forest 684-9760; River Rd., Windsor; 1,626 acres.

North County

Clarksburg State Park 664-9030; Middle Rd., Clarksburg; 346 acres.

Savoy Mtn. State Forest 663-8469; Rte 2, Florida and Rte. 116, Savoy; 10,500 acres.

For more detailed information on the county's 21 state parks, write: ***Massachusetts Department of Environmental Management*** (617-727-3180; 100 Cambridge St., Boston, MA 02202) or its Region V office (442-8928; Box 1433, Pittsfield, MA 01202).

History of The Trustees of Reservations

In 1890, long before the present national interest in the environment, a young landscape architect returned from study in Europe with a deepening concern for the need to preserve the natural beauty and historic sites of his community.

Early that year, Charles Eliot (1859-1897), just 31 years old and son of Charles W. Eliot, then president of Harvard University, proposed the establishment of an organization "empowered to hold small and well distributed parcels of land..., just as the Public Library holds books and the Art Museum pictures for the use and enjoyment of the public."

The Trustees of Reservations was incorporated by the Massachusetts General Court a year later, 1891, the first independent organization in the United States established for the purpose of preserving land.

The Trustees of Reservations; 572 Essex St., Beverly, MA 01915.

Excellent hiking opportunities await you at the following properties of the Trustees of Reservations:

Bartholomew's Cobble 229-8600; Weatogue Rd., (Rte. 7A), Ashley Falls (Sheffield).

Monument Mtn. Stockbridge Rd. (Rte. 7), Gt. Barrington.

Notchview Reservation 684-0148; Rte. 9, Windsor.

Tyringham Cobble 298-3239; Jerusalem Rd., Tyringham.

Berkshire County Land Trust

The Berkshire County Land Trust and Conservation Fund is an offshoot of Berkshire Natural Resources Council, a private, not-for-profit environmental advocacy group, established in 1967. Led by director-lobbyist, George Wislocki, this group believes that the wealth of Berkshire lies in its quality of life, in its natural environment and cultural heritage. Of the 600,000 acres in Berkshire, some 120,000 are parkland. The council works with state and local agencies to ensure that those lands are properly protected from abuse.

There are about 200 land trusts in America, many of them in New England. By all counts, Berkshire's is one of the more successful. In Pittsfield, the Trust was responsible for increasing the Pittsfield State Forest by 1,800 acres. Along the Housatonic, south of Pittsfield, the Resources Council is coordinating the creation of a 12-mile-long river park, reaching to Woods Pond in Lenox. The Land Trust facilitated the preservation of Gould Meadows, that gorgeous 95-acre pasture reaching from Tanglewood to Stockbridge Bowl. The Stockbridge-Yokun Ridge Reserve is another land corridor the Trust is assembling to remain forever wild, an eight-mile-long, 6,300-acre spread of Berkshire park.

The Land Trust helps keep Berkshire beautiful.

Berkshire County Land Trust and Berkshire Natural Resources Council, Inc.
Director: George Wislocki; 499-0596; 10 Bank Row, Pittsfield, MA 01201.

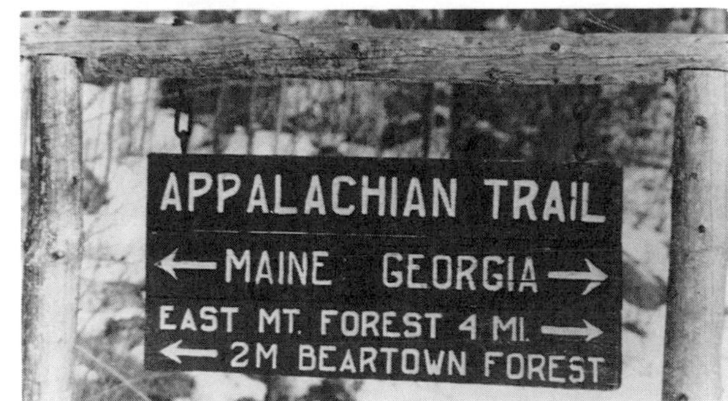

The Berkshires on foot — en route to Maine or Georgia.

David Emblidge.

There are several hiking clubs in the Berkshires, and among them, ***the Berkshire Knapsackers*** (447-7840), ***the Appalachian Trail Club*** and ***the Williams Outing Club*** (597-2317) are the most active. Each runs organized hikes through the county. The map at the end of the book shows the entire length of the Appalachian Trail in Berkshire County.

A new outfit, ***Berkshire Hiking Holidays,*** offers to guide you along the Appalachian and Taconic Range trails in half- or whole-day hikes. Snacks and lunches are included, as are stopovers at scenic vistas and cascading waterfalls. From a long, vigorous hike up a mountain to a slow meander through a birch-shaded path, Berkshire Hiking may have just the day-trip you're after. ***Berkshire Hiking Holidays*** (499-9648; P.O. Box 2231, Lenox, MA 01240).

Two excellent books on Berkshire hiking are available: *Hikes & Walks in the Berkshire Hills* by Lauren Stevens; and for North County, *The Williams College Outing Club Trail Guide*, first published in 1927 and now in its seventh edition. Stevens' book covers not only a wide variety of challenging hikes for the energetic and ambitious, but also a large number of easy strolls for those with less time or gumption; and there's a section on walks for the blind and physically handicapped. There is also the extremely detailed *Appalachian Mountain Club Trail Guide*. See the Bibliography for further details on all these books.

Various literati have climbed Berkshire mountains and recorded their impressions. In his *Notebooks*, H.D. Thoreau wrote perhaps the most rhapsodic passage of all, about awakening after a night alone on top of Mt. Greylock.

> *As the light increased I discovered around me an ocean of mist, which by chance reached up exactly to the base of the tower, and shut out every vestige of the earth, while I was left floating on this fragment of the wreck of a world.... As the light in the east steadily increased, it revealed to me more clearly the new world into which I had risen in the night, the new terra-firma perchance of my future life. There was not a crevice left through which the trivial places we name Massachusetts, or Vermont, or New York could be seen, while I still inhaled the clear atmosphere of a July morning, — if it were July there. All around beneath me was spread for a hundred miles on every side, as far as the eye could reach, an undulating country of clouds, answering in the varied swell of its surface to the terrestrial world it veiled. It was such a country as we might see in dreams, with all the delights of paradise.*

HORSEBACK RIDING

There's a slew of riding academies and stables in and around Berkshire County. A quick look in the Yellow Pages opens the barn door to information on horse breeders, dealers, trainers, shoers and saddle shops. The following is a list of riding possibilities.

Aspinwall Riding School 637-0245; 279 Pittsfield Rd. (Rte. 7), Lenox; English lessons, indoor and outdoor rings; year-round.

Bonnie Lea Farm 458-3149; 511 North St. (Rte. 7), Williamstown; private and group lessons; English, dressage; indoor and outdoor rings, guided trail rides; year-round.

Eastover 637-0625; 40 East St., Lenox; trail rides for guests only at Eastover resort; year-round.

Overmeade School of Horsemanship 499-2850; 822 East St., Lenox; English private and group lessons; year-round.

Stepping Stone Stable 684-3200; 619 East St., Dalton; summer riding program, year-round lessons.

Talbot Stables 637-2996, 655-8162; Rte. 7 (at Foxhollow Resort), Lenox; English and Western riding, English lessons, trail rides; May through November.

Undermountain Farm 637-3365; Undermountain Rd., Lenox; English lessons, trail rides; spring through fall.

HUNTING AND FISHING

The first settlers found Berkshire teeming with fish and game; and though the wildlife is presently less plentiful, there are still so many deer they must frequently be avoided on the roadways, still enough wild turkey, bear, pheasant, quail, rabbit, raccoon, fox, coyote and grey squirrel to satisfy nearly every hunter's aim. In Berkshire's waters, large and small mouth bass, northern pike, white and yellow perch, horned pout, and trout of all varieties still swim in abundance. Numerous brooks, rivers, ponds and lakes are stocked with trout each year.

Essential equipment for any hunting or fishing is a pamphlet containing abstracts of the *Massachusetts Fish and Wildlife Laws*, available free at local sporting goods shops; from the *Division of Fisheries and Wildlife* (617-727-3151; 100 Cambridge St., Boston 02202); or from the *Western Wildlife District Manager*, Tom Keefe (447-9789; Hubbard Ave., Pittsfield, 01201). This pamphlet carefully outlines the rules and regulations of Massachusetts fishing and hunting, and without it, you may well violate the law or risk injury. Also essential is a license, and this can be obtained through either city or town clerks, through the Division of Fisheries and Wildlife at the Boston address above, or through many local sporting goods stores.

Such a license permits hunting, fishing or trapping, but in no way permits trespassing on private property, whether posted or not. Permission to hunt or fish on private property must be obtained from the landowner. State lands impose no such restriction, and the game population there is generally higher. A chat with the local sporting goods proprietor or with fellow hunters at early morning coffee will often yield secrets about the most reliable hunting areas.

A LIST OF TROUT-STOCKED BERKSHIRE WATERS

South County

Alford Seekonk Brook, Green River.

Egremont Green River, Hubbard Brook.

Great Barrington Green River, West Brook, Thomas & Palmer Brook, Williams River, Lake Mansfield.

FISH, EXCLUSIVE OF TROUT, IN BERKSHIRE WATERS

TOWN	WATER	NP	LMB	SMB	CP	WP	YP	BB
South County								
Egremont	Prospect Lake				√		√	√
Lee	Goose Pond		√	√	√		√	√
Lee	Laurel Lake		√		√	√	√	√
Monterey	Benedict Pond		√				√	√
New Marlborough	Thousand Acre Swamp			√	√		√	√
Otis	Benton Pond			√	√	√	√	√
Otis	East Otis Reservoir		√	√	√	√	√	√
Stockbridge	Stockbridge Bowl		√	√	√		√	√
Central County								
Becket	Center Pond		√	√	√	√	√	√
Becket	Yokum Pond		√				√	√
Hinsdale	Ashmere Lake		√	√			√	
Pittsfield	Onota Lake	√	√		√		√	√
Pittsfield	Pontoosuc Pond		√		√		√	√
Pittsfield	Richmond Pond		√	√	√		√	√
Windsor	Windsor Pond		√		√		√	√
North County								
Cheshire	Cheshire Reservoir	√	√		√		√	√
Clarksburg	Mauserts Pond					√		√

Symbols

NP— Northern Pike
LMB— Largemouth Bass
SMB— Smallmouth Bass
CP— Chain Pickerel
WP— White Perch
YP— Yellow Perch
BB— Brown Bullheads (Horn Pout)

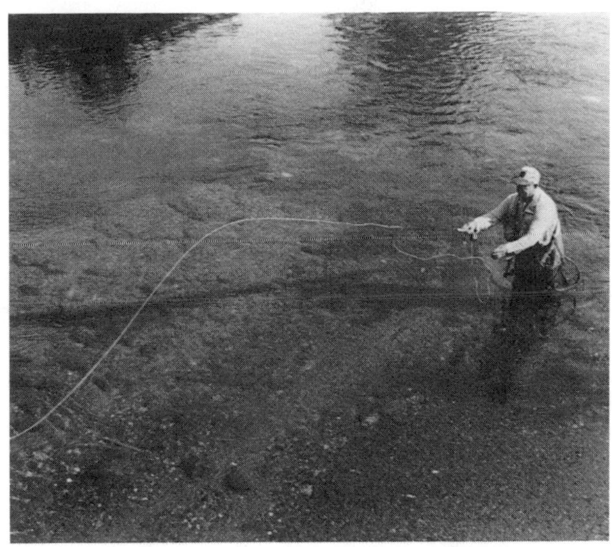

Fly fishing in the Green River.

Lee Beartown Brook (west branch), Hop Brook, Goose Pond, Greenwater Brook, Laurel Lake, Washington Mountain Brook.

Monterey Lake Buel, Lake Garfield, Rawson Brook, Konkapot River.

New Marlborough Konkapot River, Umpachene Brook, York Pond.

Otis Farmington River, Otis Reservoir, Dimock Brook, Little Benton Pond, Big Benton Pond.

Sandisfield Buck River, Clam River, Farmington River.

Sheffield Hubbard Brook, Konkapot River.

Stockbridge Marsh Brook, Stockbridge Bowl.

Tyringham Hop Brook, Goose Pond Brook, Goose Pond.

West Stockbridge Williams River, Cone Brook, Flat Brook.

Central County

Becket Shaker Mill Brook, Greenwater Pond, Yokum Brook, Westfield River (west branch), Walker Brook.

Dalton Sackett Brook, Housatonic River (east branch), Wahconah Falls Brook.

Hancock Kinderhook Creek, Berry Pond.

Hinsdale Bennet Brook, Housatonic River (east branch), Plunket Reservoir.

Lanesborough Town Brook, Sachem Brook, Lake Pontoosuc.

Lenox Sawmill Brook, Marsh Brook, Yokum Brook, Laurel Lake.

Peru Trout Brook.

Pittsfield Daniel Brook, Housatonic River (southwest branch), Lulu Cascade Brook, Sackett Brook, Smith Brook, Onota Lake, Lake Pontoosuc, Jacoby Brook.

Richmond Cone Brook, Furnace Brook, Richmond Pond, Mt. Lebanon Brook.

Washington Depot Brook.

Windsor Westfield River (east branch), Windsor Jambs Brook, Windsor Pond, Windsor Brook, Westfield Brook.

North County

Adams Anthony Brook, Hoosic River (south branch), Tophet Brook, Southwick Brook.

Cheshire Hoosic River (south branch), Dry Brook, Kitchen Brook, South Brook, Thunder Brook, Penniman Brook.

Clarksburg Hoosic River (north branch), Hudson Brook.

Florida Deerfield River, North Pond.

North Adams Notch Brook, Windsor Lake.

Savoy Chickley River, Cold River, Westfield River (east branch), Center Brook.

Williamstown Broad Brook, Hemlock Brook, Green River (west branch), Green River, Roaring Brook.

NATURE PRESERVES

In addition to its vast forests, Berkshire is blessed with seven nature preserves, each of which shows off the county's flora and fauna. Half a dozen of them provide miles of rich trail life, while Bartholomew's Cobble features geologically ancient stone outcroppings.

Checking the trails, at Bartholomew's Cobble.

South County

Bartholomew's Cobble 229-8600; Weatogue Rd. (Rte. 7A), Ashley Falls (Sheffield). Bartholomew's Cobble, a National Natural Landmark is a 277-acre sanctuary with outcroppings of marble and quartzite, about 500 million years old. The terrain supports wildflowers, trees and ferns in great variety and number. It's a fine place to view the Housatonic River and its surrounding valley. On the site is the Bailey Museum of Natural History (Closed: Mon., Tues.). Group tours on request; picnic privileges available. Season: Apr. 15 - Oct. 15; Fee.

Berkshire Garden Center 298-3926; Junction of Rtes. 102 & 183, Stockbridge. (Recently renamed Berkshire Botanical Garden) For more than 50 years, the Berkshire Garden Center has been the foremost botanical complex in the county. Spread over 15 acres of gently rolling land, the magnificent plantings include primroses, conifers, day lilies, perennials and shrubs. There's a terraced herb garden, a rose garden, raised-bed vegetable gardens and exotic flowers in abundance. And the Garden Center has greenhouses (one of them is a well-designed passive solar model) growing seedlings, cuttings and plants of all sorts. It has a Visitor Center, where you may join the club or ask a few questions; and it has a Garden Gift Shop and an Herb Products Shop, both of which offer garden items, some of them practical, some merely beautiful or sweet smelling.

The Garden Center runs a full schedule of activities, May through October, ranging from flower shows and herb symposiums to lectures on flower arranging and on English Country gardens. They also have a fine reference library, filled with books, magazines and the latest seed catalogs. This library is open to the public, and its staff is available for your gardening questions.

The Garden Center calendar culminates with the Harvest Festival in early October. Besides cider and apples, donuts and cakes of all kinds, and an ever-expanding luncheon menu, the day's fare includes rides on a 1923 fire truck, mazes, face-painting and balloons for the kids, and a book and clothing tag sale where it's still possible to buy a good-as-new Brooks Brothers suit for a few dollars.

Ice Glen Ice Glen Rd., Stockbridge. Cross the footbridge over the Housatonic River, follow the trail southward and walk a primeval path of glacial boulders. The trail is tricky and not recommended for the weak-kneed. Traditionally, the townsfolk of Stockbridge walked this path, bearing torches, on Halloween night.

Central County

Canoe Meadows Wildlife Sanctuary 637-0320; Holmes Rd., Pittsfield; 242-acre preserve of forest, ponds, streams, the Housatonic River banks and flood plain; owned and managed by the Massachusetts Audubon Society; Fee.

Dorothy Francis Rice Sanctuary South Rd. (off Rte. 143), Peru; 300-acre preserve of woodland trails, owned and managed by the New England Forestry Foundation; Free.

Notchview Reservation Rte. 9, Windsor; 3,000 acres of forest, crossed by miles of trails; owned and managed by The Trustees of Reservations; Fee.

Pleasant Valley Wildlife Sanctuary 637-0320; 472 West Mountain Rd. (off Rte. 7, opposite All Seasons Inn), Lenox; 700 acres of forest, field, ponds (beaver dams) and streams with miles of trails; educational programs; owned and managed by the Massachusetts Audubon Society; Fee.

North County

Duvall Nature Trail Rte. 116 (at Hoosac Valley High School), Adams; two miles of nature trails overlooking the Greylock Range; Free.

Hopkins Memorial Forest 458-3080; Bulkley St. (off Rte. 7), Williamstown; 2,500 woodland acres on the slopes of the Taconic Range with miles of hiking trails; Free.

POLO

Come hear the thwack of mallet on ball, the thunder of hooves on turf at ***Berkshire Polo Club***. Two or three times a week, May through Labor Day, area horsemen play together or host visiting teams, usually in conjunction with the Millbrook Polo Club from Pine Plains, NY. Berkshire Polo also hosts visiting players, and recently their team has included horsemen from Argentina and Pakistan. The Club runs a polo school as well, where lessons are given by qualified instructors. Scrimmages and clinics are held at Blue Hill Rd., Monterey. For schedules and information, contact Jed Lipsky at 528-0762. Whether you ride or watch, come for a chucka or two at Berkshire Polo.

RACQUET SPORTS

RACQUETBALL

There's a lively racquetball scene in Berkshire, with courts in Lenox, Pittsfield, New Ashford, and North Adams. The **North Adams YMCA** (663-6529; 22 Brickyard Court), has two nice courts. At the **Brodie Mtn. Racquet Club** (458-4677; Rte. 7), in New Ashford, there are five courts, open from 9 a.m. to 10 p.m. **Pittsfield YMCA** (499-7650; 292 North St.) has four; and **Berkshire West** (formerly the Racquet Club at Bousquet; 499-4600; Dan Fox Dr., Pittsfield) has four. Both Pittsfield facilities offer top-flight teaching programs.

SQUASH

Squash in Berkshire? Yes, but it's mostly the garden variety. As for the sporting type, the situation is decidedly less bountiful. Many squash courts do exist, but, alas, most are open only to people associated with the private schools maintaining them. For travelers and locals alike, there is only one squash facility in Berkshire offering public access: the **Pittsfield YMCA** (499-7650; 292 North St.). Luckily the Y's court is new, well built and lively.

TENNIS

In the Berkshires' Gilded Age, at the close of the 19th century, tennis was played on lawns, close-cropped and lined with lime. Wheatleigh was an especially favored site, and the lawn tennis parties there featured men in long, white linen trousers and ladies in ankle-length tennis dresses. Most of the grass courts are front lawns now, and though a few Berkshire connoisseurs still play on turf, tennis, here as elsewhere, is now played principally on clay, composites and hard courts.

Several tournaments are annual events and can be counted on to test the best skills or provide exciting viewing. Starting in late summer, tournaments are run by the ***YMCA's Ponterril facility*** (447-7405 or 499-0640 Rte. 7, Pontoosuc Lake, Pittsfield).

TENNIS FACILITIES

South County

Egremont Country Club; 528-4222; Rte. 23, S. Egremont; 4 hard-surface courts; Fee.

Monument Mtn. Motel 528-3272; Rte. 7, Gt. Barrington (opposite Friendly's); 1 lighted all-weather court; Fee. Call for reservation.

Greenock Country Club 243-3323; W. Park St., Lee; 2 clay courts; Fee.

Oak n' Spruce Resort 243-3500; Off Rte. 102, S. Lee; 2 clay courts; Fee.

Prospect Lake Park 528-4158; Prospect Lake Rd., N. Egremont; 2 courts; Fee.

Simon's Rock College of Bard 528-0771; Alford Rd., Gt. Barrington; 4 hard courts plus backboard; Summer memberships available.

Stockbridge Golf Club Pro: Jenna Marcovicci; 298-3838; Main St., Stockbridge (behind Town Hall); 3 clay, 2 hard-surface courts; non-members may arrange for lessons only.

Stockbridge Public Courts Pine St., 2 hard courts; The Plain School, Main St. (Rte. 7); 2 hard courts; For town residents and registered hotel guests.

Central County

Berkshire West (formerly the Racquet Club at Bousquet) Pro: Dave Bell; 449-4600; Dan Fox Dr., Pittsfield; 8 outdoor courts and 5 indoor hard courts; Memberships available.

Pittsfield Public Courts free to the public when school is not in session; all are asphalt courts.

BERKSHIRE RECREATION SITES

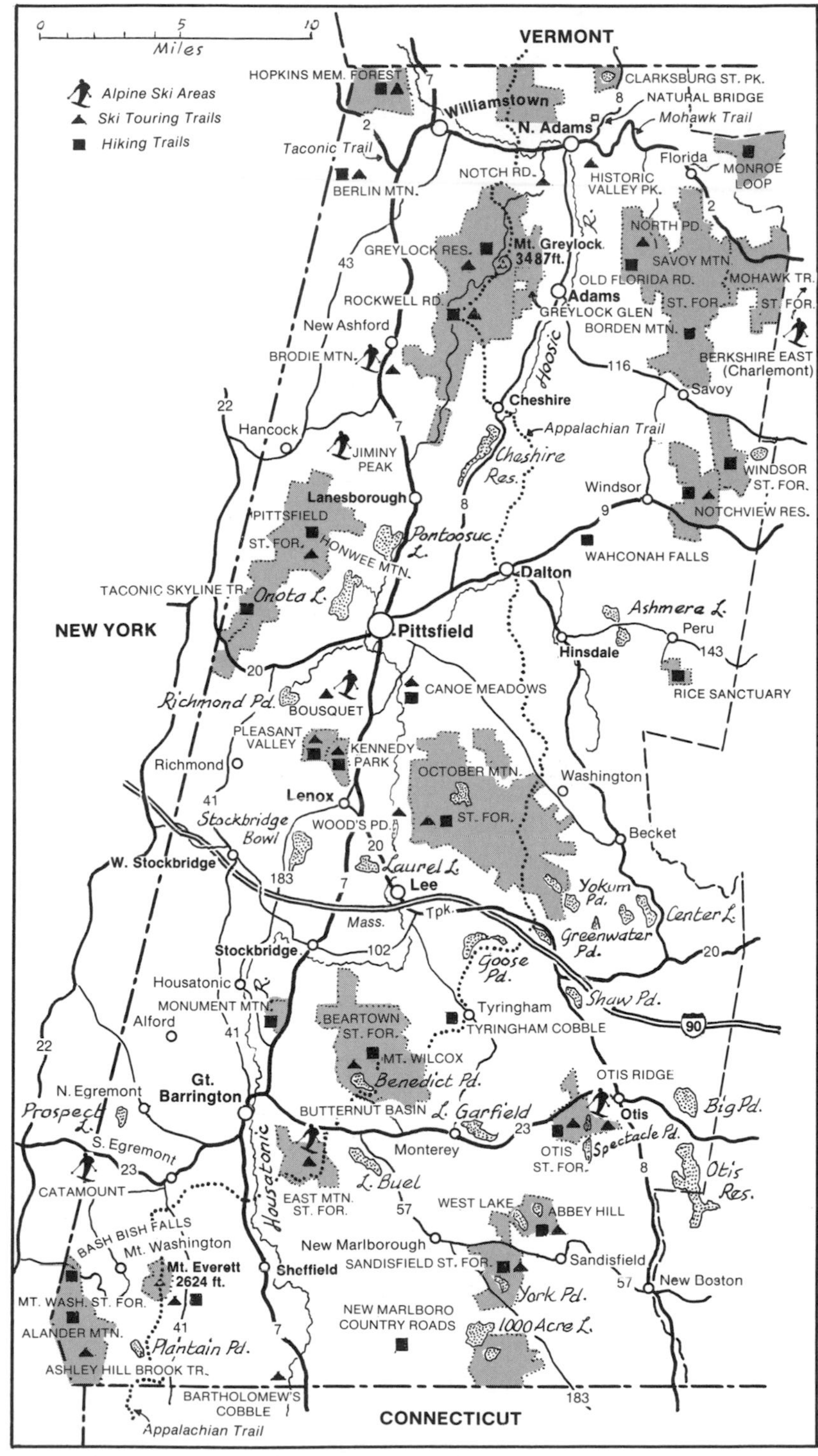

Herberg Middle School Pomeroy Ave.; 4 courts.

Lakewood Park Newell St.; 2 courts.

Pittsfield High School East St.; 4 courts.

Reid Middle School North St.; 4 courts.

Taconic High School Valentine Rd.; 4 courts.

Ponterril/YMCA Pro: Barbara Mills; 447-7405 or 499-0640; Rte. 7, Pontoosuc Lake, Pittsfield; 6 outdoor clay courts; Members only, but when courts are free, nonmembers may use them for a fee, and summer memberships are available.

North County

Brodie Mountain Tennis & Racquetball Club Pro: Barbara Mills; 458-4677; Rte. 7, New Ashford; 5 indoor courts; Memberships available.

North Adams Public Courts free to the public; all courts are asphalt.

Greylock Recreation Field Protection Ave. (off Rte. 2), 2 courts.

Noel Field; (in back of Child Care of the Berkshires); State St. (Rte. 8A); 2 courts.

Williams College 458-4260; Main St. (Rte. 2), Williamstown; 12 clay and hard-surface courts; Summer memberships available.

RUNNING

If you're a runner, you've run into the right neck of the woods in the Berkshires. With terrain and roadways of all types, clean mountain air and inspiring vistas

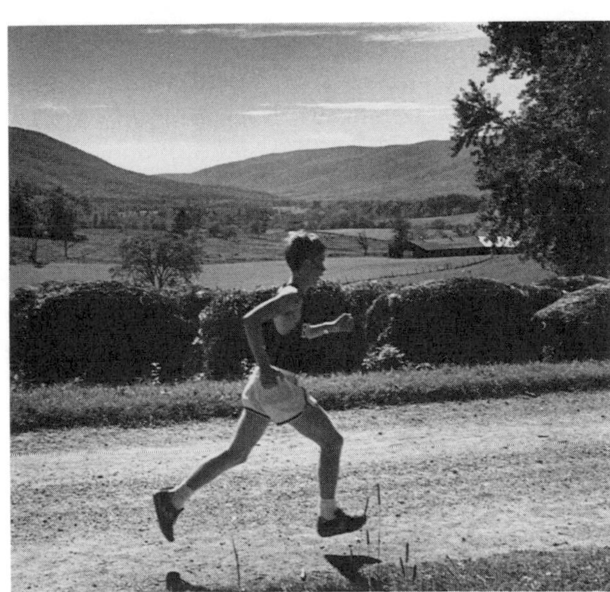

Airborne at Mount Hope Farm, Williamstown.

William Tague.

at every turn, Berkshire draws out the relaxed runner in you, that meditative runner who can run forever. Most back roads and byways have little traffic, and for all the jogs we've taken, each new jaunt refreshed the impression of running through one giant park. For the rugged cross-country runner, some of the trails outlined in the "Hiking" section are suitable, though it must be remembered that these trails are basically for hikers. If you're a racer, or yearn to be, many towns and organizations across the county run road races; exact dates and entry information for these can be obtained from local Chambers of Commerce.

SKATING

For ice skaters, there are many smooth and slippery possibilities in the Berkshires, most of them framed by the hills. There are three rinks open to the public, one at the ***Pittsfield Boys Club*** (448-8258; 16 Melville St.); the other at ***Chapman Rink*** (597-2433) in Williamstown *(**Williams College**)*, and the third in North Adams at the ***Vietnam Veterans Memorial Skating Rink*** (664-9474; S. Church St.). All the rinks offer low-priced children's programs. Outdoor skating on flooded fields is a Berkshire tradition, and during the colder months, you can do that both day and night on The Common in Pittsfield, at the Dalton Community House and on the Stockbridge Town Field. Lake and pond skating is exquisite in Berkshire, and many of the "Swimming" sites noted later in this chapter are partially cleared after the snow flies. Occasionally, all the elements work together to produce natural rinks of glass ice or "black ice."

For those who prefer their skating on wheels, many of the county's smoother back roads make for ideal blacktop cruising. And there is one roller rink in Berkshire: ***Roller Magic*** (458-3659; Rte. 2, Colonial Shopping Center, Williamstown).

SKIING — DOWNHILL

Berkshire downhill ski areas go back to the 1930s, and there's some evidence that three significant advances in modern skiing had their origins in the Berkshires: the surface ski lift, snowmaking, and the ski bar. Now, with Brodie Mountain's "Master Blaster" snowguns and Jiminy Peak's "Snow-Coat," a vinyl blanket to protect the snowy slopes in rain, Berkshire ski areas continue to be innovative, always questing for better, more consistent conditions over a longer season.

But it's not the technology that makes Berkshire skiing so appealing, so increasingly popular. The Berkshire hills are challenging yet picturesque, without being imposing. From the summits of the area's ski mountains, the vistas are splendid — mountains on the horizon (like the Catskills, seen from atop Butternut) and skinny bands of civilization below. With seven major ski areas in the region to choose from, skiers in the Berkshires can pick their mountain for a week or tour the hills and ski a different area on different days. Each ski mountain has its own character, each caters to a slightly different skier yet always welcomes all.

Jiminy Peak and Berkshire East have the highest proportion of trails suited to advanced skiers only; but Butternut, Catamount, and even Bousquet have dicey runs, demanding enough for many experts. Every Berkshire ski area offers instruction, and some make a specialty of ski training for youngsters, such as Bousquet with its ski school or Otis Ridge with its ski camp.

Courtesy Berkshire Atheneum.

The ski train from New York arrives at Pittsfield in the 1940s; buses then shuttled skiers to Bousquet.

BERKSHIRE SKI INFORMATION

From ***Outside*** Massachusetts: 802-457-3330.

Berkshire Ski Conditions: 499-7669. New England Ski Council reports are broadcast twice daily, Tues. through Sat., from radio station ***WBEC-AM***, 1420 on the dial, Pittsfield.

WHERE TO BUY AND RENT SKI EQUIPMENT

Besides the ski areas themselves, all of which have fully stocked ski shops, renting and selling equipment, the following specialty shops sell skis and related paraphernalia.

Arcadian Shop 637-3010; 333 Pittsfield-Lenox Rd., Lenox.

Besse Clarke 499-1090; 273 North at Summer St., Pittsfield.

Kenver Ltd. 528-2330; Rte. 23, S. Egremont.

The Mountain Goat 458-8445; 130 Water St., Williamstown.

Plaine's Ski & Cycle Center 499-0294; 55 W. Housatonic St., Pittsfield.

Sports, Inc. 442-1824; Rtes. 8 & 9 (Allendale Shopping Center), Pittsfield.

Tonon's Ski Haus 443-0671; Rte. 7, Lanesborough.

South County

BUTTERNUT BASIN
528-2000.
Rte. 23, Gt. Barrington, MA 01230.
2 mi. E. of town, toward Monterey.
Trails: 21 Downhill (6 Beginner, 9 Intermediate, 6 Expert).
XC trails (7 km.).
Lifts: 6 Chairlifts (5 double-chair, 1 triple-chair), 1 Poma.
Vertical drop: 1,000 ft.
Snowmaking: 100% of area.
Tickets: 1991 Adults $33, Junior $27, Senior $25, Children $10.
Open: Wkdays 9-4; Wkends 8:15-5.
Ski school pro: Einar Aas.

Few entrepreneurs can realize their business dreams in their own backyards. Ski-resort developer Channing Murdoch, who lives at the foot of Warner Mountain, in between Great Barrington and Monterey, is one such lucky man.

Murdoch designed and built Butternut Basin Ski Area right there on a site that has become one of the Berkshires' premier winter recreation meccas. At Butternut there are challenging downhill runs, a separate beginner's slope and extensive cross-country ski trails. The area offers ideal options for every kind of skier — from first-timer to serious racer.

But Butternut is more than terrific trails and the welcoming charm of its two lovely lodges. From the top of Warner Mountain, there are extraordinary views of the distant Catskills in the west and of Mt. Greylock at the northern end of Berkshire County. The mountain's timed slalom course is open to everyone, making a potential Olympic class racer — at least in fantasy — out of even a beginner. Whether you're an advanced skier or on the slopes for your debut, you'll find just the guidance you need from Butternut's personable ski pro, Einar Aas, and his team of expert ski instructors. And should you want the latest in skiwear and equipment, you'll find that, too, at Butternut's ski shop, one of the most extensive and stylish at any Berkshire mountain.

From the mogul fields of the expert run, "Downspout," to the meandering path of the novice "Pied Piper's Trail," Butternut is a delight to the eye and a refreshing test of athletic skill. "A showcase," said *Ski Magazine*, presenting Butternut with a first place award "in recognition of outstanding environmental planning and excellence of design." "It's a graceful, tasteful area," added *Ski's* Bill Berry. *The New York Times* sportswriter William Wallace went even further, saying "Butternut is a Godsend . . . . The best nearby skiing I know of as to snowmaking, lifts, trails and ambience".

Choosing an alpine trail at Butternut.

Even the famous skiing senator from Massachusetts, Edward Kennedy, has joined the chorus: "Butternut gets more beautiful every year."

CATAMOUNT
528-1262, 518-325-3200.
Rte. 23, S. Egremont, MA 01258.
On New York State border.
Trails: 24 Downhill (Novice to Expert); No XC.
Lifts: 4 Chairlifts; 1 T-Bar; 1 J-Bar.
Vertical drop: 1,000 ft.
Snowmaking: 90% of area.
Tickets: 1991 Wkdays, $26 Adults, $20 Junior/ Senior; Wkends/ Holidays $32 Adults, $25 Junior $20 Senior; Night Skiing, Wed.-Sat. $18 Adults, $14 Junior.
Open: 8:30-4 Wkends/ Holidays; Midwk./ Non-holidays, 9-5; Night Skiing, Wed.- Sat., 3:30-10:00.
Ski school pro: Shy Reeves.

"On the cutting edge of Berkshire ski country," as *Skiing Magazine* put it, Catamount straddles two states and offers magnificent views of four: Massachusets, New York, Connecticut and Vermont. The slopes are primarily novice and intermediate, but seasoned skiers can find quite a bit of challenge through the glades near the summit, and down on through Flipper and Dipper trails.

Called by some a vest-pocket Killington, Catamount is convenient, especially to New Yorkers. Not your trendiest, competition-minded ski resort, there's a pleasant quaintness here, right down to the Swiss Hutte restaurant at the mountain's base. Snowmaking equipment at Catamount has just been overhauled and expanded, and they're now firing state-of-the-art equipment onto 85% of their 25 trails and slopes. Furthermore, the area has added several new grooming vehicles to its fleet. Night skiing is also an attraction at Catamount.

Central County

OTIS RIDGE

Otis Ridge is the molehill among the mountains, but few slopes do so much to cater to beginners and youngsters. Famous for its winter ski camp, the area takes on a special character on frosty weekends and holiday periods when camp's in session. Snowmaking covers 90% of the 11 trails at Otis, and their lift system consists of a double-chair, T bar, J Bar, a pony tow, excellent for beginning skiers and an old- fashioned rope.
Otis Ridge 269-4444; Rte. 23, Otis, MA 01253.

BOUSQUET
442-8316.
Dan Fox Dr., Pittsfield, MA 01201.
Access off South St. (Rte. 7)
Trails: 21 Downhill (Novice to Expert); No XC.

It was 1932 when a group of winter enthusiasts first approached Clarence Bousquet about using the slopes of Bousquet Farm for some skiing. Three years later, the fledgling Bousquet Ski Area put together one of the Berkshires' greatest travel promotions ever: ski trains from New York to Pittsfield (with bus connector to Bousquet) for $2 round trip.

Lifts: 2 Chairlifts; 3 Rope tows; Snowboarding half-pipe.
Vertical drop: 750 ft.
Snowmaking: 100% of area.
Tickets: $15 Wkday, Wkend, Night.
Open: 10-10 Wkday; 9-10 Wkends; 9-4 Sun.; Night Skiing, Mon.-Sat. 5-10.
Ski school pro: Court McDermott.

Now, over 50 years later, the Berkshires' oldest ski area continues to provide friendly slopes, primarily for novice and intermediate skiers. There are, however, several very demanding runs, and from the summit of Bousquet, there's a fine view of Mt. Greylock's whalelike profile (nearly the same view that so inspired Melville; see "Arrowhead" on p. 94). Bousquet is well known for its effective ski school, a corps of some 50 teachers under the direction of Court McDermott.

EASTOVER

For its guests only, Eastover, a resort hotel in a converted mansion, offers alpine ski runs suitable for beginners and intermediates. Because of the convenience of Eastover's lodging-dining-recreation facilities, learning to ski can be a pleasure at this Lenox resort. The vertical drop is gentle; the longest run about 3/4 mi. Besides skiing, Eastover offers tobogganing and skating, and on a warmer note, indoor swimming and sauna.

Eastover 637-0625; 430 East St., Lenox, MA 01240.

JIMINY PEAK
738-5500.
Corey Rd., Hancock, MA 01237.
Access from Rte. 7, Lanesborough, or Rte. 43, Hancock, via Brodie Mt. Rd.
Trails: 25 Downhill (Novice to Expert); No XC.
Lifts: 4 Chairlifts; 1 J-Bar.
Vertical drop: 1,140 ft.
Snowmaking: 95% of area.
Tickets: 1991 Adult wkday, $30; Junior & Seniors, $24.
Open: Wkdays, 9-10:30; Wkends, 8:30-10:30.
Ski school pro: Jay Barranger.

Jiminy is committed to long seasons of well-groomed slopes, and to that end, they go to extraordinary lengths. Frequently opening early in November and staying open well into March, Jiminy not only utilizes advanced snowmaking equipment but also lays out what they call a Sno-Coat, essentially a giant tarp to protect vulnerable areas from rainy washouts.

This is one of the area's most demanding mountains, with 40% of its trails being suitable for advanced skiers only. Those with such talents will greatly enjoy the North Glade, Upper Lift Line and Whirlaway. For intermediates, there's the 360, the WestWay and the Ace of Spades. From these last two trails, you can see a magnificent vista of the Jericho Valley, northwards toward Vermont.

In addition to a full calendar of ski events (races, clinics and demonstrations), Jiminy also runs a race team just for children, a more serious tri-state race team, a freestyle team, a night adult program and a ski school. When you go to ski at Jiminy, you'll spend most of your time skiing: liftlines are carefully monitored so that you'll rarely have to wait more than 12 minutes. And, they close the parking lots when the area nears its capacity of 3,500 skiers.

The biggest news at Jiminy Peak is the completion of its $8.5 million 105-room condominium. Now there's quality lodging and a restaurant right at the base of the mountain.

North County

BERKSHIRE EAST

Billing itself as "Southern New England's most challenging ski area," Berkshire East's steep terrain lives up to that claim. With only 20% of its trails suited to novice skiers, this mountain is demanding, especially down the steep Flying Cloud and Lift Line trails, both of which are over 4,000 feet long. For beginners, three separate open slopes around the west lodge provide plenty of room to learn the basics.

From the summit of Berkshire East, midst the pines, you can get a fine view of the Deerfield River valley (to the east) with mountains all around it. The area offers day and night skiing, and has a rustic lodge with a bar upstairs.
Berkshire East 339-6617; Rte. 2 (near Savoy town line), Charlemont, Franklin County, MA 01339.

BRODIE MOUNTAIN
443-4752.
Rte. 7, New Ashford, MA 01237.
Trails: 24 Downhill (Novice to Expert); XC (25 km.).
Lifts: 4 Chairlifts; 2 Rope Tows.
Vertical drop: 1,250 ft.
Snowmaking: 95% of area.
Tickets: 1991 Adult Midwk $25; Wkend, $30.
Open: 9-11; Twilight Skiing, 3-11; Night Skiing, 7-11.
Ski school pro: John Koch.

One of the oldest ski areas in the Berkshires, Brodie Mountain started out under the direction of Gregory Makeroff, and now has quite a different flavor under the guidance of the Kelly clan. "Kelly's Irish Alps," they call Brodie; and a more Irish slope you could not imagine, right down to the occasional staff leprechaun dressed in green and shushing downhill. Brodie is a fun area, and has always had tremendous appeal to singles and younger skiers.

Three-quarters of Brodie's 20-odd trails and slopes are geared to novice and intermediate skiers, and one slope (Tipperary) offers a not-too-demanding 2 1/4-mi. glide. For experts, there's Mickie's Chute, Gilhooley's Glade and Danny Boy's Trail. Brodie is committed to its snowmaking, pioneering large-scale snowmaking in 1965 and now covering 95% of its slopes. They utilize state-of-the-art equipment, employing various systems and a super arsenal of Hedco Snow Cannons. In addition, Brodie invented its own "Master Blaster" snowgun and now has the capability to be the first area open in all of New England, a feat once accomplished in late October.

At sundown especially, the views from Brodie across the valley are stunning, and of particular note is the view northward to Mt. Greylock's whalelike silhouette. But the skiing doesn't stop at sundown at Brodie; for Kelly's Irish Alps is one of the largest night skiing areas anywhere, with over 17 mi. of trails and four chairlifts fully illuminated.

And after skiing, off the slopes, Brodie keeps the fun going, with five indoor tennis courts, five racquetball courts (racquets and sneakers can be rented for both), and a sauna. After sports, there's the Blarney Room and Kelly's Irish Pub.

Snowboarders Sighted on Berkshire Slopes

Another new creature has made its appearance on Berkshire mountainsides, this one vaguely resembling the now-thriving downhill skier, but zipping down the snowy slopes on just one wide ski. Combining skateboarding, surfing and skiing, snowboarding now has half a million enthusiasts, and most Berkshire ski areas can rent or sell you a board, and follow up with instruction. Hey, Dude! Get your board! Snow's up!

SKIING - CROSS COUNTRY

Berkshire is made to order for cross-country skiers — from flat runs along the Housatonic to steep trails up Mt. Greylock, from tours in town, such as Kennedy Park in Lenox and Heritage Park in North Adams, to wilderness paths like the one around North Pond in Savoy Mountain State Forest.

There are no lines, no chair lifts and most of Berkshire's ski touring is free, dependent only on the whims of the weather. Since Nordic skiing has gained in popularity, private touring centers have multiplied in the Berkshires, and if you prefer your trails groomed, your warming and waxing huts warm, there are now half a dozen such places to cross country ski.

It's best never to ski alone, especially in a wilderness area. If you're planning to ski in a state forest, check in at forest headquarters first. They usually have a map and some helpful hints; besides, it's a good precaution to let someone know you're out there. Be sure to carry a compass and extra clothes. Snacks and drinks are also nearly required equipment on the trail, and the really well prepared also carry a first-aid kit, knife, whistle, flashlight and space blanket.

Dozens of public trails are described below, most with sufficient directions for a short tour. More detailed descriptions for some of these tours, including maps, can be found in the excellent and compact *Skiing in the Berkshire Hills* by Lauren Stevens, (Berkshire House Publishers).

South County

Southern Berkshire ski touring is a bit more benign than in the other parts. The wilderness down south is a trifle less rugged, the snowmobilers fewer in number, the variety of groomed trails much higher. Yet there's plenty of challenge, exciting views, and several long downhill runs that are pure pleasure.

PUBLIC SKI-TOURING

Many trails in the Mt. Washington State Forest offer quintessential Berkshire ski touring. No snowmobiles are allowed, so the whistle of the wind will be the loudest noise you hear all day. From the forest headquarters (East St.), The Ashley Hill Brook Trail runs south along the brook towards New York State, a four-mi., slightly uphill trip suitable for intermediate skiers. Nearby, from the parking lot just outside the Mt. Everett Reservation, you can ski up that

2,600-ft.-tall mountain, the Dome of the Taconics. The climb up is gentle, passing Guilder Pond; the run down, long and exhilarating without being unduly dangerous.

Bartholomew's Cobble in Ashley Falls (Sheffield) has an interesting system of trails, with the runs on the far side of Weatogue Rd. being the best. A map is posted in the parking lot.

Beartown State Forest in Monterey has some lovely trails, starting at Benedict Pond and circling through the 14,000 acres of forest preserve. Maps are available at the ***State Forest Headquarters*** (528-0904; Blue Hill Rd., off Rte. 23.) Triangular red blazes or wooden markers designate the ski-touring trail in Beartown, with a blue-blazed trail circling Benedict Pond, the white-blazed Appalachian Trail passing through, and the orange-blazed trails for snowmobilers.

The West Lake area of the ***Sandisfield State Forest*** is a fine site for Nordic skiing. No snowmobiles are allowed on the Abbey Hill Foot Trail (marked with blue blazes), and from the state forest headquarters and parking area, just off West St., a beautiful tour of about two hours will circle you around Abbey Lake, up Abbey Hill (1,810 ft.) and then down past West Lake. The area around York Lake in the forest also has some good trails.

You can ski the Knox Trail in the ***Otis State Forest*** if you take Rte. 23 to Nash Rd. in Otis. Where Nash joins Webb Rd. is a good place to wax up, and as you ski, watch for red K's and red blazes marking the trail.

PRIVATE TOURING CENTERS

Butternut Basin (528-0610; Rte. 23) in Gt. Barrington has seven km. of groomed novice and intermediate trails. In addition to their lovely lodges, to comfort you they also offer a pondside warming hut. ***Otis Ridge*** (269-4444; Rte. 23, Otis) has over six km. of packed, but not tracked, trails. And ***Oak n' Spruce Resort*** (243-3500; off Rte. 102, South Lee) has six km. of Nordic trails.

Central County

John MacGruer.

Central Berkshire ski trails are generally gentle with moderate slopes and climbs. Several "Nature Preserves" (see that section) maintain trails, and these are excellent and beautiful places to gain Nordic experience. And Bucksteep Manor maintains private, groomed trails.

PUBLIC SKI-TOURING

Lenox is graced with beautiful ski-touring areas, the most popular of which is ***Kennedy Park.*** Its 500 acres were once the site of the grand old Aspinwall Hotel (which burned to the ground in 1931). Now its long, rising driveway and its bridle paths are used for ski-touring. The Main Trail (white blazes) is the widest and simplest, with Lookout Trail (red blazes) being more of a challenge. Stately oaks dot this very pretty highland, and you gain access either at the Church on the Hill (Main St., Rte. 7A) or behind the Lenox House Restaurant (north of town on Rte. 7), where you can rent equipment from the Arcadian Shop..

Pleasant Valley Wildlife Sanctuary (see "Nature Preserves"), also in Lenox, has a trail system laid out by the Massachusetts Audubon Society. For $2 ($1 for kids), you can ski, going out on the trail marked with blue blazes and back on the one marked in yellow. There's also Yokun Brook Trail, Nature Trail and others. Maps are free at the office next to the parking area (Closed: Mon.). The ***Woods Pond*** area in Lee and Lenox has a pretty, mostly flat trail running along the southern shore of Woods Pond, then north along the eastern bank of the Housatonic River for just over two mi. Enter via Woodland St. in Lee. The trail is best skied on weekdays due to weekend snowmobile traffic. ***Canoe Meadows*** (see "Nature Preserves") is another Massachusetts Audubon Society area, and it too has some lovely trails. On weekends, there is a $1 fee, which includes a map.

For more advanced Nordic skiers, the ***Honwee Mtn.-Turner Trail*** circuit is a challenge for the best skills. Park just off Cascade Rd. in Pittsfield State Forest. Check in at forest headquarters, get oriented, then start up the Mountain Trail, initially marked in orange, then in white. This trail has some great views, tough climbs and steep descents. Closer to the center of the city, in ***Sackett Brook Park*** (Williams St.), there are four mi. of marked trails.

Northeast of Pittsfield on Rte. 9 is the ***Notchview Reservation***, in the town of Windsor. Trails are well marked and maintained, and there is a modest 50-cent charge for touring. Maps are available for 20 cents; on weekends and holidays, the Budd Visitor Center is open as a warming and waxing shelter. Notchview is owned by The Trustees of Reservations.

PRIVATE TOURING CENTERS

South of Lenox on Rte. 20, ***Cranwell***, (637-1364; 55 Lee Rd.) has a network of trails, crisscrossing their golf course. And at the ***Canyon Ranch*** (637-4100; Kemble St.) closer to town, ski touring and instruction is available for spa guests, the trails sweeping across the majesty of the Bellefontaine estate.

In the hilltown of Washington, east of Pittsfield, ***Bucksteep Manor*** (623-5535; Washington Mt. Rd.) operates a long ski-touring season. Set on over 250 acres, at 1,900 ft., Bucksteep has 25 km. of looped, interconnecting trails. There's a waxing room, a ski shop which sells and rents, as well as on-site lodging and dining. Nearby in Becket, ***Canterbury Farm*** (623-8765; Fred Snow Rd.) grooms 11 mi. of trails for its inn guests and daily cross-country ski guests. There is a ski shop for rentals, lessons are available, and the ski fee is $6.

North County

PUBLIC SKI-TOURING

Up at 2,000 ft., where the snows come early and stay late, ***Savoy State Forest*** has miles of cross-country trails, best navigated with a map obtainable at ***State Forest Headquarters*** (663-8469). Enter the forest from Rte. 2 (Florida) or Rte. 116 (Savoy). A 2 1/2-mi.-long trail (blue blazes) makes a challenging circuit around North Pond and then South Pond. In North Adams itself, ***Historic Valley Park*** offers ski touring quite close to downtown. The trail starts at the parking area next to Windsor Lake and is well marked by blue blazes and signs which even describe the degree of difficulty of the next stretch of trail.

On ***Mt. Greylock***, many opportunities for fine ski touring exist. Here again though, it's best to ski during the week, because weekends tend to draw much snowmobile traffic. Depending on your skills and fitness, you can ski part or all the way to the summit. It's an 8-mi. round trip up Rockwell Rd. to Jones Nose and back, 15-mi. round trip to Stony Ledge, or 17-mi. round trip to the summit. The views are breathtaking, the skiing sometimes testy, and the weather ever-fickle. With this last factor in mind and given the height of your ascent, be sure to take warm clothing and some snacks. Check in at the Visitor Center on Rockwell Rd., off Rte. 7, Lanesborough.

The area in and around ***Williamstown*** is striped with trails, most of them novice or intermediate but at least one, Brooks Trail, is quite demanding. Brooks, and the Berlin Mtn. Trail near it, get heavy use from Williams College skiers. The trails begin off Berlin Rd., west of Rte. 2. The four-mi. Stone Hill Loop in Williamstown is probably the area's most popular: it's relatively easy and offers all the splendor of the best ski touring. The trail starts and finishes in the ***Clark Art Museum*** parking lot (South St.), and circles the 1,100-ft. Stone Hill, with its wonderful views. Finally, in ***Hopkins Forest***, Williams College maintains a network of trails just off Northwest Hill Rd. Although the trails are groomed and maps are available at the forest "Carriage House," facilities are minimal. All the best cross-country ski trails in the area are described in the *Williams Outing Club's Trail Guide*. And further information might possibly be had by calling the club itself (597-2317; Baxter Hall, Williams College).

PRIVATE TOURING CENTERS

Brodie Mountain Ski Area in New Ashford (Rte. 7) maintains a 25-km. trail network, of which 10 km. are groomed daily. Training site of the Williams College Cross-Country Ski Team, Brodie's trails were laid out by ski coach Bud Fisher. Many of the trails are double-tracked and wind through field and wood. If you're adventurous enough for a guided ski tour to the summit of Mt. Greylock, Brodie can arrange it (443-4752; call well in advance).

SOARING

Your attitude controls your speed, which is ideally 51 mph. In this unearthly quiet, half a mile high, the Berkshires seem like a Swiss landscape, all rolling patterns of farm and woodland. "Nice to be rich," said my instructor, Walt, admiring a gracious spread below, replete with pool and tennis court. "Nice to own one of these estates."

"This is the great estate," I replied, admiring the sky.

"You like it, eh?"

"Like it?"

"Keep your nose up, nose up! You're going too fast!"

You can try the ***Berkshire Soaring Society***, out of the Pittsfield Municipal Airport (443-6700; Tamarack Rd.), or the ***Mohawk Soaring Club*** out of Harriman West Airport, North Adams (458-8650). If you wish to soar, it's best to hang out with the glider pilots at the far edge of the airstrip on weekends. Watch, ask a few questions. You could end up floating on air.

Should you feel an aircraft to be an awful encumbrance, but still want to soar, people are regularly jumping off the top of Mt. Greylock in Adams, and just as often off a steep slope of the Taconic Range, on Rte. 2, west of Williamstown — with only lightweight ***hang gliders*** to support their flight. We recommend watching only.

A LUXURY SPA

CANYON RANCH AT BELLEFONTAINE 637-4100; 91 Kemble St., Lenox

A world-class spa in the Berkshires! It's an idea whose time has come, and health entrepreneurs Mel and Enid Zuckerman have taken their highly successful Tucson, Arizona, Canyon Ranch formula, and transferred it to the sculpted hills of Lenox. Sparing no expense in their $45 million creation, they transformed and built upon Giraud Foster's splendid "cottage," Bellefontaine, which is itself an exact replica of the French Le Petit Trianon.

The result is a spa that rivals any other, a spectacular facility smoothly run by a group of skilled and friendly professionals. Whether you come for a short cool-out, a vacation, a chance to drop a few pounds and tone up, or an invigorating change of pace, Canyon Ranch lives up to its self-proclaimed billing as "The Spa that never leaves you." With over 50 fitness classes to choose from daily, swimming, racquet sports of all kinds and a state-of-the- art gymnasium, the 3-level spa complex offers a physical workout that you can custom tailor to your needs. Add to that, hiking, mountain biking, and cross-country skiing in winter, and you have indoor/outdoor fitness possibilities unimaginable in your average spa.

Besides sumptuous jacuzzis, steam rooms, and saunas, Canyon Ranch offers inhalation rooms (combining steam and eucalyptus) and a range of personal services to pamper yourself as never before. Want a massage to soothe tired muscles? Choose from Swedish, shiatsu, Reflexology, cranial, Jin Shin Jyutsu, Trager and Reiki. How about a herbal wrap, an aroma wrap, clay or salt treatment or some hydrotherapy? Each of these ancient, exotic treatments is performed by experts, leaving you revitalized, inside and out. The healthful opportunities go on and on, from skin and beauty treatments, to dietary education and stop-smoking hypnosis. And speaking of diets, you're automatically on one when you stay at Canyon Ranch, a low-fat, low- cholesterol regime that's as delicious as it is healthy.

You dine, play and work out in swell company, too, meeting a corporate, artistic and social elite that gathers at such an internationally renowned renewal spot. Expect celebrities and all manner of fine regular folk as well.

While Canyon Ranch is sensational for many, it's not for everybody. Prices vary seasonally, but are always substantial. Access to the facility is limited to guests only, and should you wish to tour the spa, special arrangements must be made.

Getting in shape is good clean fun at Canyon Ranch. "I've taken lots of fitness classes in New York," said one recent guest, "but these girls are better." Fine by design, fine in maintenance, and fine in staffing, that's the Canyon Ranch system at Lenox. Says *Vogue* magazine: "Not a fitness factory or fat farm...you go to Canyon Ranch anticipating short-term results...and return with a long-term resolve." "A cross between boot camp and heaven," says *Self*. Said Berkshire humorist Roy Blount, in a report to *Gentlemen's Quarterly*: "Made me feel like a jackrabbit!"

The vast and luxurious indoor spa, at Canyon Ranch.

SPELUNKING

For you cave men and women out there, Berkshire is like stumbling onto the Mother Lode. The hills are riddled with caves, each of which has a colorful name and legend to go with it. ***French's Cave***, west of Williamsville in West Stockbridge, is 450 ft. deep, the longest cave in the whole of Massachusetts. Other Berkshire caves of note include ***Radium Springs Cave*** in Pittsfield; ***Bat's Den Cave*** in Egremont; ***Cat Hole Caves*** in New Marlborough; ***Pittibone Falls Cave*** in Cheshire; ***Belcher's Cave*** in Gt. Barrington; ***Tory Cave*** in Lenox; ***Peter's Cave*** in Lee; and the caves of western Lanesborough.

The ***Williams College Outing Club***, Williamstown (597-2317) occasionally goes a-caving. Notable Berkshire cavemen of the Present Age include *Berkshire Eagle* ace photographer Joel Librizzi, and Stockbridge Chief of Police Rick Wilcox.

Caving is great adventure, but it is also dangerous and should not be attempted alone or without an experienced guide.

SPORTS CAR RACING

Drivers, start your engines!

On the edge of Berkshire is the renowned **Lime Rock Race Track**, and an outfit even closer, the **Skip Barber Racing School** based in Canaan, CT, can teach you how to drive safely at very high speeds. Barber operates two schools actually, the **BMW Advanced Driving School** and the Skip Barber Racing School, both of which utilize the Lime Rock, CT, track as their training course. The Advanced Driving School uses specially prepared BMWs and takes you through accident evasion, performance braking, controlled slides and the limits of lateral acceleration. The Racing School seats you in specially prepared, low-slung Formula Fords, teaching you to drive at speeds you'd never consider on the highway. With either course, your driving skills are greatly enhanced, making you safer and more effective out on the road.

If you've been yearning to put the pedal to the metal, step on it and get on over to **Skip Barber Racing School** (203-824-0771; Rte 7, Canaan, CT).

SWIMMING

Berkshire is blessed with countless magical swimming spots, some secluded and known only to the likes of otter, and some quite public. There are sizable lakes and ponds, rushing green rivers, and deep, chilly quarries. For wintertime, and for those who prefer their water sport in a more controlled setting, there are numerous swimming pools, both indoor and out.

South County

Benedict Pond Beartown State Forest; 528-0904; Gt. Barrington; follow signs from Rte. 23 or from Rte. 102 in South Lee.

Berkshire Motor Inn 528-3150; Main St., Gt. Barrington; Indoor pool and sauna.

Eden Hill Recreation Center (298-5222; Congregation of the Marians, Prospect Hill, Stockbridge) Olympic-size heated indoor pool; Hours 6 a.m. to 8 p.m. Mon.-Fri., 12:30 p.m. to 5 p.m. on Sat., closed on Sun.

Egremont Country Club 528-4222; Rte. 23, S. Egremont; outdoor Pool.

Green River Off Rte. 23, 1 mi. west of Gt. Barrington; and off Hurlburt Rd., between Alford Rd. and Rte. 71; Clearest of the clear, greenest of the green, purest of the pure — a summer treat not to be missed.

Lake Garfield, Kinne's Grove, Rte. 23, Monterey.

Lake Mansfield 528-2610; off Christian Hill Rd., Gt. Barrington.

Oak n' Spruce Resort 243-3500; Off Rte. 102, S. Lee; Heated outdoor and indoor pools, saunas, whirlpool bath, physical fitness room; memberships available.

Otis Reservoir Tolland State Forest; 269-6002 or 269-7268; Off Rte. 23, Otis; camping, fishing, picnicking, boating.

Prospect Lake 528-4158; Prospect Lake Rd. (3/4 mi. west, off Rte. 71), N. Egremont; Camping, day picnics, adult lounge; open to 6 p.m. daily.

Spectacle Pond Cold Spring Rd., Sandisfield.

Berkshire swimming in full swing.

Paul Rocheleau, courtesy the Berkshire Hills Conference.

York Lake Sandisfield State Forest; 528-4774; Off Rte. 57, New Marlborough; Picnicking, fishing, hiking.

Central County

Ashmere Lake Ashmere Beach, Rte. 143, Hinsdale.

Berkshire West 499-4600; Dan Fox Drive, Pittsfield; Outdoor pool open June - Sept. Bath house, snack bar, showers; Memberships available.

Boy's Club 448-8258; 16 Melville St., Pittsfield. (Under 18) Indoor pool open to members only; memberships available. Free swimming early eves. wkdays; Sat. 1 - 3.

Onota Lake Lakeway Dr., Pittsfield; Free municipal beaches, supervised, 12 to 8 p.m., daily.

Pontoosuc Lake Rte. 7, Pittsfield; Free municipal beach.

Pittsfield Girls' Club 442-5174; 165 East St., Pittsfield; Indoor pool open for recreational swimming eves., Mon.-Fri.; Sat. 1 - 2:15.

Pittsfield State Forest 442-8992; Cascade St., Pittsfield; Swimming (lifeguards on duty 10 a.m. to 6 p.m.), picnicking, hiking and nature trails.

Pittsfield YMCA 499-7650; 292 North St., Pittsfield.

Plunkett Lake Lion's Club Beach, Church St., Hinsdale.

Ponterril 442-3342; Pontoosuc Lake, Rte. 7, north of Pittsfield; Operated by the Pittsfield YMCA (pool open to members only); Season memberships available).

Wahconah Falls State Park Off Rte. 9, Dalton.

North County

Clarksburg State Park Rte. 8, Clarksburg, near Vermont line; Camping, picnicking.

Hoosac Valley High School 743-5200; Rte 116, Cheshire; indoor pool open Sept. through June.

Jiminy Peak 738-5500; Corey Rd., off Rte. 7, Hancock; outdoor pool.

Margaret Lindley Park 458-5985; Rte. 2, Williamstown; swimming pond.

North Pond Savoy Mountain State Forest, Florida; Follow signs from Rte. 2 (in Florida) or Rte. 116 (in Savoy); $3 day-use, $20 season pass.

Northern Berkshire YMCA 663-6529; Brickyard Ct., N. Adams.

Sand Springs Pool and Spa 458-5205; off Rte. 7, near Vermont line, Williamstown; 50x75-ft. mineral pool (year-round temperature of the spring, 74); 2 mineral whirlpools (temperature of 102), mineral showers, sauna, shuffleboard, picnic area, beach. Pavilion for private party use.

Windsor Lake North Adams; Access via Bradley St. from North Adams State College or via Kemp Ave. from E. Main St.; Municipal swimming area; Supervised daily; Residents, $3 with car sticker, non-residents, $15 with car sticker; One-time use, $2.00.

Windsor Jambs State Forest 684-9702; Windsor; Follow signs from Rte. 9 in West Cummington or Rte. 116 in Savoy.

YMCAS

PITTSFIELD YMCA 499-7650; 292 North St., Pittsfield.

With its North St. facility and Ponterril Outdoor Recreation Center (see below), Pittsfield's YMCA undoubtedly serves more public recreational needs than any other complex in the county. At the North St. Y, the range of fitness and sports programs is staggering, if not revitalizing. Here you can enjoy aerobics, Aeoreflex (musical aerobics with hand-held weights); here, too, you can swim and scuba dive, both with instruction if you wish, and play racquetball, handball and squash. The racquetball program is particularly fine, being led by top teaching-pro Roger Gauchione, who even offers a videotaped analysis of your game. There are Nautilus machines and programs; special classes for kids, in basketball, gymnastics, swimming and Indian lore. To smooth things out, the Y has a sauna, a steam room, sunlamps and a lounge with color TV.

From Memorial Day through Labor Day, the Pittsfield Y's Ponterril Outdoor Recreation Center (499-0640; Rte. 7 at Pontoosuc Lake) really comes to life, and here, too, the facilities are inviting, the programs enriching. There's an Olympic-sized pool, a wading pool and a tot's spray pool; and swim lessons are offered. Down at the lake, the Y has a marina with moorings for 50 boats; they offer canoe, rowboat and sailboat rentals, and sailing lessons. There's a tennis camp and a soccer camp, a day camp and a preschool camp. And up at Ponterril's six, fast-dry clay courts, some of the best tennis in the county is played.

NORTHERN BERKSHIRE YMCA 663-6529; 22 Brickyard Ct., North Adams.

North County's Y is another center of vitality in Berkshire, a facility that has continued to improve and upgrade its sports complex. There's a six-lane pool, a full gymnasium, a weight room and Nautilus, a new gymnastics room for children, and two new handball/racquetball courts, all with programs to match. As with the Pittsfield Y, other Y memberships are honored (with a slight surcharge), and special short-term guest passes can be arranged.

A YOGA RETREAT

KRIPALU CENTER FOR YOGA AND HEALTH 637-3280; Rte. 183 (just south of Tanglewood and actually in Stockbridge); Mailing address: Lenox, MA 01240.

One of the grandest of Berkshire's summer "cottages" was Shadowbrook, a 100-room Tudor house with a one-acre floor plan. Built by Anson Phelps Stokes, the gargantuan house passed to Andrew Carnegie in 1917 and burned to the ground in 1956. The view southwards from Shadowbrook was and still is among the Berkshires' most inspiring: a panoramic sweep of the sky, the lake (Mahkeenac, or Stockbridge Bowl) and the mountains (including Monument Mtn., off to the right). Though the red brick structure built to replace Shadowbrook is among Berkshires' least inspiring, the estate nevertheless feels like hallowed ground and continues to have a deeply moving effect on many who visit. It was a Jesuit monastery for several years.

How appropriate then that such a facility be turned into a residential center for yoga and health with a staff of 150. Under the leadership of the ever-youthful Yogi Amrit Desai, Kripalu ("compassionate one") has emerged as a holistic health retreat of substantial importance. Successfully treading the fine line between cultic commune and a truly open facility, this center for yoga and health offers a comprehensive program of physically and spiritually rejuvenating practices. Facilities include spacious aerobic dance and yoga studios; saunas, whirlpools and flotation tanks; 300 acres of forests, meadows, meditation gardens, and miles of woodland trails; private beach on the Bowl; bookstore and gift shop; special health services including facial, foot and body massage; medical offices specializing in biofeedback, homeopathy and holistic health care; and a natural foods kitchen serving quite tasty, well-balanced vegetarian meals.

Many of Kripalu's programs are out on the lawns of the estate, and here, high over the lake and ringed by mountains, all the Center's therapeutic programs seem to have heightened effect. There are now many more than the original Shadowbrook's 100 rooms, and, increasingly, people who come to Kripalu sign on for short-term room and board combined with the programs. Local day-visitors are welcome as well. With its healthy ways, Kripalu enhances the hills, and may well enhance you, too.

FOR KIDS ONLY

As far as most kids are concerned, Berkshire is one neat county. Besides the dozens of children's camps here (see Camps), most of the ski slopes operate children's ski schools. In between the summer camping and winter skiing, dozens of little events are happening on a small scale all over the county. Most local libraries have story hours, most of the museums have kids' programs, and many of the local theaters have innovative children's productions. If you're serious about having a full calendar for the kids, *Adventures In the Berkshires — Places to Go with Children* by Patti Silver and Vivienne Jaffe is highly recommended reading. This spiral bound $7.95 paperback, available at some bookstores or through Berkshire Country Day School, is chockful of fun things to do.

South County

In Great Barrington, at the ***Mixed Company Theatre*** (528-2320; Rosseter St.), The ***Robbins-Zust Family Marionettes*** often perform a full range of "classic tales for children of all ages." Bringing out the heavyweight dramas such as "Three Little Pigs," "Rumpelstiltskin" and "The Emperor's New Clothes," the Robbins-Zust troupe also performs in Lenox and Pittsfield. For more information, call the Marionettes themselves (698-2591). They are "the smallest, established, permanent, floating repertory company in America."

In Great Barrington, the ***Barrington Ballet*** (528-4963) runs ballet classes for children Tues. through Sat. ***Dos Amigos*** Mexican Restaurant (528-8884; Stockbridge Rd.) often hosts David Grover, who sings and invites you to sing along, captivating kids of all ages. Across the way, at the Cove Bowling Lanes on Rte. 7, is the ***Rainbow's End Miniature Golf Course***, an indoor extravaganza to test even the deftest little putter. Other miniature golf courses are: ***Baker's Driving Range & Miniature Golf*** (442-6102; Rte. 7, Lanesborough), and ***Jiminy Peak*** (738-5500; Corey Rd., off Rte. 7, Hancock).

The ***Stockbridge Library*** (298-5501; Main St., Stockbridge) has a large and cozy children's section, and story hours are a regular event. During the summer, the ***Berkshire Theatre Festival*** (298-5536; Rte. 102, just east of the junction of Rte. 7, Stockbridge) gives Children's Theatre performances of plays written by local kids.

Central County

In Lenox, those little rascals the ***Robbins-Zust Marionettes*** act out again, performing their engaging histrionics at the ***Berkshire Performing Arts Center*** (637-4718; 40 Kemble St., Lenox). The ***Lenox Library*** (637-0197; 18 Main St.) has a terrific children's room, which always seems to be brimming with kid energy.

Creature comforts, at the Berkshire Museum.

Lisa Gamble Bartle, courtesy the Berkshire Museum.

Shakespeare & Company (637-3353; The Mount) recently offered "Entering the World of Shakespeare," a workshop for kids, and invited kids to be their guests at performances on Sun. nights. ***Pleasant Valley Wildlife Sanctuary*** (637-0320; 472 W. Mountain Rd.) runs a History Day Camp, one- and two-week sessions, featuring exciting educational outdoor activities for boys and girls, Grades One through Nine.

Central County's other Massachusetts Audubon Society property, ***Canoe Meadows Wildlife Sanctuary*** (637-0320; Holmes Rd., Pittsfield), runs a one-week native American Camp for boys and girls, ages 3, 4 and 5. ***Hancock Shaker Village*** (443-0188; Rte. 20, Hancock) offers a series of children's programs around the "Hands to Work" theme. These include tours for youngsters five to eight, focusing on Shaker work areas; children in the Shaker Kitchen for small folks, ages six to nine, and young people's natural history, for those ages nine to twelve, "a morning of fun exploring fields and woods."

In downtown Pittsfield, the ***Berkshire Athenaeum's*** (499-9483; Wendell Ave. at East St.) children's library, 499-9483, has a wide range of programs, from story hours to films. The ***Berkshire Museum*** (443-7171; South St.) also has a extensive series of educational children's events, including "Music, Motion and Make-Believe", — theater, dance and story-telling for the whole family.

In town at the ***Berkshire Public Theatre*** (445-4631; Union St.), it's those miniature magicians again, the Robbins-Zust Marionettes doing their little thing anew for little ones of all ages. Jack was there, and so was his beanstalk; and Hansel was recently seen there with Gretel. The Public Theatre also has a Youth Ensemble, which now develops plays by children for children. ***Either/Or Bookstore*** (499-1705; 122 North St.) pays lots of attention to the little ones, with a regular children's series featuring authors, illustrators and musicians.

North County

Up-county a ways, at ***Jiminy Peak*** (738-5500; Rte. 43, Hancock), the fun goes right into summer with their ***Alpine Slide***, a scenic 15-minute ride up, and an exhilarating 5-minute slide down. Jiminy also has a miniature golf course, trout fishing and a separate tennis program. Over in North Adams, at the ***Heritage Gateway State Park*** (663-6312; Furnace St.) a recent feature was a "Kid's Korner" craft workshop. In Williamstown, there's an extensive playground program, including swimming lessons at ***Margaret Lindley Park***. Information can be had by calling the program's operators, the Youth Center (458-5925; Cole Ave.). Also offered through the ***Youth Center*** are tennis lessons for kids in Grades Three through Six at ***Brodie Racquet Club*** (458-4677, 499-3038; Rte. 7, New Ashford). And music, dance and puppetry are some of the offerings at the ***Clark Art Institute***, through ***Northern Berkshire Council of the Arts'*** (663-3651) Imagine That!

CHAPTER SEVEN
Antique, Boutique and Untique SHOPPING

Master potter, Richard Bennett, working the clay at his Great Barrington Pottery.

Stores where you can buy local, regional, American and international creations of all kinds dot the Berkshire landscape. There are old things in Berkshire, antiques of every variety for sale in shops or at auction. Do you collect bottles, old lace, duck decoys or walking sticks? There are dealers in Berkshire who can oblige you, with such antique exotics and much more, ranging from Chinese export porcelain and Delft china to Colonial and Shaker furniture. American 19th-century paintings are the specialty of one shop, antique scientific instruments the mainstay of another.

There are more than a dozen bookstores selling new books in Berkshire, some shops quaint and highly selective, others huge and comprehensive. Many of them host readings and book signings by authors, and some will keep you informed of just who and when via mailing lists. The county has clothing shops both funky and elegant, and several that are both; many of them feature antique clothes from a jazzier age. There are fabric outlets and weavers aplenty. Those interested in current textile arts will find much to please them here. There are old-time general stores, suffused with the essence of New England. And many county towns have shopping streets or mews, where you can wander from shop to shop, enjoying the glorious Berkshire air in between.

There have been major shop closings since our first edition — both the legendary England's and the timeless Jennifer House were forced to close their doors, but plans are already afoot for revitalization. Many others, however, are just opening their doors. Just north of Pittsfield, in the wilds of Lanesborough, is the brand spanking new ***Berkshire Mall***, a shopping city that boasts 85 specialty shops, a 10-screen cinema, and a food court as well as ***Hills, JCPenney, Sears*** and ***Steigers***.

Lenox has had two new shopping centers come to fruition, with the ***Brushwood Shops*** offering an eclectic and exciting range of goods, and the ***Lenox House Country Shops,*** just up the road, bringing to Berkshire a wonderful array of factory outlets. And in the hinterlands of Southfield, looking decidedly more antique, is the ***Buggy Whip Factory***, an 18th-century structure that's been converted to a dozen shops and a restaurant. Here, in Colonial rusticity, you can shop for clothing, crafts and antiques, then snack or dine at the ***Boiler Room Cafe***, where it's first-class country dining all the way.

ANTIQUES

If you're coming to Berkshire with the idea that you'll visit all its antique shops, you'd better rent your room on a weekly basis. For Berkshire is blessed with a mind-boggling array of antiques. During an afternoon's random sampling, you'll likely see very fine early furniture and accessories, as well as jewelry, vintage clothing, paper goods, dolls, pottery, glassware and a host of other collectibles. These all range in age and character from the 18th-century classics, through the Victorian era with its abundance of oak and wicker, to those sharp, clean lines of the Art Deco period. If what you really had in mind was 1950s collectibles, don't despair; you'll find those, too.

You might well wonder: where are all these antiques from? If you posed the question to ten locals, you'd likely get seven different explanations and a few blank looks. In fact, much of what is offered is original to the area, and these items continue to surface in the marketplace as local families slowly wind down. Vast quantities of European household items arrived here during Berkshire's Gilded Age, furnishings for the many grand "cottages" that crowned the hillsides. Other antiques come and go by various means, and sometimes even come back again. When this happens, folks in the antique trade refer to them as "old friends."

What is an antique? New antiques are born every year. According to U.S. Customs Law, an object reaches the status of an antique when it is 100 years old. Thus, any item made prior to 1891 is now considered a bona fide antique and may enter the country from abroad, duty-free. Formerly, the year 1830 was the fixed date for defining antiquity. Symbolically, 1830 marked the end of an era, a convenient watershed separating the earlier handcrafted work of independent artisans from the later mass-produced objects made in factories during the Industrial Revolution.

A common challenge facing all Berkshire antique hunters involves strategies for stalking the prey. You might wish to begin your hunt with the annual brochure of the ***Berkshire County Antique Dealer's Association***. This pamphlet includes a handy reference map showing where to find over 60 dealers in 25 area towns, together with brief descriptions of what you might expect to find, their business hours and telephone numbers. Members of this Association "take pride in their merchandise and guarantee its authenticity." Their brochure is available in member shops or by mail (send SASE to: BCADA Directory, RD 1, Box 1, Sheffield, MA 01257).

Of course, there are dozens of other fascinating antique sources throughout the area which shouldn't be overlooked. Still to be discovered are those one-of-a-kind bargains tucked into the corner on the side porch of a hilltown shop. Perhaps you'll find your treasure masquerading beside a used toaster at a roadside tag sale or quietly sleeping in a box lot at auction.

As you motor south through Berkshire villages, noting one roadside "Antiques" shingle after another, you'll soon see how Rte. 7 got the nickname, "Antique Alley." Main St. in Stockbridge is worth a stroll for its shops, and antique-hunting opportunities are even more numerous in Great Barrington.

As you pass through Great Barrington, you can't help but notice the ***Little Store*** across from the cemetery (State Rd., Rte. 7). It's a tiny shop bulging at the seams with 19th-century painted furniture, baskets, art pottery and even 1940s collectibles. The ***Little Store*** has no phone but is open most days by chance. And in the center of town, artfully occupying the space formerly occupied by Shelley's Art Supplies is ***Memories*** (528-6380), a place that now stocks antique scooters, kitchen stoves, lanterns and a fine selection of John Sanderson's rare books.

Portraits on the block, under the big top, at Robert Herron's, Austerlitz, NY.

Auctions, of course, have their own importance in Berkshire. Some auctions are specialty sales, focusing on a given category of antiques; while others, such as an estate sale, offer everything that a household may have possessed, from the Queen Anne highboy to the family car.

If you've never attended an auction, you're in for a treat. It needn't be intimidating. When you arrive, ask the auctioneer any questions you might have concerning the bidding procedure. You are likely to find the auctioneer, the staff and even the other auction-goers friendly and helpful. Be sure to arrive in plenty of time to examine the merchandise. It's nearly impossible to judge an item's worth if you haven't looked at it closely.

An on-site, outdoor estate auction is often an event in itself. These sales are usually fast-moving yet relaxed affairs in which everything that comes out of the house is sold, and when that's finished, everyone moves to the barn to start all over again.

There is often a weekend auction scheduled in Berkshire County. You may be able to attend one at ***Caropreso Galleries*** (243-2434; 136 High St., Lee). Louis Caropreso conducts antiques auctions often at his gallery/church, itself a treat. Louie (as mostly everyone refers to him) is probably best known for his auctions of Americana and New England country wares.

Cheryl Hutto, of ***Hutto Auction Company*** (274-6052; North St., Housatonic), conducts auctions also on a regular basis. These auctions are often eclectic groupings of antiques, catering to varied tastes and collectors. Generally, her auctions are held in Sheffield at the American Legion Post on Rte. 7; she does several on-site auctions each summer.

The ***Bradford Galleries*** (229-6667; Rte. 7, Sheffield) are run by auctioneer Bill Bradford who regularly offers merchandise such as oriental rugs, fine furniture and accessories of all types. You may also attend one of the ***Bradford Galleries'*** ever-popular tag sales, scheduled between auction dates.

When you arrive in the Berkshires, you'll be able to find out quickly when and where the auctions, tag sales and flea markets are happening for the weekend by picking up a few publications, usually found free on store counters. Among the surefire ***South County*** standbys is the *Shopper's Guide*, a weekly publication from Great Barrington with a wide circulation. You'll find at least a dozen tag sales in summer months, scattered as tiny listings throughout its pages. Auctions, flea markets and antique shows are a bit easier to find because they are always listed in the "Entertainment" section. ***Central*** and ***North County*** publications include the *Berkshire Trader, Yankee Shopper*, and the *Penny Saver*, all of which are free weekly "shoppers." *The Berkshire Eagle*, the largest daily paper for the county, has complete classified listings for antiques, tag sales and auctions.

Some of the best antiquing is done at organized antique shows, where the chance to visit 50 or more shops in one place is well worth the price of admission. Because strict rules are usually laid down by the management, items tend to be of dependable quality, age and condition. Dealers who only sell at shows follow a circuit, and their steady customers look forward to seeing what new items will be offered.

However you look at it, Berkshire antiquing has a lustrous patina to it, a quality that's gotten better with age.

ANTIQUES DEALERS AND SHOPS

All shops are open year-round unless otherwise indicated.

South County

SOUTH EGREMONT

Bird Cage Antiques (Managers: Arnold & Marilyn Baseman; 528-3556; Main St., Rte. 23, next to post office.) Country furnishings with folksy accent. Toys and dolls, old collectible china and glass, spongeware, samplers, silver and jewelry. The unusual in 18th-century through the 1950s. Open daily 9-5.

Country Loft Antiques (Managers: Carol & Thomas Millott; 528-5454; Rte. 23.) American country furniture, early pattern glass, lamps, mirrors, woodenware, and other accessories. Open summer 10-5 daily. Other seasons, Thurs.-Sun. 10-5 and by chance.

Douglas Antiques (Manager: Douglas Levy; 528-1810; Rte. 23; P.O. Box 571.) Victorian (walnut/pine), turn-of-the-century oak furniture and quilts 1820-1940. Rolltop, flattop desks, office pieces, Hoosiers, tables, chests. Open daily 10-5:30, Tues. by chance.

Elliott and Grace Snyder (528-3581; Undermountain Rd., Rte. 41, 1/2 mi. south of Rte. 23) 18th- and early 19th-century American furniture, accessories and folk art, with emphasis on textiles and metalwork. Open by chance or appt.

Geffner/Schatzky Antiques and Varieties (528-0057; Rte. 23, at the sign of the Juggler.) Jewelry, pottery, glass, folk art, furniture. Open May-Aug. daily 10-5:30, Sept.-April, Fri.-Sun. 10-5:30 and during the week by chance.

Howard's Antiques and Bix Furniture Refinishing (Managers: Jeff & Linda Howard; 528-1232; Rte. 23.) 18th- and 19th-century American country furniture, brass lamps and accessories. Open daily 9-5, closed Tues.

Little House Studio (Managers: Libby & Milt Fett; 528-9517; Old Sheffield Rd.) Country furniture and decorative accessories. Specializing in painted and cut lampshades. Open most days year-round.

The Splendid Peasant (Managers: Martin & Pamela Jacobs; 528-5755; Rte. 23 and Old Sheffield Rd.) 18th- and 19th-century country furniture, folk art, whimsy and kitchenalia. Open daily 9:30-5.

GREAT BARRINGTON

Compass Antiques (Manager: Edward & Bridget Lotz; 528-1353; 224 State Rd., at Belcher Square.) Antique scientific instruments, scales, weights, measures, fine metalware and unusual collector's items. Open daily 11-6, call ahead is advisable.

Corashire Antiques (Managers: Nancy & John Dinan; 528-0014; Rte. 7 & 23, at Belcher Square.) American country furniture and accessories in the red barn. Open 9-5.

The Kahn's Antique and Estate Jewelry (Managers: Steven & Nancy Kahn; 528-9550; 38 Railroad St.) Specialists in antique jewelry, appraisals, diamond grading, gem identification; two jewelers on premises for fine repairs and custom work. Open daily 10-5:30; Sun. 12-3.

Mullin-Jones Antiquities (Managers: Patrice Mullin & Robert Jones, Jr.; 528-4871; 525 S. Main St., Rte. 7.) Importers of country French 18th- and 19th-century furniture and objects: armoires, buffets, tables, mirrors, pottery, architectural elements, French decorator fabrics, wallpapers, window lace. Open April-Oct. 10-5 daily (Tues. by appt.); Nov.-March always open weekends, otherwise by chance or appt.

Susan and Paul Kleinwald, Inc. (528-4252; 578 S. Main St.) 18th- and 19th-century American and English furniture, paintings and decorative accessories. Insurance and estate appraisals. Open anytime by chance or appt.

Snyder's Store (Manager: Shirley Snyder; 528-1441; 945 S. Main St.) Rustic furniture, country and oak. Also stock mantels, architectural details and garden pieces, quilts, linens and jewelry. April-Dec. open most days 12-5, Jan.-March weekends and by appt.

LEE

Aardenburg Antiques (Managers: David Hubregsen & Douglas Howes; 243-0001; 144 W. Park St.) American furniture and accessories of the early 19th century. Open weekends by chance, or anytime by appt.

Ferrell's Antiques and Custom Woodworking (Managers: Glenn & Deborah Ferrell; 243-0041; 67A Center St.) Always a fine line of country furniture and accessories in original condition. Expert antique repair, and all types of chair seating. Open daily 9-5. Closed Sun.

Henry B. Holt (243-3184; P.O. Box 699.) 19th- and early 20th-century paintings purchased and sold. Advisory services available for the disposition of estates or single works or art. Member Appraisers Association of America. Call for appt.

Kingsleigh 1840 (Managers: Linda & Arthur Segal; 243-3317; 32 Park St., Rte. 20.) Antique and American Indian jewelry, vintage watches, chains and fobs, small furniture, mirrors and collectibles. Open daily 11-5 or call for appt.

Pembroke Antiques (Manager: Morton Dobson; 243-1357; Rte. 20.) Shaker furniture and accessories, 18th- and 19th-century folk art, paintings and furniture. Open weekdays, Sat.-Sun. by appt.

MONTEREY

Tea Room Antiques (Manager: Judy Durlack; 528-4415; Rte. 23.) Country furniture and collectibles. Open mid-May to mid-Oct., 10:30-4:30, closed Wed.

SANDISFIELD

Country Antiques (Managers: Elaine & Bob Ziegler; 258-4834; Corner of New Hartford and Dodd rds., from Gt. Barrington take Rte. 23 to Rte. 57 and look for sign.) Country and primitive furniture. Cupboards, tables, benches, blanket boxes. Antique farm engines. Open weekends 8-5. Weekdays by chance or appt.

SHEFFIELD

Note: The following antique shops are in the township of Sheffield where there are two villages — Ashley Falls and Sheffield proper.

Ashley Falls

Don Abarbanel (229-3330; E. Main St., at Lewis & Wilson.) Antiques and accessories of the 17th, 18th and 19th centuries, including needlework, brass and metalwork, English pottery, English and Dutch Delft, Chinese export porcelain. Open daily 10-5; in winter call ahead.

Ashley Falls Antiques (Managers: The Cherneffs; 229-8759; Rte. 7A.) Large selection of fine period American furniture and accessories. Carefully selected and authenticated antique jewelry for the collector and dealer. Open daily 9:30-5:30.

Circa (229-2990; Rte.7A.) Majolica & Canton. 18th- and 19th-century furniture and accessories. Open daily 10-5.

Lewis and Wilson (Managers: Don Lewis, Tom Wilson; 229-3330; E. Main St.) English 18th- and 19th-century furniture. English, Continental and Chinese accessories. Open most days 10-5; in winter call ahead.

The Vollmers (Managers: Diana & Henry Vollmer; 229-3463; Rte. 7A.) 18th- and 19th-century furniture, both country and formal, firearms, paintings, and period accessories. Open daily 10-5, Tues. by chance or appt.

Sheffield

Centuryhurst Antiques (Managers: Ronald & Judith Timm; 229-8131; Main St., Rte. 7.) Specializing in clocks, Wedgewood, country furniture, primitives and accessories. Open daily 9-5.

Corner House Antiques (Managers: Thomas & Kathleen Tetro; 229-6627; Rte. 7, corner N. Main St. & Old Mill Pond Rd.) General selection of antiques and country accessories for the decorator, collector and dealer. Specialists in antique wicker furniture. Open most days.

Darr Antiques and Interiors (Managers: Donald Cesario, Robert Stinson; 229-7773; S. Main St., Rte. 7.) A 7-room house full of fine quality 18th- and 19th-century American, European and oriental furniture, paintings, lamps, rugs and other accessories displayed in elegant room settings. Open daily, May-Oct.; open Thurs. thru Mon., Nov.-April.

Dovetail Antiques (Managers: David & Judith Steindler; 229-2628; N. Main St., Rte. 7.) American clocks, country furniture and accessories. Repair and restoration of antique clocks. Open daily, Tues. by chance or appt.

E.G.H. Peter, Inc. (Managers: Peter Ermacora & Evan G. Hughes, 229-8881; N. Main St., Rte. 7.) 18th- and 19th-century American painted country furniture, folk art, and related decorative arts. Open Fri.-Mon. Other days by chance or appt.

Falcon Antiques (Managers: Peter & Annette Habicht; 229-7745; 176 Undermountain Rd., Rte. 41.) Country furniture and accessories. Good selection of period brass, copper, pewter, tin and treen (wooden things). Open daily 10-5; Jan., Feb. 12-5; other times by appt.

Frederick A. Hatfield Antiques (Managers: Fred & Eve Hatfield; 229-7986; S. Main St., Rte. 7.) 18th-, 19th- and-20th century antiques and accessories, including jewelry, silver, paintings and formal furniture. Open daily 9-5:30 and by appt.

Good & Hutchinson (Managers: David Good, Robert Hutchinson; 229-8832, 258-4555; Main St., Rte. 7, on the Green.) Specializing in American, English and Continental furniture, paintings, fine pottery and china for museums and antiquarians. Open Mon.-Sat. 10-5, Sun. 1-5.

Kuttner Antiques (Manager: Kathy Immerman; 229-2955; N. Main St., Rte. 7.) English and American furniture and decorative accessories. Open daily 10-5, closed Tues. Mail: P.O. Box 741.

Lois W. Spring (229-2542; Ashley Falls Rd., Rte. 7A.) 18th- and 19th-century American furniture both country and formal plus appropriate accessories. Open Sat. and Sun. 10-5, weekdays by chance or appt.

1750 House Antiques (Manager: Frances Leibowitz; 229-6635; S. Main St., Rte. 7.) Specializing in American, French and European clocks; music boxes and phonographs. Fine glass, china, furniture and decorative accessories. Open daily. Dealers welcome.

Susan Silver Antiques (229-8169; N. Main St., Rte. 7.) English and American 18th- and 19th- century furniture and decorative accessories. Open daily 10-5, Tues. by chance or appt. Mail: P.O. Box 621.

David Weiss Antiques (229-2716; N. Main St., Rte. 7.) Specializing in 18th- and early 19th- century formal and country furniture, china and accessories. Open daily by chance or appt.

STOCKBRIDGE

Encores Antiques (Manager: Pauline F. Nault 298-4765; Main St.) Bamboo, faux-bamboo and art deco. Normally open Wed.-Sun., 11-5. Mail: P.O. Box 518.

Tom Carey's Place (Manager: Lucille Nickerson; 298-3589, 298-4893; Sergeant St., off Main St.) Specializing in American clocks, country furniture of the 18th- and 19th-century, lamps, glass and unusual accessories. Open daily by appt.

WEST STOCKBRIDGE

Sawyer Antiques (Managers: The Sawyers; 232-7062, 698-3315 evenings; Depot St.) Early American furniture and accessories — formal, Shaker and country. Member American Society of Appraisers. Fri.-Sun. 10-5, other days call ahead.

Courtesy Hancock Shaker Village.

Shaker boxes, on display and for sale, at Hancock Shaker Village.

Central County

LANESBOROUGH

Amber Springs Antiques (Managers: Gae & Larry Elfenbein; 442-1237; Main St., Rte. 7, 5 mi. N. of Pittsfield.) American country furniture, pottery, tools, advertising, country store items. Open daily. Call ahead advisable.

Walden's Antiques and Books (Manager: William C. Walden; 442-5346, 499-0312; 1 Main St., Rte. 7.) General line of antiques and books. Appraisals and estate liquidations. Open daily May-Nov. by chance or appt.

LENOX

Charles Flint Antiques (637-1634, 637-0583, 243-9835; 83 Church St.) Broker, consultant and dealer in Shaker, paintings, and Americana. No retail shop. Open daily 10-5, Sun. by chance, always by appt.

October Mountain Antiques (Managers: Betty & Sidney Fleishman; 637-0439; 136 East St.) Country and Shaker furniture and folk art. Open May-Dec. 10 by chance or appt.

Stones's Throw Antiques (Manager: Sydelle Stone Shapiro; 637-2733; 57 Church St.) 19th- century American, English, French and oriental antiques; including furniture, china, glass, silver, prints and unusual collector's items. May-Oct.: open daily, Nov.-Apr.: open Thurs. thru Mon.

North County

WILLIAMSTOWN

Library Antiques (Manager: Sue Ellen Raiff; 458-3436; 70 Spring St.) Victorian antiques quilts, porcelain, lamps and antique prints. Open daily.

BOOKS

Many of the gift shops at the museums and performance centers of the Berkshires sell books, and some have extensive inventories of titles related to their organization's purposes, for example: the shop at ***Hancock Shaker Village*** (books on the Shakers and their crafts) or ***the Mount*** (books on and by Edith Wharton), or ***Chesterwood*** (books on architecture and sculpture), or the shop at the ***Clark Art Institute*** (art books).

South County

GREAT BARRINGTON

The Bookloft (Managers: Debby Reed, Eric Wilska; 528-1521; Barrington Plaza, Stockbridge Rd., Rte. 7.) Completely revised, updated, expanded, and gentrified, this longstanding Berkshire book outlet has moved a few doors down, and is now the classiest emporium in the area. Wooden bookcases frame the intelligent selection, all dramatically highlighted by track lighting. Wall-to-wall carpeting, soothing music and framed graphics all contribute to the sense of being in a fine library. Bookseller Eric Wilska's dream-come-true, with the able assistance of Debbie Reed.

LEE

Apple Tree Books (243-2012; 87 Main St.) Books, magazines, cards, gifts, stationery and audio.

STOCKBRIDGE

Books 'n Things (298-4687; in the Mews, off Main St.) This colorful shop fills every bit of its tiny space with books, men's accessories, a children's learning corner, cards, gifts and Norman Rockwell collectibles. While it's not a general bookstore with something in every category, you will find many illustrated "coffee table" and gift-book items here amidst the other attractions.

Stockbridge Books (Managers: Brant & Jamie Keller; 298-3115; 2 Elm St.) A whole new look and personality has emerged since Railroad Street Books in Great Barrington moved to this cozy new location across from the Stockbridge post office. Brant and Jamie Keller are devoting one whole room to magazines, stationery, greeting cards and other gift items, while still another room is a children's playhouse, packed with books, games and things kids love.
All this and a fireplace, too, Oh yes, and many books.

Central County

LANESBOROUGH

Lauriat's (445-5191; Berkshire Mall.) Huge selection of oversized illustrated books, publishers' overstocks, and the latest magazines of every persuasion make this a great browse, an almost irresistible opportunity to buy the newest and neatest in print. Strong travel section for the armchair adventurer or gung-ho globe-trotter.

Waldenbooks (499-0115; Berkshire Mall.) Mega-chain store sells books like a supermarket, but gets the titles soon after publication and frequently has books others don't.

LENOX

The Book Maze (637-1701; 333 Pittsfield-Lenox Rd., Lenox House Country Shops.) Special order, mail order, phone order. Lasersearch, booksearch. Cassettes, compact discs. Books too!

The Bookstore (Managers: Jo Baldwin, Matthew Tannenbaum; 637-3390; 9 Housatonic St.) "The world's oldest, permanent literary establishment, serving the community since last Tuesday," as their motto says, ***The Bookstore*** is by no means an ordinary shop. Of course you can choose from an extensive selection of hardcovers and paperbacks, but this is also the place where people gather to meet and chat. In fact, the owner, Matthew Tannenbaum, proudly points out the bulletin board, filled with community information; customers have even been known to leave messages for friends and neighbors who might pass by later. Book-signing parties are regular events where you might rub elbows with anyone from Alice Brock to Gene Shalit. **The Bookstore** keeps titles in stock longer than most bookshops, has a marvelous small-press collection (be sure to look upstairs), a lively children's corner and, in Tannenbaum and Baldwin, two of the best reader's advisors you'll find anywhere.

PITTSFIELD

Berkshire Bookshop (442-0165; 375 North St., and 664-4986, N. Adams Center, N. Adams.) A pleasant surprise, with scope and brightness. Both stores offer extensive selections of paperbacks and popular magazines, plus cards, posters and other gifts.

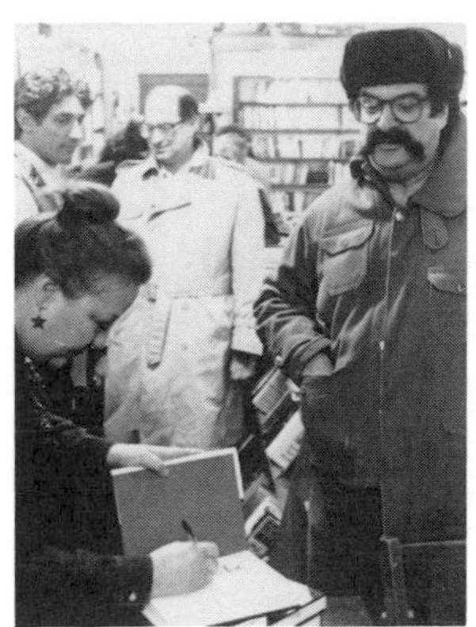

Ruth Bronz, who was chef-owner at Miss Ruby's Cafe, a Berkshire eatery formerly located in New York, signs her "Miss Ruby's Regional Cooking," for Berkshire resident, Gene Shalit, as Bookstore owner Matthew Tannenbaum looks on.

Either/Or Bookstore (Manager: Steve Satullo; 499-1705; 122 North St.) One of the most extensive and best book shops in the Berkshires. A sign on the door says the manager "reserves the right to rearrange sections at his discretion without prior notice" but you should still look at the map by the front door which will guide you through over 40 different categories of reading, ranging from women, history and nature to sports, children and food. There is a special section just on New England.

North County

NORTH ADAMS

Berkshire Bookshop (See Pittsfield.)

WILLIAMSTOWN

The College Bookstore/Erasmus Cafe (458-4808; 76 Spring St.) The inventory at the College Bookstore was built by the Renzi family over many years at a location just up the street. The collection here is still intelligently chosen and diverse, serving both the student and general reader very well. A good first place to look for current best sellers and how-to books.

Water St. Books (Manager: Keith Terwillegar; 458-8071; 26 Water St.) Do you like your bookstore to feel like a private library? Then this new store on Water St. is the place. The wide, open space bounded by 10-foot-high wooden shelves offers great browsing among an excellent selection of academic books and an extensive collection of titles in art, literature, theater, criticism, poetry and subjects for children.

Outside the County

SALISBURY, CONNECTICUT

Lion's Head Books (203-435-9328; Academy St.) A fine literary bookstore with a staff that knows its stock well and loves beautiful books.

CLOTHING

If you came to Berkshire with an empty suitcase or even an empty car, you could easily go home overloaded, with new or antique clothing — in almost any style. The shops described in this section are among the most interesting and best of the Berkshires, but they're not necessarily the best known. You may also want to explore the more popular alternatives for other fine clothing: for example, ***1884 House*** (298-5159; Main St., Stockbridge); Lenox; ***Talbots*** (637-3576; 46 Walker St., Lenox); ***Elise Farar*** (637-1131; Rte. 7, north of Lenox); ***Chase Ballou*** (two shops: 637-2133; Rte. 7, north of Lenox and ***Allendale Shopping Center,*** Pittsfield); ***The Cottage*** (two shops: 447-9643, 31 South St., Pittsfield; 458-4305, 96 Water St., Williamstown); ***Besse-Clarke*** (447-7361; 273 North St., Pittsfield); ***The***

Gap (442-5151; Berkshire Mall, Lanesborough); and in Williamstown, the ***House of Walsh*** (458-8088; 39 Spring St.).

South County

GREAT BARRINGTON

Decades (528-2950; 42 Railroad St.) A bonanza of classy & funky vintage clothing, jewelry and accessories. Good, clean, cheap fun. ***T.P. Saddle Blanket & Trading Co.*** (528-6500; 152 Main St.) The Southwest comes to the Northeast! An awesome array of cowboy boots, blanket-appliqued denim shirts, moccasins and fringed deerskin gloves are among the intriguing clothing options at this new outpost, which also offers bath oils, candles, saddles, saddle blankets, twig furniture, pillows and other Southwestern gear.

SOUTHFIELD

The ***Buggy Whip Factory*** (229-3576; Main St.) The Mother Lode for Berkshire-born sweaters! At the ***Neuma Sweater Factory Outlet***, choose from a host of Neuma's original, playful designs, beautifully translated into handcrafted, all-cotton sweaters. While you're clothes shopping at the Buggy Whip, you might also want to check out ***Dudley's***, a men's factory outlet, and ***Devoted to Children***, which offers some neat kid's clothes. Even more intriguing clothes can be found downstairs, at the ***Artisans Gallery***. Here, among an array of other beautiful crafts, you can look over the gorgeous shawls and ponchos by weaver Jade Lamb of Chatham, NY.

STOCKBRIDGE

Sweaters, Etc. (Manager: Fred Wallhauser; 298-4286; South St.) This lovely old house holds a family industry started by Bill & Fred Wallhauser. Classic designs are created here and then sent to Uruguay, where sweaters are hand-knitted, using soft wool from Romney Marsh sheep. Each sweater is unique, with patterns and craftsmanship seldom found anywhere else. These sweaters are sold wholesale under the name South Wool. There is a smaller line of hand-knit cotton sweaters, and during the last two weeks of October the shop holds a special sale.

Vlada Boutique (Manager: Vlada; 298-3656; Elm St.) At this unusual and distinctive shop, you'll find great clothes by Putamayo, Eileen Fisher, Reminiscences, and Pandemonium, jewelry by Ed Levin and John Michael Richardson, an extensive selection of lovely scarves and hats, and an exciting array of perfume oils, soaps, lotions, shampoos, gifts, greeting cards, and lots more. Vlada creates her own unique and beautifully crafted handbags in many designs and fabrics.

Central County

LENOX

Glad Rags (Managers: Lee Everett & Lynn West; 637-0088; 76 Church St.) One of Berkshire's funkiest clothing experiences, Glad Rags continues to delight and inspire. Looking for those special berets? Glad Rags has them, in two dozen colors, and in leather too. For you ladies who want to combine the antique look with New Wave, how about some lace-lined clear plastic shoes, also available in pink? Here, too, you'll find raccoon coats, lace dresses and top hats. Jewelry and accessories, and a wide range of Kiehl's oils, essences and lotions are also featured in Central County's hippest thread emporium.

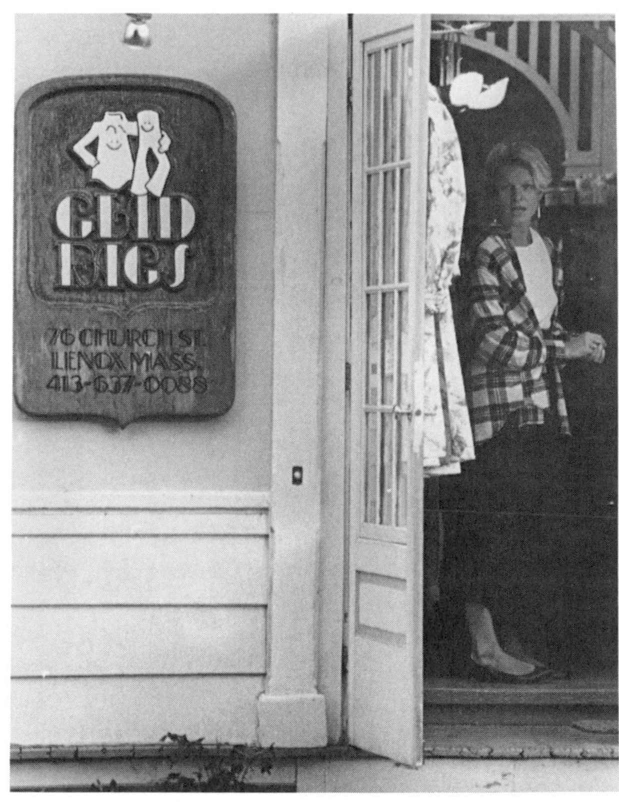

PITTSFIELD

Greystone Gardens (Manager: Carla Lund; 442-9291; 436 North St.) Vintage Victorian clothing and accessories for men and women. Fedoras, lace lingerie and other curious wearables. Quite fun.

North County

ADAMS

Harbor Woolens (Managers: The Bussieres; 743-1222; Grove St., Rte. 8.) For three generations, the Bussiere family has manufactured and designed textile products throughout New England. Now this family-owned-and-operated business stocks first-quality, seconds, thirds, discontinued and irregular clothing at tremendous savings. Bernat yarns, Levi, Timberland, Woolrich and Hudson's Bay are just a few of the names you will find in this outlet.

NORTH ADAMS

Alliance Editions (664-6318; Windsor Mill.) The all-cotton fashions that are stencil-dyed and silk-screen printed here are sold throughout the country and in Canada. Their new retail shop attractively displays women's clothing in a full line from dresses to separates.

Windsor Mill Outlets (664-6318; 121 Union St., Rte. 2.) This converted mill now houses several outlet shops, and the savings are terrific. Not very many people realize that one of the country's premiere designer-manufacturers of women's cotton clothing has this factory outlet. With savings of 40%-70%, you can find hand-silk screened tops and skirts, turtlenecks and T-shirts; and, depending on the season, corduroy skirts, blazers, dresses and accessories such as bags and sweaters.

FABRICS AND WEAVERS

South County

ASHLEY FALLS

Maplewood Fabrics (229-8767; Rte 7A.) One of the largest selections of quality fabrics in New England, in one of the region's sleepiest hamlets! Choose from Liberty of London, Scalamandre, Schumacher, and other major manufacturers in a low-key setting. Unbeatable, personalized attention will assure success in your next sewing project.

STOCKBRIDGE

Country Curtains (298-4938; the Red Lion Inn, Main St.) Located behind the Red Lion is the home of this nationally known mail-order firm. Years of old-fashioned quality are displayed in the curtains, dust ruffles, bedspreads and canopy covers. There are many fabrics available with the added attractions of kitchen and dining room accessories, pillows and dolls.

WEST STOCKBRIDGE

Undermountain Weavers (Managers: The Pinkstons; 274-6565; Rte. 41, south of Williamsville; Mail: RR 1, Box 26, Housatonic, MA 01236.) Stop by this restored barn where you can watch weavers Dutch and Anne Pinkston design cloth, using traditional patterns and wools from the Shetland Islands. They also use rare Chinese cashmere. The shuttles fly on century-old hand looms as the cloth appears, strand by strand, before your eyes. The Pinkstons will arrange tailoring for you or you may purchase fabric by the yard.

Skillful hands and tools of the trade at Undermountain Weavers, Housatonic.

Central County

LENOX

Tanglewool (Manager: Aline Sosne; 637-0900; 59 Church St.) Aline Sosne has added new dimensions to her exclusive line of wools by Patricia Roberts and Yarnworks. Sweaters, plus sophisticated and playful leather clothing, as well as accessories and makeup, abound here. Trips to Europe have inspired these additions, and you can either shop in this attractive store or order by mail.

Weaver's Fancy (Managers: Barbara Caplin, Catherine Pincus; 637-2013; 69A Church St.) There is a real sense of warmth, color, texture and quality in this shop. The owners have over 30 years of weaving experience, and they weave natural fibers into exclusive and original designs.

North County

ADAMS

Old Stone Mill Factory Outlet (743-1015; Rte. 8.) A beautiful old stone mill housing a wealth of wall coverings and fabrics that have been discontinued or are slightly irregular. The staff is very helpful in figuring out measurements, and they will snip a few samples of the wallpapers if you would like to try them out at home before deciding on a purchase.

Waverly Fabrics Outlet Store (743-1986; 5 Hoosac St). This outlet store is right in front of the Waverly Mill complex. There are remnants and seconds in fabric, upholstery, bedspreads, draperies, pillows, quilted yardage and wallpaper. They have also started selling oriental carpets, dhurries, hooked and braided rugs.

NORTH ADAMS

Novtex (664-4207; 459 State Rd., Rte. 2.) Located in a white house across the street from the Novtex Mill, this factory store has everything for a craft or sewing project: it's all on sale at 30%-90% off regular retail prices.

FURNITURE AND WOOD PRODUCTS

South County

GREAT BARRINGTON

Rooms (Manager: Laurie MacMakin; 528-5827; 291 Main St.) Strong emphasis on summery furniture, light in weight and look. Bright upholstery, often in jazzy patterns. Designer doodads. Very refreshing.

WEST STOCKBRIDGE

Anderson & Son's Shaker Tree (Managers: The Andersons; 232-7072; Rtes. 41 & 102.) Peter Anderson has been a master craftsman in the fine art of Shaker furniture for 18 years, and with his wife, Beverlee, and their three sons, Peter, Paul and Mark, owns and operates the Shaker Tree. The main workshop is in Staffordville, CT; in 1981, they opened their shop in W. Stockbridge. Their craftsmanship is so perfect that they were entrusted with permission to measure Shaker pieces in the Andrew's Collection at the Metropolitan Museum of Art in New York. A remarkable New England tradition lives on in the Andersons.

Central County

DALTON

Specialty Wood Company (Manager: Craig Walton; 684-2431; 484 East Housatonic St.) Craig Walton had been in the importing business for 15 years before opening this shop. Catering to hobbyists and contractors, he sells 26 "species" of wood from all over the world including South America, the Philippines and Indochina. He also stocks some of the more common woods from the United States such as pine, oak, mahogany and cherry.

GENERAL STORES

South County

NORTH EGREMONT

Old Egremont Store (Manager: Craig Elliott; 528-4796; Rte. 71.) Like his father before him, Craig Elliott runs the Old Egremont Store, the post office, the gas station and a dowsing service that can mysteriously pinpoint underground water veins. In an era when supermarkets seem to be exploding into hypermarkets and America is being "malled" east and west, the Old Egremont Store is an outpost from another era — a country store that is as much a gathering place as a provision company. Soups and sandwiches are served from the store's deli, and for your dining pleasure, the front yard boasts a couple of picnic tables. On a good day at morning coffee time, you'll meet local farmers and woodcutters, toddlers and doggies, mothers and policepeople, campers and hunters, and one fellow who's a dynamiter.

MONTEREY

Monterey General Store (528-4437; Rte. 23.) One of just a handful of shops in Monterey, this one isn't as general as it used to be but is still an oasis in southeastern Berkshire. Besides beer and wine, the store stocks fresh vegetables, cold cuts, preserves and locally made maple syrup, along with corkscrews and toenail clippers. There's a lunchroom in the back, but the front porch is best, with its two benches overlooking all this tiny town's action.

Jane McWhorter.

North County

WILLIAMSTOWN

Phillips' General Store (458-3723; 11 Water St.) "Dry Goods, Sporting Goods, Garden Supplies, Toys, Kitchenware, Hardware, Plumbing, Paint" says the sign outside this holdover from another era. But inside, the categories fade as you wander on creaky wooden floors, down aisles crammed with cookie cutters, 9-foot-long ostrich feather dusters, wooden hay rakes, rabbit and skunk repellents, post diggers, sledgehammers and jawbreakers. From waders to pink flamingos, this 126-year-old institution continues to supply necessaries, both exotic and ordinary.

The Store at Five Corners (458-3176; 6 New Ashford Rd., Rtes. 7 & 43.) Pull up to the pumps at this 19th-century building and you're likely to end up getting more than gas. Inside are wines and beers, a full deli, fresh homemade pastries, homemade soup, jams and jellies as well as homemade candies and fresh-ground coffee. An old-time (and better) answer to today's so-called convenience stores.

GIFTS

See also "Shopping Streets" at the end of this chapter where other special gift shops, among the dozens in Berkshire County, are mentioned.

South County

GREAT BARRINGTON

The Berkshire Cupboard (Managers: Mimi MacDonald & Nancy Hecker; 528-1880; 297 Main St.) A treasure-trove of locally made goods and goodies, from maple syrup and herb assortments, to beautifully marbled blank books and all manner of neat crafts. A Berkshire potpourri, The Berkshire Cupboard.

Bullwinkel's (Manager: Laura Soderland; 528-0388; 50 Stockbridge Rd.) Actor Bob Brolli has assembled the most intriguing mini-department store in Berkshire, a quaint shop housed in a real house, with everything from English Wellingtons, slickers and "brollies," to sensational local paper cuttings, from Irish handknits to imported toys. Everything's top quality, everything just a little different.

Crystal Essence (Manager: Adrienne Cohen; 528-2595; 39 Railroad St., Great Barrington.) Awesome array of magnificent geodes, gemstones, ceramics, jewelry, Central American clothing, New Age books, calendars, and a whole school of Paleolithic minnows who got fossilized in the layers of some sedimentary rock. Listen carefully, and you can hear a minnow's famous last words: "So I was out one day, with my schoolmates, wiggling around a puddle, and the sun gets hot, the puddle evaporates, and next thing I know, we're in some New Age shop in Great Barrington, dead!"

NORTH OTIS

Otis Poultry Farm (269-4438; Rte. 8.) Ask for a tour of this farm and you will see a lot more than chickens. Their country store features shearling hats, gloves, vests and slippers, sheepskin rugs, suede and leather handbags and French rabbit jackets.

SHEFFIELD

Blueberry Hill Antiques and Gifts (229-3575; Main St.) A fun shop, especially well stocked with local crafts, like hand-painted trays, quilts, and rocking horses, all made in Berkshire.

Central County

LENOX

The Silver Sleigh (Manager: Carol Schauer; 637-3522; Rtes. 7 & 20, Lenox, at Brushwood Farm, just north of village.) Carol Schauer was born on Christmas Day, and though she only remembers one early childhood birthday, she has many happy memories of the holidays, working with her family, who were florists. Now, in a restored carriage barn, she has captured everyone's imagination by filling her enchanting shop with holiday and other decorations from countries all over the world.

North County

NORTH ADAMS

International Outlet (664-4580; 121 Union St.) With a small retail showroom leading into a warehouse, this importer's outlet features savings up to 70% on crystal, china, cookware, toys, pottery, baskets, rugs and brassware, with many additional items that are either closeouts or odd lots. Take the time to wander down the warehouse corridors, and check the building's directory. There are other artisans here, such as Stephen Suave and Karl Housaker, who handcraft and repair guitars at Suave Guitars (663-3060).

HANDCRAFTS

South County

GREAT BARRINGTON

The Great Barrington Pottery (274-6259; Rte. 41.) Using traditional methods and a wood-fired kiln, potter Richard Bennett has created oriental-style pottery with a dramatic yet subtle range of glazes. The pottery (both practical dishware and objets d'art) is complemented by a large collection of silk flowers which can be purchased individually; floral arrangements are also made to order. The grounds are attractively landscaped and the courtyard of the teahouse has a Japanese garden. Tours of the workshop and grounds are available; during the summer, a tea ceremony is performed daily. See "Seasonal Events" in Chapter Four, *Culture*.

Evergreen Crafts (Manager: Barbara Watkins; 528-0511; 34 Railroad St.) An exciting collection of American handcrafts, including jewelry, wooden boxes, turned wooden vases by Pittsfield craftsman Warren Vienneau, magic brass kaleidoscopes from Northampton, beautiful table settings, playful table accessories such as cow creamers, splendid hand-painted silks, excellent toys for your favorite little person. Be prepared: you'll want to spend both time and money here.

Out of Hand (Manager: Gail Anderson; 528-3791; 81 North Main St.) This multileveled shop was started by Katherine Shanahan 14 years ago. Importing from Africa, Asia and the Americas, she stocks women's clothing and accessories made from natural fibers. There is also a wide range of baskets, both functional and decorative, and many other items for home decor. As you wander through the displays, you will find collector's pieces from Africa and South America.

Wonderful Things (Managers: Deborah & Harry Sano & Lucille Tanguay; 528-2473; 232 Stockbridge Rd., Rte. 7.) This amazing building is indeed full of wonderful things. A labyrinth that's fun to explore, there are yarns and needlework, art and craft supplies, and American- made handcrafted gifts. Owned and operated by three craftspeople, there is always someone available for advice.

MONTEREY

Joyous Spring Pottery (Manager: Michael Marcus; 528-4115; Art School Rd.; call for appointment.) *Bizen Nobori Gama* is a multichambered climbing kiln named after the Japanese town of its origin, where unglazed pottery called *yaki-shime* has been produced for over 1,000 years. The potter here, Michael Marcus, fires the kiln's load of raw, unglazed objects, and the pieces emerge dramatically glazed by flame and ash.

SOUTHFIELD

The Artisans Gallery (Manager: Robin Schmitt; 229-6686; Buggy Whip Factory.) South County's Grand Central for fine regional handcrafts, the Artisans Gallery is a lovely showcase for locally crafted pottery by Jane Burke and others, handweavings by Jade Lamb, wood-turned objects by Warren Vienneau, and scores of other intriguing crafts that magically blend art with utility.

STOCKBRIDGE

Seven Arts Antiques (Managers: Andy Talbot & Amy Johnson; 298-5101; Main St.) Berkshire's premier source for dugout canoes, coconut monkeys, and flying Indonesian babies. Looking for Shiva, or some other god? They're here.

Dolphin Studios (Managers: The ffrenches; 298-3735; West Main St.) You can't miss this cheerful house or its sign, and when you step into the studio, you will meet the imaginative and creative ffrench family. Each member of the family is an artist, and collectively they have produced ceramics, calendars, cards, batiks, collages, woolens, knitted sweaters and hats, and silk screening. Be sure and check out Crispina's Capreatures, wooly, capricious little creatures. Expect the unexpected at the sign of the Dolphin.

Marsters Pottery (Owner/Managers: Peter Marster & Amy Shapiro; 298-5240; Elm St.) Predominantly pottery and ceramics, this shop displays dozens of ways you can dress up your table. From the simple to the grandiose, offering ample range to please particular friends as well.

The Pink Kitty (Manager: Paula Hall; 298-3134; located in the Red Lion Inn.) Berkshire books, sporting ties, country dresses, lamps, throw pillows, sporty umbrellas, unusual playthings.

WEST STOCKBRIDGE

G/M Galleries (Managers: George & Marie Bonamici-Woodcock; 232-8519; Main St.) Fine American and international crafts, with an emphasis on jewelry. Almost anything you purchase here will be of museum quality, of major beauty.

New England Stained Glass (Manager: Raymond Dorazio; 232-7181; Depot St.) With over 20 years at his art, Raymond crafts stained glass windows, boxes, and lamps. His Tiffany-design lamps are especially pleasing, and in particular, his dragonfly lamp is a stunner. Brass dragonflies flit over the aqua-colored tile base, while several larger dragonflies watch from the stained glass shade, their eyes glowing a ruby red.

Central County

LENOX

Brushwood Studio (637-2836) World-traveler Dudley Levenson offers his museum quality collection of carvings, baskets, art. An adventure.

Potala (Managers: Andrew Failes & Rachel Park; 637-4147; 25 Housatonic St.) Magnificent kilims, jewelry, furniture and miniature rocking elephants from Asia. A journey into the art of craft.

Lacquerware at Potala, Pittsfield.

PITTSFIELD

Potala (Managers: Andrew Failes & Rachel Park; 443-5568; 148 North St.) Considerably larger quarters and more stock than the Lenox outlet, but less ambiance. Still, an outstanding collection of moderately priced Asian art and craft.

Pottery Plus (448-2362; 122 North St.) Sophisticated American crafts, with the emphasis on pottery and baskets. Also, a nice selection of Pittsfielder Warren Vienneau's splendid turned wooden vases.

North County

NORTH ADAMS

Up Country Artisans' Showroom (663-5802; Heritage State Park.) The most complete collection of Berkshire arts and crafts, from the lovely pen-and-ink nature drawings by Gene Matras to the thick, cabled afghans by Martha Struthers of North Adams. Also, stained glass, wood turnings, sweaters, pottery, quilts, toys, and scores of other beautiful Berkshire creations. Up Country, uplifting!

WILLIAMSTOWN

J-Cubs Bear Co. (Managers: The Jacobs; 663-3335; 610 N. Hoosac Rd.) Paula & Bill Jacobs (note the company name) have lovingly created bears, bears and more bears. These are not your average teddies. Each one is made from different patterns and materials, and they are more decorator pieces than toys. In fact, if you have a favorite tartan or piece of material, the Jacobs will create your very own bear. Throughout the shop, there are a number of other complementary crafts collected throughout New England, such as dried wreaths and miniature furniture with rush seats.

The Potter's Wheel (458-9523; 84 Water St.) Sensational, museum-quality collection of American crafts will have you cooing, and probably quickly reaching for your wallet. Riverside location and open gallery space enhance aesthetic experience. Astonishing and delightful array of jewelry, pottery, toys, and other crafts makes for a delicious, if expensive, expedition.

Hey Diddle Diddle (458-2855; 96 Water St.) Potter's Wheel owner Adelaide England's shop for kids features yummy handknits, adorable toys, and supercool wooden rocking boats by Buckley Smith.

JEWELRY

South County

WEST STOCKBRIDGE

L'Artisant (Managers: Jean & Patricia Khalaf; 232-7187; Main St.) Unique, elegant, one-of-a-kind custom gold and silver pieces. Artisan's shop on premises.

Central County

LENOX

L & R Wise Goldsmiths (637-1589; 81 Church St.) Laurie Wise Donovan, is the main designer and creator in this workshop-gallery, which features original and one-of-a-kind gold jewelry. Laurie's design for a brooch received the 1991 Spectrum Award, one of 15 nationwide, presented by the American Gem Trade Association. It will be part of a one-year national tour. Richard Wise is a gemologist. Together they have established a reputation as major sellers of rare gems. Going directly to the source, Richard brings back fine sapphires from Burma, Kashmir and Ceylon, and rubies from Burma and Thailand. The Wises also sell and show work by other jewelers. A visit to these goldsmiths deserves high priority, because each piece is beautifully displayed, showing creative and perfect workmanship.

KITCHENWARE

South County

GREAT BARRINGTON

Resources (Manager: Marjorie Blair; 528-4002; 312 Main St.) A treasure trove for the trendy kitchen. Designer everything, from dishracks to dinnerware. Cookbooks, wooden wine racks, beautiful stemware. Your best-dressed kitchen could start here.

Central County

PITTSFIELD

Your Kitchen (Manager: Susan Gordon; 442-0602; 170 North St.) Susan Gordon promises that if you can't find it at Your Kitchen, she will get it for you or tell you where else to look for it. Known as the cook's hardware store, there is a full range of gadgets, cookware and tools, cookbooks and gifts. A browser's paradise.

RECORDS

South County

LEE

Berkshire Record Outlet (243-4080; Rte. 102, Pleasant St.) A new location houses this wonderful collection in even more prosaic warehouse surroundings. A record collector's dream. If you are searching for a special recording, whether classical, popular or folk, or if you need help trying to locate a certain performance by your favorite recording artist, look no further. The chances are good that you will succeed right here; and if what you want is not in stock, the Record Outlet will find it for you. Want the option of six or more versions of the Brandenburg Concerti to choose from? Come here!

SHOPPING STREETS, MEWS AND MALLS

There are a number of streets or shopping clusters in Berkshire where you can literally shop till you drop. Here then, are close to a dozen prime possibilities to leave the car behind and go exploring on foot. Though window-shopping and browsing are certainly possible, it helps to bring a bit of cash, or credit cards, and good walking shoes.

South County

GREAT BARRINGTON

Railroad Street

This small street in the center of town packs in everything for the shopper. There are three lovely restaurants, several professional offices and the Barrington Ballet School, too. ***Decades*** (528-2950), near the high end of the street, is a vintage clothing and jewelry store. ***Kahn's Antique and Estate Jewelers*** (528-9550) and ***Byzantium*** (528-9496; women's clothing) are on either side of ***Evergreen*** (528-0511), a craft shop operated by Bob and Barbara Watkins. His pottery is displayed next to crafts from all over the country; the shop features jewelry and blown glass. Just upstairs is Steve Myrowitz's ***Sprout House*** (528-5200), a unique, health-oriented supply store with a splendid selection of juicers, sprouts, sprout seeds, full spectrum bulbs and other holistic accouterments. ***Petcetera*** (528-3487) has pet supplies, fish and Cosmic Catnip; and ***Initially Yours*** (528-9402) provides monograms and initials, with an incredibly colorful array of wool and accessories for sale. At the ***Snap Shop*** (528-4725), Tony and Steve will supply you with the latest and greatest in photo equipment, as well expert advice on how to take fine photos.

Across the street, you'll find ***Crystal Essence*** (528-2595) an astounding collection of fossils, figurines, clothing and crystals for the New Age. ***J.C. Wheeler Country Classics*** (528-2110), women's clothing. ***Leatherwoods Ltd.*** (528-4884) is one of the oldest shops on the street. Larry Newey calls his shop "an outlet for my craft." Quality is emphasized as he and his wife, Selma, search out leather clothing, footwear, handbags and gloves. ***Hilde B's*** (528-0331), nearby, is an eclectic selection of crafts, from pretty peasant and designer clothing to jewelry, from pottery to leather backpacks. ***Gatsby's*** (528-9455) clothing boutique, offers a wide range of clothes, shoes and sneakers, and also has shops in Lee and Williamstown. ***Farshaw's*** (528-1890), the Fun Store presents a mind-boggling array of the latest fad gear, such as primo Zube Tubes, Koosh and Mini-Koosh, as well as high-tech skateboard trucks and supplies, every variety of pen and pencil available in the Free World, paper, office supplies, groovy toys, wacky gags, boffo doo-dahs. Feeling dull or blue? A visit to Farshaw's can quickly rearrange your reality.

SOUTHFIELD

The Buggy Whip Factory (229-3576)

In 1792, the Thompson Whip Company established its factory in Southfield, helping to speed horsedrawn traffic throughout New England. The Factory is still thriving 200 years later, now as a community of unique shops in a superb setting. Here's a great way to spend a Berkshire morning or afternoon, with or without the kids. For the little ones, there's ***Devoted to Children***, with imaginative toys and clothing. Outside, there's a splendid pond with ducks, and an incredible pint-sized wooden train, just waiting for your little conductor. Here, also, you'll find scores of county antique dealers, offering everything from classic jewelry to inscribed first editions.

Other shops at Buggy Whip include the ***Neuma Sweater Factory Outlet***; ***Dudley's Clothing; Surroundings***, a country gift shop and interior design studio; the ***Music Man***, chockful of records, old and new, tapes, and CDs. A highlight at the Buggy Whip is the ***Artisans Gallery***, filled with beautiful weavings, wood turnings, pottery, jewelry, sweaters and duck decoys by New England craftspeople.

For those born to shop, Buggy Whip's a must; for all others, Buggy Whip is great fun.

An elegant, antique hobby horse at the Buggy Whip Shops.

STOCKBRIDGE

The Mews

Just off Main Street, the Mews incorporates five small and colorfully different shops. ***Books & Things*** (see "Bookstores") starts this lively walkway. **Heirlooms** (298-4436) displays a wide collection of antique, period and new jewelry; and in adjoining shops, you will find **Currier & I** (298-4840), a contemporary dress shop and **Hodge Podge** (298-4687) which has custom-made ladies' clothing plus children's hand-smocked dresses. Follow your nose back around the corner to the aromas of freshly baked bread and coffee beans waiting to be ground at **Williams and Sons** (298-3016), a country store with a large selection of penny candy and various other gifts. The Mews is pretty and sits right at the heart of Stockbridge, but at peak tourist times, the crowds are overwhelming.

Central County

LANESBOROUGH

The Berkshire Mall

At first we resented the malling of Lanesborough, feeling strongly that such concentrations of commercialism were clearly a blight on the landscape, something Berkshire could do fine without, thank you. Now that we've been malled, it doesn't feel quite so bad, and our first few mall crawls have been rather neat. Main Street America has been conspicuously absent in Central County, Berkshire, of late, but it's arisen again in Lanesborough, in the Mall. With over 85 specialty shops, a ***Hoyts' Cinema 10***, a food court, ***Hills, JCPenney, Sears*** and ***Steigers***, an instant community was created, and comes to life every day and night. Here, amidst broad climate-controlled avenues, browse and stroll much of Berkshire, some shopping for the latest stuff, some shopping for each other. There are wooden benches for sitting beneath potted trees, and huge, vaulted pyramid skylights, making the place feel like a gargantuan spacecraft, in orbit.

Whatever your orientation, there's something here for you, from half a dozen sneaker shops, with fab gear even for infants, to ***Same Bat Channel***, offering a devilish selection of classic comics; from ***Pinches and Pounds***, selling every kind of coffee, nut, grain, and candy imaginable to dozens of clothing stores, two book shops (***Lauriat's*** and ***Waldenbooks***), toy stores, drug stores and five jewelry stores. No wonder the Mall is the new village green for so many; no wonder we've learned to appreciate it.

LENOX

The Brushwood Shops

On the site of one of Berkshire's oldest surviving farms, Brushwood Shops offers more than a dozen specialty shops, among the most intriguing of which are: ***Silver Sleigh***, a dazzling Christmas shop; the ***Nature of Things***, a fascinating collection of nature and science stuff; and Dudley Levenson's fantastic ***Brushwood Studio***, a skylit wonderland of handcrafted wooden horses, baskets, weavings, paintings, Buddhist gods and goddesses.

The Curtis Shops (Walker St.)

One of the ***Grande Dames*** of Berkshire lodging got spruced up in the 1970s, and recently, a covey of shops has lighted on the first floor. ***The Hand of Man***, a craft gallery (637-0632), commands the post position, as you enter. Around the bend is ***Celtic Origins*** (637-1296), for beautiful Irish and Scottish clothing; ***Danae*** (637-2545), a sleek step into high fashion boudoir furnishings and accouterments; ***Andina*** (637-4705), top grade leather fashions for men and women; ***Alston*** (637-3676), a perfumery; and ***Stritch Gallery***, an outlet for the works of Berkshire artist John Stritch.

Lenox House Country Shops (Rtes. 7 & 20, north of town.)

This newly expanded commercial center has dozens of shops offering predominantly clothes, shoes, and gifts. Among the most interesting are: the ***Arcadian Shop*** (637-3010), specializing in sporting equipment (strong on cross-country skiing), and the ***Different Drummer*** (637-0606) which has everything from wind chimes to candles and other contemporary crafts. This is Berkshire's center for factory outlets, where you can choose from the likes of Bass and Bannister for shoes, Van Heusen and Manhattan for shirts.

PITTSFIELD

North Street

If you browse through this whole *Shopping* chapter, you will notice that several of the most interesting stores we have highlighted are located on Pittsfield's main downtown shopping street, called North Street. And there's more on North Street to make it worth an occasional visit. Along the street, you'll find sporting goods, shoes, clothing shops of several kinds, home appliances and hardwares, candies, an Italian gourmet shop, a camera store, furniture both contemporary and traditional. In general, North Street is less chic but far more comprehensive in its possibilities than the other special "Shopping Streets" we describe.

North County

NORTH ADAMS

The Marketplace at Heritage State Park

A cluster of shops in a historic, reconstructed railway yard. The double whammy includes fascinating exhibits on the railway yard and the construction of the Hoosac Tunnel, together with a jampacked ***General Store*** (663-3907), the ***Station House Antiques*** (662-2961), and the exciting ***UpCountry Artisans*** (663-5802), a showcase for regional crafts.

WILLIAMSTOWN

Spring Street

Just opposite Williams College, Spring Street has a whopping 223 free parking spaces nearby and includes restaurants, deli, bar, bakery, news stand, barbers, hair designer, movie house, service station, cleaners, optician, banks, accountant, architect, bookstores and pharmacy. Shops sell clothing, food, liquor, gifts, shoes, records, insurance, flowers, travel services, office supplies, furniture, real estate, jewelry, and sports clothing and equipment. Among the highlights are: ***The Cowbell*** (458-5437), ***House of Walsh*** (458-5010) and ***Gatsby's*** (458-5407).

Water Street

This historic street was opened in 1761, and Water Street today (which is also Rte. 43) still carries on the tradition of small businesses, most of which are located in old buildings. The ***Potter's Wheel*** (458-9523), owned by Adelaide England, offers an outstanding collection of work by America's finest craftspeople. Perched high above the Green River, this shop displays a selection of stoneware, jewelry, glass, prints, woods and fibers. Next door is Adelaide's latest venture, ***Hey Diddle Diddle*** (458-2855), a craft gallery for kids featuring woolen handknit sweaters, hats and mittens, as well as incredible rocking boats by Buckley Smith. ***The Cottage*** (458-4305) is marketplace for gifts and clothing. ***The Mountain Goat*** (458-8445) will look after all your needs for outdoor activity. Cross the street to ***Toonerville Trolley*** (458-5229), which carries a wide variety of records at discount prices; for the collector, there are jazz and rock "cutout" LPs. ***Rita's Custom Fashions*** (458-8485), is a shop where a rich array of fabrics can be fashioned into individual designs.

CHAPTER EIGHT
Practical Matters
INFORMATION

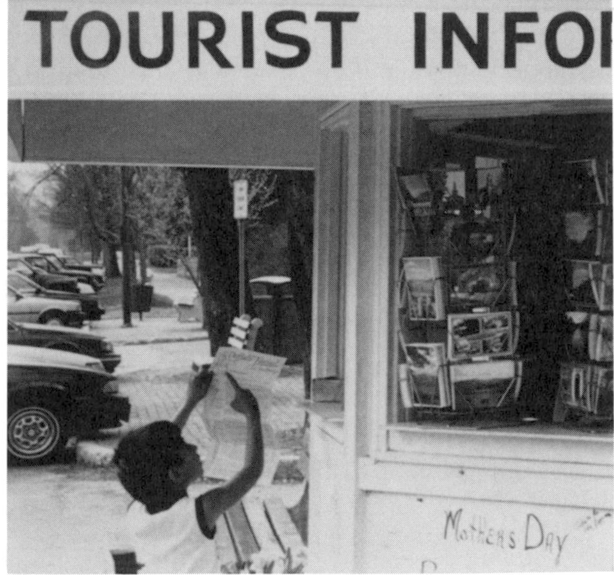

Checking the way, at the Stockbridge Information booth.

We offer here a little encyclopedia of useful information to help facilitate everyday life for locals and vacation time for visitors in the Berkshires. This chapter provides information on the following topics.

AMBULANCE, FIRE, POLICE

The general emergency number for Pittsfield is 911. For the rest of Berkshire County, each town has its own specific emergency numbers for ambulance, fire, or police. These numbers can be obtained by consulting your local phone book. In an emergency situation anywhere in the county, dial "O" and the operator will connect you directly to the correct agency.

Another county-wide set of emergency numbers is:

Fire	445-4559
Poison Control	800-682-9211
Police	442-0512
Rape	443-3521

AREA CODES, TELEPHONE EXCHANGES, ZIP CODES, TOWN HALLS/LOCAL GOVERNMENT

AREA CODES

The Area Code for all of Berkshire County is 413. Area codes for adjacent counties are as follows.

Massachusetts

Franklin, Hampden and Hampshire Counties — 413

Connecticut

Litchfield County and all of Connecticut — 203

New York

Columbia and
Rensselaer Counties — 518

Vermont

Bennington County and all of Vermont — 802

TOWN HALLS

Except for Adams, North Adams and Pittsfield, each of which has a City Hall, all Berkshire communities have Town Halls as the seats of local government. Most townships are governed by Boards of Selectmen; a few have Town Managers. For general information, call the Town Offices at the following numbers or write to the Town Clerk, c/o Town Hall in the village in question.

Town	*Telephone Exchange*	*Zip Code*	*Town Hall Office*
Adams	743	01220	743-0684
Alford	528	01230	528-4536
Ashley Falls	229	01222	229-8752 (Sheffield)

Town	*Telephone Exchange*	*Zip Code*	*Town Hall Office*
Becket	623	01223	623-8934
Berkshire County Commissioners	Pittsfield	01201	448-8424
Cheshire	743	01225	743-1690
Clarksburg	663	01247	663-7940
Dalton	684	01226	684-0203
Egremont	528	01258	528-0182
Glendale	298	01229	298-4714 (Stockbridge)
Florida	662	01247	662-2448
Gt. Barrington	528	01230	528-3140
Hancock	738	01237	738-5225
Hinsdale	655	01235	655-2245
Housatonic	274	01236	528-3140 (Gt. Barrington)
Lanesborough	499	01237	442-1167
Lee	243	01238	243-2100
Lenox	637	01240	637-1511
Lenoxdale	637	01242	637-1511 (Lenox)
Middlefield	623	01243	623-8934 (Becket)
Mill River	229	01244	229-8116 (New Marlborough)
Monterey	528	01245	528-1443
Mt. Washington	528	01258	528-2839
New Marlborough	229	01244	229-8116
N. Adams	662, 663, 664	01247	663-6685
N. Egremont	528	01252	528-0182 (Egremont)
Otis	269	01253	269-4052
Peru	655	01235	655-8027
Pittsfield	442, 443, 445 446, 447, 448 494, 499	01201 01202 (Post Office)	499-9361
Richmond	698	01254	698-3355
Sandisfield	258	01255	258-4711
Savoy	743	01256	743-4290
Sheffield	229	01257	229-8752
S. Egremont	528	01258	528-0182 (Egremont)
Southfield	229	01259	229-8116 (New Marlborough)

Town	*Telephone Exchange*	*Zip Code*	*Town Hall Office*
S. Lee	243	01260	243-2100 (Lee)
Stockbridge	298	01262	298-4714
Tyringham	243	01264	243-1749
Washington	623	01223	623-8383
W. Stockbridge	232	01266	232-7080
Williamstown	458, 597	01267	458-5358
Windsor	684	01270	684-3878

BANKS

Several Berkshire County banks are linked electronically to banking systems elsewhere in the United States. If you are visiting here, you may find these options quite helpful — especially if you need extra cash or traveler's checks. It's best to inquire with your home bank to see which system you can use and which Berkshire bank can serve you.

Adams Co-operative Bank
93 Park St., Adams; 743-0720. Branch: N. Adams.

Bank of New England West
66 West St., Pittsfield; 499-1600. Branches: Adams, Gt. Barrington, Lee, N. Adams, Stockbridge, Williamstown.

Berkshire County Savings Bank
Park Square, Pittsfield: 443-5601. Branches: Gt. Barrington, N. Adams.

City Savings Bank
116 North St., Pittsfield; 443-4421. Branch: Gt. Barrington.

Comfed Savings
5 North St., Pittsfield; 447-8400. Branch: N. Adams.

First Agricultural Bank
99 West St., Pittsfield. 499-3000; Branches: Adams, Dalton, Gt. Barrington, Lanesborough, Sheffield, Williamstown.

First National Bank of the Berkshires
76 Park St., Lee; 243-0115; Branches: Gt. Barrington, Otis.

Great Barrington Savings Bank
Main St., Gt. Barrington; 528-1190. Branches: Sheffield, W. Stockbridge.

Lee Bank
75 Park St., Lee; 243-0117. Branch: Stockbridge.

Lenox National Bank
7 Main St., Lenox; 637-0017.

Lenox Savings Bank
35 Main St., Lenox; 637-0147.

North Adams-Hoosac Bank
93 Main St., N. Adams; 663-5353.

Pittsfield Co-operative Bank
70 South St., Pittsfield; 447-7304. Branches: Dalton, Gt. Barrington.

Williamstown Savings Bank
795 Main St., Williamstown; 458-8191.

BIBLIOGRAPHY

Here are two lists of books about the Berkshires, many of which we used in researching this book.

"Books You Can Buy" shows titles available either through Berkshire bookshops, bookstores elsewhere or from the publishers. For information on Berkshire booksellers, see "Bookstores" in Chapter Seven, *Shopping*.

"Books You Can Borrow" suggests a wealth of other reading in earlier publications now no longer for sale. Some of the more rarefied material on this list does not circulate outside the libraries, and its use may be restricted to those with professional credentials. Several popular items here will especially interest history buffs. The best sources for book borrowing are described under "Libraries" in Chapter Four, *Culture*.

Books You Can Buy

LITERARY WORKS

Howard, Walter. *Sisyphus in the Hayfield - Views of A Berkshire Farmer*. Cobble Press, 1988. 128 pp., photos, $14.00.

Melville, Herman. *Great Short Works of Herman Melville*. NY: Harper & Row, 1969. 507 pp., bibliog, $3.95.

Wharton, Edith. *A Backward Glance*. NY: Charles Scribner's Sons, 1985 reprint. 379 pp., index, $12.95, pap.

Wharton, Edith. *Ethan Frome*. NY: Scribner's, 1988 reprint. $5.95.

LOCAL HISTORIES

Chapman, Gerard. *Eminent Berkshire Women*. Gt. Barrington: Attic Revivals Press, 1988. 32 pp., $5.00.

Chapman, Gerard. *A History of the Red Lion Inn in Stockbridge, Massachusetts*. Stockbridge: Red Lion Inn, 1987. 54 pp., illus., $12.00.

Drew, Bernard A. *Spanning Berkshire Waterways.* Gt. Barrington: Attic Revivals Press, 1990. 32 pp., photos, maps, $5.00.

Drew, Bernard A. *History of The Mahaiwe Theatre in Great Barrington, Massachusetts.* Gt. Barrington: Attic Revivals Press, 1989, 48 pp., illus., $5.00.

Drew, Bernard A. *William Cullen Bryant's "A Border Tradition."* Gt. Barrington: Attic Revivals Press, 1988, 32 pp., bibliog., $6.50.

Drew, Bernard A. *A History of Notchview Reservation: The Arthur D. Budd Estate in Windsor, Massachusetts.* Gt. Barrington: Attic Revivals Press, 1986, 48 pp., illus., maps, $5.00.

Drew, Bernard A. and Donna M. *Mapping the Berkshires.* Gt. Barrington: Attic Revivals Press, 1985. 48 pp., illus. maps, $5.00.

Drew, Donna M. *A History of Monument Mills in Housatonic, Massachusetts.* Gt. Barrington: Attic Revivals Press, 1984. 32 pp., illus., photos, maps, bibliog, $3.50.

Miller, Amy Bess. *Hancock Shaker Village/The City of Peace: An Effort to Restore a Vision 1960-1985.* Hancock: Hancock Shaker Village, 1984. 170 pp., illus., photos, appendices, bibliog., index, $12.00, pap.

Owens, Carole. *The Berkshire Cottages: A Vanishing Era.* Englewood, NJ: The Cottage Press, 1984. 240 pp., photos, illus., index, $21.95, pap.

Parish, Lila S. *A History of Searles Castle in Great Barrington, Massachusetts.* Gt. Barrington: Attic Revivals Press, 1985. 32 pp., illus., maps, bibliog., $5.00, pap.

Pincus, Andrew L. *Scenes from Tanglewood.* Boston: Northeastern University Press, 1989. 287 pp., photos, $14.95, pap.

The Stockbridge Story, 1739-1989. Stockbridge: Town of Stockbridge, 1989. 209 pp., illus., photos, index, $24.95.

PHOTOGRAPHIC STUDIES

Bazan, John. *Rails Across the Berkshire Hills. Railroad Photography, 1890-1984.* Pittsfield: The Author, 1984. Photos, $9.95, pap.

Binzen, Bill. *The Berkshires.* Chester, CT: Globe-Pequot Press, 1986. 90 color photos, $19.95.

Butler, Linda & June Sprigg. *Inner Light: The Shaker Legacy.* NY: Knopf, 1985. Photos, $32.50.

Gilder, Cornelia Brooke. *Views of the Valley-Tyringham 1739-1989.* Tyringham: the Hopbrook Community Club, 1989. 142 pp., photos, $15, pap.

Scott, Walter. *The Norman Rockwell Bicycle Tours of Stockbridge.* Stockbridge: SnO Publications, 1980. 32 post cards, $10.95.

RECREATION

A Canoe Guide to the Housatonic River, Berkshire County. Pittsfield: Berkshire County Regional Planning Commission. Illus., maps, $3.50.

Cuyler, Lewis C. *Bike Rides in the Berkshire Hills.* Gt. Barrington: Berkshire House, Publishers, 1991. 200 pp., photos, maps, $8.95, pap.

Silver, Patti, and Vivienne Jaffe. *Adventures in the Berkshires – Places to go with Children.* Lenox: Berkshire Country Day School, 1991. 144 pp., illus., map, $7.95, pap.

Stevens, Lauren. *Hikes & Walks in the Berkshire Hills.* Gt. Barrington: Berkshire House, Publishers, 1990. 200 pp., maps, $8.95, pap.

Stevens, Lauren. *Skiing in the Berkshire Hills.* Gt. Barrington: Berkshire House, Publishers, 1991. 228 pp., maps, $8.95, pap.

Appalachian Trail Guide to Massachusetts-Connecticut. Harpers Ferry, WV: Appalachian Trail Conference, 1988. 160 pp., maps.

TRAVEL

The Berkshire Hills-A WPA Guide, with a new foreword by Roger Linscott. Boston: Northeastern University Press, 1987. 360 pp., illus., photos, maps, lore, history, $11.95, pap.

Davenport, John. *Berkshire-Bennington Locator.* Madison, WI: First Impressions, 1988. 112 pp., maps, $10.95, pap.

Whitman, Herbert S. *Exploring the Berkshires.* NY: Hippocrene, 1988. 168 pp., illus., $9.95, pap.

Books You Can Borrow

Annin, Katherine Huntington. *Richmond, Massachusetts: The Story of a Berkshire Town and Its People, 1765-1965.* Richmond: Richmond Civic Association, 1964. 214 pp., photos, illus., index. Only complete readable history of town.

Birdsall, Richard. *Berkshire County, A Cultural History.* NY: Greenwood Press, 1978 reprint. 401 pp., notes, bibliog., index. Only cultural study of region; emphasis on first half of the 19th-century. Chapters cover development of law, newspapers, education, religion. Special attention to the literary heritage.

Bittman, Sam and Steven A. Satullo, eds. *Berkshire: Seasons of Celebration.* Pittsfield: Either/Or Press, 1982. 112 pp., photos.

Boltwood, Edward. *The History of Pittsfield, Massachusetts from the Year 1876 to the Year 1916.* Pittsfield: The City, 1916. Covers history of most important county communities to early 20th century.

Bulkeley, Morgan. *Mountain Farm: Poems From the Berkshire Hills.* Chester: Hollow Springs Press, 1984. 95 pp., illus.

Collections of the Berkshire Historical and Scientific Society. Pittsfield: Sun Printing Co., 1892-1899. Papers on historical topics read at Society meetings. Often composed by local authorities, subjects range from Berkshire geology to glass manufacture in Berkshire. Often unique and usually reliable.

Consolati, Florence. *See All the People: Or, Life in Lee*. Lee: The Author, 1978. Colorful, quaint history of the town and its citizens. 442 pp., photos, bibliog., index.

Coxey, Willard D. *Ghosts of Old Berkshire*. Gt. Barrington: The Berkshire Courier, 1934. Legends and folktales of Berkshire people and places.

Drew, Bernard A. *Berkshire Between Covers: A Literary History*. Gt. Barrington: Attic Revivals Press, 1985. 32 pp., illus., bibliog. Brief biographical sketches of deceased fiction writers with significant connections to the Berkshires.

Drew, Bernard A. *Berkshire Off the Trail*. Gt. Barrington: Attic Revival Press, 1982. 96 pp., illus., index. Informal history of less traditional subjects.

Emblidge, David, ed. *The Third Berkshire Anthology: A Collection of Literature and Art*. Lenox: Berkshire Writers, Inc., 1982. 185 pp., illus.

Field, Stephen, ed. *A History of the County of Berkshire, Massachusetts*. Pittsfield: Samuel W. Bush, 1829. Perhaps the first history of the Berkshires, sponsored by the Berkshire Association of Congregational Ministers. A general history of the county, followed by accounts of individual towns, each written by its minister.

Jones, Electa F. *Stockbridge, Past and Present: Or, Records of an Old Mission Station*. Springfield: Samuel Bowles & Co., 1854. History of early Stockbridge (early Indian mission and Stockbridge Indians).

Kupferberg, Herbert. *Tanglewood*. NY: McGraw-Hill, 1976. 280 pp., photos, bibliog., index. Most thorough history of the Berkshire Music Festival.

Lewis, Joseph W. *Berkshire Men of Worth*. 4 Vols. Scrapbook of newspaper articles. From 1933 until well after Lewis' death in 1938, over 300 columns on Berkshire notables were published in the *Berkshire Evening Eagle*. Series featured penetrating biographical sketches of men whom Lewis regarded as important historical figures. Perhaps the most comprehensive biographical treatment of historical Berkshire figures.

Oakes, Donald, ed. *A Pride of Palaces: Lenox Summer Cottages, 1883-1933*. Lenox: Lenox Library, 1981. 83 pp., illus., photos.

Perry, Arthur L. *Origins in Williamstown*. NY: Charles Scribner's Sons, 1896. Detailed, well-researched history of early Williamstown and other segments of northern Berkshire.

Preiss, Lillian E. *Sheffield, Frontier Town*. Sheffield: Sheffield Bicentennial Comm., 1976. 188 pp., photos, illus., bibliog., index. Good, traditional town history.

Resch, Tyler, ed. *Berkshire, The First Three Hundred Years 1676-1976*. Pittsfield: Eagle Pub. Co., 1976. 163 pp., photos, illus., maps, bibliog., index. Photographs and illustrations of significant and interesting historical events and people, with concise captions.

Sedgwick, Sarah Cabot & Christina Sedgwick Marquand. *Stockbridge, 1739-1939: A Chronicle.* Stockbridge: The Authors, 1939. 306 pp., photos, illus., bibliog. Popular, readable history.

Smith, J.E.A., ed. *History of Berkshire County, Massachusetts, With Biographical Sketches of Its Prominent Men.* 2 Vols. NY: J.B. Beers & Co., 1885. Wide-ranging history covering every aspect of Berkshire life. Nine chapters on individual towns. Most comprehensive, reliable history of the first 200 years of Berkshire development.

Smith, J.E.A. *The History of Pittsfield (Berkshire County), Massachusetts, From the Year 1734 to the Year 1800.* Boston: Lee & Shepard, 1869. *The History of Pittsfield (Berkshire County), Massachusetts, From the Year 1800 to the Year 1876. Springfield: C.W. Bryan & Co., 1876.* The most detailed, thorough town histories for the county. Smith had access to much material since lost; covers surrounding communities as well.

Taylor, Charles J. *History of Great Barrington (Berkshire), Massachusetts 1676-1882. Part II, Extension 1882-1922* by George Edwin MacLean. Gt. Barrington: 1928. Detailed, accurate history of town, particularly the Taylor segment.

Wood, David H. *Lenox, Massachusetts Shire Town.* Lenox: 1968. Similar to Sedgwick history of Stockbridge but more detailed.

CLIMATE AND WEATHER REPORTS

CLIMATE

"If you don't like the weather in New England, wait five minutes...." That was Mark Twain's opinion (he summered in Tyringham), and there are plenty of days when his exaggeration seems pretty close to reality. How the Berkshire climate strikes you depends on what you're used to. People visiting from outside the region may be helped by the following information.

In general, while summers are blessedly mild due to the elevation of the Berkshire hills, winters can be fiercely cold and snowy with tricky driving conditions. Of course, what one fellow (who doesn't ski) finds annoying in a New England winter, another (who does ski) will praise to the skies. Summer visitors should remember that nights can be quite cool; bring sweaters. And those in search of great snow should note that spring comes to South County well before it does up north and up higher. One day, we went cross-country skiing in the morning on good snow at Notchview in Windsor and then ran the rototiller in the garden at home in Great Barrington that same afternoon!

TEMPERATURE AND PRECIPITATION

Average Temperature	October	49.3°
	January	21.2°
	April	44.3°
	July	68.3°

Average Annual Total Precipitation		43.14"
	Snow	70"
	Rain	36.14"

For people who are really into statistics, the source for this information and a great deal more, *The Berkshire Data Book*, is available (for $25.00 plus $2.00 postage) from the Berkshire County Regional Planning Commission (442-1521; 10 Fenn St., Pittsfield, MA 01201).

Weather Reports

Great Barrington	528-1118
Lee/Stockbridge	243-0065
Pittsfield	499-2627
Adams/Cheshire	743-3313
North Adams	662-2221
Williamstown	458-2222

DAY CARE

There's a patchwork quilt of day-care options in the Berkshires, with numerous small operations in churches and private homes plus several elaborate programs set up as nurseries and preschools. There is no central organization which can make recommendations to parents, so careful personal investigation is advised. Here is a representative sample of the options.

Child Care of the Berkshires 499-4660 Ext. 278. This organization, through its South, Central or North County offices, will provide information about seven other day-care facilities it operates for infants to preschoolers.

South County

GREAT BARRINGTON

Bear Care Centers, Ltd. 777 S. Main St., 528-4470.

LEE

The Learning Center, Rte. 102, 243-1573.

STOCKBRIDGE

Children's Center at St. Paul's Church, Main St., 298-4913.

Southern Berkshire Early Childhood Center, Main St., 298-3444.

Central County

LENOX

Lenox Children's Center, 9 School St., 637-0321.

PITTSFIELD

Bear Care Centers, Ltd. 1450 W. Housatonic St., 442-3300.

Brigham Children's Center, Pittsfield Girls Club; 442-5174.

Dorothy Amos Association for Child Development, Inc., 43 Francis Ave., 499-2320.

Norman Rockwell Early Childhood Center, West St., 443-3487.

The Tot Spot, 217 2nd St., 447-7971.

Wee Kare Kiddie Kollege, 850 Williams St., 442-3581.

North County

NORTH ADAMS

Child Care of The Berkshires, 210 State St., 663-6593.

WILLIAMSTOWN

Williamstown Community Day Care Center, First United Methodist Church, 458-4476.

GUIDED TOURS

If you want to be bused directly to Berkshire's high spots by an informed guide, there are hosts of possibilities, some based here in the hills, some coming from New York and Boston. From the big cities, there are fall-foliage tours, Tanglewood tours and ski tours, all of which provide transport, tickets, meals and lodging plus background on the sites. For an individual, these tours offer a taste of the area's delights in a perfectly packaged form. For groups, the tours turn a possible logistical nightmare into a fun-filled holiday.

Should you be coming from New York or Boston, a travel agent may be very helpful in choosing the right tour. The best of the commercial tour companies belong to the National Tour Association. The best of the charter bus companies belong to the American Bus Association. Here are a few of the most experienced Berkshire guided-tour companies operating from New York and Boston.

NEW YORK

Casser Tours 212-840-6500, 800-251-1411; 46 W. 43rd St.

Parker Tours 718-459-6566, 800-833-9600; 98-12 Queens Blvd., Forest Hills.

Tauck Tours 800-468-2825; 11 Wilton Rd., Westport, CT.

BOSTON

Collette Tours 617-542-1794; Pawtucket, RI.

WITHIN THE BERKSHIRES

Within Berkshire, there are also a number of guided tour options. For something relatively brief and informal, a local cab driver can usually be persuaded to drive you around, adding colorful histories that only a cabbie might know. For more organized, detailed tours, consider the following.

Berkshire Cottage Tours (637-1899; The Mount, Plunkett St., Lenox.) This step-on guide service focuses on the mansions of the Gilded Age. Starting at the Mount, the tour takes you by your own group's tour bus through Lenox and Stockbridge, filling you in on the fabulous histories as you view more than twenty of the "cottages." Light refreshments served in the garden of Naumkeag are a highlight of this three-hour tour.

Berkshire Walking Tours (443-5017, 800-244-5017; Box 33, Pittsfield.) Berkshire native Nancy C. Henriques has created a series of walking tours through Stockbridge and Lenox that is informative, entertaining, inexpensive and good exercise to boot. Operating weekends in June, September and October, and daily in the high summer season, the tours are led by professional guides, steeped in the colorful history of both Berkshire towns. Tours are one hour in length, the Lenox tour usually beginning with complimentary continental breakfast or cheesecake and coffee at Cheesecake Charlies, the Stockbridge tour concluding with complimentary appetizers at Michael's Restaurant. Be sure to phone ahead for schedules and prices.

The Travel Store (499-3770; 180C Elm St., Pittsfield.) Packages, special interest tours, creative theme parties. Transport, hotel and tour management. Sole American Express representative for Berkshire County.

Willa Tours (458-9503; 53 Belden St., Williamstown.) Choice of twelve planned tours with Berkshire travel writer Willa Petschek.

HANDICAPPED SERVICES

Although Berkshire is a mountainous region with lots of rough terrain, handicapped people will find access quite easy to most cultural sites and events, to many lodgings and restaurants, and to most shops. In Chapter Three, *Lodging*, we specify those places where we know handicapped access is either feasible or not. Elsewhere, to confirm the situation, use the phone numbers we provide to get information.

The Berkshire Visitors Bureau (443-9186; Berkshire Common, Pittsfield, MA 01201) publishes seasonal brochures listing many Berkshire services and attractions, in many cases, specifying access to handicapped people. The *AAA Tour Guide*, available through the Auto Club of Berkshire County (445-5635; 196 South St., Pittsfield) also designates restaurants, lodging, etc. with handicapped access.

As for transportation, the ***Berkshire Regional Transit Authority*** (499-2782 or 800-292-2782) runs the public bus system throughout the major towns in the county and has many buses in service which are equipped with wheelchair lifts.

See Chapter Two, *Transportation*, "Getting Around the Berkshires," for more information.

HOSPITALS

South County

GREAT BARRINGTON
Fairview Hospital 528-0790; 29 Lewis Ave.

Central County

PITTSFIELD
Berkshire Medical Center 447-2000; 725 North St.
Hillcrest Hospital 443-4761; 165 Tor Court.

North County

NORTH ADAMS
North Adams Regional Hospital 663-3701; Hospital Ave.

LATE NIGHT FOOD AND FUEL

Berkshire Truck Plaza (food and fuel): Rte. 102, W. Stockbridge. Restaurant closes at 11 p.m. on Fri. and Sat.

Convenience Plus (food and fuel); open all night: 84 Tyler St., Pittsfield; 241 Main St., Lee.

Cumberland Farms (food and fuel); open all night: 885 Dalton Ave., Pittsfield.

Depot 22 (food and fuel): Rte. 22, Canaan, NY. 518-781-4400.

Diesel Dan's (food and fuel): Rte. 102, Lee. Restaurant closed Fri.-Sat., pumps close at 11 p.m. Sat.

Dunkin' Donuts (food); open till midnight: 5 Union St., N. Adams; 18 First St., Pittsfield.

Grampy's Convenience Store (food and fuel); open all night; 223 Columbia St., N. Adams; 41 Housatonic St., Lee.

Joe's Diner (food); open till midnight except Sat. and Sun.; Main St., Lee.

Price Chopper Supermarkets are all open till midnight. Branches: Stockbridge Rd., Rte. 7, Gt. Barrington; Park St., Lee; Pittsfield Rd., Rte. 7, Lenox; Merrill Rd., Pittsfield.

Salt & Pepper North (food); open Tues.-Sat. till 4 a.m., Sun. till 3 a.m.; 641 North St., Pittsfield.

Stop & Shop Supermarket (food); open all night Mon.-Fri.; Sat. till midnight; Merrill Rd., Pittsfield.

The Texan Restaurant (food); open till 3 a.m., 437 Curran Hwy., N. Adams.

MEDIA: MAGAZINES AND NEWSPAPERS; RADIO STATIONS

MAGAZINES AND NEWSPAPERS

The Advocate 458-5713; 38 Spring St., Williamstown; Wednesday. Highly readable, well-researched articles, mostly on community-related topics for northern Berkshire and southern Vermont. Now also available in a separate, South Berkshire edition, published in Lenox, 637-2225; 25 Housatonic St.

Berkshire Business Journal 499-3400; 74 North St., Pittsfield. Berkshire's answer to the *Wall Street Journal*. Lively up-to-date news of Berkshire business doings. Monthly freebie.

The Berkshire Courier 528-3020; 335 Main St., Gt. Barrington; every Thursday. An oldie but goodie among town newspapers, with informative articles on all local topics.

The Berkshire Eagle

The Berkshire Eagle 447-7311; 75 S. Church St., Pittsfield. The county's newspaper of record, a Pulitzer Prize-winning publication with extensive world, national, state and local news, plus features and comics ("Doonesbury"!). During the summer the *Eagle* also publishes *Berkshires Week*, a supplementary magazine-in-newsprint containing colorful articles, a calendar of events and lots of ads from local dining and entertainment places. Recently the *Eagle* has added a Sunday edition chockful of interesting features of global, national and local significance.

Berkshire Magazine 298-3791; Box 617, Stockbridge; bimonthly. Newly revitalized, graphically exciting, regional. Feature stories and information calendar in a glossy, full-color format.

The Berkshire Record 528-5380; Castle St., Gt. Barrington; weekly. Newest Southern Berkshire weekly features current affairs and articles of historic note.

Berkshire Senior 499-1353; 100 North St., Pittsfield; monthly. Articles by and about Berkshire senior citizens.

Country Journal 667-3211; 25 Main St., Huntington, Hampshire County; Thursday. Covers the central hill towns.

New Visions 443-4817; 10 Taconic St., Box 2336, Pittsfield; seasonally. Articles, announcements and ads about alternative healing, psychological growth and spiritual transformation.

The Penny Saver 243-2341; 14 Park Pl., Box 300, Lee; weekly. Central County's shopping guide, including classifieds, TV listings, nightlife, comprehensive business service listings.

Shopper's Guide 528-0095; Bridge St., Box 89, Gt. Barrington; weekly. Southern Berkshire's shopping guide, including enticing sections on real estate and automobiles.

The Transcript 663-3741; American Legion Dr., N. Adams; weekday afternoons, Saturday morning. Local, some state and national news; covers northern Berkshire County and southern Vermont.

Yankee Shopper 684-1373; 839 Main St., Box 96, Dalton; weekly. Central and Northern Berkshire's shopping guide, including scads of used cars, rototillers, computers, vacuum cleaners, baby bunnies as well as a business/professional services directory.

RADIO STATIONS

National Public Radio: There are two stations receivable in the Berkshires:

WAMC-FM, 90.3; 518-465-5233; Albany, NY.
WFCR-FM, 88.5; 545-0100; Amherst, MA.

Other Local Radio Stations:

WBEC-AM, 1420; 499-3333; Pittsfield. General.
WBEC-FM, 105; 499-3333; Pittsfield. Rock music.
WBRK-FM, 101; 442-1553; Pittsfield. General.
WMNB-AM, 1230 and **FM** 100.1; 663-6567; N.Adams. General.
WSBS-AM, 860; 528-0860; Gt. Barrington. General.
WBBS-FM, 105.1 528-0860; Gt. Barrington. Contemporary.
WTBR-AM, 499-1483; Pittsfield. General.
WUHN-AM, 1110; 499-1100; Pittsfield. General.
WUPE-FM, 96; 499-1531; Pittsfield. Rock and other music.

Television

There are no Berkshire-based network television stations, and unless your place has access to cable TV or installs a satellite dish, reception in these parts is usually spotty. The cable TV companies appear in the Yellow Pages.

REAL ESTATE

What's your dream house? An isolated cabin, deep in the woods? A late 20th-century split level, suburban tract house? A lakeside condo for time-sharing? Or a forty-room Gilded Age mansion that just needs a couple-of-hundred grand in handyman repairs? Berkshire County has them all.

Window shopping for a home in the Berkshires.

If you are shopping for Berkshire real estate, you can obtain information as follows.

Lists of realtors: Consult the Yellow Pages of the telephone book or, if you're far away, contact any of the three Chambers of Commerce. ***Southern Berkshire Chamber of Commerce*** 528-1510; 362 Main St., Gt. Barrington, MA 01230. ***Central Berkshire Chamber of Commerce*** 499-4000; Berkshire Common, Pittsfield, MA 01201. ***Northern Berkshire Chamber of Commerce*** 663-3735; 69 Main St., N. Adams, MA 01247. All three organizations will send a list of their realtor members. The seasonal tourist information brochures from the ***Berkshire Hills Conference*** (443-9186; Berkshire Common, Pittsfield, MA 01201) also list numerous realtors.

Once you're into the process of buying land or a house, it is essential to check with the local town government about zoning laws, building permits, etc. Such regulations vary widely from town to town. See: "Area Codes," in this chapter, for town hall telephone numbers.

You can also follow the real estate market in the newspapers; see "Media," in this chapter. *The Berkshire Home Buyers Guide* is a free monthly publication, distributed in local shops or available from 637-4333; P.O. Box 2096, Lenox, MA 01240. And the single, most comprehensive resource is *Buying or Building a House in the Berkshires*, published each spring and available at newsstands (or from P.O. Box 2048, Lenox, MA 01240) for $3.00. This is an almanac of information on taxes, zoning laws, "perc" tests, property values, police and fire coverage, and many other public services.

RELIGIOUS SERVICES AND ORGANIZATIONS

Berkshire County has an active and unusually diverse religious community. The best source for information about church and synagogue services is the Saturday edition of *The Berkshire Eagle*. The Berkshire County Telephone Directory has a comprehensive list of all mainstream religious organizations, under the headings "Churches" and "Synagogues." For nontraditional groups, a helpful publication to consult is *New Visions*, published seasonally and distributed through various shops. Also, keep an eye on community bulletin boards at the area's colleges and in towns such as Great Barrington, Stockbridge, Lenox, Pittsfield and Williamstown.

ROAD SERVICE

Emergency road service from ***AAA***, anywhere in the county, can be obtained by calling 442-2422, Pittsfield. For non-AAA drivers, the following is a listing of some 24-hour emergency towing services throughout the county.

South County

Decker's Auto Body, Gt. Barrington	528-1432
Mac's Garage, Gt. Barrington	528-1234
Steve's Auto Repair, Gt. Barrington	528-9833
R W's Inc., Lee	243-0946

Central County

Sayers' Auto, Pittsfield	443-1635
Southgate Motors, Pittsfield	447-7694

North County

West End Auto Body & Glass, N. Adams	664-6708

SCHOOLS

PUBLIC SCHOOL DISTRICTS

South County

Berkshire Hills Regional School District, Stockbridge; 298-3711
Lee Public Schools; 243-0276
Southern Berkshire Regional School District, Sheffield; 229-8778

Central County

Central Berkshire Regional School District, Dalton; 684-0320
Lenox Public Schools; 637-0204
Richmond Consolidated Schools; 698-2207
Pittsfield Public Schools; 499-9512

North County

Adams-Cheshire Regional School District; 743-2939
Town of Clarksburg School Department; 664-8735
Town of Florida School Department; 664-6023
Town of Lanesborough Schools; 442-2229
Town of New Ashford School Department; 458-5461
City of North Adams Public Schools; 663-3793
Town of Savoy School Department; 743-1992
Town of Williamstown School Department; 458-5707

PRIVATE AND RELIGIOUS SCHOOLS

South County

Berkshire School, Sheffield; 229-8511
De Sisto School, Stockbridge; 298-3776
Great Barrington Rudolf Steiner School, Gt. Barrington; 528-4015
St. Mary's School, Lee; 243-1079

Central County

Berkshire Country Day School, Lenox; 637-0755
Berkshire County Christian School, Pittsfield; 442-4014
Miss Hall's School, Pittsfield; 443-6401
Sacred Heart School, Pittsfield; 443-6379
St. Agnes School, Dalton; 684-3143
St. Joseph's Central High School, Pittsfield; 447-9121

North County

Buxton School, Williamstown; 458-3919
The Highcroft School, Williamstown; 458-8136
Pine Cobble School, Williamstown; 458-4680
St. Stanislaus, N. Adams; 743-1091

COLLEGES

South County

Simon's Rock College of Bard, Gt. Barrington; 528-0771

Central County

Berkshire Community College, Pittsfield; 499-4660. South County Branch: Gt. Barrington; 528-4521.

North County

North Adams State College, N. Adams; 664-4511
Williams College, Williamstown; 597-3131

Index

Index

LODGING BY PRICE

Price Codes

Inexpensive	Up to $65
Moderate	$65 to $95
Expensive	$95 to $150
Very Expensive	Over $150

South County

RESTAURANTS BY PRICE

Price Codes

Inexpensive	Up to $15
Moderate	$15 to $20
Expensive	$20 to $30
Very Expensive	Over $30

RESTAURANTS BY CUISINE

Note: For your convenience, we list here restaurants serving specific ethnic cuisines. Restaurants featuring American and/or Continental cuisine are many in number, and their definitions of cooking styles are hard to pin down. See Chapter 5, *Restaurants*, under the town where you expect to dine.

RESTAURANTS WITH OUTDOOR DINING

RESTAURANTS OPEN LATE

MAPS

A Note on the Author and Principal Photographer

Jonathan Sternfield is a writer, photographer, inventor and tennis pro. Born in New York City, he has lived in the Berkshires since shortly after graduating from the University of Pennsylvania in 1969. Residing in and around Great Barrington, he has also traveled extensively in Europe, living for periods in England and France. As a writer he has worked in Hollywood, developing screenplays for feature films, as well as for the "College Bowl" television show, Rockefeller Center and General Electric, among other clients. His publishing credits include *The Complete Book of Mopeds* (Funk and Wagnalls), *Starring Your Love Life* (Lynx), *The Look of Horror* (Running Press), and numerous articles for *Berkshire Magazine* as well as pieces on electric cars and solar energy for other publications. His non-fiction exploration, *Firewalk,* will be published by Berkshire House in 1991. As a photographer, he has created images for advertising, for actors, for book illustration and for rock videos. His book of color views of New Yorkers, *Apple of My Eye,* is awaiting publication. When he's not writing or photographing, Jonathan Sternfield is a tennis pro at Canyon Ranch in Lenox.

The pages of this book were composed on Pagemaker by Graphic Innovations, Pittsfield. The typeface, Palatino, created in the mid-20th century by Hermann Zapf, is named for the famous 16th-century calligrapher, Giambattista Palatino. Design of original text for the Great Destination series was by Janice Lindstrom of Stockbridge. BookCrafters printed and bound the book.

Berkshire Town Maps

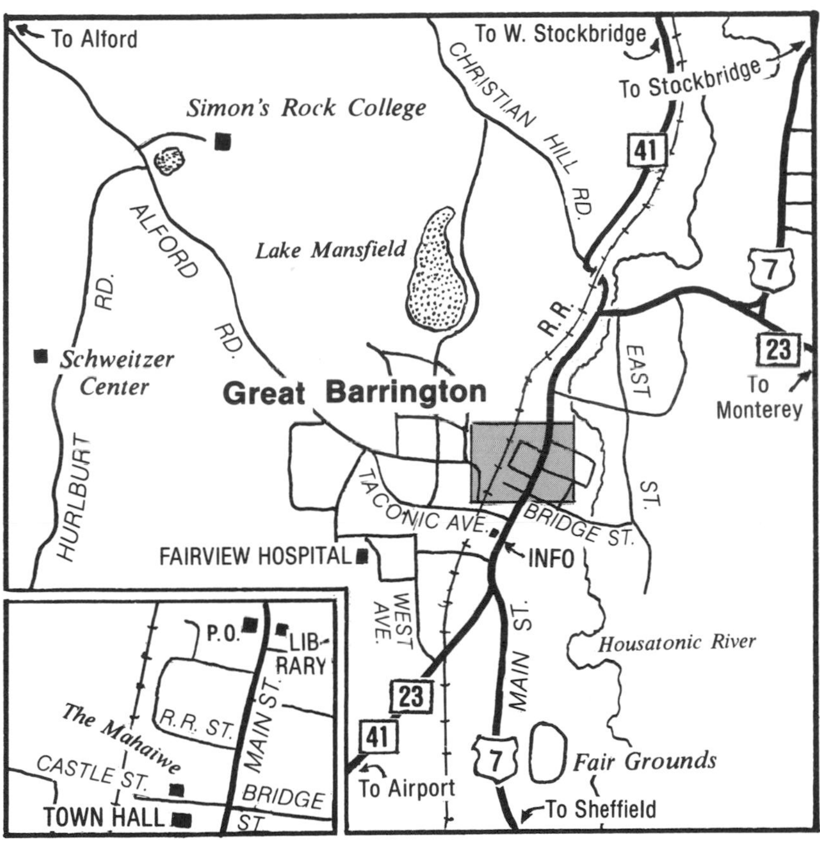

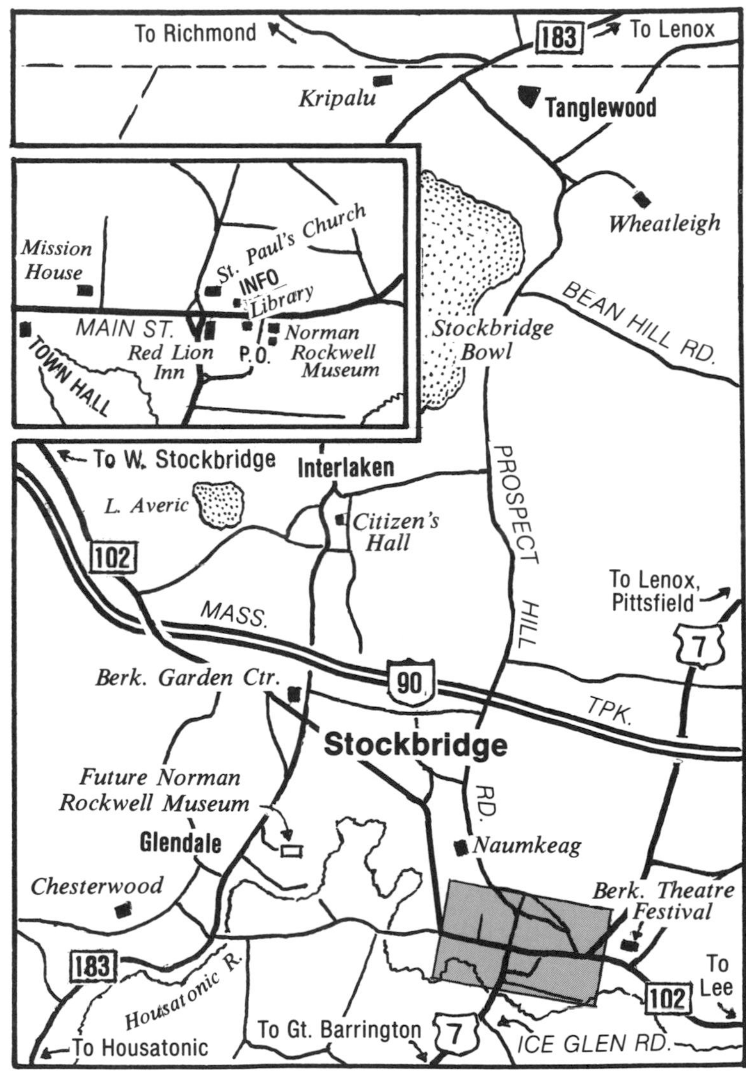

To Richmond
183
To Lenox
Kripalu
Tanglewood
Wheatleigh
BEAN HILL RD.
Mission House
St. Paul's Church
INFO
Library
MAIN ST.
Red Lion Inn
P.O.
Norman Rockwell Museum
TOWN HALL
Stockbridge Bowl
To W. Stockbridge
Interlaken
L. Averic
Citizen's Hall
PROSPECT HILL RD.
102
MASS.
To Lenox, Pittsfield
7
Berk. Garden Ctr.
90
TPK.
Stockbridge
Future Norman Rockwell Museum
Glendale
Naumkeag
Chesterwood
Berk. Theatre Festival
183
Housatonic R.
To Lee
102
To Housatonic
To Gt. Barrington
7
ICE GLEN RD.

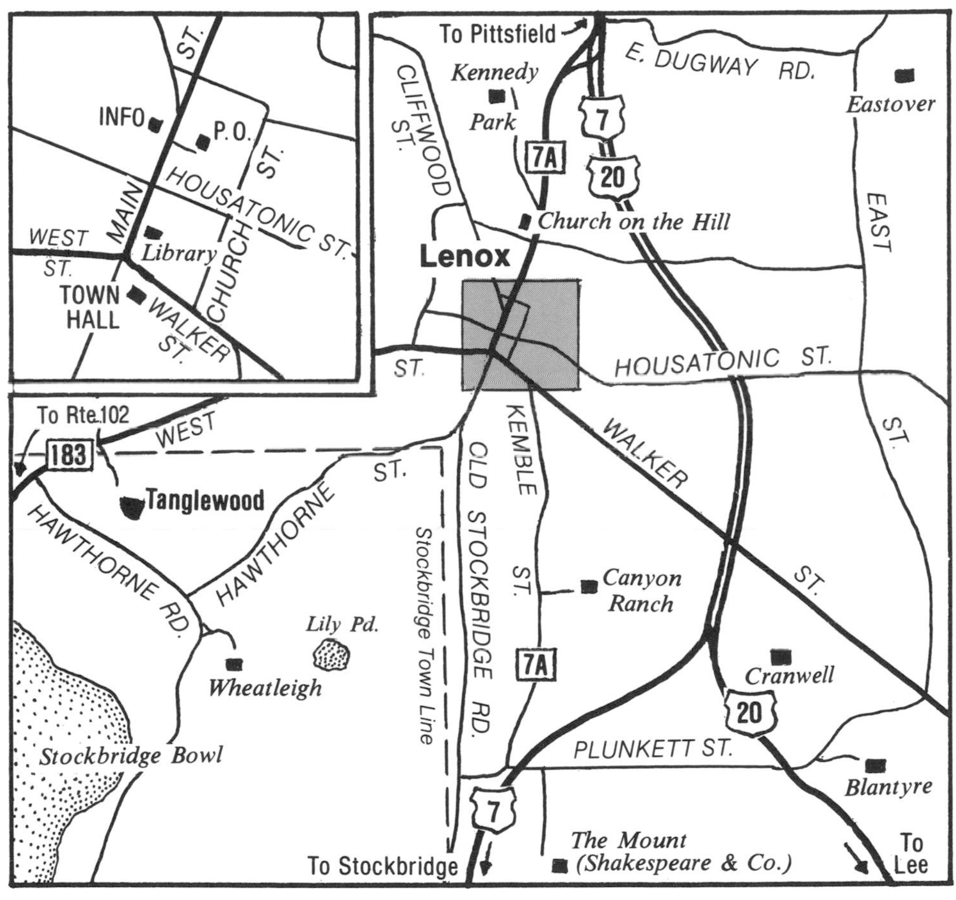

To Pittsfield
Kennedy Park
CLIFFWOOD ST.
E. DUGWAY RD.
Eastover
7
7A
20
Church on the Hill
Lenox
EAST ST.
HOUSATONIC ST.
WALKER ST.
ST.
KEMBLE ST.
OLD STOCKBRIDGE RD.
To Rte.102
183
WEST
Tanglewood
HAWTHORNE ST.
HAWTHORNE RD.
Stockbridge Town Line
Canyon Ranch
Lily Pd.
Wheatleigh
Cranwell
Stockbridge Bowl
PLUNKETT ST.
Blantyre
The Mount (Shakespeare & Co.)
To Stockbridge
To Lee
INFO
P.O.
MAIN
CHURCH ST.
WEST ST.
Library
TOWN HALL

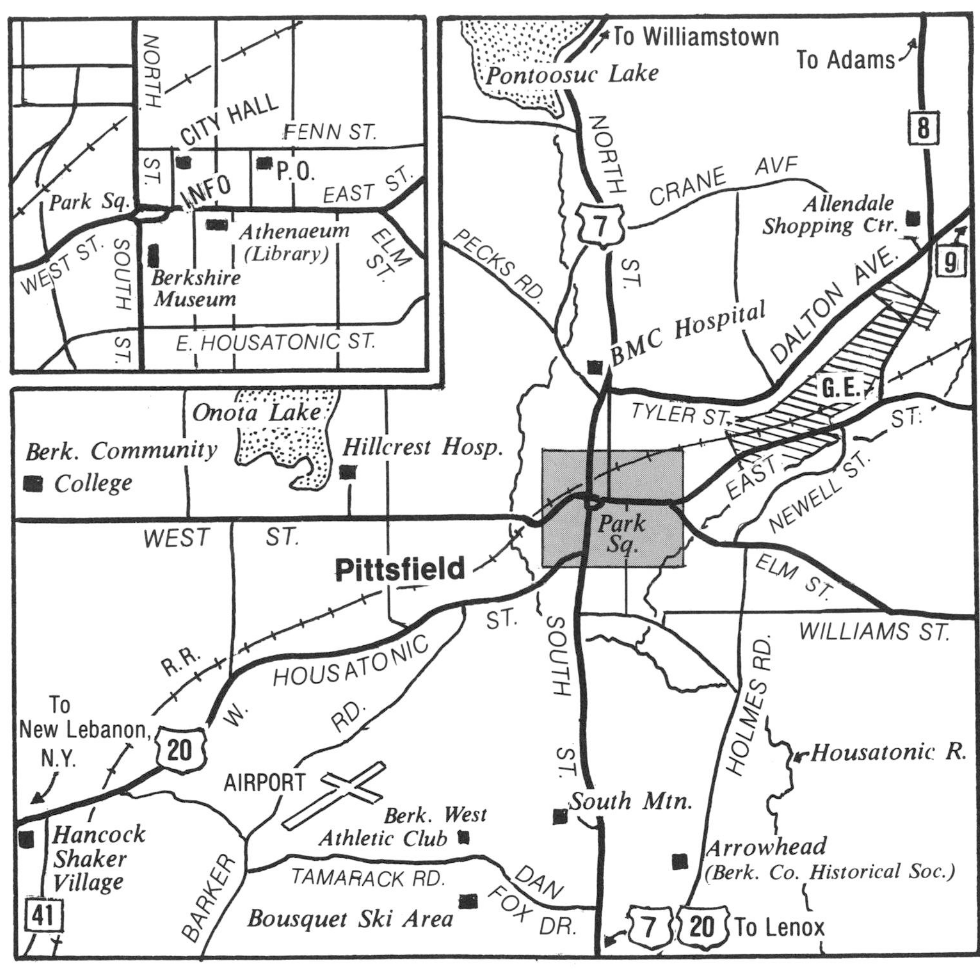

NORTH
ST.
CITY HALL
FENN ST.
P.O.
INFO
EAST ST.
Park Sq.
Athenaeum
(Library)
ELM ST.
WEST ST.
SOUTH ST.
Berkshire
Museum
E. HOUSATONIC ST.
To Williamstown
To Adams
Pontoosuc Lake
NORTH ST.
8
CRANE AVE
Allendale
Shopping Ctr.
7
PECKS RD.
DALTON AVE.
9
BMC Hospital
G.E.
TYLER ST.
Onota Lake
Berk. Community
College
Hillcrest Hosp.
EAST ST.
NEWELL ST.
Park
Sq.
WEST ST.
Pittsfield
ELM ST.
WILLIAMS ST.
R.R.
HOUSATONIC ST.
W.
SOUTH ST.
HOLMES RD.
To
New Lebanon,
N.Y.
20
RD.
Housatonic R.
AIRPORT
South Mtn.
Berk. West
Athletic Club
Hancock
Shaker
Village
Arrowhead
(Berk. Co. Historical Soc.)
TAMARACK RD.
DAN FOX DR.
BARKER
41
Bousquet Ski Area
7
20
To Lenox

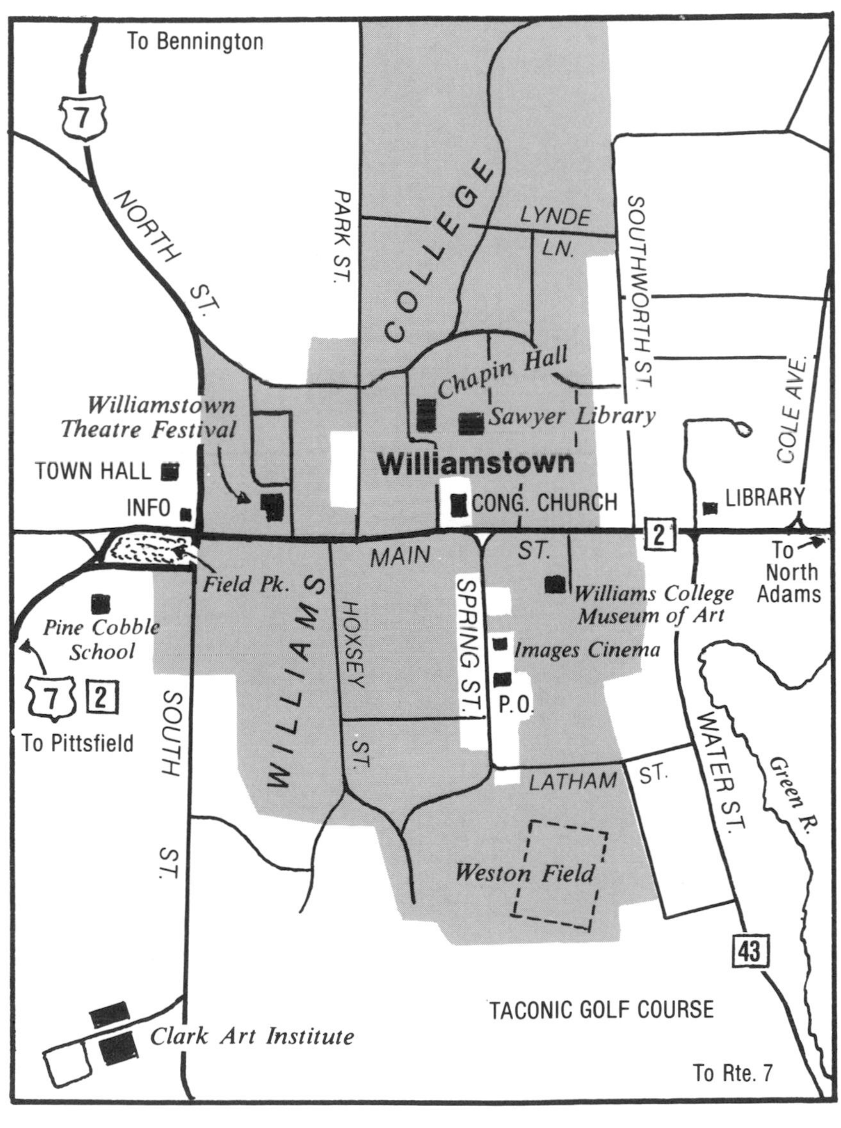
To Bennington
7
NORTH ST.
PARK ST.
COLLEGE
LYNDE LN.
SOUTHWORTH ST.
COLE AVE.
Chapin Hall
Sawyer Library
Williamstown Theatre Festival
Williamstown
TOWN HALL
INFO
CONG. CHURCH
LIBRARY
2
To North Adams
MAIN ST.
Field Pk.
WILLIAMS
HOXSEY ST.
SPRING ST.
Williams College Museum of Art
Images Cinema
P.O.
Pine Cobble School
7 2
To Pittsfield
SOUTH ST.
LATHAM ST.
WATER ST.
Green R.
Weston Field
43
TACONIC GOLF COURSE
Clark Art Institute
To Rte. 7

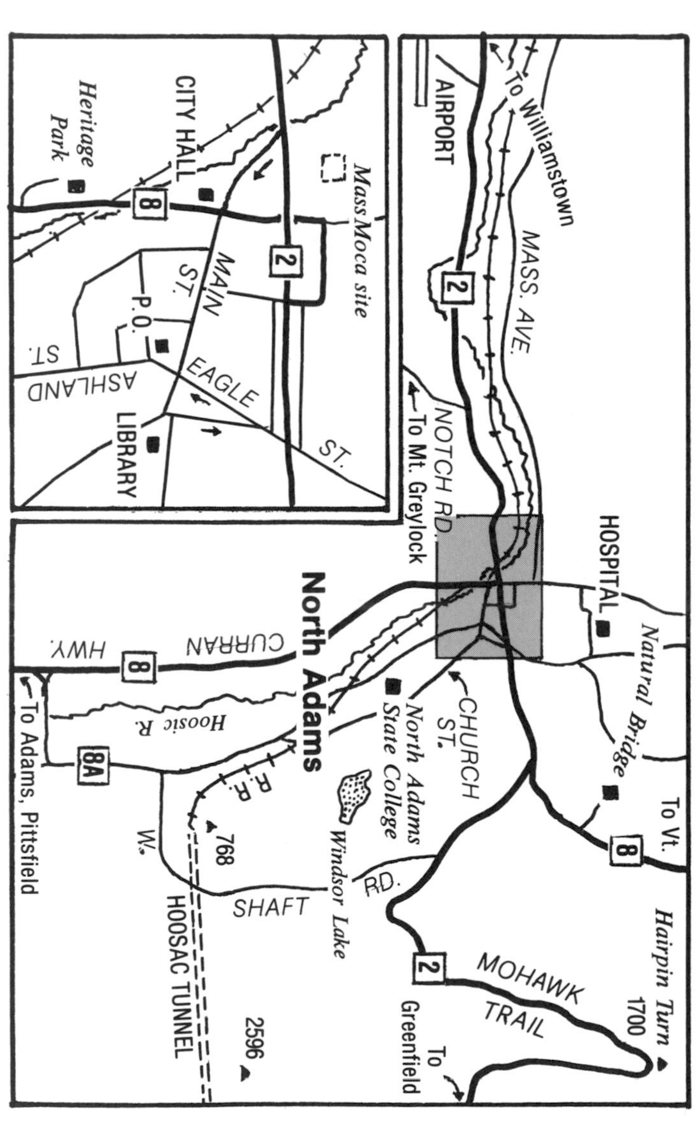
Mass Moca site
CITY HALL
Heritage Park
8
2
MAIN ST.
P.O.
EAGLE ST.
ASHLAND ST.
LIBRARY
AIRPORT
To Williamstown
MASS. AVE.
2
NOTCH RD.
To Mt. Greylock
HOSPITAL
Natural Bridge
To Vt.
8
North Adams
CURRAN HWY.
8
CHURCH ST.
North Adams State College
Windsor Lake
Hoosic R.
R.R.
8A
W.
SHAFT RD.
768
HOOSAC TUNNEL
2596
To Adams, Pittsfield
2
MOHAWK TRAIL
To Greenfield
Hairpin Turn
1700

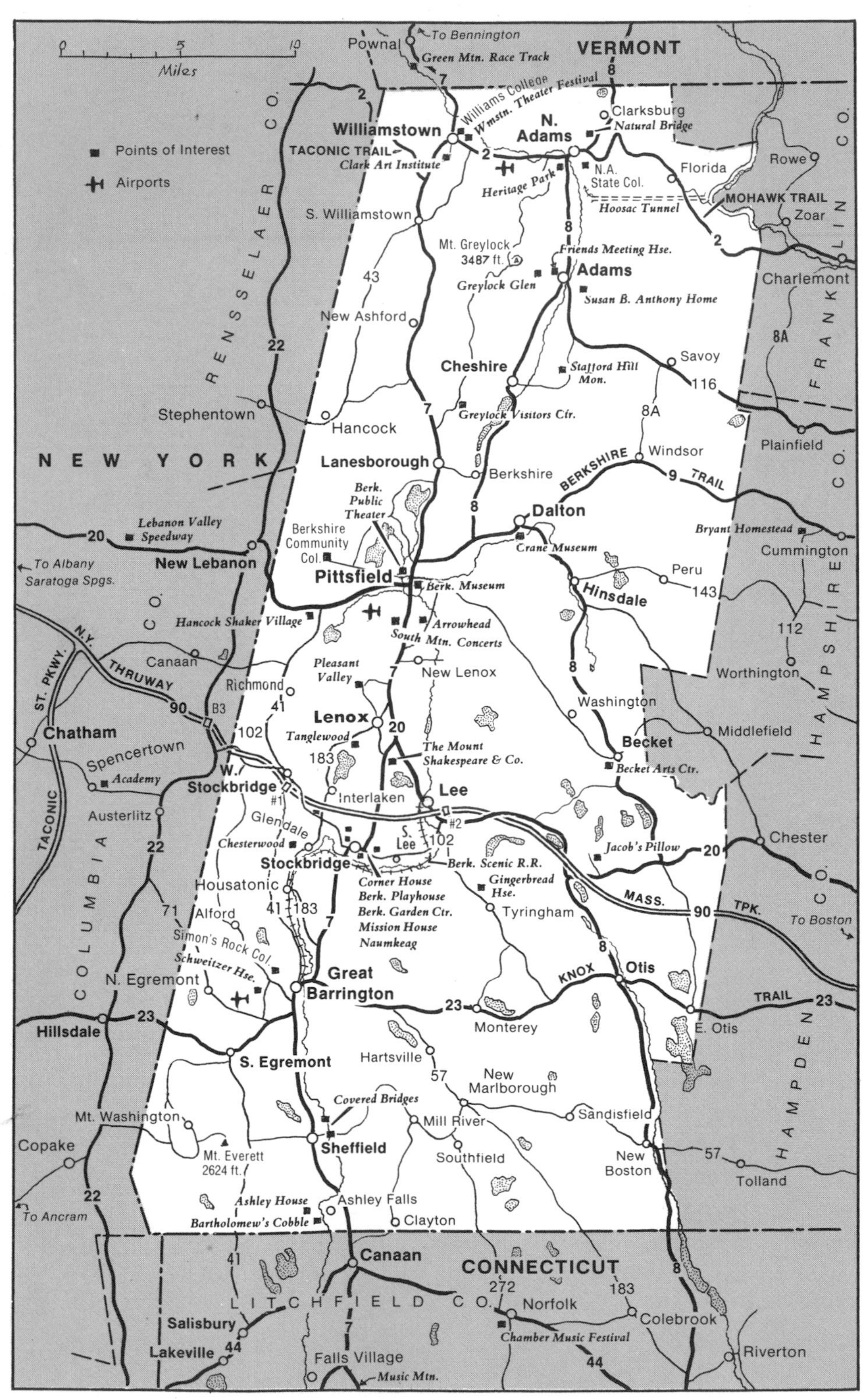
Miles
Points of Interest
Airports
To Bennington
Pownal
Green Mtn. Race Track
VERMONT
Williams College
Wmstn. Theater Festival
Williamstown
Clarksburg
Natural Bridge
N. Adams
TACONIC TRAIL
Clark Art Institute
Heritage Park
N.A. State Col.
Florida
Rowe
Hoosac Tunnel
MOHAWK TRAIL
Zoar
S. Williamstown
Mt. Greylock 3487 ft.
Friends Meeting Hse.
Adams
Greylock Glen
Susan B. Anthony Home
Charlemont
New Ashford
Cheshire
Savoy
Stafford Hill Mon.
Stephentown
Hancock
Greylock Visitors Ctr.
Windsor
Plainfield
NEW YORK
Lanesborough
Berkshire
BERKSHIRE TRAIL
Berk. Public Theater
Dalton
Berkshire Community Col.
Crane Museum
Bryant Homestead
Cummington
Lebanon Valley Speedway
New Lebanon
To Albany Saratoga Spgs.
Pittsfield
Berk. Museum
Peru
Hinsdale
Hancock Shaker Village
Arrowhead
South Mtn. Concerts
N.Y. THRUWAY
Canaan
New Lenox
Pleasant Valley
Richmond
Worthington
ST. PKWY.
Washington
Chatham
Lenox
Tanglewood
Middlefield
Becket
Spencertown
The Mount
Shakespeare & Co.
Academy
W. Stockbridge
Becket Arts Ctr.
Interlaken
Lee
Austerlitz
Glendale
S. Lee
Jacob's Pillow
Chester
TACONIC
Chesterwood
Stockbridge
Berk. Scenic R.R.
Corner House
Berk. Playhouse
Berk. Garden Ctr.
Mission House
Naumkeag
Gingerbread Hse.
Housatonic
Tyringham
MASS. TPK.
To Boston
Alford
Simon's Rock Col.
Schweitzer Hse.
Otis
KNOX TRAIL
N. Egremont
Great Barrington
Monterey
Hillsdale
E. Otis
S. Egremont
Hartsville
New Marlborough
Covered Bridges
Mt. Washington
Mill River
Sandisfield
Copake
Sheffield
Mt. Everett 2624 ft.
Southfield
New Boston
Tolland
To Ancram
Ashley House
Ashley Falls
Bartholomew's Cobble
Clayton
Canaan
CONNECTICUT
LITCHFIELD CO.
Norfolk
Colebrook
Salisbury
Chamber Music Festival
Lakeville
Falls Village
Riverton
Music Mtn.
RENSSELAER CO.
COLUMBIA CO.
FRANKLIN CO.
HAMPSHIRE CO.
HAMPDEN CO.